Fran[...]

Für Michael,

mit herzlichen Grüßen

Thomas

BEING A BOARD MEMBER IN GERMANY

BEING A BOARD MEMBER IN GERMANY

A manual for English-speaking
members of management boards
and supervisory boards of German AGs,
SEs and GmbHs

CHRISTOF VON DRYANDER
KLAUS W. RIEHMER (EDS.)

CHRISTOF VON DRYANDER,
KLAUS W. RIEHMER, JENS HAFEMANN,
TOBIAS KIRCHER, DIRK MATTHES

GLP
German Law Publishers
www.germanlawpublishers.com

ISBN 978-3-941389-07-6

The Deutsche Nationalbibliothek lists this publication in the Deutsche Nationalbibliografie; detailed bibliographic data are available on the Internet at http://dnb.de.

Typesetting: GreenTomato GmbH, Stuttgart
Printing and binding: Druckhaus »Thomas Müntzer«, Neustädter Straße 1–4, 99947 Bad Langensalza

Table of Contents

Table of Contents: Long Version

PREFACE

As one of the consequences of the recent Global Economic Crisis, corporate boards have increasingly become the focus of public scrutiny. Major companies have initiated reviews of their corporate governance structures in order to satisfy enhanced compliance standards. Corporate laws providing for board members' duties become ever more rigid. Additional obligations are being created through governance rules of industry bodies, stock exchanges or quasi-governmental organizations. Also, law suits against board members account for a larger part of the calendars of courts and lawyers. At the same time, as a consequence of the globalization of the businesses of many companies, the composition of corporate boards is now much more international compared to a few years ago.

These developments are having a significant effect in Germany as well. The recent changes to German corporate law have increased the obligations of, and risks for, management and board members of both the Aktiengesellschaft (AG) and the GmbH. The German Corporate Governance Code has also been revised, which has resulted in new compliance questions, such as the development of strategies for enhancing diversity in German board rooms.

Diversity is not limited to the question of gender, but also refers to internationalizing board membership to better reflect the global scope of German trade and industry. Good corporate governance today is hardly possible without taking into account the views of experienced managers and other experts who are familiar with the geographic markets in which the company operates.

Foreign board members in particular require access to English-language sources that help them navigate through the myriads of legal and other requirements that provide the framework in which board members of German companies work.

In such an increasingly complex international environment, we hope that this book will serve as a source of general guidance and specific reference for board members in Germany. Our focus is on the rights and duties of members of the management and supervisory boards of an AG and the boards of a SE, as well as those of the general managers of a GmbH. In addition, we discuss general corporate law topics with which board members and other senior managers of German companies should have some familiarity.

For their invaluable help in preparing this book our special thanks go to our Cleary Gottlieb colleagues or alumni, in particular, Andrea Baller, Steve Benham, Alice Blezinger, Janine Bonn, Katherine Braddock, Manuela Krach, Christian Kutschmann, Daniel Panajotow, Nicole Rothe, Katharina Simon and Philip von der Meden.

Last but not least we thank our co-authors Jens Hafemann, Dr. Tobias Kircher and Dr. Dirk Matthes for their contributions and the excellent cooperation.

This publication is current as of 1 April 2011.

Frankfurt am Main, April 2011

Christof von Dryander   Klaus W. Riehmer

CHAPTER ONE
INTRODUCTION TO
THE GERMAN AG

§ 1 General

The German stock corporation (*Aktiengesellschaft*/"AG") is a corporation that has a nominal share capital denominated in euros, which is divided into shares. As a corporation it may, in its own name, acquire property and other rights and conduct legal proceedings. The AG generally is subject to full liability for all actions taken by its corporate bodies and employees in the course of the exercise of their duties. The shareholders of an AG cannot be held personally liable for liabilities of the AG.

The AG has three corporate bodies: the shareholders' meeting (*Hauptversammlung*), the management board (*Vorstand*) and the supervisory board (*Aufsichtsrat*). The AG is subject to the most rigid legal regime of all German corporation types: the shareholders may deviate from or supplement the statutory requirements by way of different or additional provisions in the articles of association only in the cases expressly provided by law.[1] In particular, none of the statutory requirements designed to ensure creditor protection may be changed.

Historically, the AG was created in order to provide a vehicle for a joint business undertaking by a large group of investors. By contrast, the German limited liability company (*Gesellschaft mit beschränkter Haftung*/"GmbH") presents an option for a small number of persons intending to set up a business. Due to simplifications of the formation requirements, it is now, however, possible for a single individual to form an AG.

The European stock corporation (*Societas Europaea*/"SE") and the limited partnership represented by shares (*Kommanditgesellschaft auf Aktien*/"KGaA") are alternatives to the AG, which in many respects are subject to the same legal regime as the AG.

§ 2 Share capital

The AG must have a nominal share capital of at least EUR 50,000. The share capital may be subscribed by way of contribution in cash or in kind. If the AG's founders contribute cash, at least one-quarter of the nominal share capital must immediately be paid-in. Contributions in kind must be fully contributed. A special valuation report must generally be prepared by an accounting expert for non-cash contributions. Shareholders generally have no obligation to contribute additional capital or other funds to an AG if the AG needs additional capital during its term.

---

1   Aktiengesetz [AktG] [Stock Corporation Act] 1965 § 23, ¶ 5 (F.R.G.).

The shares of an AG may be registered or bearer shares. In recent years, registered shares have become more popular even for listed AGs because they facilitate the identification of and the communication with shareholders.[2] Shares are generally represented by certificates, which, in the case of listed AGs are global certificates usually deposited with Clearstream Banking AG, the German central securities depositary.[3]

The Stock Corporation Act (*Aktiengesetz*/"Stock Corporation Act") provides for two basic types of shares: shares with voting rights, *i.e.*, common shares (*Stammaktien*), and shares without voting rights. Most AGs have issued only common shares. In Germany, the primary purpose of non-voting shares is to raise new capital while enabling the holders of the voting shares (or one or more such holders) to preserve their influence on the AG. Non-voting shares are only permissible under German law if their holders are given preferential dividend rights in order to compensate for the lack of voting rights.[4] By definition, non-voting shares of an AG are thus preferred shares (*Vorzugsaktien*). Shareholders owning preferred shares may vote at shareholders' meetings only if their rights are affected or the preferential dividend has not been paid in full for two consecutive fiscal years. Compared to Anglo-Saxon jurisdictions, the terms of both common and preferred shares of AGs are highly standardized. In particular, shares generally are not redeemable. AGs also rarely issue different classes of common or preferred shares, although from a legal perspective this would be possible.

§ 3 Shareholders' rights

The shareholders of an AG exercise their rights primarily in shareholders' meetings. Shareholders' meetings require physical attendance by a shareholder (or his proxy) in order to exercise voting rights, although the Stock Corporation Act was changed recently to allow AGs to provide for online participation in shareholders' meetings.

AGs must hold an ordinary general shareholders' meeting once a year, at which the shareholders vote on recurring agenda items, such as the appropriation of profits and the general discharge (*Entlastung*) of the acts of the management and supervisory board. Extraordinary items, such as capital and structural measures (*e.g.*, mergers, spin-offs or carve-outs) as well as fundamental changes, may also be resolved at the ordinary annual meeting or a separate extraordinary general shareholders' meeting. Due to the administrative effort and cost of preparing and holding shareholders' meetings, extraordinary general shareholders' meetings are only called if the interest of the corporation so requires (*e.g.*, the measures to be resolved cannot wait until the next ordinary meeting or the AG is in financial difficulties).

---

2   The draft of the Act amending the Stock Corporation Act as of November 2010 contemplates that unlisted AGs must have registered shares. Existing bearer shares must be transformed into registered shares until December 31, 2014. The reason is that greater transparency is desired in the combat against money laundering and terror financing.

3   *Cf.* § 6 as to the term "listed AG".

4   The draft of the Act amending the Stock Corporation Act as of November 2010 contemplates that non-cumulative preferred shares are introduced, *i.e.*, preferred shares that do not bear the right that unpaid dividends are accumulated and must be paid at a later stage.

Generally, each voting share grants one vote. For AGs that are not listed, the articles of association may limit the voting rights of the common shareholders, providing that irrespective of the individual shareholders' number of shares, a single shareholder cannot control the AG (*Höchststimmrecht*).[5] Granting individual shareholders more votes than which correspond to their capital participation (*Mehrfachstimmrecht*) is not permitted regardless of whether the AG is listed or not.[6]

The powers of the shareholders' meeting are limited to those provided by law.[7] The shareholders' meeting cannot issue instructions to the supervisory board or the management board. Only in exceptional circumstances, it may adopt resolutions regarding management measures.

Apart from voting, the shareholders of an AG have a right to information.[8] Shareholders also may challenge unlawful resolutions adopted by the shareholders' meeting.[9] That right often gives rise to frivolous claims by minority shareholders and (potentially lengthy) lawsuits.

In certain cases, shareholders can be liable to an AG for exerting undue influence on the affairs of the AG.[10]

§ 4 Management board and supervisory board

The administration of an AG is assigned to two bodies, the management board and the supervisory board (so-called two-tier system).

The management board manages the AG and represents the AG *vis-à-vis* third parties. It has an obligation to serve the interests of the AG.[11] Members of the management board are appointed and removed from office by the supervisory board.[12] If a management board member violates his duties *vis-à-vis* the AG by failing to exercise the due care of a conscientious business manager, the member is liable to the AG for damages and may be dismissed.

The principal role of the supervisory board is to supervise the management board. The supervisory board may also provide advice to the management board. It may not, however, issue instructions to the management board. By contrast, it is permissible (and general practice) to subject certain actions of the management board, such as major investments or financings, to the prior consent of the supervisory board.[13]

---

5   Aktiengesetz [AktG] [Stock Corporation Act] 1965, § 134, ¶ 1, sentence 2 (F.R.G.).
6   Aktiengesetz [AktG] [Stock Corporation Act] 1965, § 12, ¶ 2 (F.R.G.).
7   Aktiengesetz [AktG] [Stock Corporation Act] 1965, § 119 (F.R.G.).
8   Aktiengesetz [AktG] [Stock Corporation Act] 1965, § 131 (F.R.G.).
9   Aktiengesetz [AktG] [Stock Corporation Act] 1965, §§ 241 *et seq.* (F.R.G.).
10   Aktiengesetz [AktG] [Stock Corporation Act] 1965, §§ 117, 302, 311, 317 (F.R.G.).
11   Aktiengesetz [AktG] [Stock Corporation Act] 1965, § 93 (F.R.G.).
12   Aktiengesetz [AktG] [Stock Corporation Act] 1965, § 93, ¶ 2 (F.R.G.).
13   Aktiengesetz [AktG] [Stock Corporation Act] 1965, § 111, ¶ 4 (F.R.G.).

The members of the supervisory board are elected by the shareholders' meeting.[14] If the number of employees of an AG exceeds certain thresholds, the supervisory board is also comprised of employee representatives in addition to shareholder representatives (co-determination). Depending on the size and structure of the AG, the employees select a maximum of half of the supervisory board's seats (co-determination on a parity basis). In a supervisory board co-determined on a parity basis, the chairman, who as a result of the statutory election process generally is a shareholder representative, has a casting vote.

§ 5 Capital increase

German law provides for various forms of capital increases of an AG: ordinary capital increase against contribution in cash or kind, issuance of new shares out of authorized capital, issuance of new shares out of conditional capital and capital increase out of company funds. Conditional capital may be used only for the specific purposes provided by law. In an ordinary capital increase or an increase out of authorized capital, the existing shareholders are generally entitled to acquire the newly issued shares (subscription rights). The subscription rights can only be excluded in limited circumstances. There is a large body of case law by the German courts dealing with the requirements for excluding subscription rights in different circumstances.

In practice, the management board is frequently authorized by the ordinary shareholders' meeting to increase the capital within a period of up to five years at one or more points in time chosen by the management board (*genehmigtes Kapital*/"authorized capital"). This flexible form of raising new capital enables the management board to procure new equity at times, when market conditions are favorable or the AG requires additional capital (*e.g.*, for an acquisition). The issuance of new shares by an AG (whether by the use of authorized capital or on another legal basis) is a complex process, generally requiring action by the supervisory board in addition to the management board, as well as registration in the commercial register.

§ 6 Listed and privately-held AGs

AGs may apply for admission of their shares for trading on a stock exchange. The principal stock exchange in Germany is the Frankfurt Stock Exchange. The Frankfurt Stock Exchange has different markets for the admission and trading of shares and other securities: Large AGs (including all companies included in the DAX, the MDAX and the SDAX) are listed on the regulated market in the so-called Prime Standard. Smaller AGs can opt for the General Standard of the regulated market. The main difference between the two standards is the scope of ongoing listing obligations. In particular, only AGs listed in the Prime Standard must publish quarterly reports and issue corporate information in the English language (in addition to the German language). Issuers whose shares or other securities are admitted to and traded on a regulated market of a German securities exchange are subject to a variety of statutory obligations, in connection with the initial listing or the issuance of additional shares as well as on an ongoing basis, to ensure the adequate information of the capital market (in addition to obligations imposed by the exchange).[15] By contrast, issuers whose shares and other securities

---

14   Aktiengesetz [AktG] [Stock Corporation Act] 1965, § 101, ¶ 3, § 133 (F.R.G.).
15   *Cf.* §§ 117 *et seq.*

(if any) are only listed and traded in the unofficial market (called regulated unofficial market by the Frankfurt Stock Exchange), are primarily subject to capital market-related disclosure obligations imposed by the exchange. AGs that have shares listed and traded on the regulated market of a German stock exchange or a stock exchange of another member country of the European Economic Area are hereinafter referred to as "listed AGs" (*börsennotierte* AGs). As a legal matter, some of the statutory provisions applicable to listed AGs also apply to AGs whose shares are only listed on a stock exchange in a third country (*e.g.*, the New York Stock Exchange) and not listed on an European Economic Area stock exchange. Given the very small number of such AGs, the provisions that also apply to non-European Economic Area listed AGs are not specifically identified.

There are also AGs in Germany that are privately-held, but have issued bonds or other securities that are listed and traded on a regulated market (*e.g.*, privately-held banks in the form of an AG that issue bonds for funding purposes). Such AGs are subject to some of the statutory requirements that apply to listed AGs, such as the ad-hoc disclosure obligations of the Securities Trading Act (*Wertpapierhandelsgesetz*/"Securities Trading Act") and the requirement of the Commercial Code to prepare consolidated financial statements based upon international accounting standards.[16]

---

16   *Cf.* §§ 117 *et seq.*

CHAPTER TWO
MANAGEMENT BOARD
OF THE GERMAN AG

§ 7 The management board of the AG

An AG has a tripartite corporate structure: the shareholders' meeting (*Hauptversammlung*) is responsible for the most fundamental decisions regarding the AG such as amendments to its articles of association (*Satzung*), changes to the corporate structure and the decision regarding the appropriation of the annual profits, the supervisory board (*Aufsichtsrat*) is in charge of control and oversight, and the management board (*Vorstand*) determines the corporate strategy and manages the AG on a day-to-day basis.

The Stock Corporation Act vests each of these corporate bodies with rights and obligations *vis-à-vis* the other two bodies to ensure that all corporate bodies are able to perform their tasks. For example, the shareholders' meeting has the power, based upon the articles of association, to limit the management board's authority to act by requiring the consent of the supervisory board for certain actions. The supervisory board, among other things, has the right to require the management board to supply information necessary to perform its control-related duties.

I. Composition of the management board

§ 8 Number of members of the management board

The management board may consist of one or more natural persons.[17] An AG's articles of association must provide for the number of members on its management board, or the rules for determining such number. It is possible to specify a minimum or maximum number of board members, thus giving the supervisory board the power to determine such number within the given range. The management board of an AG with a share capital of over EUR 3 million must consist of at least two members, unless the articles of association provide that it consists of only one. The management board also must have at least two members if an AG is subject to employee co-determination on a parity basis and thus is required to appoint a labor director.[18] AGs that are banks, financial services firms or insurance companies must have at least two members of the management board pursuant to applicable regulatory requirements (irrespective of their co-determination status).

---

17   Aktiengesetz [AktG] [Stock Corporation Act] 1965, § 76, ¶ 2 (F.R.G.).
18   The role of the labor director is discussed further in § 11.

§ 9 Chairman of the management board

If the management board consists of more than one member, the supervisory board may appoint a chairman of the management board (*Vorstandsvorsitzender*).[19] Only the supervisory board as a whole may make such appointment. This authority cannot be delegated to a committee of the supervisory board. The supervisory board may also appoint a deputy chairman of the management board.

The Stock Corporation Act does not provide much guidance with respect to the chairman's legal status, function or authority. In practice, an AG's articles of association and/or the rules of procedure of the management board (*Geschäftsordnung*) govern the chairman's position. The tasks assigned to the chairman usually include representing the AG in public, coordinating the management board's work with the supervisory board and exercising certain formal functions within the management board, such as chairing board meetings.

The chairman may not issue instructions to other management board members. He may be given the right to cast the tie-breaking vote with respect to resolutions passed by a majority of the management board provided that the management board consists of more than two members. It is uncertain whether the chairman may be given the right to veto majority resolutions passed by the management board. A temporary veto right postponing the agenda item in question to the next management board meeting should be permissible, at least in an AG that is not co-determined on a parity basis and thus has no labor director.[20] However, even in a co-determined AG the chairman may call for a repeat vote on one and the same subject within a short time frame.

§ 10 Spokesman of the management board

If the supervisory board does not appoint a chairman of the management board, either the supervisory board or the management board itself may appoint a spokesman (*Vorstandssprecher*) of the management board. The spokeman's legal status is not expressly dealt with in the Stock Corporation Act. His duties and powers should be set forth in the rules of procedure of the management board. The Corporate Governance Code (which applies to AGs that have their shares listed on a regulated market) recommends that listed AGs appoint a spokesman or a chairman of the management board.[21]

§ 11 Labor director

The German Co-Determination Act (*Gesetz über die Mitbestimmung der Arbeitnehmer/*"Co-Determination Act") requires AGs that are subject to co-determination on a parity basis (more than 2000 employees of the AG or the corporate group of the AG) to appoint a board member responsible for personnel matters, the so-called labor director (*Arbeitsdirektor*).[22] The labor director plays a key role in all personnel matters and social responsibility issues.

---

19   Aktiengesetz [AktG] [Stock Corporation Act] 1965, § 84 (F.R.G.).
20   Cf. § 69.
21   Cf. § 6 as to the term "listed AGs".
22   Aktiengesetz [AktG] [Stock Corporation Act] 1965, § 76, ¶ 2 and § 84, ¶ 4 (F.R.G.).

The labor director has the same rights as the other members of the management board and is appointed and dismissed in the same way as other members, *e.g.*, by the supervisory board.[23] Neither the AG's workforce nor the employee representatives on the supervisory board or trade unions have any special rights with regard to the labor director's appointment, such as rights to propose or veto the appointment (or dismissal). An exception to this rule applies to AGs that operate in the coal and steel industry (and thus are subject to a special co-determination regime, the Coal and Steel Co-Determination Act), whose labor director may not be appointed contrary to a majority vote by the employee representatives on the supervisory board.

§ 12 Deputy management board members

The supervisory board may also appoint deputy management board members.[24] The term "deputy management board member" is, however, misleading. Under the Stock Corporation Act, deputy board members have all the rights and duties of ordinary board members and are "genuine" members of the management board. Deputy members do not act as *Prokuristen*[25] or holders of a commercial power of attorney (*Handlungsbevollmächtigter*), or assume the responsibilities of absent or indisposed ordinary board members. The designation "deputy" merely indicates an internal hierarchy within the management board based upon the internal rules of procedure of the management board, which usually restrict the authority of deputy management board members to manage the AG's affairs.

Some companies use the title "divisional board member" (*Bereichsvorstandsmitglied*). In many cases, such divisional board members are not members of the management board, but senior executives with regional or divisional responsibility below the level of the management board.

II. Appointment to the management board

§ 13 Distinction between appointment and service agreement

Management board members generally have two legal relationships with the AG:[26] the appointment (*Bestellung*) to the management board as an act of corporate law and the service agreement (*Anstellungsvertrag*) creating the contractual relationship between the AG and the board member.[27] The appointment makes a person a member of the management board, creates the rights and duties under corporate law, and grants legal authority to a management board member to represent the AG *vis-à-vis* third parties. The service agreement sets out the terms of the contractual relationship between the management board member and the AG, including the rights to compensation and benefits.

---

23   The appointment procedures are set forth in more detail in §§ 22 *et seq.*, the dismissal is discussed in §§ 30 *et seq.*
24   Aktiengesetz [AktG] [Stock Corporation Act] 1965, § 94 (F.R.G.).
25   An authorized signatory with a general commercial power of attorney defined by law.
26   Aktiengesetz [AktG] [Stock Corporation Act] 1965, § 84 (F.R.G.).
27   The service agreement is discussed in more detail in §§ 36 *et seq.*, *cf.* Form of Service Agreement for management board members of the AG attached in Chapter Seven: Annex I.A.

Although the appointment to the management board and the execution of the service agreement often coincide, these two legal relationships differ in terms of the requirements to make them effective, and their commencement and duration. An effective board appointment can be made without a service agreement. Conversely, terminating the service agreement does not necessarily terminate the appointment as a member of the board (and *vice versa*). However, it is standard practice to draft the service agreement in order to achieve a correlation between the appointment and the service agreement, *e.g.*, by specifying that dismissal from the management board automatically terminates the service agreement.

A. Prerequisites for becoming a board member

§ 14 Natural person with full legal capacity
The supervisory board generally has broad discretion in its choice of persons to serve on the management board. Such persons must be natural persons, whose legal capacity is unrestricted.[28] Specific requirements apply to AGs that engage in regulated activities such as banking.[29]

§ 15 No convictions
Anyone convicted of a certain type of insolvency offense is barred from serving on the management board of an AG for five years after the conviction becomes legally binding.[30] In addition, a candidate for the management board may not be subject to a court or other governmental order prohibiting the conduct of a business similar to the activities of the AG. If such conviction or prohibition takes effect while a management board member is in office, the appointment becomes ineffective, and the management board member is barred from reappointment for five years.

§ 16 Nationality, residence and work permits
Candidates of all nationalities may become members of the management board of an AG. However, the candidate must be able to fulfill the legal duties of a management board member, at least to a material extent, within Germany. Therefore it is generally advisable to appoint only persons who may freely reside and work in Germany.

§ 17 Additional qualifications for banks and insurance companies
Management board members at banks, financial services firms and insurance companies must meet certain additional qualifications. Whenever the supervisory board has the intention of making an appointment to the management board of such banks, financial services firms and insurance companies, the German Federal Financial Supervisory Authority (*Bundesanstalt für Finanzdienstleistungsaufsicht*, "BaFin") must be notified, together with the submission of the candidate's *curriculum vitae* and other supporting documentation. The BaFin may veto the appointment if the candidate lacks sufficient qualifications or personal reliability. In practice,

---

28   Aktiengesetz [AktG] [Stock Corporation Act] 1965, § 76, ¶ 3 (F.R.G.).
29   *Cf.* § 17.
30   Aktiengesetz [AktG] [Stock Corporation Act] 1965, § 76, ¶ 3 (F.R.G.).

it is common to discuss a proposed appointment formally with the BaFin prior to submitting a formal notice in order to exclude the risk of a negative decision.

§ 18 Additional qualifications specified in the articles of association

Although less common in practice, the articles of association of an AG may specify additional personal qualifications. Such requirements may, however, not impose undue restrictions on the supervisory board's discretion.

§ 19 Memberships on multiple management boards

German law does not prohibit persons from serving on the management boards of two or more AGs at the same time.[31] However, the supervisory boards of both (or all) AGs must agree to the multiple appointments. This rule also applies to multiple intra-group appointments or to appointments to the management boards (or equivalent bodies) of other German or foreign companies. In certain circumstances, a member of the management board who is also appointed to another management board (or an equivalent body) of another company may be barred from voting in management board meetings of one or both companies in order to avoid conflicts of interest.

§ 20 Simultaneous and successive membership on management and supervisory board

The supervisory board's task is to control and advise the management board.[32] It cannot do so effectively if management board members are simultaneously also members of the supervisory board of the same AG. Such simultaneous appointments are thus prohibited as they conflict with the two-tier structure of the AG.[33]

The supervisory board may, in exceptional circumstances, however, appoint one of its members to substitute for an indisposed management board member to fill a vacancy on the management board for a fixed period of time. The appointment may be renewed or extended provided that the aggregate term does not exceed one year. Supervisory board members delegated to serve on the management board are barred from actively serving on the supervisory board while being members of the management board. During their term on the management board, their powers are the same as those of the management board members for whom they act as a substitute.

Within a group of AGs, a member of the management board of the controlled AG may not serve on the supervisory board of the controlling AG. By contrast, it is permissible, and indeed common, for management board members of a parent AG to be appointed as members of the supervisory board (or equivalent bodies) of group companies.[34]

Overlapping board memberships are also impermissible outside the context of intra-group relationships: a person may not be a member of the management board of AG "A" if he is a member of the supervisory board of AG "B" and at the same time a management board member

---

31   Aktiengesetz [AktG] [Stock Corporation Act] 1965, § 88 (F.R.G.).
32   Aktiengesetz [AktG] [Stock Corporation Act] 1965, § 111, ¶ 1 (F.R.G.).
33   Aktiengesetz [AktG] [Stock Corporation Act] 1965, §§ 100, 105 (F.R.G.).
34   Cf. § 205.

of AG "B" serves on the supervisory board of AG "A". Such an arrangement could result in
the two persons controlling each other, and thus could potentially render the separation of
management and supervision in the two-tier system ineffective.[35]

To ensure effective supervision and prevent potential conflicts of interest, a management board
member of an AG whose shares are listed and traded on a regulated market may not be appointed to the supervisory board of the AG within a two-year period after having served on the
management board of the AG.[36] This cooling-off period does not apply if the former management board member is elected to the supervisory board based upon a proposal of shareholders
whose shareholding exceeds 25% of the voting rights of the AG.[37]

§ 21 Legal consequences of failing to meet prerequisites for membership
The appointment of a management board member is null and void if any of the personal qualifications prescribed by statute are not met at the time of the appointment. If, following a valid
appointment, a qualification ceases to be fulfilled, the appointment automatically becomes
legally invalid. If, in any such case, the management board member takes up or continues his
board position despite lacking the proper qualification, the consequences for the AG and third
parties are uncertain. If the management board member acted knowingly, he may be liable to
the AG and third parties for any actions taken in his capacity as a board member.

If personal qualifications set forth in the articles of association were disregarded when the appointment was made, the appointment is valid, but the supervisory board is entitled to revoke
the appointment for cause.

Appointing a supervisory board member to the management board in violation of a statutory
restriction makes the appointment null and void.[38] However, the appointment of a supervisory
board member to the management board is effective if the supervisory board member gives up
the seat on the supervisory board before taking up the position on the management board. Corresponding rules apply in the opposite case of a management board member being appointed to
the supervisory board (unless the two-year cooling-off rule applies).[39]

B. Appointment procedures

§ 22 Appointment by supervisory board resolution
Management board members are appointed by resolution of the supervisory board of the AG
acting as a whole.[40] The supervisory board has the sole authority to make such appointments.

---

35   *Cf.* § 206.
36   *Cf.* § 207.
37   Aktiengesetz [AktG] [Stock Corporation Act] 1965, § 100, ¶ 2, sentence 1, no. 4 (F.R.G.).
38   Please note the exception for members of the supervisory board seconded to the management board,
      in exceptional circumstances, as discussed in § 20.
39   *Cf.* § 208.
40   Aktiengesetz [AktG] [Stock Corporation Act] 1965, § 84 (F.R.G.).

The task of appointing the management board may not be delegated to a supervisory board committee.[41] The supervisory board's authority to appoint the management board members cannot be transferred to, or subjected to the approval of, third parties, such as the parent company or a majority shareholder. In practice, a parent company as major shareholder will usually be consulted prior to the appointment.

The supervisory board appoints the management board members by majority vote. Appointment resolutions must be passed explicitly. No member can be appointed to the management board simply by acquiescence.

In AGs that are subject to employee co-determination on a parity basis, the appointment generally requires a special majority: on the first ballot, a resolution to appoint a management board member requires the majority of two thirds of the votes cast. If the required majority has not been obtained, the supervisory board may immediately take a second vote, provided that all members consent thereto. Should the second vote not result in the required majority, the matter is delegated to the supervisory board's mediation committee, whose members have the task of agreeing on a candidate to be presented in the next supervisory board meeting. Subsequently, a new ballot on the candidate nominated by the mediation committee takes place with the supervisory board deciding by simple majority of the votes cast. In case of a dead-lock situation, the chairman of the supervisory board, who usually is a shareholder representative, has the casting vote. As a consequence, the board members who represent the shareholders are in effect able to appoint their candidate, but the appointment process may require several meetings and ballots.

In order to take effect, the appointment must be accepted by the candidate. The appointment to the management board as such does not assign the member to any particular business area or function.

§ 23 Appointment by court

Appointments to the management board may be made by court order if the management board does not have the required number of members.[42] This power is granted to the court only in urgent cases, and is exercised only upon application. The test is whether it is necessary to fill the position(s) on the management board in order for the AG to be managed properly or to be able to act *vis-à-vis* third parties.[43] Furthermore, there must be an urgent reason for appointing a replacement member by court order. This applies only if the supervisory board is unable to appoint the new management board member(s) quickly enough to avert potentially adverse consequences for the AG, shareholders, employees, creditors or the public.

Examples of court appointments of management board members include vacancies on the management board due to death, dismissal or resignation of a board member. In each case, the

---

41   Aktiengesetz [AktG] [Stock Corporation Act] 1965, § 107, ¶ 3, sentence 3 (F.R.G.).
42   Aktiengesetz [AktG] [Stock Corporation Act] 1965, § 85 (F.R.G.). A vacancy on the management board may also be filled by delegating a supervisory board member to the management board, *cf.* § 243.
43   §§ 81 *et seq*. deal with the representation of an AG.

application to the court has to demonstrate that the appointment of a new member is necessary for the proper functioning of the management board. Typical examples include the resignation of the chief financial officer in the midst of the preparation of the annual accounts or the appointment of a second management board member of a co-determined AG in order to ensure compliance with statutory co-determination requirements.

The competent court of jurisdiction is the local court (*Amtsgericht*) responsible for the AG's registered office. The application may be filed by anyone with a legitimate interest in the appointment. Such persons typically include members of the management or supervisory board, shareholders, creditors or employees. In practice, one or more members of the management board and/or the supervisory board file the application.

Court-appointed management board members have the same rights and duties as the other board members. They may claim compensation for their activities on the management board and reimbursement of expenses. If the AG and the court-appointed member fail to reach an agreement, the court determines the level of compensation and expenses. The term of office of a court-appointed member of the management board ends automatically, without explicit dismissal, when the (former) vacancy on the management board is filled by appointment of a new member by the supervisory board. Management board members appointed by the court may be removed from office at an earlier time, but only by the court itself and not by the supervisory board. The supervisory board may, however, apply to the court to have the board member removed.

§ 24 Deficient appointments

The appointment to the management board of an AG is a legal act, and as such may have deficiencies affecting its validity. Such deficiencies include, for example, the absence of a resolution passed by the supervisory board acting as a whole. Despite having a deficiency, the appointment of a management board member is not invalid. Instead, unless the appointee lacks statutorily-required qualifications,[44] the appointment is regarded as a provisional appointment, with the result that the board member concerned has the same rights and duties as a correctly appointed member. The provisional appointment can only be terminated with future effect by revocation or resignation. Furthermore, a management board member whose appointment is deficient is entitled to contractually agreed compensation, even if his service agreement is not valid.

§ 25 Commercial register filing

All changes to the composition of the management board and all changes to the members' authority to represent the AG *vis-à-vis* third parties must be notified to and registered in the commercial register.[45] The management board members are responsible for the registration and must sign the application for registration. Commercial register applications are filed through a German notary. If the sole member of the management board departs, his successor is re-

---

44   *Cf.* § 21.
45   Aktiengesetz [AktG] [Stock Corporation Act] 1965, § 81 (F.R.G.).

sponsible for filing the change. When filing changes, the AG may generally be represented by an authorized representative based upon a publicly certified or notarized[46] power of attorney granted by the management board.

C. Term of office and end of the appointment

§ 26 Term of office

The term of office of a management board member begins at the beginning of the term of office as specified in the appointment resolution, which may differ from the day of the appointment.[47] The registration in the commercial register may occur after the appointment has taken effect.[48]

There is no statutory minimum term of office for management board members. Management board members may be appointed for a maximum term of five years. A renewal of the appointment is permitted. There is no statutory limitation on the maximum period that a member of the management board may serve. There is also no mandatory retirement age, although AGs may provide for mandatory retirement at a certain age in their articles of association.

Reappointment requires a new supervisory board resolution, which in general may be adopted no earlier than one year prior to the expiration of the current term of office. However, in the case of an appointment for less than five years, the initial supervisory board resolution may provide for an extension of the term of appointment up to an aggregate term of five years. If the aggregate term will exceed five years a new supervisory board resolution is required. These principles also apply for the service agreement. However, the service agreement may provide that it shall remain in effect in the event of a reappointment.[49]

§ 27 End of the appointment

In addition to a termination of the appointment by expiration of the designated term, the appointment also ends by resignation of the management board member, mutual agreement or revocation of the appointment (dismissal) by the supervisory board. It should be kept in mind that termination of the appointment does not necessarily also result in the termination of the board member's service agreement with the AG.

§ 28 Resignation of a management board member

An appointment to the management board may be terminated by resignation of the member. Resignation is a unilateral declaration by the member to leave the board, which is usually made in writing. The declaration must be addressed to and actually received by the supervisory board. Receipt by the chairman of the supervisory board is sufficient. The resigning board

---

46 Handelsgesetzbuch [HGB] [Commercial Code] 1897, § 12, ¶ 1, sentence 2 (F.R.G.).
47 Aktiengesetz [AktG] [Stock Corporation Act] 1965, § 84, ¶ 1 (F.R.G.).
48 Cf. § 25.
49 The service agreement is discussed in more detail in §§ 36 *et seq.*, *cf.* Form of Service Agreement for management board members of the AG attached in Chapter Seven: Annex I.A.

member need not specify reasons or show cause for the resignation to be effective. Untimely resignations, such as a resignation that renders the management board incapable of acting during an urgent situation, should be avoided as they may give rise to damage claims by the AG. Further, resignation from the management board without cause may represent a breach of the board member's service agreement, entitling the supervisory board to revoke the appointment and terminate the service agreement for cause.

Typical examples of cause for resigning from office as a management board member are the unjustified refusal of the shareholders' meeting to discharge the acts of the management board member, failure to make payments to which the management board member is entitled, severe and lasting disputes among the management board members undermining their collaboration, or undue interference by the supervisory board in the management of the AG. The management board member does not also have to declare the termination of the service agreement at the time of resigning from the management board. It is recognized that a management board member has the right to leave the board for cause without automatic loss or other adverse effect on his contractual rights.[50]

§ 29 Mutual agreement to terminate
Membership on the management board may be terminated by mutual agreement between the management board member and the AG, represented by the supervisory board, at any time without cause. Such termination requires a majority resolution passed by the supervisory board acting as a whole.

§ 30 Revocation by supervisory board resolution
A management board member can be removed from the management board for cause by way of revocation of the appointment (dismissal).[51] A revocation must be made by majority resolution of the supervisory board acting as a whole. The management board mandate ends when the member is notified of the supervisory board's resolution. In an AG that is subject to employee co-determination on a parity basis, the supervisory board must comply with the procedure applicable for the appointment of management board members *mutatis mutandis*.[52]

§ 31 Revocation: Cause
Revoking the appointment of a management board member is only possible for cause.[53] This requirement is intended to ensure the independence of the management board. Cause exists when retaining the member on the management board until the end of his term of office would be unacceptable for the AG. Whether this is the case is determined by weighing the interests of the AG against the interests of the management board member concerned. Cause does not have to be associated with the member as a person, nor does it require that the management board member has acted culpably in the sense of being personally responsible. Cause may also

---

50   The management board member's service agreement is discussed further in §§ 36 *et seq.* below.
51   Aktiengesetz [AktG] [Stock Corporation Act] 1965, § 84, ¶ 3 (F.R.G.).
52   *Cf.* § 22, Mitbestimmungsgesetz [MitbestG] [Co-Determination Act] 1976, § 31, ¶ 2–4 (F.R.G.).
53   Aktiengesetz [AktG] [Stock Corporation Act] 1965, § 84, ¶ 3 (F.R.G.).

be based upon the management board member's conduct outside of board activities or prior to taking office.

The Stock Corporation Act lists the following examples of cause: a gross violation of duties, inability to manage the AG properly, and a vote of no-confidence by the shareholders' meeting.[54] This list, however, is not exhaustive.

The question of whether cause exists is a question of fact, which is subject to full review in court. The burden of proof lies with the AG. The supervisory board has no discretion to apply its own judgment. The articles of association may not contain an exhaustive list of what constitutes cause. If cause exists, the supervisory board must decide in the interests of the AG whether to revoke the management board member's appointment. The revocation is effective, unless it is declared invalid by a court ruling.

If an appropriate period of time has passed since the cause arose, and the management board member can in good faith assume that the supervisory board will not revoke his board appointment on the basis of the facts and circumstances that gave rise to cause, the supervisory board forfeits its right of revocation. Similarly, a revocation may not be based on grounds that were already known to the supervisory board at the time the appointment was made.

§ 32 Revocation: Gross violation of duties

A gross violation of duties is presumed in case of serious misconduct, either in relation to the board member's duties or in the private sphere, which harms the AG at least indirectly.[55] Possible misconduct by a management board member constituting a gross violation of duties includes breach of fundamental management board duties, personal financial difficulties, insider dealing, venality, or other types of criminal activity.

§ 33 Revocation: Inability to manage the AG properly

Inability to manage the AG properly typically exists if a board member lacks the knowledge required to manage the AG, there are lasting disputes among the management board members undermining their collaboration, a serious rift exists between the management board and the supervisory board or long-term illness prevents the management board member from performing his duties.[56] Dismissal of a board member on the ground of inability to manage the AG properly often will result in a dispute between the AG and the dismissed board member and, therefore, requires thorough analysis and detailed substantiation. The burden of proof lies with the AG.

§ 34 Revocation: Vote of no-confidence by shareholders' meeting

A vote of no-confidence by the shareholders' meeting constitutes cause for revoking an appointment.[57] No further justification for the revocation is required. In particular, it is not nec-

---

54   Aktiengesetz [AktG] [Stock Corporation Act] 1965, § 84, ¶ 3, sentence 2 (F.R.G.).
55   Aktiengesetz [AktG] [Stock Corporation Act] 1965, § 84, ¶ 3 (F.R.G.).
56   Aktiengesetz [AktG] [Stock Corporation Act] 1965, § 84, ¶ 3 (F.R.G.).
57   Aktiengesetz [AktG] [Stock Corporation Act] 1965, § 84, ¶ 3 (F.R.G.).

essary to show a violation of duties on the part of the management board member. However, the shareholders' vote of no-confidence may not be made on the basis of obviously unfounded reasons. Accordingly, the withdrawal of confidence may not be arbitrary or used as an excuse for lack of other grounds that would constitute cause. Failure to discharge the acts of the management board member does not constitute a vote of no-confidence by the shareholders' meeting and is not otherwise sufficient to revoke the management board member's appointment.

§ 35 Suspending a management board member from office
Temporarily suspending a management board member's appointment (as opposed to terminating the appointment) is not expressly provided by law. There is no accepted best practice for suspension. Therefore, suspension of board membership is a legally uncertain measure. It should be permissible to suspend a member of the management board if all prerequisites for revocation of the appointment are met. By contrast, it is unclear whether a suspension would be permissible if cause for revocation is only suspected. The AG bears the burden of proof. For this reason, suspension is generally not advisable, especially in cases of doubt. Also, if cause exists, the supervisory board is likely to be under an obligation to revoke the management board member's appointment to protect the AG. In practice, the supervisory board and the member of the management board affected should aim towards reaching a mutual agreement on terminating the management board appointment if possible or, if there is cause, the supervisory board should revoke the member's appointment to the management board.

III. Service agreement

§ 36 Scope of the service agreement
The service agreement is a contract between the AG and the management board member, similar to an employment agreement, governing individual rights and duties, as opposed to the corporate rights and duties resulting from the position on the management board of the AG. Yet the management board member is not an employee of the AG in a technical sense as he represents the corporation. In particular, the supervisory board may not give instructions to the management board.

The service agreement may cover a wide range of matters such as compensation, benefits (*e.g.*, pension rights and bonus payments), vacation, post-contractual non-compete obligations, D&O insurance, expense reimbursement policy, or ancillary and outside activities (*e.g.*, active membership in industry organizations).[58]

---

58   *Cf.* Form of Service Agreement for management board members of the AG attached in Chapter Seven: Annex I.A.

A. Conclusion and termination of the service agreement

§ 37 Conclusion of the service agreement

The service agreement is concluded between the management board member and the AG, represented by the supervisory board.[59] It does not require any particular form but is generally made in writing. The supervisory board is also responsible for all amendments to the service agreement. The negotiation and execution of the service agreement between the AG and the management board member may be (and often is) delegated to a supervisory board committee, which must have at least three members. Following recent changes in the Stock Corporation Act, a supervisory board committee may not, however, execute the service agreement before the supervisory board acting as a whole has approved the service agreement. Decisions on management board compensation require action by the full supervisory board.[60] The service agreement may not provide for the appointment of the management board member or make any promise as to such appointment.[61] The supervisory board acting as a whole must either decide upon the appointment prior to the execution of the service agreement, or the service agreement is executed subject to the condition of later appointment.

If the service agreement is invalid or ineffective for any reason, but the management board member has already accepted the appointment to the management board, the service agreement, in principle, is nevertheless regarded as effective until the appointment is terminated. Details depend on the reason why the service agreement lacks legal effect.

§ 38 Service agreement with another entity in a corporate group

Within a corporate group the question may arise whether it is permissible to conclude the service agreement with another group company instead of the AG on whose management board the member is to serve. Concluding the service agreement with the parent company generally is not advisable due to potential conflicts of interest. The board member of the subsidiary must serve the interest of "his" AG and, on the other hand, would have contractual obligations to the parent company.[62] In such a case, the group-wide interests would not override the interests of the AG. Tax issues also need to be considered when separating the contractual service relationship from the corporate relationship (*e.g.*, hidden profit distributions under German corporate income tax law may occur). However, in case a control agreement (*Beherrschungsvertrag*) between the controlling parent and the controlled AG exists, the service agreement of the management board member of the controlled AG may be concluded with the controlling parent. It may, however, be necessary to modify or terminate the service agreement if the control agreement between the group companies is terminated.

§ 39 Termination of the service agreement

The appointment to the management board as an act of corporate law and the conclusion of the service agreement as the execution of a contract result in two different legal relationships

---

59 Aktiengesetz [AktG] [Stock Corporation Act] 1965, §§ 84, 112 (F.R.G.).
60 Aktiengesetz [AktG] [Stock Corporation Act] 1965, § 107, ¶ 3, sentence 3 (F.R.G.), § 87, ¶ 1, 2.
61 § 22 deals with the appointment of the management board member by resolution of the supervisory board.
62 Aktiengesetz [AktG] [Stock Corporation Act] 1965, § 317 in connection with §§ 308, 309 (F.R.G.).

between the AG and the management board member.[63] As a consequence, in the absence of specific contractual priorities the service agreement is not automatically terminated when the appointment ends and *vice versa*. However, it is common practice to tie the service agreement to the appointment. Therefore the service agreement will generally be terminated automatically when the appointment to the board ends.

§ 40 Termination by the supervisory board: Notice of termination

If the AG has the contractual or statutory right (*e.g.*, in case of cause) to terminate the service agreement,[64] such termination requires a resolution of the supervisory board and notice of termination to the management board member.[65] The task of resolving the termination of a management board member's service agreement may be delegated to a supervisory board committee.

Note, however, that if the appointment to the management board is still valid, which would be the case if no resolution revoking the appointment has been passed in advance[66] and the appointment has not ended for other reasons, a supervisory board committee may not decide on the termination of the service agreement in order not to preempt the decision by the full supervisory board on whether to revoke the appointment of the management board member. Although the revocation of the corporate appointment by the supervisory board could be interpreted as implicitly giving notice of termination of the service agreement, a separate notice of termination regarding the service agreement is advisable.

The notice of termination must be delivered to the management board member. Evidence of the delivery should be kept on file.

§ 41 Termination by the supervisory board: Cause

Unless the termination of the service agreement is permitted by the terms of the agreement, the termination requires cause. Cause for termination exists if a continuance of the service agreement until the end of the term or the next contractual termination date would be unacceptable for the AG. Cause for the revocation of the management board member's appointment[67] also generally constitutes cause for the termination of the service agreement. However, revocation of the appointment due to a vote of no-confidence by the shareholders' meeting[68] is cause for termination of the service agreement only if the management board member has committed a serious breach of his duties.

The notice of termination must be given within two weeks after the supervisory board has received information on all of the facts constituting cause for the termination of the service

---

63   § 13 deals with the distinction between the appointment and the service agreement in general.
64   The end of the appointment to the management board is covered further in §§ 27 *et seq.*
65   Cause for the revocation of the management board member's appointment is dealt with in § 31.
66   The revocation of the appointment by the supervisory board is further discussed in §§ 30 *et seq.*
67   Revocation of the appointment for cause is dealt with in § 31.
68   Revocation of the appointment based on a vote of non-confidence is dealt with in § 34.

agreement.[69] If the facts given to the supervisory board are incomplete, the board must take steps to cure this problem on an urgent basis. The two-week period begins to run only after all supervisory board members have been informed of the facts constituting cause. In any event, the AG bears the burden of proof for compliance with the two-week period.

§ 42 Termination by the management board member

A management board member wishing to terminate his service agreement must provide notice of termination to the supervisory board. Delivery of the notice of termination to only one supervisory board member, preferably the chairman, is sufficient. The notice should be given in writing and evidence of its receipt should be retained by the AG.

In general, a management board member may only terminate his service agreement based on cause, unless the contractual terms permit termination for other reasons. Circumstances justifying early resignation from the corporate office as a management board member[70] generally also represent cause for terminating the service agreement with immediate effect. In practice, the termination of the service agreement for cause often is a matter of intense negotiation between the AG and the management board member. Given the concept that appointment and service agreement are two separate legal relationships,[71] in practice the necessity arises to analyze whether both relationships are terminated simultaneously. Generally, a provision in the service agreement that ties the service agreement to the appointment is permissible, but in practice provisions of this type are often challenged in the event of a termination for cause.

§ 43 Termination by mutual agreement

The service agreement may be terminated at any time by mutual agreement. The termination agreement has to be executed on behalf of the AG either by the full supervisory board or by a committee.

B. Compensation

§ 44 Recent developments regarding compensation

Recently, new statutory rules governing the compensation of management board members entered into force. The new rules were adopted in response to the criticisms raised against executive compensation schemes in the wake of the world-wide financial crisis, and are designed to ensure that the compensation of executives is better aligned to the fortunes of the businesses that they run. The following sections provide an overview of the new rules. Banks, financial services firms and insurance companies are subject to additional regulatory requirements for setting the compensation of their executives and employees.

---

69   Bürgerliches Gesetzbuch [BGB] [Civil Code] 1896, § 626, ¶ 2 (F.R.G.). The notice of termination is dealt with in § 40.
70   Resignation by the management board member is dealt with in § 28.
71   The concept is outlined in § 13.

§ 45 Entitlement to compensation

The service agreement governs the management board member's entitlement to payment of the agreed compensation.[72] The compensation generally includes all monetary components, that is, in particular fixed salary, bonus, stock options, expense allowances, insurance premiums and any commissions. It may also include other agreed items, such as post-contractual compensation following termination of the board membership and benefits in kind (*e.g.*, use of company property such as cars, flats, planes etc.).

§ 46 Determination of the compensation by the full supervisory board

The compensation must be determined by the supervisory board acting as a whole.[73] Delegation to a committee is not permissible.[74] The management board compensation may also not be stipulated in the articles of association of the AG. The statutory framework is designed to ensure that the individual financial arrangements provide incentives in favor of a sustainable development of the company and to prevent unduly high levels of compensation. The supervisory board has a legal duty to ensure that the compensation is appropriate in relation to the duties and performance of a management board member,[75] on the one hand, and the situation of the AG, on the other hand.[76] This duty includes the obligation to make sure that the total compensation of a management board member does not exceed the customary compensation without good reasons.[77] These principles also apply to pension entitlements and similar benefits.

The Stock Corporation Act provides that the shareholders' meeting of an AG whose shares are listed and traded on a regulated market may adopt a non-binding resolution on the AG's compensation regime for management board members.[78] A shareholder vote on compensation is only possible if the management board and the supervisory board have included such a vote as an agenda item of the shareholders' meeting, which a substantial number of listed AGs have done.

Shareholder approval of the management board compensation does not give rise to specific rights or duties and, therefore, the tangible benefits of obtaining such approval are limited. In particular, approval by the shareholders' meeting does not have any effect on the obligation of the supervisory board to comply with the statutory requirements of the Stock Corporation Act in setting and adjusting the compensation of the members of the management board.[79]

---

72   § 51 deals with bonus payments. § 53 deals with stock options. § 54 deals with pensions and payments to dependants of a deceased management board member, *cf.* Form of Service Agreement for management board members of the AG attached in Chapter Seven: Annex I.A.

73   Compensation of management board members appointed by the local court is dealt with in § 23.

74   Aktiengesetz [AktG] [Stock Corporation Act] 1965, § 107, ¶ 3, sentence 3 (F.R.G.).

75   Aktiengesetz [AktG] [Stock Corporation Act] 1965, § 87, ¶ 2, sentence 1 (F.R.G.).

76   The appropriateness of compensation is further discussed in §§ 57 *et seq.*

77   Aktiengesetz [AktG] [Stock Corporation Act] 1965, § 87, ¶ 2, sentence 1 (F.R.G.).

78   Aktiengesetz [AktG] [Stock Corporation Act] 1965, § 120, ¶ 4 (F.R.G.).

79   Aktiengesetz [AktG] [Stock Corporation Act] 1965, § 120, ¶ 4 (F.R.G.).

§ 47 Reducing compensation: statutory obligation of the supervisory board

The Stock Corporation Act requires the supervisory board to reduce the management board's compensation if the AG's financial position deteriorates so that it would be unreasonable to expect the AG to continue compensating board members at the agreed level.[80] However, in order to protect retired management board members, the supervisory board's obligation to reduce the compensation extends only to adjustment of pension commitments, payments to dependants of deceased members of the management board or other retirement-related payments within the first three years after the retirement of the management board member from the management board.[81]

The supervisory board may only reduce compensation due to adverse economic developments. Such developments can, for example, be evidenced by the need to make pay cuts or dismissal or by the insolvency of the AG, but also by the fact that the AG will not be able to pay dividends to its shareholders. A reduction may not be made based on a disappointing performance by the individual management board member or the entire management board or because the supervisory board determines the benefits were set at an inappropriately high level at the outset. However, a reduction is possible if the management board member did not fulfill his duties and as a result caused the AG's adverse economic development, or if the adverse development occurred while the management board member was (jointly with other management board members) in charge of the AG's affairs. The reduction is effected by way of unilateral declaration by the supervisory board.[82] The management board member concerned may challenge the decision by filing an action for specific performance claiming full payment of the contractually agreed compensation. The compensation must be increased to the level before the reduction once the AG's financial position has improved.

Reducing compensation has no effect on the validity of the management board member's service agreement. In case of a reduction of compensation, the management board member is, however, entitled to extraordinary termination of his service agreement by giving six weeks' notice to the end of the next calendar quarter.[83] If the board member terminates his service agreement, he also has to declare his resignation from the management board.

§ 48 Increase of compensation

A major improvement in the AG's financial condition does not entitle management board members to any increase of their compensation (unless the compensation had previously been reduced in light of a deterioration of the AG's financial position).[84] Service agreements frequently provide for the supervisory board to reassess the management board member's compensation on a regular basis (e.g., every one or two years) without granting the management board member a right to claim an increase of compensation. For pension commitments, there are generally adjustment clauses adapting the level of pensions to the rate of inflation or a similar

---

80   Aktiengesetz [AktG] [Stock Corporation Act] 1965, § 87, ¶ 2 (F.R.G.).
81   Aktiengesetz [AktG] [Stock Corporation Act] 1965, § 87, ¶ 2 (F.R.G.).
82   Aktiengesetz [AktG] [Stock Corporation Act] 1965, § 107, ¶ 3, sentence 3 (F.R.G.).
83   Aktiengesetz [AktG] [Stock Corporation Act] 1965, § 87, ¶ 4 (F.R.G.).
84   Reducing of the compensation is dealt with in § 47.

measure. Additional compensation by way of special bonus payments generally is an adequate tool to reward special efforts and achievements by members of the management board.[85]

§ 49 Mandatory disclosure of compensation

The total compensation paid to all management board members (as opposed to the compensation received by an individual board member) must be disclosed in the annex to the AG's individual or consolidated annual financial statements. The number and current market value of stock options and other equity-based compensation must be indicated at the time it is granted. Later changes in value that result from a change in the conditions of exercise must be taken into account.

AGs whose shares are listed and traded on a regulated market must disclose the aggregate compensation of each individual management board member, broken down into fixed and performance-related components, and those with long-term incentive effects. The disclosure duty also applies with respect to compensation to which a board member is entitled in the event of termination of his appointment to the management board (*e.g.*, as a result of change of control provisions)[86] as well as with respect to changes agreed thereto during the financial year.[87] If a management board member ceased to be a member of the board during the financial year, the benefits agreed in conjunction with the departure of the board member as well as the benefits actually paid during the financial year have to be disclosed.[88] Finally, benefits promised or provided to a board member by third parties in relation to his activity as a management board member are also subject to the disclosure duty.

The disclosure of individual board members' compensation is not required if the shareholders' meeting opts out of disclosure by adopting a resolution with a majority of at least three-quarters of the share capital present at the shareholders' meeting.[89] Opting out is only possible for a maximum period of five years. It is not possible to opt out of disclosing the aggregate amount of all management board members' total compensation. AGs whose shares are listed and traded on a regulated market also must provide details of the basic principles of the compensation system in their annual report or the group annual report.

Non-listed German AGs are not required to disclose the total compensation of the management board if such disclosure would enable the reader to calculate the individual members' compensation from such information. Generally, this would only be possible if the approximate individual compensation could be calculated by dividing the total compensation by the number of board members. No such calculation could be made if individual board members,

---

85   Compensation awarded at the end of or following the appointment is further discussed in § 52 and § 54.
86   Handelsgesetzbuch [HGB] [Commercial Code] 1897, § 285, no. 9, lit. a), lit. aa), bb), § 314, ¶ 1, no. 6, lit. a), lit. aa), bb) (F.R.G.).
87   Handelsgesetzbuch [HGB] [Commercial Code] 1897, § 285, no. 9, lit. a), lit. cc), § 314, ¶ 1, no. 6, lit. a), lit. cc) (F.R.G.).
88   Handelsgesetzbuch [HGB] [Commercial Code] 1897, § 285, no. 9, lit. a), lit. dd), § 314, ¶ 1, no. 6, lit. dd) (F.R.G.).
89   Handelsgesetzbuch [HGB] [Commercial Code] 1897, § 286, ¶ 5 (F.R.G.).

such as the chairman of the management board, receive significantly higher compensation than the other board members.

The Corporate Governance Code recommends that AGs whose shares are listed and traded on a regulated market publish a compensation report explaining the system of compensation for management board members.[90] This is also advisable if the shareholders' meeting decides to opt out of the disclosure requirements.

§ 50 Right to payment of compensation in case of illness

The Continuation of Pay Act,[91] which provides for the continuation of salary payments in case of illness, does not apply to management board members. If the service agreement does not give a management board member contractual rights to continued compensation in the event of illness, accident or death, the board member is entitled only to continued payment if he is indisposed for a relatively short period (generally no longer than six weeks, but it is unclear how long the period is). Continued payment of compensation should be (and generally is) addressed in the service agreement.

1. Components of compensation
§ 51 Bonus payments

Management board members often receive annual bonus payments as part of their total compensation depending on the AG's economic success. Bonus payments also must meet the criteria for the appropriateness of the compensation.[92]

Agreements on bonus payments vary greatly. The service agreement generally specifies the conditions under which the supervisory board can award bonus payments. The amount of the bonus payment may be linked to financial parameters such as ROCE (return on capital employed) or EBITA (earnings before interest, taxes and amortization) or on achieving separately agreed targets for the individual management board member (target bonus payments). Awarding bonus payments can also be linked to stock-price performance (in absolute terms or in relation to a designated peer group) or be placed at the discretion of the supervisory board. In this way, the supervisory board can take the individual contribution of a management board member into account when deciding on the level of the bonus payment. The fact that the decision to award (or not to award) a bonus payment may, in general, be reviewed by a court mitigates the risk of arbitrary decisions.

§ 52 Appreciation awards

The supervisory board may retroactively award special compensation of services previously rendered if the contractually agreed compensation appears insufficient in light of the extraordinary performance of a management board member. A payment for services already rendered to the AG or the retroactive increase of compensation can raise legal concerns, unless the service

---

90   Deutscher Corporate Governance Kodex [DCGK] [German Corporate Governance Code] 2010, 4.2.5. (F.R.G.).
91   Entgeltfortzahlungsgesetz [EFZG] [Continuation of Pay Act] 1994 (F.R.G.).
92   Appropriateness of compensation is discussed in detail in §§ 57 et seq.

agreement specifically provides that the supervisory board, in its discretion, may grant special bonus payments for past services as a means of rewarding a board member. In the highly-publicized Mannesmann/Vodafone case, the public prosecutor even brought criminal charges with respect to the appreciation awards paid to members of the Mannesmann's management board in connection with the takeover by Vodafone.

If the service agreement is silent on retroactive increases of compensation or appreciation awards, a stricter test applies. The German Supreme Court ruled in the Mannesmann/Voda-fone case that payment of an appreciation award not contemplated in the service agreement is not permitted if it merely rewards past services that do not result in any advantages to the AG in the future. Furthermore, a clause in the service agreement on retroactive increases in compensation and potential payment of appreciation awards does not relieve the supervisory board of its duty to examine the appropriateness of the compensation granted in each individual case.

§ 53 Stock options, share awards and other equity-linked compensation

Equity-compensation plans take various forms, which can raise complex legal and tax issues.[93] Such plans enable the AG to structure part of the variable compensation of a management board member as a long-term incentive. In its purest form, an equity-compensation plan grants the beneficiaries the right (option) to acquire a certain number of shares of the AG at a fixed price within a certain period of time. The fixed price generally corresponds to the stock exchange price on the day when the option is granted, thus giving the beneficiaries the chance of benefitting from future increases in the stock price. Under the Stock Corporation Act, there is a mandatory waiting period of four years before a stock option may be exercised and the shares acquired thereby may be sold. Shares to be delivered upon the exercise of stock options generally are newly issued by the AG out of the AG's so-called conditional capital (*bedingtes Kapital*). As a legal matter, the AG may, however, also use treasury stock or shares acquired under hedging arrangements with third parties to fulfill its obligations under stock option programs. *In lieu*, or as an additional feature, of stock option programs, AGs may offer or require direct investments in the AG's stock by members of the board of management.

An alternative are virtual programs: Management board members participating in such programs receive additional compensation in cash based upon the development of the AG's stock price. Such plans are often labeled "phantom stocks" or "stock appreciation rights".

The issuance of new shares to board members or employees, whether directly or in accordance with the terms of a stock option program, generally requires a resolution of the AG's shareholders' meeting, adopted with a majority of at least three-quarters of the share capital represented at voting, regarding an increase of the share capital. In the case of stock option programs, the shareholders' resolution must specify the number of shares available for the program and the allocation of the subscription rights to the management board members, members of the management of subsidiaries, and employees of the AG and subsidiaries. The shareholders' meeting

---

93   Taxation of compensation is dealt with in §§ 59 *et seq.*

also must decide upon the basic parameters of the program, such as the targets (*e.g.*, a certain share price), the periods for acquiring and exercising rights, and the waiting periods until exercise of the stock options (at least four years). The supervisory board is responsible for specifying the details of the program, in particular the amount of management board compensation covered by stock options, and the grant of options to individual members of the management board.[94] By contrast, virtual programs can in most cases be implemented by the supervisory board without a shareholder resolution.

§ 54 Retirement pensions and benefits for dependants of a deceased board member

A management board member is entitled to retirement benefits only if the service agreement or a separate retirement pension agreement provides for such benefits. In absence of such an agreement, the board member is not entitled to retirement benefits even if it has become the custom of the AG to provide all management board members with such benefits. In practice, management board members often receive retirement pensions including a widow's and orphans' pension, and disability benefits. The requirement as to the appropriateness of the level of compensation also applies to retirement pensions and related benefits.[95]

Pension commitments may be static in that the board member is to receive a fixed recurring amount on reaching a pensionable age. By contrast, dynamic pension commitments link the amount of the retirement pension to indices, inflation or provide for fixed increases of the pension.[96]

It is important that the contractual pension arrangements set out the precise basis for calculating the retirement pension, in particular which parts of the board member's compensation are taken into account for calculating the amount of the retirement pension. The retirement pension arrangements may provide that compensation for contractual non-compete obligations are offset against the retirement pension.

The Improvement of Company Pension Schemes Act applies to most management board members who are entitled to retirement pensions.[97] The statutory provisions, *inter alia*, do not apply to management board members who hold a significant interest in the AG. If the statutory provisions are applicable, a pension commitment generally results in a vested right that does not lapse in case a board member leaves the management board prior to having reached a pensionable age.

Serious misconduct of a management board member towards the AG, such as accepting bribes or engaging in other serious criminal conduct in the course of performing professional duties, may justify a refusal by the AG to honor its retirement pension commitment. However, the rescission or reduction of retirement benefits is an exceptional measure. Even gross misconduct

---

94   Aktiengesetz [AktG] [Stock Corporation Act] 1965, § 192, ¶ 2, no. 3, § 193, ¶ 2, no. 4 (F.R.G.).
95   Appropriateness of overall compensation is dealt with in §§ 57 *et seq.*
96   Clauses that provide protection against inflation are discussed in § 55.
97   Gesetz zur Verbesserung der betrieblichen Altersversorgung [BetrAVG] [Improvement of Company Pension Schemes Act] 1974 (F.R.G.).

often does not justify a complete rescission of the retirement pension agreement. Less serious violations of a board member's duties, on the other hand, may not even be a basis for reducing retirement benefits.

If the retirement pension agreement contains a "survivor clause", which names the spouse of the management board member as beneficiary, the spouse acquires a direct right to payment against the AG upon the board member's death. The widow's pension is usually 50–60% of the management board member's retirement pension entitlement. It is often agreed that the claim to a widow's pension requires that the board member was married to the surviving spouse for a certain period of time.

Historically, pension liabilities of German companies were on-balance sheet obligations similar to other liabilities. In recent years, many companies have, however, used contractual trust arrangements (CTAs) to improve balance sheet ratios or credit ratings. The use of CTAs and other techniques to achieve the off-balance treatment of pension liabilities raises a number of accounting, labor law and tax issues.

§ 55 Inflation protection of retirement pensions

Retirement pension arrangements often provide for protection against inflation. Other components of compensation may also be protected against inflation. Germany has adopted strict statutory limitations on the permissibility of indexation clauses providing for automatic adjustment of the pension entitlement to a cost of living index or other parameters. Some clauses that protect against inflation require approval by the German Federal Bank (*Deutsche Bundesbank*). An alternative to automatic indexation is to grant board members the right to claim appropriate adjustment of retirement pensions in the discretion of the supervisory board. The exercise of such discretion is subject to court review.

A method often used for inflation protection, which does not require regulatory approval, are clauses providing for the pension to be adjusted based upon increases to the salary or pension of a specified civil servants' salary group, collective bargaining group or old-age social security benefits.

If contractual provisions do not require an adjustment of a retirement pension, the AG may still be under an obligation (based on the Improvement of Company Pension Schemes Act or the principle of good faith) to review the retirement pension with respect to possible adjustment every three years, and to make what it considers to be a fair decision. In doing so, it must take into account the economic situation of the recipient and that of the AG.

§ 56 Loans to members of the management board

Loans granted by the AG to a management board member require approval by the supervisory board.[98] The supervisory board may delegate the decision on whether to grant such approval

---

98   Aktiengesetz [AktG] [Stock Corporation Act] 1965, § 89 (F.R.G.), with the exception of loans not exceeding a one month gross salary.

to a supervisory board committee. The approval resolution must relate to a particular loan or particular type of loan and may not be adopted more than three months before the loan is paid out. The resolution must set out the interest rate and the terms of repayment of the loan, although a specific repayment date need not be specified.

These approval requirements also apply to other financial arrangements that are similar to loans in an economic sense, such as, trade credit and acceptance credit, current account credit, guarantees or extensions beyond customary periods for the reimbursement of monies owed by a board member to the AG.

Loans to natural persons or companies related to, or affiliated with, a management board member (*e.g.*, spouses or children and, arguably, legal entities or partnerships in which the board member holds a significant interest) or anyone acting for the account of the board member, must also be approved by the supervisory board. The same applies to loans to other companies if a management board member of the AG is at the same time a senior executive or a member of the supervisory body of the borrower.[99] Special rules apply for AGs that are banks or financial services firms.

If a loan is made without the required supervisory board approval, the loan agreement is nonetheless valid. However, unless the supervisory board approves the loan retroactively, the loan must be repaid immediately.[100] By contrast, if the loan agreement itself was not properly executed by the supervisory board (*e.g.*, signed by a supervisory board member without proper authorization), the loan agreement is void and any funds that have been disbursed thereunder must be repaid according to the rules of general civil law.

2.   Appropriateness of compensation
§ 57 Parameters for assessing appropriateness

When setting the management board's compensation, the supervisory board must ensure that the level of total compensation payable to an individual board member is appropriate.[101] The question of appropriateness is assessed at the time when the compensation is fixed. Special requirements apply to later adjustment of the compensation.[102]

The test is whether the total compensation of a management board member is appropriate to his tasks and performance, on the one hand, and the AG's financial position, on the other hand. Moreover, the supervisory board has to verify that the total compensation of a management board member does not exceed the customary compensation without good reasons. Pension benefits, including retirement compensation, payments to dependants and similar benefits, must also be appropriate in light of all circumstances.

---

99   Aktiengesetz [AktG] [Stock Corporation Act] 1965, § 89, ¶ 4, sentence 1 (F.R.G.). A supervisory board
     resolution is not required in case of group companies or if the loan is granted for the payment of goods [AktG]
     [Stock Corporation Act] 1965, § 89, ¶ 4, sentence 2 (F.R.G.).
100 Aktiengesetz [AktG] [Stock Corporation Act] 1965, § 89, ¶ 5 (F.R.G.).
101 Aktiengesetz [AktG] [Stock Corporation Act] 1965, § 87, ¶ 1, sentence 1 (F.R.G.).
102 Adjustment of compensation is dealt with in § 47, § 48.

Factors to be taken into account include the scope and significance of the tasks given to a management board member (*e.g.*, role of chairman of the management board, special areas of responsibility), his qualifications, the size, economic situation and future prospects[103] of the AG as well as the level of compensation that is customary in the region, in the sector and for a company of comparable size, on the one hand, and the general structure of worker and employee compensation within the AG, on the other hand. Generally, the level of compensation may be based on the prevailing compensation in comparable AGs. The easiest way to ensure that the board's compensation is appropriate in relation to the AG's financial position is through variable compensation components linked to the AG's (long-term) success. Such components should contain elements combining long-term incentives and elements of risk, such as share awards with vesting or lock-up periods of at least four years,[104] stock options or virtual equity-linked compensation programs.[105] Given the recent adoption of new statutory requirements relating to the long-term nature of variable compensation components, there is little guidance on how to apply the criteria in practice. Thus, the supervisory board has to make a reasonable decision based on the circumstances of each specific case.

For AGs whose shares are listed and traded on a regulated market, the compensation structure has to be linked to the sustainable success of the company.[106] Therefore, variable elements of the compensation must be based upon the AG's performance measured over several years and taking into account any negative developments within that period.

§ 58 Legal consequences of excessive management board benefits

Excessive management board compensation does not render the service agreement invalid or ineffective. The board member still has a contractual claim to the full compensation. A board member who is awarded and accepts excessive compensation by the supervisory board may, however, be held liable for damages to the AG. If supervisory board members acted culpably in granting the excessive compensation, they are liable to damages for violating their fiduciary duties to the AG.[107]

Under German tax law, excessive benefits to management board members who are also shareholders of the AG may qualify as hidden profit distributions. Hidden profit distributions are not deductible from the AG's taxable income and therefore subject to corporate income and trade tax.

3.   Overview of taxation of compensation
§ 59 Liability of management board members to German tax authorities

The compensation received by management board members of an AG is subject to German personal income tax (*Einkommensteuer*), a solidarity surcharge (*Solidaritätszuschlag*) thereon

---

103 Deutscher Corporate Governance Kodex [DCGK] [German Corporate Governance Code] 2010, 4.2.2 (F.R.G.).
104 Aktiengesetz [AktG] [Stock Corporation Act] 1965, § 193, ¶ 2, no. 4 (F.R.G.).
105 Stock options are dealt with in § 53.
106 Aktiengesetz [AktG] [Stock Corporation Act] 1965, § 87, ¶ 1, sentence 2 (F.R.G.).
107 Aktiengesetz [AktG] [Stock Corporation Act] 1965, § 116, sentence 3 (F.R.G.).

and, if applicable, church tax (*Kirchensteuer*).[108] The tax is collected by way of withholding from the AG's payments.[109] The combined tax rate is progressive and varies between approximately 14.77% – 50%, depending on the board members' personal income situation.

Taxation of board members may also raise questions of international tax law. Citizenship is irrelevant for determining the liability to German personal income tax. A board member's compensation is subject to German personal income tax in any case, but it is important to note that residence or habitual abode of a board member in Germany triggers so-called unlimited liability to German income tax (*unbeschränkte Steuerpflicht*). A management board member generally meets this test if he maintains an apartment under circumstance that justify the conclusion that he will maintain and use the apartment or, alternatively, if he stays in Germany for more than six months during a calendar year. Short-term absences are not taken into account.[110] Details should be discussed with a personal tax advisor. If a board member is subject to unlimited tax liability, his worldwide personal income (*e.g.*, all domestic and international earnings, whether or not related to the position on the management board) are generally subject to German income tax. By contrast, a management board member who does not reside in Germany and does not have his habitual abode in Germany is taxed in Germany only on his German source income.[111] However, it has to be noted that even in case of unlimited German tax liability in most cases double taxation of income is mitigated or totally avoided due to applicable double tax treaties concluded between Germany and many countries or German unilateral tax provisions. Board members are urged to discuss their personal income tax situations with a personal tax advisor.

§ 60 Taxable income

Generally, all components of compensation are subject to German personal income tax. Special rules apply for the taxation of retirement pensions.[112]

If a company car is made available to a management board member, the monetary benefit attributed to the private use constitutes taxable income. The monetary benefit from the private use of company-owned computers or other telecommunication devices, such as telephones, mobile phones or BlackBerrys, is generally tax-free.[113] By contrast, the transfer of ownership of such equipment to a board member free of charge or at a reduced price constitutes taxable income.

In general, the management board member is not entitled to deduct input-VAT for services or supplies received and does not qualify as entrepreneur for German value added tax purposes. However, due to recent changes in the case law, management board members may under certain prerequisites be viewed as entrepreneurs thus potentially being able to deduct input-VAT.

---

108 Einkommensteuergesetz [EStG] [Income Tax Act] 1934, §§ 1, 49 (F.R.G.).
109 Social security contributions are dealt with in § 62.
110 Einkommensteuergesetz [EStG] [Income Tax Act] 1934, § 1, ¶ 1, sentence 1. (F.R.G.), Abgabenordnung [AO] [General Tax Code] 1976, §§ 8, 9 (F.R.G.).
111 Einkommensteuergesetz [EStG] [Income Tax Act] 1934, § 49, ¶ 1, no. 4, lit. c) (F.R.G.).
112 Art. 18 of the OECD Model Convention on Income and Capital.
113 Einkommensteuergesetz [EStG] [Income Tax Act] 1934, § 3, no. 45 (F.R.G.).

§ 61 Timing of taxation

Personal income tax is an annual tax. Taxable income is taxed in the calendar year in which the income is received by the board member. Bonus payments, for instance, are not taxed when the contractual claim to the bonus payment arises, but at the time the bonus payment is actually paid. Under certain prerequisites, payments may be treated as income received for more than one tax period subject to a preferential tax rate.

The timing for taxing share awards and stock options is complex and depends upon their specific features. To mention a few guiding principles, freely transferable stock options are generally taxed at the time the stock option is either exercised or sold by the board member (although an older view that is sometimes still followed by the tax authorities takes the position that a freely transferable stock option is taxed at the time it is granted to the board member). The tax is generally levied on the difference between the fair market value of, and the lower purchase price paid for, the stock option or the underlying shares. If stock options are structured such as that they are not freely transferable (e.g., the options may not be sold, transferred or pledged) by the management board member for a specified blocking period, the options are generally taxable after the expiration of the blocking period, or, if earlier, when the stock options become exercisable assuming that the shares received upon exercise are freely transferable. Payments under phantom stock and similar cash-settled programs are generally taxed when the cash payment is received by the board member.

§ 62 Social security contributions

Management board members are exempt from making contributions to the German statutory pension and old age insurance (*Rentenversicherung*)[114], statutory unemployment insurance (*Arbeitslosenversicherung*)[115] and statutory personal accident insurance (*Unfallversicherung*) with regard to compensation received for their management board services. Management board members will also generally be exempt from making contributions to the statutory health insurance (*Krankenversicherung*) and nursing care insurance (*Pflegeversicherung*) but under certain prerequisites an obligation to contribute may arise depending on the individual circumstances. Any contributions payable by the AG to the board member for private insurance contracts should be addressed in the service agreement.

C. Other rights and duties arising from the service agreement[116]

§ 63 Vacation entitlement

In relation to a management board member's vacation entitlement, the statutory provisions concerning vacation[117] are not applicable because the board member is not an employee of the AG. If the board member's service agreement does not provide for vacation, he is still

---

114 Sozialgesetzbuch VI [SGB VI] [Social Security Act VI] 1989, § 1 sentence 4 (F.R.G.).
115 Sozialgesetzbuch III [SGB III] [Social Security Act III] 1997, § 27, ¶ 1, no. 5 (F.R.G.).
116 *Cf.* Form of Service Agreement for management board members of the AG attached in Chapter Seven: Annex I.A.
117 Bundesurlaubsgesetz [BUrlG] [Federal Holiday with Pay Act] 1963 (F.R.G.).

entitled to appropriate vacation time, which is to be determined by the supervisory board in its reasonable discretion. It is advisable to include the key elements of the vacation arrangement in the service agreement. For example, a vacation clause may specify the amount of vacation to which the management board member is entitled, how long an individual vacation may last, when the vacation may be taken (*e.g.*, in consultation with the other management board members), and when vacation entitlements lapse.

§ 64 Rights to inventions
Service agreements often also include provisions concerning the management board members' rights to their inventions. If an agreement does not contain any such provisions, and does not specify that the board member's regular compensation is considered to satisfy all claims for compensation for rights arising from inventions, the board member should be entitled to appropriate compensation for such rights. The statutory provisions relating to inventions of employees are not applicable.

§ 65 Prohibition of competition
Management board members are subject to a statutory prohibition on competitive activities for the duration of their appointment. From the AG's perspective, a contractual provision extending restrictions on competition beyond the term of the appointment is often desirable. There are strict statutory limitations on the permissibility of such contractual provisions.[118] For example, the restriction must protect legitimate interests of the AG and may not unfairly restrict the place, time or scope of the former management board member's professional or financial activities. The maximum permissible duration of a post-contractual non-compete clause is about two years. Furthermore, the management board member must be adequately compensated for the non-competition obligation, although details of the compensation requirement are unclear. Compensation for post-contractual non-compete obligations is often addressed in the service agreement.

IV. Managing the AG

§ 66 The management board's role as corporate management body
The management board has the duty to manage the AG in its own responsibility.[119] The management board, in general, is the sole body authorized to conduct business in the name and on behalf of the AG. It is responsible for formulating and implementing the AG's strategy (which includes corporate policy, business development, decisions on business-related and financial risks along with coordination, control and financing) as well as for taking day-to-day actions and decisions. By contrast, the supervisory board is responsible for control and oversight of the management board's activities. The shareholders' meeting, the third corporate body of the AG, adopts the articles of association of the AG, elects the representatives of the shareholders on

---

118   Gesetz gegen Wettbewerbsbeschränkungen [GWB] [Act against Restraints of Competition], 1998, § 1 (F.R.G.), Bürgerliches Gesetzbuch [BGB] [Civil Code] 1896, § 138 (F.R.G.).
119   Aktiengesetz [AktG] [Stock Corporation Act] 1965, § 76, ¶ 1 (F.R.G.).

the supervisory board, and resolves on important corporate decisions which are allocated to it by statute, such as dividend distributions, issuance of new shares or corporate reorganizations, or on which the management board requests a shareholder vote. The mandatory division of powers among the three bodies of the AG cannot be altered by the articles of association or otherwise.[120] The dual board structure distinguishes the AG from stock corporations in most other jurisdictions, which provide for only one body, the "board of directors," with responsibility for managing and overseeing the AG's affairs.[121]

The management board's duty to manage the AG is the joint obligation of all members of the board.[122] Managing the AG comprises all decisions and actions serving the purpose of the AG, irrespective of whether an action constitutes a legal transaction having external effects or merely an internal matter. In particular, the term "managing" includes entrepreneurial and steering responsibility, oversight of the activities of the employees of the AG, and compliance with all of the AG's legal obligations. Tasks that fall within the core area of management may not be delegated to subordinate levels within the AG or outsourced to third parties. Management board members have a duty to the AG to comply with the restrictions imposed by law, the articles of association, the supervisory board, the shareholders' meeting and the rules of procedure of the management board.[123] Violating any such restrictions may render the management board members personally liable for damages to the AG or may constitute cause for revoking a management board member's appointment.[124]

§ 67 Principle of joint management

The Stock Corporation Act requires the management board members to manage the AG jointly ("principle of joint management").[125] Joint management means that either all board members act together, or that the other board members consent to the actions of the acting member(s). Management decisions are taken in the form of management board resolutions.[126]

§ 68 Deviations from the principle of joint management

The AG's articles of association or the rules of procedure of the management board[127] may provide that the management board's resolutions may be adopted by majority vote. In addition, or alternatively, the AG's articles of association or the supervisory board may allocate certain responsibilities to individual management board members. Even if different responsibilities are allocated among the board members, generally by way of a schedule of responsibilities

---

120   Aktiengesetz [AktG] [Stock Corporation Act] 1965, § 23, ¶ 5 (F.R.G.).
121   The situation may differ in the case of a German SE, which need not have a separate supervisory board, cf. §§ 354 et seq.
122   Aktiengesetz [AktG] [Stock Corporation Act] 1965, § 76, ¶ 1, § 77, ¶ 1 (F.R.G.).
123   Aktiengesetz [AktG] [Stock Corporation Act] 1965, § 82, ¶ 2 (F.R.G.).
124   §§ 137 et seq. deal with the liability of management board members, § 31 deals with revocation of the appointment based upon cause.
125   Aktiengesetz [AktG] [Stock Corporation Act] 1965, § 77, ¶ 1 (F.R.G.).
126   Management board resolutions are covered in further detail in §§ 78 et seq.
127   The rules of procedure of the management board are covered in further detail in § 73.

(*Geschäftsverteilungsplan*),[128] the basic principle that the management board is a cooperative body with joint responsibility for managing the AG remains valid.[129] All management board members therefore have a duty of oversight and control with respect to all decisions and actions taken by the management board as a whole or individual board members.[130] Matters of fundamental importance to the AG must always be submitted for discussion and decision to the management board as a whole.

§ 69 Majority decisions

The rules of procedure of the management board (or the AG's articles of association) may provide that all decisions or decisions concerning certain subjects require only a simple or qualified majority (instead of unanimity). Decisions taken on the basis of such provisions nevertheless bind those management board members who were outvoted or did not participate in the decision.[131] The AG's articles of association or rules of procedure may also provide that, in the event of a tie vote, the chairman of the management board has a casting vote.[132] By contrast, individual management board members may not be given the right to take decisions or actions contrary to the board's majority.[133] With respect to an AG that is not subject to co-determination on a parity basis, it should, however, be permissible to give a minority (or even an individual member) of the management board the right to veto decisions taken by the majority of the board members. In co-determined AGs, minority veto rights are impermissible as the role of the labor director whose position must be equal to that of the other board members could be undermined.[134]

§ 70 Individual management authority

The articles of association of the AG or the rules of procedure for the management board may grant individual board members the authority to take decisions without the need for authorization by the full management board. In addition or as an alternative, the articles of association or the rules of procedure may give a board member the right to object to management decisions and actions taken by another board member (veto right). If such a veto right is used, the decision or action has to be discussed by the management board as a whole before it may be carried out.

§ 71 Allocation of tasks within the board: Schedule of responsibilities

In practice, management activity is so extensive and diversified that it becomes necessary to allocate specific responsibilities among the management board members. This is generally

---

128 The schedule of responsibility is covered in further detail in § 71.
129 Aktiengesetz [AktG] [Stock Corporation Act] 1965, § 76, ¶ 1 (F.R.G.); Bürgerliches Gesetzbuch [BGB] [Civil Code] 1896, §§ 164 *et seq.* (F.R.G.).
130 The duty of oversight and control is dealt with in further detail in § 72.
131 However, an exception are management board decisions that are damaging the AG: In that case the dissenting management board members must try to protect the AG from damages in order to avoid personal liability. *Cf.* § 152.
132 A casting vote is not permissible in case the management board has only two members as this would factually result in the chairman of the management board having individual management authorization which would render the other management board member incapable of exerting influence.
133 Aktiengesetz [AktG] [Stock Corporation Act] 1965, § 77, ¶ 1, sentence 2 (F.R.G.).
134 Mitbestimmungsgesetz [MitbestG] [Co-Determination Act] 1976, § 33 (F.R.G.). *Cf.* § 11.

done by the rules of procedure of the management board, supplemented by a schedule of responsibilities.

Responsibilities and related management authority of the individual management board members are often allocated based on different corporate functions, *e.g.*, research & development, human resources, compliance & legal, finance, sales, production, etc. It is also common to arrange responsibilities according to lines of business, such as product groups or regional markets.

The schedule of responsibilities may be adopted and changed in the same way as the rules of procedure of the management board. The management board itself thus may adopt a schedule of responsibilities, unless the supervisory board decides to do so. In any event, the supervisory board always retains the power to change the schedule of responsibilities.

§ 72 Duties of oversight and control

If specific responsibilities have been allocated to individual management board members, such board members have a duty to report to the management board as a whole on a regular basis or in case of important developments in their area of responsibility, or upon request of the management board. In light of the principle of joint management, management board members also have a duty to oversee and control the activities not assigned to them. Based on this duty, they are entitled, and in certain cases may be required, to object to decisions or actions by other management board members. In such a case, either the decision or action in question may not be carried out, or the management board as a whole must resolve the matter.

§ 73 Rules of procedure of the management board

In practice, the rules of procedure of the management board govern the day-to-day procedures and interactions of the management board members.[135] The management board's rules of procedure or the AG's articles of association may contain rules deviating from the principle of joint management and the requirement to adopt board decisions by unanimous resolutions.[136] Typically, the rules of procedure set out principles for the collaboration among the management board members as well as details of the interplay between the management board and the supervisory board. The schedule of responsibilities often forms an integral part of the rules of procedure. Also, the rules of procedure generally contain a list of decisions and actions that require the consent of the supervisory board.[137]

The management board itself may adopt its rules of procedure, unless the articles of association allocate responsibility therefore to the supervisory board or the supervisory board has decided to adopt the rules of procedure of the management board. It is also permissible that rules of procedure adopted by the management board itself are made subject to the consent of the supervisory board before entering into effect. Specific aspects of the rules of procedure may be contained in the AG's articles of association.[138] Management board resolutions regarding the

---

135   Aktiengesetz [AktG] [Stock Corporation Act] 1965, § 77, ¶ 2 (F.R.G.).
136   The principle of joint management is dealt with in further detail in § 67.
137   Required consent of the supervisory board is dealt with in further detail in § 75.
138   Aktiengesetz [AktG] [Stock Corporation Act] 1965, § 77, ¶ 2, sentence 2 (F.R.G.).

adoption or amendment of the rules of procedure must be adopted unanimously.[139] If the supervisory board decides to override the rules of procedure adopted by the management board, the rules of procedure previously adopted by the management board cease to be effective.

Once adopted, the rules of procedure remain in force irrespective of any changes in the composition of the management board. Accordingly, the rules of procedure also apply to newly appointed members of the management board who have not explicitly consented to such rules prior to their appointment.

A. Independent management of the AG

§ 74 Independence of the management board members

As a general rule, the management board manages the AG on its own responsibility.[140] Board members are free from instructions of the supervisory board or individual shareholders. The management board is, however, required to implement the resolutions adopted by the shareholders' meeting of the AG within its scope of authority.[141] Even if certain types of transactions require the consent of the supervisory board,[142] the supervisory board is not authorized to give instructions to the management board.

The management board exercises its business discretion when taking decisions and actions. Its guiding objective must be to serve the interests of the AG.[143] In exercising its discretion, the management board must consider the interests of all stakeholders of the AG, including those of the shareholders, the employees and the general public. In case of conflicts, the management board must weigh the different interests. Decisions and actions by the management board will generally be in the corporate interest if they serve the continued existence and long-term profitability of the AG.

The management board's duty to base its decisions and actions on the corporate interest of the AG also applies if the AG is a subsidiary within a corporate group or otherwise is subject to the control of another company or person. As a general matter, the management board of the controlled AG may not take any decisions or actions detrimental to the AG even if they are in the interest of the group.[144] If a controlling shareholder insists that the controlled AG take a decision or measure that is prejudicial to the AG, the management board of the controlled AG may only take such decision or action if it has ascertained that the controlling shareholder is willing and able to compensate the AG for any adverse consequences.[145] Different rules apply, however, if the AG is subject to a control agreement.[146]

---

139 Aktiengesetz [AktG] [Stock Corporation Act] 1965, § 77, ¶ 2, sentence 3 (F.R.G.).
140 Aktiengesetz [AktG] [Stock Corporation Act] 1965, § 76 (F.R.G.).
141 Aktiengesetz [AktG] [Stock Corporation Act] 1965, § 83, ¶ 2 (F.R.G.).
142 Consent requirements applicable to the management board are discussed in further detail in § 75.
143 Aktiengesetz [AktG] [Stock Corporation Act] 1965, § 93, ¶ 1, sentence 2 (F.R.G.).
144 Aktiengesetz [AktG] [Stock Corporation Act] 1965, §§ 316, 317 (F.R.G.).
145 Aktiengesetz [AktG] [Stock Corporation Act] 1965, §§ 311, 317 (F.R.G.).
146 For further details, *cf.* below § 77.

If decisions of the management board are within the range of good business judgment, the members of the board are deemed to have acted as diligent and conscientious managers and may not be held liable even if the supervisory board is in favor of another decision (business judgment rule).[147]

§ 75 Decisions requiring consent of the supervisory board

The general rule is that the responsibility for managing the AG is solely in the hands of the management board, *i.e.*, the management board is not bound to follow instructions issued by other corporate bodies, individual shareholders or third parties.[148] However, the articles of association or the supervisory board, by way of resolution, may define certain types of management decisions or actions requiring the prior consent of the supervisory board.[149] The underlying rationale is to enable the supervisory board to control the management of the AG effectively. In case of a dispute between the management board and the supervisory board, the management board may call for the shareholders' meeting to grant its consent to the management board's proposal. The shareholders' resolution requires a majority of at least three-quarters of the votes cast.[150]

§ 76 Decisions requiring consent of the shareholders' meeting

The Stock Corporation Act sets forth the authority of the shareholders' meeting. Among other things, the shareholders have to adopt resolutions on the distribution of dividends, the issuance of new shares (unless the shareholders' meeting has previously authorized the board of management to issue a certain number of new shares in specified circumstances – authorized capital or conditional capital), mergers, spinoffs, so-called company agreements (*Unternehmensverträge*), dissolution and liquidation. There are very few matters that must be submitted to a vote by the shareholders' meeting, which are not specified in the Stock Corporation Act. Such matters include the hive-down or disposal of important subsidiaries or other core assets if the value of such assets or their contribution to revenues or income exceeds certain thresholds (so-called *Holzmüller* or *Gelatine* requirements, based upon cases decided by the Federal Supreme Court for Civil Matters (*Bundesgerichtshof, BGH*)). Resolutions of the shareholders' meeting on such matters require a majority of three-quarters of the shareholders present and voting. It is possible that the courts will take the position that the shareholders' meeting has other unwritten powers with respect to decisions on matters that have a significant effect on the rights of the shareholders. The board of management should therefore carefully consider whether to submit a matter to the shareholders' meeting even in the absence of an express statutory requirement if the matter is of great importance to the AG. The Stock Corporation Act permits the board of management to seek a vote of the shareholders even outside the express statutory powers of the shareholders' meeting.[151] Requesting a vote of the shareholders may be advisable in cases in which a particular course of action involves significant risks for

---

147   *Cf.* § 144.
148   *Cf.* § 74.
149   Aktiengesetz [AktG] [Stock Corporation Act] 1965, § 111, ¶ 4, sentence 2 (F.R.G.).
150   Aktiengesetz [AktG] [Stock Corporation Act] 1965, § 111, ¶ 4, sentences 3–5 (F.R.G.).
151   Aktiengesetz [AktG] [Stock Corporation Act] 1965, § 119, ¶ 2 (F.R.G.).

the AG because the discharge by shareholder vote of decisions or actions taken by the board of management may eliminate liability of the board members.[152]

If a decision or action falling within the unwritten powers of the shareholders' meeting is taken by the board of management without the consent of the shareholders' meeting, such decision or action is in principle nevertheless valid. However, management board members may be held personally liable to the AG for any damages arising from such decision or action.[153]

§ 77 Binding instructions for the management board in corporate groups

The principle that the management board manages the AG independently and free from instructions by shareholders or third parties is subject to an exception in corporate groups. An AG that is a subsidiary of another company may enter into a profit transfer and control agreement (*Gewinnabführungs- und Beherrschungsvertrag*) or only a control agreement with its parent company. Based upon such an agreement, the controlling shareholder may issue binding instructions to the management of the controlled AG.[154] Such instructions may be issued to advance the interest of the group as a whole and may be detrimental to the AG. The board of management (or equivalent body) of the controlling shareholder is, however, subject to a statutory obligation to compensate the controlled AG for any loss suffered by the AG as a result of instructions given by the controlling shareholder.

The shareholders of the controlled AG benefit from various statutory protections in the event that a controlling shareholder wishes to enter into a profit transfer and control agreement (or only control agreement) with the AG. First, the shareholders' meeting of the controlled AG must approve the agreement with a qualified majority of three-quarters of the shareholders present and voting. Second, the controlling shareholder must make an offer to the shareholders of the controlled AG to acquire their shares for cash or in exchange for shares of the controlling shareholder (or if the controlling shareholder itself is subject to control by another company shares of such company). Compensation in shares is not possible if the controlling shareholder (or the company controlling it) has its registered office (*Sitz*) outside the European Economic Area. Each shareholder may seek a review of the adequacy of the compensation in appraisal proceedings. Third, the agreement must provide for an adequate periodic compensatory payment to the minority shareholders of the controlled AG that do not sell or exchange their shares.

Special limitations with respect to control agreements apply in the financial and insurance sector. The use of a control agreement may not undermine the regulatory responsibility of the board of management of the controlled AG.

---

152 For further details, *cf.* below § 148.
153 Aktiengesetz [AktG] [Stock Corporation Act] 1965, § 93, ¶ 2 (F.R.G.).
154 Aktiengesetz [AktG] [Stock Corporation Act] 1965, § 291, ¶ 1, § 308, ¶ 1, 2 (F.R.G.).

B.   Management board resolutions

§ 78 Resolutions adopted by the management board

The management board, as a collective body, acts by adopting resolutions. Based upon the principle of joint management, all decisions and actions of the board of management (unless specific tasks are allocated to individual members of the management board as is common in larger companies) require the adoption of a resolution by the management board.[155]

Pursuant to the Stock Corporation Act, management board resolutions generally have to be adopted unanimously.[156] It is, however, permissible to provide for decisions by majority vote in the articles of association of the AG or the rules of procedure for the board of management.[157] There is no prescribed form for adopting board resolutions. Thus, they may be taken at a meeting, by telephone, by circular, in a videoconference or by email. Often, the articles of association or the rules of procedure provide for the form in which management board meetings may be held and resolutions may be adopted. Even if the statutory unanimity rule applies, in cases in which prompt action is required to avoid serious risks for the AG, management board members that are absent and cannot be reached do not have to consent.[158] The absent members must, however, be informed promptly and may object to the proposed action as long as it has not been carried out.

§ 79 Conflicts of interest

The Stock Corporation Act does not contain specific provisions on conflicts of interest with respect to management board members. Accordingly, it is often difficult to determine whether a board member should abstain from voting. Scenarios involving dual board memberships in a parent company and a subsidiary do not necessarily disqualify the board member concerned from voting on a matter that concerns the relationship of the two companies.[159]

In practice, it is advisable to ensure transparency by disclosing all potential conflicts of interest to the other board members. Section 4.3.4 of the Corporate Governance Code requires members of the board of management to make such disclosure. Based upon such disclosure, the board member concerned should discuss the appropriate course of action with his colleagues on the board of management and the chairman of the supervisory board. If in doubt, a board member should abstain from voting. If necessary to ensure that the board can have a frank discussion on a matter in which a member of the board has a personal interest, the board member should excuse himself from the discussion.

---

155   The principle of joint management is covered in further detail in § 67.

156   An exemption applies in case of the convening of a shareholders' meeting. Here, a simple majority resolution of the management board is sufficient, Aktiengesetz [AktG] [Stock Corporation Act] 1965, § 121, ¶ 2, sentence 1 (F.R.G.).

157   Cf. above § 69.

158   Handelsgesetzbuch [HGB] [Commercial Code] 1897, § 115, ¶ 2, (F.R.G.) *mutatis mutandis.*

159   Indeed, the Banking Act, which requires a unanimous resolution of all members of the board of management of the AG for credit decisions with respect to related parties, requires a board member who has a personal interest in the matter to participate in the vote. Cf. Kreditwesengesetz [KWG] [Banking Act] 1961, § 15 (F.R.G.).

If the vote to be taken by the board of management concerns a legal transaction or a legal dispute between the AG and a member of the board of management, the board member concerned may not participate in the vote. Otherwise, the vote is invalid.[160] This prohibition on voting also applies to a member of the management board of a parent company who at the same time is a board member of a subsidiary in respect of a resolution by the board of management of the parent company discharging the acts of the board of the subsidiary during the previous fiscal year.

§ 80 Deficiencies in adopting resolutions

If error, misrepresentation or any other deficiency affects the vote cast by a management board member, the resolution will not be invalid, unless it would not have been adopted without such vote.

C. Representation of the AG *vis-à-vis* third parties

§ 81 General principles

German law distinguishes between the (external) power to represent the AG *vis-à-vis* third parties (*i.e.*, the power to enter into contractual relationships with third parties for and on behalf of the AG) and the (internal) authority to manage the AG. The power of representation and the authority of management are not necessarily coextensive. Often, the power of representation exceeds the authority to manage.

The power of representation is reflected in the records of the commercial register, on which counterparties of the AG may rely on. Legal actions taken by a management board member in the exercise of the power of representation are binding upon the AG.[161] The AG is required to file all changes in the power of representation for registration with the commercial register.[162] The authority to manage the AG is a purely internal matter and therefore generally is not communicated to third parties.

The Stock Corporation Act empowers (and obligates) the management board to represent the AG *vis-à-vis* third parties.[163] This statutory power of representation of the management board member, in principle, is unlimited. Unlike the laws of other jurisdictions, German law does not provide for a concept of *"ultra-vires"*. The power of representation of a management board member is not (and cannot be) limited by the AG's articles of association or the AG's corporate purpose or scope of business. The AG is protected against a management board member exceeding his authority to manage the AG or acting to the detriment of the AG by

---

160 Bürgerliches Gesetzbuch [BGB] [Civil Code] 1896, §§ 134, 28, ¶ 1 (F.R.G.).
161 Aktiengesetz [AktG] [Stock Corporation Act] 1965, § 82, ¶ 2 (F.R.G.).
162 Aktiengesetz [AktG] [Stock Corporation Act] 1965, § 37, ¶ 3, no. 2, § 39, ¶ 1, sentence 3, § 81, ¶ 1 (F.R.G.).
163 However, the supervisory board represents the AG *vis-à-vis* the members of the management board, *e.g.*, the power of representation of the management board members does not include the right to represent the AG toward another member of the management board, *cf.* Aktiengesetz [AktG] [Stock Corporation Act] 1965, § 112 (F.R.G.).

the statutory provisions on (i) personal liability for civil damages and (ii) criminal liability of the management board member.

If the AG is dissolved, the liquidators (rather than the management board members) are authorized to represent the AG.[164] Similarly, if insolvency proceedings are opened with respect to the AG, the insolvency trustee replaces the management board members as the person entitled to represent the AG.

The power of representation, which is a statutory right inherent to the position of a management board member, must not be confused with a power of attorney granted to employees of an AG, which follows separate rules.

It is sufficient if declarations to be made by third parties *vis-à-vis* the AG are delivered to only one management board member.[165]

§ 82 Joint power of representation
The statutory concept is that all management board members are authorized to represent the AG acting jointly.[166] Joint power of representation is exercised through (i) joint declarations of the management board or (ii) several separate declarations by all management board members with identical content. If the declaration by the AG requires a particular legal form (*e.g.*, written form or notarization), the declarations of each management board member must also satisfy the form requirement. If the management board consists of only one person that person is authorized to represent the AG acting alone.

The statutory requirement of joint representation by all management board members is impracticable for larger AGs. It is thus possible for the articles of association of an AG to provide for rules of representation that deviate from the principle of joint representation. Alternatively, the articles of association of an AG may authorize the supervisory board to grant some or all members of the management board power of representation that deviates from the statutory concept.[167] It is possible to differentiate among the different board members with respect to the power of representation granted to them.

Common structures are individual representation (*i.e.*, each board member has the right to represent the AG individually), representation by two management board members jointly (so-called modified joint representation) or representation by one or more management board members jointly with a Prokurist (in addition to the joint power of representation of such board member(s) with the other board member(s)).[168]

---

164   Aktiengesetz [AktG] [Stock Corporation Act] 1965, §§ 265, 269 (F.R.G.).
165   Aktiengesetz [AktG] [Stock Corporation Act] 1965, § 78, ¶ 2 sentence 2, § 81, ¶ 1 (F.R.G.).
166   Aktiengesetz [AktG] [Stock Corporation Act] 1965, § 78, ¶ 2, sentence 1 (F.R.G.). However, each management
        board member is empowered severally to file for insolvency of the AG (if the conditions for such a filing are met).
        [InsO] [Insolvency Code] 1994, § 15, ¶ 1, sentence 2 (F.R.G.).
167   Aktiengesetz [AktG] [Stock Corporation Act] 1965, § 78, ¶ 2, sentence 1, ¶ 3, sentence 2 (F.R.G.).
168   Aktiengesetz [AktG] [Stock Corporation Act] 1965, § 78, ¶ 3, sentence 1 (F.R.G.).

No management board member may be entirely excluded from representing the AG.

§ 83 Limited authorization for certain specific business transactions[169]

Management board members holding joint power of representation may grant limited authorization to individual management board members empowering them to execute a specific business transaction or certain specific types of business transactions. Such limited authorization must be sufficiently precise and restricted to a single transaction or at most to certain areas of business. Otherwise, the underlying concept of joint representation would be circumvented. Therefore, a delegation of authority limited solely based upon a maximum monetary amount is not permissible. Such an individual limited authorization may be revoked at any time by any of the board members who participated in granting it without providing specific reasons.

§ 84 Restrictions on the power of presentation

Internal restrictions on the authority of the management board (*e.g.*, the assignment of an area of competence by the rules of procedure or the requirement for internal consents by the supervisory board) do not affect the board's external power of representation *vis-à-vis* third parties.[170] If a board member uses his power of representation in violation of internal restrictions, the resulting contract or transaction generally is valid and binding upon the AG, but the board member may be liable for damages to the AG. Very limited exceptions to the principle of the external validity apply in the event of an abuse of the power of representation.[171]

Management board members may not represent the AG in transactions with themselves or other management board members. Only the supervisory board may represent the AG *vis-à-vis* a management board member.[172]

German law also provides for restrictions on self-dealing:[173] A management board member may not enter into a contract or transaction acting on the one hand as representative of the AG and at the same time based upon a power of attorney for a third party, unless both the AG and the third party have granted an exemption from the self-dealing restrictions. In the case of the AG, such exemption must be set forth in the articles of association or a resolution of the supervisory board, and must be registered in the commercial register.

§ 85 Absence of management board members

If a management board member is not available for any reason, such absence does not change or otherwise affect the rules governing the power of representation of the AG. In urgent cases, a new or an additional management board member has to be appointed by the supervisory board or the local court at the registered seat of the AG.[174]

---

169   Aktiengesetz [AktG] [Stock Corporation Act] 1965, § 78, ¶ 4 (F.R.G.).
170   Aktiengesetz [AktG] [Stock Corporation Act] 1965, § 82, ¶ 1 (F.R.G.).
171   *Cf.* § 88 below.
172   Aktiengesetz [AktG] [Stock Corporation Act] 1965, § 112 (F.R.G.).
173   Bürgerliches Gesetzbuch [BGB] [Civil Code] 1896, § 181 (F.R.G.).
174   Aktiengesetz [AktG] [Stock Corporation Act] 1965, §§ 84, 85 (F.R.G.); *cf.* § 23.

§ 86 Representation in court proceedings

In court proceedings, the AG must be represented by the management board as its legal representative.[175] This also applies for all filings with the commercial register.[176]

In actions contesting the resolutions of the shareholders' meeting, the AG is jointly represented by its management board and its supervisory board. If an action is brought against the AG by a management board member, the AG is represented by the supervisory board; if an action is brought by a supervisory board member, the AG is represented by the management board.[177] If the AG is represented by the management board, court documents must be addressed to the management board, although it is sufficient to deliver them to one management board member only.[178]

§ 87 Knowledge of management board members imputed to the AG

Good faith, knowledge or negligent lack of knowledge of a management board member results in the AG being treated as if it had known about the circumstances in question; the management board member's knowledge (or negligent lack of knowledge) is imputed to the AG, irrespective of whether the AG has a concept of individual or joint power of representation, whether the board member in question actually was involved in the business transaction, and whether the board member had knowledge of the business transaction.

§ 88 Abuse of the power of representation

The concept of abuse of power of representation is a narrow exception to the principle that the power of representation of the management board may not be restricted. An abuse of the power of representation involves a scenario in which it is known (or should have been obvious) to the contractual partner that the management board member exceeds his internal authority (*e.g.*, violates the articles of association, rules of procedure or the schedule of responsibilities). A typical case of abuse of the power of representation involves fraudulent collusion of a management board member with a third party to the detriment of the AG. An abuse of the power of representation renders the resulting legal transaction null and void.

V. Duties

§ 89 Introduction

Management board members are subject to a variety of statutory and implied duties. Due to the principle of joint management, the duty of control and oversight is one of the most important duties of a management board member. A violation of duties can give rise to a claim for damages or, if the violation is serious, dismissal.

---

175   Aktiengesetz [AktG] [Stock Corporation Act] 1965, § 78, ¶ 1 (F.R.G.).
176   In some cases, the chairman of the supervisory board is required to participate in the filing as a co-signatory.
177   Aktiengesetz [AktG] [Stock Corporation Act] 1965, § 246, ¶ 2, sentence 2, 3, § 249, ¶ 1, § 275, ¶ 4 (F.R.G.).
178   Zivilprozessordnung [ZPO] [Civil procedure statute] 1950, § 170, ¶ 3 (F.R.G.).

A management board member must fulfill the general duties discussed in the following sections when carrying out his specific duties as a management board member. The general duties include the requirement to exercise due care and the duty of loyalty to the AG, which is expressed in a prohibition of competition and the doctrine of corporate opportunities.

§ 90 Duty to exercise due care

When performing management tasks, management board members are bound by law to exercise a high degree of care.[179] The applicable standard requires management board members to act in the same way as a dutiful, independent manager of a comparable AG in similar circumstances, who does not conduct business with his own funds but, similar to a custodian, acts in accordance with the pecuniary interests of others.

As a management board member has to take business decisions for which he is responsible, he must have wide-ranging discretion when performing his duties, *i.e.*, he must be allowed to take acceptable risks. There is a statutory presumption that a management board member does not violate his duties if the decision constitutes a "business decision", taken in the interest of the AG without regard to any interests of other persons (including without regard to the board member's own interest) and based upon adequate information, and if the management board member acted in good faith.[180] "Business decisions" are decisions that require entrepreneurial judgment. By contrast, performance of a board member's statutory duties does not involve any business decision.

§ 91 Fiduciary duty

Appointment to the management board results in fiduciary duties requiring the board to place corporate interests before private interests and not to abuse the appointment to gain personal advantage. In practice, the main limitations and obligations arising from a board member's fiduciary status relate to dealings with the assets of the AG, corporate opportunities and the duty to cooperate with the other corporate bodies of the AG in a spirit of trust.

§ 92 Doctrine of corporate opportunities

The doctrine of corporate opportunities is one of the principal obligations resulting from the fiduciary duty. According to this doctrine, the management board members are required to act solely in the interest of the AG when performing their tasks. If business opportunities arise for the AG while a board member is performing his tasks, such as the possibility of acquiring a plot of land that is of interest to the AG, he must attempt to use this opportunity for the benefit of the AG, and is not permitted to exploit the opportunity for his own benefit. If the AG does not have sufficient liquid funds available when the opportunity arises, the management board member must inform the other board members and the supervisory board of the opportunity to enable them to consider potential financing options.

---

179   Aktiengesetz [AktG] [Stock Corporation Act] 1965, § 93, ¶ 1, sentence 1 (F.R.G.).
180   Aktiengesetz [AktG] [Stock Corporation Act] 1965, § 91, ¶ 1, sentence 2 (F.R.G.).

§ 93 Statutory prohibition of competition

The statutory prohibition of competition prohibits management board members from oper-ating a business or conducting business transactions in the same line of business as the AG without the consent of the supervisory board.[181] This includes any participation in commercial activity aimed at generating a profit, including acting as a member of the management board or in a similar capacity for a company that is a competitor of the AG. The prohibition of com-petition does not apply to portfolio investments, such as the purchase of shares for investment purposes. Violations of the statutory prohibition of competition constitute a basis for a claim for damages by the AG. The AG may, *in lieu* of claiming damages, demand that the board member treat the transaction in question as a transaction for the account of the AG or, if the board member engaged in competition with the AG for the account of a third party, relinquish his compensation.[182]

§ 94 Duty to observe secrecy

Management board members are bound to secrecy concerning the AG's confidential informa-tion and company secrets that become known to them in their capacity as management board members.[183] Company secrets include, among others, customer base, financial plans, personnel decisions and manufacturing or production processes. In addition, other information whose disclosure could be detrimental from the AG's point of view (confidential information) must also be kept secret.

The duty to observe secrecy applies not only *vis-à-vis* business partners and other third parties but also in dealings with shareholders, employees, trade unions and other employee representa-tives. By contrast, there is no restriction on making confidential information available to col-leagues on the management board. However, the supervisory board should receive confidential information only in accordance with the process generally applicable to communications be-tween the two boards. Advisers, consultants and the statutory auditors of the AG may be given access to confidential information within the scope of their engagement and duties.

In principle, the duty of secrecy also applies within a corporate group of companies. According-ly, the board member of an AG that is a subsidiary of another company may not freely disclose information to the management or the board of the parent company or a sister company. There are, however, exceptions in a group context in that disclosure of information is permissible to the extent required in order to enable the parent company to manage the group or to comply with legal obligations (*e.g.*, information needed to prepare consolidated financial accounts or fulfill group-wide regulatory duties).

The duty to observe secrecy also does not apply if a management board member is required by law to disclose information (*e.g.*, in the event the board member is required to testify in court or to provide information to a regulatory authority). The duty to observe secrecy continues to

---

181   Aktiengesetz [AktG] [Stock Corporation Act] 1965, § 88, ¶ 1 (F.R.G.).
182   Aktiengesetz [AktG] [Stock Corporation Act] 1965, § 88, ¶ 2 (F.R.G.).
183   Aktiengesetz [AktG] [Stock Corporation Act] 1965, § 93, ¶ 1, sentence 3 (F.R.G.).

be in force beyond the termination both of the member's appointment and service agreement. Violation of the duty to observe secrecy is a criminal offence.[184]

§ 95 Duty to observe secrecy in connection with M&A transactions

Questions regarding the scope of the duty to observe secrecy often arise when an investor who intends to take a stake in an AG or a potential acquirer of an AG wishes to conduct a due diligence review. It is usually advisable for the management board of the target AG to adopt a resolution setting out the scope of the due diligence and the process for conducting the due diligence. The due diligence process should generally be preceded by the conclusion of a confidentiality agreement which requires the recipient of the information to treat such information confidential. If a member of the management board has a personal interest in the transaction (*e.g.*, as a seller), it is advisable to have the supervisory board approve any decision to permit the potential investor or acquirer to conduct due diligence.

In deciding whether to allow a due diligence review, and what process to follow, the management board must act solely in the best interests of the AG. Questions to be considered include whether the transaction is in the interest of the AG, its employees, shareholders and creditors.

The management board also may permit a due diligence review in order to enable a major shareholder of the AG to sell its stake in the AG, unless there are overriding interests of other constituencies of the AG arguing against permitting such review.

Management board members will have no liability for disclosing confidential information in connection with M&A transactions if they follow the principles for making business decisions.[185] Accordingly, they must first determine whether the recipient of the information has a genuine interest in acquiring the AG or a stake in the AG (*e.g.*, by entering into a letter of intent). It may also be advisable, depending on the sensitivity of the information to be disclosed, to proceed in stages, which means that access to particularly sensitive information will be given only later in the process when a high degree of confidence that the transaction will materialize has been reached.

A.   Reporting to the supervisory board

§ 96 Reporting duty

The supervisory board is only capable of performing its task of overseeing the management board effectively if it receives information about the management of the AG's affairs. Therefore, the management board has certain statutory reporting duties. The Corporate Governance Code recommends that the supervisory board specifies the information and reporting duties of the management board in greater detail.[186] The rules of procedure for the management board

---

184   Aktiengesetz [AktG] [Stock Corporation Act] 1965, § 404, ¶ 1, no. 1 (F.R.G.).
185   *Cf.* § 74 above.
186   Deutscher Corporate Governance Kodex [DCGK] [German Corporate Governance Code] 2010, 3.4, ¶ 3 (F.R.G.).

thus often contain detailed provisions on how and when the management board has to inform and report to the supervisory board. It is not permissible, however, to reduce the information and reporting duties below the statutory minimum or to eliminate them altogether.

§ 97 Reporting process

The reporting obligations of the management board run to the supervisory board as a whole. Each management board member has a duty to ensure conscientious reporting to the supervisory board, and if necessary, to report to the supervisory board in person. In practice, the management board (generally acting through its chairman or speaker) maintains regular contact with the chairman of the supervisory board to manage the flow of information from the management board to the supervisory board. The management board fulfills its reporting duty if it passes information to the chairman of the supervisory board, who then has an obligation to inform the supervisory board as a whole. Each member of the supervisory board has, however, an individual right to require the management board to provide information to the supervisory board as a whole. It is not permissible for a supervisory board member to request that information should only be provided to himself. Reports should generally be made in text form (*e.g.*, in writing or by email or fax).[187] In urgent cases, it is, however, common practice for the chairman or speaker of the management board to provide oral information to the chairman of the supervisory board.

§ 98 Content of reports

Reports must be true and complete.[188] No material information or facts may be withheld from the supervisory board. The reporting duty is limited to what the supervisory board requires to fulfill its own duties. Therefore, as an exception, no report must be given (or information may be omitted) if there is clearly no functional connection between the subject matter on which the report is requested and the tasks of the management board. Reports need not include original documents on the matter to which a report relates. The supervisory board has, however, a separate statutory right to require the submission of books and records by the management board.[189] The reporting duty also does not apply in exceptional cases involving an abusive demand for information, for example, if a supervisory board member works at a company that is a competitor of the AG and it is feared that he will pass on information to his employer. Management board members should keep records documenting the reasons in instances in which they did not provide full information to the supervisory board to be able to refute any claim that they violated their duties.

§ 99 Regular reports

The Stock Corporation Act sets forth various areas on which the board of management must report to the supervisory board on a regular basis.[190] At least once a year, a report is due on the AG's intended business policy and other fundamental questions concerning business planning

---

187   Aktiengesetz [AktG] [Stock Corporation Act] 1965, § 90, ¶ 4, sentence 2 (F.R.G.), Aktiengesetz [AktG] [Stock Corporation Act] 1965, § 90, ¶ 1, sentence 3 (F.R.G.).

188   Aktiengesetz [AktG] [Stock Corporation Act] 1965, § 90, ¶ 4 (F.R.G.).

189   *Cf.* below § 249.

190   Aktiengesetz [AktG] [Stock Corporation Act] 1965, § 90 (F.R.G.).

(in particular, finance, investments and personnel). Any deviations between actual developments and targets reported earlier have to be explained. Furthermore, at the supervisory board meeting at which the annual financial statements are discussed, the management board must report on the AG's profitability, in particular on the return on shareholders' equity. In addition, the management board must routinely, but at least once per quarter, inform the supervisory board of business developments, especially on the AG's turnover and financial condition. The information also has to include group-wide information if the AG is the parent company of a corporate group.

§ 100 Special reports

Special reports must be made whenever important developments occur. For example, the management board must, if reasonably practicable, inform the supervisory board on a timely basis of transactions that may have a material effect on the AG's profitability or liquidity, in order to give the supervisory board an opportunity to comment before the transaction is effected.[191] The management board also must inform the supervisory board promptly of any changes of the intended business policy given in the regular report, or changes of the business planning.[192]

In addition, the management board must report to the chairman of the supervisory board immediately whenever there is any other important development,[193] e.g., a material disruption of operations, major losses, a threat to larger receivables, a critical labor dispute, the impending commencement or negative outcome of a significant proceeding, major tax issues, serious disruptions of the collaboration within the management board or liquidity problems of the AG.

§ 101 Reports upon request

Furthermore, the supervisory board (or individual supervisory board members) may request additional reports at any time on matters concerning the AG, including legal and commercial relations with affiliated companies as well as business developments occurring at affiliated companies that are of material significance to the AG.[194]

B.   Shareholders' meeting

§ 102 Calling a shareholders' meeting

A shareholders' meeting must be called in the cases prescribed by law or the articles of association, and whenever required in the interest of the AG.[195] The Stock Corporation Act provides that a shareholders' meeting must in particular be called for the submission of the audited annual financial statements and annual reports to the shareholders, for the decision on the appropriation of the balance sheet profits (if any), for the discharge of the acts of the management board and the supervisory board, and for the selection of the auditors. These are

---

191   Aktiengesetz [AktG] [Stock Corporation Act] 1965, § 90, ¶ 1, sentence 1, no. 4, ¶ 2, no. 4 (F.R.G.).
192   Aktiengesetz [AktG] [Stock Corporation Act] 1965, § 90, ¶ 2, sentence 1 (F.R.G.).
193   Aktiengesetz [AktG] [Stock Corporation Act] 1965, § 90, ¶ 1, sentence 3 (F.R.G.).
194   Aktiengesetz [AktG] [Stock Corporation Act] 1965, § 90, ¶ 3, sentence 1 (F.R.G.).
195   Aktiengesetz [AktG] [Stock Corporation Act] 1965, § 121, ¶ 1 (F.R.G.).

the principal decisions to be taken at each annual or ordinary shareholders' meeting.[196] The articles of association of the AG may provide that the shareholders' meeting approves the annual financial statements. In practice, it is, however, common to give the management board and the supervisory board the authority for such approval, which means that these bodies make the final decision on the annual financial statements. Ordinary shareholders' meetings must be held during the first eight months of the financial year of an AG.[197] If the management board fails to call the shareholders' meeting in time, the commercial register at which the AG is registered may impose a fine on the management board.[198]

A shareholders' meeting called for any reason other than those mentioned above is referred to as an extraordinary shareholders' meeting. The management board must call an extraordinary meeting whenever required in the interest of the AG, for example if a decision is necessary at short notice on the issuance of new shares to increase the share capital or on a fundamental issue that falls within the competence (written or unwritten) of the shareholders' meeting.[199] Furthermore, the management board must call a shareholders' meeting to discuss restructuring measures if the AG has suffered a loss exceeding half of its share capital.[200]

The management board decides by simple majority of the votes cast whether to call a shareholders' meeting.[201] In exceptional cases, the supervisory board may call a shareholders' meeting with simple majority of the votes cast.[202] Further, a qualified minority of shareholders may, subject to certain prerequisites, force the calling of a shareholders' meeting.[203]

Notice of any shareholders' meeting must be published at least 30 days before the scheduled date for the meeting.[204] If the articles of association of an AG make participation in or voting at the shareholders' meeting conditional upon prior registration by shareholders, the 30-day period is extended by the period between the latest possible date of registration and the date of the shareholders' meeting. Resolutions adopted at a shareholders' meeting that was not called properly may be challenged by individual shareholders (or in the case of a violation of certain statutory requirements may even be void), unless all shareholders were present and none of them objected to the adoption of the resolutions (so called universal meeting).[205] In practice, organizing a shareholders' meeting of an AG that has a large shareholder base (which includes all AGs whose shares are traded on a securities exchange irrespective of the market segment) is a time-consuming and complex process, which should be given the required attention in order to ensure that all legal requirements are observed. Otherwise, the management board runs the

---

196   Aktiengesetz [AktG] [Stock Corporation Act] 1965, § 175, ¶ 1, § 173, ¶ 1, § 175, ¶ 3, § 234, ¶ 2, § 120, ¶ 1, sentence 1 (F.R.G.) and Handelsgesetzbuch [HGB] [Commercial Code] 1897, § 318, ¶ 1 (F.R.G.).
197   Aktiengesetz [AktG] [Stock Corporation Act] 1965, § 120, ¶ 1, § 175, ¶ 3 (F.R.G.). The articles of association may determine a shorter period.
198   Aktiengesetz [AktG] [Stock Corporation Act] 1965, § 407, ¶ 1, § 175 (F.R.G.).
199   Competences of the shareholders' meeting are discussed in further detail in § 3 and § 76.
200   Aktiengesetz [AktG] [Stock Corporation Act] 1965, § 92, ¶ 1 (F.R.G.).
201   Aktiengesetz [AktG] [Stock Corporation Act] 1965, § 121, ¶ 2, sentence 1 (F.R.G.).
202   Aktiengesetz [AktG] [Stock Corporation Act] 1965, § 111, ¶ 3 (F.R.G.).
203   Aktiengesetz [AktG] [Stock Corporation Act] 1965, § 122 (F.R.G.).
204   Aktiengesetz [AktG] [Stock Corporation Act] 1965, § 123, ¶ 1 (F.R.G.).
205   Aktiengesetz [AktG] [Stock Corporation Act] 1965, § 121, ¶ 6 (F.R.G.).

risk that shareholders' resolutions which are required to conduct the AG's business are void or subject to challenge in court proceedings.

§ 103 Publication of notice of shareholders' meeting

Notice of a shareholders' meeting must be given in the publications designated for corporate notices, including the mandatory minimum amount of information.[206] Violating the requirements for calling a shareholders' meeting provides a basis for challenging the resolutions passed at the shareholders' meeting, unless all shareholders are present and waive the requirement to correctly convene the shareholders' meeting.[207]

Special publication requirements apply with respect to certain subject matters on which resolutions are to be adopted by the shareholders' meeting, such as decisions on amending the articles of association, corporate contracts requiring the approval of the shareholders' meeting,[208] a capital increase against contribution in kind,[209] the election of supervisory board members[210] or the exclusion of subscription rights.[211] When the shareholders' meeting is called, an agenda listing the subjects of the meeting and of the resolutions to be adopted must also be published at the same time, showing the order in which they will be dealt with at the shareholders' meeting.[212] If a special publication requirement is ignored, resolutions may not be validly passed on these items.[213]

§ 104 Implementation of resolutions of shareholders' meeting

The management board must prepare the shareholders' meeting and execute and implement the resolutions adopted by the shareholders' meeting.[214]

The authority of the shareholders' meeting generally is limited to the matters enumerated in the Stock Corporation Act. The shareholders' meeting has no power to vote on management matters unless the management board has submitted a specific matter to a vote by the shareholders.[215] If the shareholders' meeting passes a resolution on management matters without such a submission by the management board, or on matters outside its statutory competence, the resolution is not binding on the management board. Furthermore, the management board is not required to implement any resolutions of the shareholders' meeting that are void or as to which a legal challenge is pending in court proceedings.

---

206 Aktiengesetz [AktG] [Stock Corporation Act] 1965, § 121, ¶ 3 (F.R.G.).
207 Aktiengesetz [AktG] [Stock Corporation Act] 1965, § 241, no. 1 (F.R.G.).
208 Aktiengesetz [AktG] [Stock Corporation Act] 1965, § 124, ¶ 2, sentence 2 (F.R.G.).
209 Aktiengesetz [AktG] [Stock Corporation Act] 1965, § 183, ¶ 1, sentence 2 (F.R.G.).
210 Aktiengesetz [AktG] [Stock Corporation Act] 1965, § 124, ¶ 2, sentence 1 (F.R.G.).
211 Aktiengesetz [AktG] [Stock Corporation Act] 1965, § 186, ¶ 4 (F.R.G.).
212 Aktiengesetz [AktG] [Stock Corporation Act] 1965, § 124, ¶ 1, sentence 1 (F.R.G.).
213 Aktiengesetz [AktG] [Stock Corporation Act] 1965, § 124, ¶ 4, sentence 1 (F.R.G.).
214 Aktiengesetz [AktG] [Stock Corporation Act] 1965, § 83, ¶ 1, sentence 1, ¶ 2 (F.R.G.).
215 Aktiengesetz [AktG] [Stock Corporation Act] 1965, § 119, ¶ 2 (F.R.G.).

In addition, the management board is required to prepare and execute agreements requiring the consent of the shareholders' meeting in order to be valid.[216] The shareholders' meeting may instruct the management board to perform a specific measure or conclude a specific agreement that is subject to the competence of the shareholders' meeting.[217] The resolution on the instruction requires the same majority as the majority required for the measure or consent to the agreement in question.[218]

§ 105 Reporting to shareholders' meeting

In certain cases, the management board must report to the shareholders' meeting. For example, the management board must submit a written report to the shareholders' meeting if the statutory subscription rights of the shareholders are to be excluded with respect to the issuance of new shares,[219] company agreements are to be concluded (such as a profit-transfer or domination agreement)[220] or a merger,[221] spin-off[222] or change of legal form is proposed.[223] The report must be signed by all management board members, unless the rules of procedure for the management board provide otherwise. Reporting duties also apply if the AG has repurchased its own shares (which in any event is subject to limitations under the Stock Corporation Act).[224] With respect to certain matters, documents concerning the transaction to which the report relates must be made available to shareholders for inspection at the time of the calling of the shareholders' meeting.[225]

§ 106 Submission and publication duties

The management board must submit to the shareholders' meeting the annual financial statements, the annual report, the supervisory board's report on its examination of the annual financial statements and the actions of the management board, and the proposal for the appropriation of the AG's balance sheet profits.[226] Sufficient copies of the relevant documents must be made available in the meeting room for inspection by shareholders. Furthermore, the

---

216 Aktiengesetz [AktG] [Stock Corporation Act] 1965, § 83, ¶ 1, sentence 2 (F.R.G.).
217 A resolution of the shareholders' meeting is, *inter alia*, required for inter-company agreements, Aktiengesetz [AktG] [Stock Corporation Act] 1965, §§ 293, 295 (F.R.G.), merger contracts (in a technical sense), Umwandlungsgesetz [UmwG] [Transformation Act], 1994, §§ 4 *et seq.*, 61 (F.R.G.), a transfer of the AG's entire assets, Aktiengesetz [AktG] [Stock Corporation Act] 1965, § 179a (F.R.G.).
218 Aktiengesetz [AktG] [Stock Corporation Act] 1965, § 83, ¶ 1, sentence 3 (F.R.G.).
219 Aktiengesetz [AktG] [Stock Corporation Act] 1965, § 186, ¶ 4, sentence 2 (F.R.G.).
220 Aktiengesetz [AktG] [Stock Corporation Act] 1965, § 293 (F.R.G.).
221 Umwandlungsgesetz [UmwG] [Transformation Act], 1994, § 8 (F.R.G.).
222 Umwandlungsgesetz [UmwG] [Transformation Act], 1994, § 127 (F.R.G.).
223 Umwandlungsgesetz [UmwG] [Transformation Act], 1994, § 192 (F.R.G.).
224 Aktiengesetz [AktG] [Stock Corporation Act] 1965, § 71, ¶ 3, sentence 1 (F.R.G.).
225 Certain documents must be made available to shareholders in case of post-formation contracts (Aktiengesetz [AktG] [Stock Corporation Act] 1965, § 52, ¶ 2 (F.R.G.)), a transfer of the entire assets of the AG (Aktiengesetz [AktG] [Stock Corporation Act] 1965, § 179a, ¶ 2 (F.R.G.)), certain intra-company agreements (in a technical sense) such as profit-transfer or domination agreements (Aktiengesetz [AktG] [Stock Corporation Act] 1965, §§ 293f, 293g (F.R.G.)), absorptions (Aktiengesetz [AktG] [Stock Corporation Act] 1965, § 319, ¶ 3 (F.R.G.)), squeeze-outs (Aktiengesetz [AktG] [Stock Corporation Act] 1965, § 327 c, ¶ 2–4, § 327d (F.R.G.)), mergers (Umwandlungsgesetz [UmwG] [Transformation Act], 1994, §§ 63, 64 (F.R.G.)), divestitures (Umwandlungsgesetz [UmwG] [Transformation Act], 1994, § 125, sentence 1, § 135, sentence 1 (F.R.G.)) and change of the AG's legal form (Umwandlungsgesetz [UmwG] [Transformation Act], 1994, §§ 230, 232, 238, 239 (F.R.G.)).
226 Aktiengesetz [AktG] [Stock Corporation Act] 1965, § 176, ¶ 1, § 175, ¶ 2 (F.R.G.).

management board is required to elaborate on its submissions during the shareholders' meeting. This is generally done by the chairman or the speaker of the management board. The elaboration should include a discussion of the material content of the submissions, an update with respect to key developments since the submissions were prepared, and an assessment of the current financial year.

C. Accounting

§ 107 Duty to keep books and records

An AG has a statutory duty to keep its books and records in accordance with applicable law.[227] This is the responsibility of all management board members. However, it is possible to allocate this responsibility to an individual board member, *e.g.*, via the schedule of responsibilities. In practice, many AGs appoint a member of the management board to the position of CFO with responsibility for accounting matters. Despite such appointment, the other members of the management board retain a duty of oversight requiring them to intervene whenever there are indications that the CFO is not fulfilling his duty properly.

The management board is also responsible for ensuring that the AG keeps copies of its business correspondence.[228] The AG also has to establish and maintain adequate bookkeeping systems and other recordkeeping procedures in accordance with the Commercial Code and tax laws. It is generally permissible to keep records on electronic data storage devices.[229] German tax laws generally require the AG to keep and store its books within Germany.[230] However, under certain prerequisites electronic accounting and electronic data storage may be transferred to another EU member state.[231]

If the books of the AG do not provide a sufficient basis for calculating the AG's income, the tax authorities are authorized to estimate the taxable profit (which may result in additional tax obligations for the AG).[232]

Certain violations of the accounting laws applicable to board members are criminal offenses.[233]

---

227 [HGB] [Commercial Code] 1897, § 238, ¶ 1, sentence 1, § 6, ¶ 1 (F.R.G.); Aktiengesetz [AktG] [Stock Corporation Act] 1965, § 3, ¶ 1, § 91 (F.R.G.). Provisions regarding accounting and maintenance of records stem from commercial and tax law.
228 Handelsgesetzbuch [HGB] [Commercial Code] 1897, § 238, ¶ 2 (F.R.G.).
229 Handelsgesetzbuch [HGB] [Commercial Code] 1897, § 257, ¶ 3, sentence 1 (F.R.G.), with the exception of the opening balance sheet and annual financials.
230 Abgabenordnung [AO] [General Tax Code] 1976, § 146, ¶ 2, sentence 1 (F.R.G.).
231 Abgabenordnung [AO] [General Tax Code] 1976, § 146, ¶ 2a (F.R.G.).
232 Abgabenordnung [AO] [General Tax Code] 1976, § 162 (F.R.G.).
233 Handelsgesetzbuch [HGB] [Commercial Code] 1897, § 331 (F.R.G.) or in case of insolvency Strafgesetzbuch [StGB] [Criminal Code] 1871, §§ 283, 283b (F.R.G.).

§ 108 Duty to prepare financial statements

An important element of the duty to keep accounts is the preparation of the financial statements at the end of each financial year. German AGs need not select the calendar year as
their financial year, although for most AGs the financial year coincides with the calendar
year. The annual financial statements must comprise at least a balance sheet showing the assets and liabilities, a profit and loss statement, and an annex containing explanatory notes.[234]
In addition, the management board has to prepare a management report (*Lagebericht*), which
discusses the performance of the business, the financial condition and the results of operations
of the AG including the risks that the AG is facing. These documents generally have to be
drawn up for each financial year within the first three months of the following financial year.[235]
Small AGs that do not exceed certain size criteria set out in the Commercial Code need not
prepare a management report and generally have six months in order to prepare their financial
statements. The members of the board of management of listed AGs have to provide certain
certifications with respect to the annual financial statements of the AG. Incorrect certifications can result in civil and criminal liability. AGs whose shares or other securities are listed
on the regulated market of a securities exchange are subject to additional publicity obligations pursuant to the Securities Trading Act, including an obligation to publish their annual
financial statements in certain ways, and an obligation to prepare and publish interim financial
information.

AGs that have subsidiaries generally also have to prepare consolidated financial statements for
their group of companies. Exceptions apply to AGs that themselves are subsidiaries within a
group of companies or to small groups of companies. The consolidated financial statements of
listed AGs have to be prepared in accordance with IFRS. Unlisted AGs may use IFRS for their
consolidated financial statements, but in practice they prefer German GAAP. By contrast,
the unconsolidated financial statements of all AGs must be prepared on the basis of German
GAAP as set forth in the Commercial Code and the Stock Corporation Act.

The difference between the unconsolidated and the consolidated financial statements of an
AG is important in that the unconsolidated financial statements, prepared in accordance with
German GAAP, are the basis for determining whether and in what amounts the AG is able to
pay dividends to its shareholders. Dividends may only be paid if and to the extent that the AG
shows a balance sheet profit (*Bilanzgewinn*) in its unconsolidated annual financial statements.
The unconsolidated financial statements are also the basis for determining whether the AG
is "overindebted", which is one of the tests requiring the initiation of insolvency proceedings
under German law.

The unconsolidated financial statements of an AG in principle are the basis for determining
the AG's tax position. German tax laws, however, require numerous adjustments, which in
practice results in substantial differences between the commercial and tax financial statements
of an AG.

---

234 Handelsgesetzbuch [HGB] [Commercial Code] 1897, § 264, ¶ 1, §§ 242 *et seq.* (F.R.G.).
235 Handelsgesetzbuch [HGB] [Commercial Code] 1897, § 264, ¶ 1, sentence 3 (F.R.G.).

§ 109 Adequate monitoring and control system

In connection with the duty to keep accounts, the management board is also required to set up a monitoring and control system to ensure the early detection of developments having a potential threat to the continued existence of the AG.[236] This system requires an organizational framework to ensure the systematic recognition and assessment of risk, the internal reporting of hazardous developments and the taking of adequate measures to avert the risk (risk control). For example, the system must provide for procedures to cause the controlling and internal audit departments to identify and report issues on a timely basis as well as for processes to ensure that reported issues are remedied. The functioning and efficiency of the system must be reviewed on an ongoing basis. The appropriate form of the monitoring and control system depends in particular on the size and structure of the AG.

Within a group of companies controlled by an AG, the controlling AG is legally required to operate a monitoring and control system for the whole group.

According to the majority view of legal commentators, an AG does not need to establish a comprehensive risk management system. Such an obligation applies only to companies in the financial and insurance sector.

D. Taxes

§ 110 Filing tax returns

German tax laws require AGs to file various tax returns and statements.[237] These include the corporate income tax return, the annual value-added tax advance return[238] and value-added tax advance returns,[239] trade tax returns,[240] wage tax statements[241] and dividend withholding tax statements.[242] Tax returns have to be signed by the AG's legal representatives, *i.e.*, the management board members, and must include the documents required by statute. The general rule is that tax returns covering a calendar year must be filed within five months of the end of the year, unless applicable tax law provides otherwise.[243] If a management board member discovers that a tax return filed previously is incomplete or incorrect, he is required to complete or correct it.[244]

---

236 Aktiengesetz [AktG] [Stock Corporation Act] 1965, § 91, ¶ 2 (F.R.G.). In case of listed AGs, the auditor has to audit whether the management board obeyed to this duty; Handelsgesetzbuch [HGB] [Commercial Code] 1897, § 317, ¶ 4 (F.R.G.).

237 Abgabenordnung [AO] [General Tax Code] 1976, § 149, ¶ 1, sentence 1 (F.R.G.).

238 Umsatzsteuergesetz [UStG] [Value Added Tax Act] 1979, § 18, ¶ 3 (F.R.G.).

239 Umsatzsteuergesetz [UStG] [Value Added Tax Act] 1979, § 18, ¶ 1 (F.R.G.).

240 Gewerbesteuergesetz [GewStG] [Trade Tax Act] 1936, § 14a (F.R.G.) in conjunction with Gewerbesteuerdurchführungsverordnung [GewStDV] [Trade Tax Ordinance] 1956, § 25, ¶ 1 (F.R.G.).

241 Einkommensteuergesetz [EStG] [Income Tax Act] 1934, § 41a (F.R.G.).

242 Einkommensteuergesetz [EStG] [Income Tax Act] 1934, § 45a (F.R.G.).

243 Abgabenordnung [AO] [General Tax Code] 1976, § 149, ¶ 2 (F.R.G.).

244 Abgabenordnung [AO] [General Tax Code] 1976, § 153 (F.R.G.).

§ 111 Withholding and timely payment of taxes

AGs are subject to various tax laws and regulations prescribing the taxes the AG has to pay or to withhold from payments made in respect of their contractual and other obligations. The management board is responsible for ensuring compliance with these laws and regulations.[245] For example, in the case of wages and salaries paid to employees, wage tax has to be withheld and paid to the tax office.[246] Dividends are subject to withholding tax,[247] and value-added tax arises for supplies and services rendered by the AG.[248] Furthermore, the appropriate tax amounts must be withheld and paid to the tax office when paying compensation for services rendered by persons that are only subject to limited tax liability in Germany (*e.g.*, persons that have their tax residence abroad).[249] In virtually all cases, in which withholding tax requirements apply, the AG itself will become liable for the tax if it does not withhold the correct amount of tax from its payments.

Management board members may be liable for damages if, willfully or through gross negligence, claims arising from the tax debtor-creditor relationship are not determined or satisfied or not determined or satisfied on a timely basis due to a breach of the duties imposed on them, or where, as a result, tax benefits or reimbursements are granted without legal basis.[250]

§ 112 Duties of notification and disclosure

In addition to the obligation to file tax returns and withhold and pay taxes, the AG is also required to submit tax-related notifications and disclose tax-related information to the tax authorities. The management board is responsible for ensuring compliance with this requirement.[251]

An AG, as a German taxpayer, has a general duty to cooperate with the tax authorities, including the disclosure of the true and complete facts relevant to taxation and the proof available to it. With respect to matters having foreign elements, AGs are under an even stricter duty to cooperate.[252] If the AG violates its duties to cooperate on tax matters, the tax authorities may estimate the AG's taxable income, potentially resulting in additional taxes for the AG.[253]

An AG is also subject to specific tax-related disclosure requirements. For example, it is required to disclose in particular, a change of legal form, change of management location or the winding up of the AG.[254] If the AG begins a commercial operation outside its registered office (*i.e.*, setting up of a branch), it is required to disclose this to the municipality.[255] Furthermore, the AG must inform the tax authorities if it establishes or acquires operations outside the

---

245 Abgabenordnung [AO] [General Tax Code] 1976, § 34 (F.R.G.).
246 Einkommensteuergesetz [EStG] [Income Tax Act] 1934, § 38, ¶ 3 (F.R.G.).
247 Einkommensteuergesetz [EStG] [Income Tax Act] 1934, § 43, ¶ 1 (F.R.G.).
248 Umsatzsteuergesetz [UStG] [Value Added Tax Act] 1979, § 13b (F.R.G.).
249 Einkommensteuergesetz [EStG] [Income Tax Act] 1934, § 50, ¶ 1, 4, § 50a (F.R.G.).
250 Abgabenordnung [AO] [General Tax Code] 1976, §§ 69, 34 (F.R.G.).
251 Abgabenordnung [AO] [General Tax Code] 1976, § 34, ¶ 1 (F.R.G.).
252 Abgabenordnung [AO] [General Tax Code] 1976, § 90 (F.R.G.).
253 Abgabenordnung [AO] [General Tax Code] 1976, § 162 (F.R.G.).
254 Abgabenordnung [AO] [General Tax Code] 1976, § 137, ¶ 1, § 20 (F.R.G.).
255 Abgabenordnung [AO] [General Tax Code] 1976, § 138, ¶ 1 (F.R.G.).

Federal Republic of Germany, acquires interests in foreign partnerships (and any termination or changes in respect of such interests), and exceeds certain thresholds for the acquisition of shares of foreign corporations.[256]

E.   Takeover and crisis

§ 113 Duties during takeovers

Takeovers place special obligations on the management board of an AG irrespective of whether the AG is the acquirer or the target. The management board of the target often is in a particularly difficult situation because, depending on whether it welcomes the takeover, it must decide whether it wishes and is legally permitted to initiate defense measures.

German corporate law does not provide explicitly how the management board of the target AG must react to a takeover approach. The board's primary duty is to manage the AG in its own responsibility.[257] In the event of a potential takeover, the management board is not subject to a strict duty to remain neutral. Instead, it is required to act in the AG's best interests, but with a certain degree of discretion.

Listed AGs are subject to the provisions of the Securities Acquisition and Takeover Act, which prohibits the management board from taking certain types of actions that could prevent the success of a takeover bid once the bidder has published its decision to launch a takeover bid.[258] Examples of actions that would be of questionable legality include issuing additional shares, selling important assets or creating antitrust obstacles for the bidder. These prohibitions do not apply if a diligent and conscientious manager of an AG, which is not subject to a takeover bid, would have taken the action in question or if the shareholders' meeting authorizes the management board to take the action in question.[259] The management board of the target also always may look for a competing bidder (white knight) without any need for specific authorization from the shareholders' meeting.[260]

If a bidder has launched a takeover bid for a listed AG, the management board of the AG is required to publish a reasoned opinion on the proposed takeover. The opinion must discuss the consideration offered, the expected impact of a successful takeover on the AG (including the AG's work force), the bidder's objectives, and the intentions of the members of the manage-

---

256   Abgabenordnung [AO] [General Tax Code] 1976, § 138, ¶ 2 (F.R.G.).
257   Aktiengesetz [AktG] [Stock Corporation Act] 1965, § 76, ¶ 1 (F.R.G.).
258   Wertpapierübernahmegesetz [WpÜG] [Securities Acquisition and Takeover Act] 2001, § 33, ¶ 1, § 10 (F.R.G.).
259   Wertpapierübernahmegesetz [WpÜG] [Securities Acquisition and Takeover Act] 2001, § 33, ¶ 1, sentence 2, ¶ 2 (F.R.G.). The shareholders' meeting, with a majority of three-quarters of the share capital represented, may empower the management board for up to 18 months in advance to take defensive actions of a type that requires authorization by the shareholders' meeting (capital increase, sale of interest in other companies, etc.). Further, any such action requires the consent of the supervisory board, Wertpapierübernahmegesetz [WpÜG] [Securities Acquisition and Takeover Act] 2001, § 33, ¶ 2 (F.R.G.).
260   Wertpapierübernahmegesetz [WpÜG] [Securities Acquisition and Takeover Act] 2001, § 23, ¶ 1, no. 2 (F.R.G.).

ment board (if they hold shares in the AG) to accept the takeover bid.[261] The management board must disclose all information that formed the basis of its opinion, excluding only information that is subject to confidentiality obligations.

The management board is liable to the AG for damages if it violates the legal prohibition on taking defensive measures.[262] Furthermore, the management board members may be fined up to EUR 1 million for taking defensive measures in violation of applicable law.[263]

§ 114 Duties in a financial crisis of the AG

If an AG has suffered or is expected to suffer losses of a certain magnitude, or if the AG is overindebted or insolvent, the Stock Corporation Act imposes certain requirements on the management board. Special rules apply to AGs that are insurance companies,[264] or banks or financial services firms.[265] The management board of such a regulated entity must notify the supervisory authority, the BaFin, which will then have to decide whether to apply for the initiation of insolvency proceedings or take other measures with a view to assessing the situation and potentially avoiding insolvency proceedings, such as the imposition of a moratorium. Under German law, the BaFin has the exclusive power to apply for the initiation of insolvency proceedings with respect to an insurance company, a bank or a financial services firm. Creditors have no right to file insolvency applications.

Apart from mandatory statutory duties (*e.g.*, obligation to call a shareholders' meeting in the event of losses amounting to half of the share capital and prohibition on making payments on behalf of the AG in the event of the inability of the AG to pay its debts),[266] the management board of an AG has no general duty to inform creditors or business partners of a crisis of the AG. Contractual agreements may however contain obligations to inform the counterparties of a deterioration of the financial situation of the AG. It is also possible that general contractual principles of good faith will require the AG to inform contractual counterparties if the AG's ability to perform its obligations under a contract is in jeopardy. Listed AGs may also be subject to public disclosure duties in the event that they are in financial difficulties.

Failure to fulfill the duties of the management board arising in the event of losses, overindebtedness or insolvency is a criminal offense.[267] In addition, management board members may be liable for damages to the AG[268] and the shareholders.[269]

---

261 Wertpapierübernahmegesetz [WpÜG] [Securities Acquisition and Takeover Act] 2001, § 27, ¶ 1, 2 (F.R.G.).
262 Aktiengesetz [AktG] [Stock Corporation Act] 1965, § 93, ¶ 2 (F.R.G.).
263 Wertpapierübernahmegesetz [WpÜG] [Securities Acquisition and Takeover Act] 2001, § 60, ¶ 1, no. 8 (F.R.G.).
264 Versicherungsaufsichtsgesetz [VAG] [Insurance Supervision Act] 1901, § 88 (F.R.G.).
265 Kreditwesengesetz [KWG] [Banking Act] 1961, § 46b, ¶ 1 (F.R.G.).
266 Aktiengesetz [AktG] [Stock Corporation Act] 1965, § 92, ¶ 1 and ¶ 2 (F.R.G.).
267 Aktiengesetz [AktG] [Stock Corporation Act] 1965, § 401 (F.R.G.).
268 Aktiengesetz [AktG] [Stock Corporation Act] 1965, § 93, ¶ 2, sentence 1, § 92 (F.R.G.).
269 Bürgerliches Gesetzbuch [BGB] [Civil Code] 1896, § 823, ¶ 2 (F.R.G.) in conjunction with Aktiengesetz [AktG] [Stock Corporation Act] 1965, § 92 (F.R.G.).

§ 115 Duties in the event of losses of the AG

If in conjunction with the preparation of the annual financial statements or interim financial information or otherwise in the course of performing its duties, the management board of an AG discovers that a loss equal to one half of the AG's share capital has occurred, the management board is required to call a shareholders' meeting promptly to inform the shareholders of the situation.[270] The management board also has an obligation to inform the chairman of the supervisory board of events that have a significant effect on the AG's financial condition.[271] A loss equal to one half of the share capital occurs if the AG's assets cover only one half of the nominal share capital. In making this determination, the management board has to compare the value of the assets with the entire equity shown in the balance sheet. A loss of nominal share capital occurs once the loss exceeds all other elements of the AG's equity, generally the capital reserves, any earnings reserves, and any profit carried forward, plus at least one half of the nominal share capital. Depending on whether it is reasonable to assume that the AG will continue to exist as a going concern, the valuation of the AG's assets may be based on German-GAAP book values. Unrealized reserves may only be realized for this purpose, if such realization would be permissible in the annual German GAAP financial statements. If it is doubtful whether the AG will continue to exist, liquidation values have to be used.[272]

The requirement to call a shareholders' meeting "promptly" means that the management board has to act as quickly as reasonably practicable. It is doubtful whether ongoing restructuring negotiations with lenders provide a basis for delaying the notice to call the shareholders' meeting. The notice must comply with the statutory requirements as to form and content.

The purpose of calling the shareholders' meeting is to enable the shareholders to decide on remedial action, such as an injection of additional capital or the liquidation of the AG.

If the management board has already filed an application for the initiation of insolvency proceedings, there is no need to call a shareholders' meeting.

§ 116 Duties in the event of overindebtedness or insolvency of the AG

If an AG is insolvent or overindebted, the management board of the AG is required to apply promptly, but in any event not more than three weeks after the insolvency or overindebtedness occurred, for an insolvency proceeding to be opened.[273] The filing obligation is a personal duty of each management board member because each board member, acting individually, is entitled to file for insolvency.[274] Insolvency occurs if the AG can no longer meet its payment obligations as they become due, unless it can be expected with considerable certainty that the liquidity shortage will be eliminated within the next three weeks, and under the circumstances the creditors can reasonably be expected to wait for payment. Overindebtedness occurs when the AG's assets no longer cover its liabilities. The determination whether the liabilities exceed

---

270 Aktiengesetz [AktG] [Stock Corporation Act] 1965, § 92, ¶ 1 (F.R.G.).
271 Aktiengesetz [AktG] [Stock Corporation Act] 1965, § 90, ¶ 1, sentence 3 (F.R.G.).
272 Handelsgesetzbuch [HGB] [Commercial Code] 1897, § 252, ¶ 1, no. 2 (F.R.G.).
273 Aktiengesetz [AktG] [Stock Corporation Act] 1965, § 92, ¶ 2 (F.R.G.).
274 Insolvenzordnung [InsO] [Insolvency Code] 1994, § 15, ¶ 1 (F.R.G.).

the assets is to be made on the basis of a special balance sheet, which differs in many respects from the year-end German GAAP-balance sheet. In principle, the balance sheet has to show the true market values, which depending on the prognosis for the continuation of the AG may be going concern or liquidation values. To mitigate the effects of the crisis in the financial markets, the German legislature modified the insolvency filing rules based upon overindebtedness for a limited period ending on July 31, 2013. According to the modified rules, overindebtedness requires no insolvency filing if the prognosis for the continuation of the AG is positive.

If insolvency or overindebtedness has occurred, the management board may not make any further payments unless they are compatible with the care of a diligent and conscientious manager.[275]

F.   Publication and notification obligations for listed AGs

§ 117 Introduction
To prevent investors from obtaining an unfair advantage on the securities markets due to possessing material non-public information, the management board of a listed AG is legally required to publish information relating to the AG or the AG's shares or other securities that could have a material effect on the price of such shares or other securities in the event of a disclosure to the market ("insider information"). Persons who are in possession of insider information (irrespective of how they obtained such information) may not disclose such information, trade in the securities to which such information relates, or recommend to others to trade in such securities on the basis of such information. Any violation of the insider prohibitions generally is a criminal offense, punishable by a fine or imprisonment up to five years.

In order to ensure compliance with the insider prohibitions, transactions in the AG's shares (or derivative instruments relating to such shares) by members of the management board and the supervisory board, senior employees of the AG, and individuals or entities closely related to any of the foregoing persons are subject to statutory directors' dealing disclosure obligations. Furthermore, the AG is subject to organizational requirements to restrict and control the dissemination of material non-public information, such as the keeping of insider lists.

1.   General publication duties
§ 118 Disclosure of share ownership in the AG or other AGs
The management board of an AG is required to make various disclosures with respect to the ownership of shares of the AG by third parties as well as with respect to shareholdings of the AG in other AGs. Similar disclosure obligations may apply with respect to shareholdings of the AG in listed foreign stock corporations.

First, shareholders of an AG whose shares are listed and traded on a regulated market are required to notify the AG and the BaFin, within a statutorily prescribed period of time, if their

---

275   Aktiengesetz [AktG] [Stock Corporation Act] 1965, § 92, ¶ 3, sentence 1, 2 (F.R.G.).

holdings of common shares of the AG reach, exceed or fall below 3, 5, 10, 15, 20, 25, 30, 50 or 75% of the common share capital of the AG.[276] There are various statutory attribution rules that create additional notification obligations for trustees, parent companies and persons that have control of votings rights based upon other arrangements with the legal owners of the shares (*e.g.*, voting pooling contracts). The AG has to publish an ownership notification within three trading days after receipt. The notification obligations also apply to treasury shares held by the AG itself. They do not apply, however, to non-voting shares. A failure to comply with the notification obligations will result in the loss of voting, dividend and other rights arising from the shares.

Shareholdings in non-listed AGs need not be notified to the BaFin or be made public. Any enterprise that owns more than 25% or more than 50% of the shares in a non-listed AG, is, however, obligated to notify the AG of such shareholding.[277] In determining whether the notification thresholds are exceeded, voting and non-voting shares are taken into account.

An AG also must disclose certain information in the notes to its annual financial statements with respect to shareholdings in other companies that reach at least 20% of the outstanding equity interests.[278] Furthermore, listed AGs must report all holdings in large corporations exceeding 5% of the voting rights in the notes to the annual financial statements and in the notes to the group financial statements.[279]

§ 119 Corporate Governance Code

In 2001, the German Federal Minister of Justice established a Corporate Governance Commission composed of leading academic scholars and representatives of issuers, institutional investors and small shareholders.[280] The Corporate Governance Commission adopted the Corporate Governance Code, which has since undergone several revisions. The objective of the Code is to make German corporate governance rules transparent to national and international investors, thus strengthening the confidence in the management of AGs. The Code only applies to AGs whose shares are listed and traded on a regulated market. In large part, the Code explains the statutory governance regime of the AG. It also contains guidance for the operation of the management and supervisory boards and the interaction between the two boards, the setting of the compensation for the members of the two boards, the disclosure and resolution of conflicts of interest, and the preparation and publication of the financial statements.

Compliance with the Corporate Governance Code is voluntary. The management board and the supervisory board of an AG that is subject to the Code are, however, required to publish an annual declaration disclosing whether and to what extent the AG has complied and will

---

276   Gesetz über den Wertpapierhandel [WpHG] [Securities Trade Act] 1994, § 21, ¶ 1 (F.R.G.).

277   Aktiengesetz [AktG] [Stock Corporation Act] 1965, § 20, ¶ 1, 4, 5, § 21, ¶ 1, 2, 3 (F.R.G.).

278   Handelsgesetzbuch [HGB] [Commercial Code] 1897, § 285, sentence 1, no. 11 (F.R.G.).

279   Handelsgesetzbuch [HGB] [Commercial Code] 1897, § 285, sentence 1, no. 11, 1. part, § 313, ¶ 2–3 (F.R.G.).

280   http://www.corporate-governance-code.de/index-e.html. *Cf.* German Corporate Governance Code attached in Chapter Seven: Annex II. E.

comply with the Code.[281] The declaration must remain accessible to the shareholders at all times.[282]

Incorrect declarations of compliance provide a basis for shareholders to challenge the resolutions of the annual general shareholders' meeting discharging the acts of the management and supervisory boards. If during the course of a year an AG ceases to be in compliance with the Corporate Governance Code, it must publish a correction of its declaration of compliance. Failure to do so may also provide a basis for a challenge of the approval resolutions at the next annual general meeting. Recent case law has, *e.g.*, upheld such challenges on the ground that the declaration of compliance was incorrect because it failed to disclose that, contrary to the guidelines of the Code, the annual report of the supervisory board to the annual general meeting did not provide information on how the supervisory board dealt with the conflict of interest of a board member.

2.   Management board member's personal disclosure duties
§ 120 Directors' dealings
In contrast to the USA and the United Kingdom, German corporate law does not impose a duty on members of the management or supervisory board to disclose their current shareholdings at the time of their appointment. However, to promote transparency of the capital markets and equal treatment of investors, management and supervisory board members and senior employees, as well as persons and entities closely related to such persons, must disclose transactions in the shares of the AG or financial instruments (in particular derivative instruments) relating to such shares to the AG and the BaFin within five working days.[283] The information must be published by the AG promptly, and the BaFin must be notified of the publication at the same time.[284]

§ 121 Persons required to make disclosures
The disclosure obligations do not apply to persons who no longer serve on the management or supervisory board, nor to members of a committee or advisory council who are not also members of either board. Within a group of companies, the duty to report transactions in the shares of the listed parent AG applies only to the members of the boards of the parent AG, and not to any management or supervisory bodies of subsidiaries or affiliated companies. The disclosure obligations, however, also apply to senior employees of the AG below the level of the management board if such employees are authorized to take significant entrepreneurial decisions for the AG and regularly have access to insider information.[285]

In addition to board members and senior employees, their spouses, children and, subject to certain conditions, other relatives are subject to the disclosure obligations. Moreover, other entities at which board members or senior employees of the AG perform managerial tasks also

---

281   Aktiengesetz [AktG] [Stock Corporation Act] 1965, § 161 (F.R.G.).
282   Aktiengesetz [AktG] [Stock Corporation Act] 1965, § 161, sentence 2 (F.R.G.).
283   Gesetz über den Wertpapierhandel [WpHG] [Securities Trade Act] 1994, § 15a, ¶ 1, 2 (F.R.G.).
284   Gesetz über den Wertpapierhandel [WpHG] [Securities Trade Act] 1994, § 15a, ¶ 4 (F.R.G.).
285   Emittentenleitfaden der Bundesanstalt für Finanzdienstleistungsaufsicht 2009, V.1.2.1.

must disclose their transactions in the AG's shares. [286] As a result, a listed AG (AG A) on whose supervisory board serves a management board member of another listed AG (AG B) has to disclose dealings in the shares of AG B (and *vice versa*). Board members and senior employees also must disclose transactions in the AG's shares by entities of which they have control or of which they are the beneficiaries.[287]

§ 122 Transactions subject to the disclosure requirements
Transactions subject to the disclosure requirements include all transactions aimed at transferring shares of the AG or financial instruments relating to such shares, in particular purchases and sales and repurchase and share lending transactions. Acquisitions by inheritance or gift are not subject to reporting.[288]

The disclosure obligations also do not apply if and as long as the *de minimis* limit of EUR 5,000 per financial year is not exceeded. In calculating whether the limit has been reached or exceeded, transactions by persons or entities closely related to the board member or senior employee are also taken into account.

Contrary to the literal wording of the statutory provisions, the BaFin has taken the view that the disclosure obligations do not apply with respect to stock options and similar financial instruments relating to the AG's shares acquired by board members or senior employees as part of their compensation.[289] By contrast, if an incentive program of an AG requires the participants to acquire shares of the AG as a condition to participating in the program, the purchase of such shares is subject to the disclosure obligation.

§ 123 Time, form and content of disclosure and publication
Persons subject to a disclosure obligation must file a notification with the BaFin and the AG within five working days after execution of the reportable transaction (not including the day on which the transaction took place). The trade date is determinative, not the (later) settlement date. If the disclosure obligation is based on the fact that the *de minimis* limit is exceeded, the deadline for disclosure of all transactions ends five working days after the trade date for the transaction that exceeded the *de minimis* limit.[290] The notification must include, among other things, specific details about the issuer, the price of the transaction, the person required to make the notification, and the shares or financial instruments traded. [291] The BaFin has made available forms to facilitate compliance with the disclosure obligations.[292] Transmittal to the BaFin must be made in writing. Telefax qualifies for this purpose, but email transmittal is not considered written form.

---

286   Gesetz über den Wertpapierhandel [WpHG] [Securities Trade Act] 1994, § 15a, ¶ 3 (F.R.G.).
287   Emittentenleitfaden der Bundesanstalt für Finanzdienstleistungsaufsicht 2009, V.1.2.6.
288   Emittentenleitfaden der Bundesanstalt für Finanzdienstleistungsaufsicht 2009, V.2.2.
289   Emittentenleitfaden der Bundesanstalt für Finanzdienstleistungsaufsicht 2009, V.2.2.
290   Emittentenleitfaden der Bundesanstalt für Finanzdienstleistungsaufsicht 2009, V.2.7.
291   Cf. Wertpapierhandelsanzeige- und Insiderverzeichnisverordnung [WpAIV] [Security Trading Announcement and Insider Register Order] 2004, § 10, no. 1–5 (F.R.G.).
292   http://www.bafin.de/EN/Home/homepage__node.html

The AG must promptly make a publication through one of the media specified by law for this purpose upon receipt of a disclosure notice. The publication must be made in the German language and include certain information about the reporting person, the issuer and the transaction.[293] The issuer is required to send written evidence of the publication to the BaFin immediately after the publication, usually within three working days.[294]

3.   Ad-hoc notifications
§ 124 Duty to publish ad-hoc notifications
In order to ensure efficient capital markets and equal treatement of market participants, listed AGs and AGs that have other securities listed on the regulated market of a securities exchange in Germany or another country within the European Economic Area are subject to a statutory obligation to publish "insider information" relating to them or to such listed securities (ad-hoc notification).[295] Any ad-hoc notification is subject to prior review by the domestic securities exchanges on which the shares of the AG (or other securities to which the notice relates) are listed and the BaFin (preliminary notification).[296]

In certain circumstances, the AG may delay the publication of insider information if immediate publication would be contrary to the legitimate interests of the AG (*e.g.*, negotiation of an M&A transaction).[297]

In practice, most ad-hoc notifications relate only to the shares of an AG because prices of shares are more volatile than prices of debt securities and react to a much wider range of facts and circumstances than debt securities. However, there may be developments that have a particular effect on outstanding listed debt of the AG (or one of the AG's subsidiaries), such as a significant deterioration of the creditworthiness of the issuer or the guarantor, or the occurrence of events that affect the rights of the holders of the debt securities. In such cases, it may be necessary to publish an ad-hoc notification with respect to such debt securities.

§ 125 Existence of insider information
The obligation to publish an ad-hoc notification relates to "insider information." This term is defined as "concrete information about circumstances not known to the public that relate to one or more issuers of insider securities or to the insider securities themselves, and that could influence the stock exchange or market price of the insider securities materially if it enters the public domain". An analysis, such as a research report on an issuer, which is based solely on information that is in the public domain, is not considered insider information, even if it may have an influence on the price of insider securities.[298]

---

293   Wertpapierhandelsanzeige- und Insiderverzeichnisverordnung [WpAIV] [Security Trading Announcement and Insider Register Order] 2004, §§ 12, 13 (F.R.G.).
294   Emittentenleitfaden der Bundesanstalt für Finanzdienstleistungsaufsicht 2009, V.3.5.
295   Gesetz über den Wertpapierhandel [WpHG] [Securities Trade Act] 1994, § 15, ¶ 1, sentence 1 (F.R.G.).
296   Gesetz über den Wertpapierhandel [WpHG] [Securities Trade Act] 1994, § 15, ¶ 1–4 (F.R.G.).
297   *Cf.* § 133 below.
298   Gesetz über den Wertpapierhandel [WpHG] [Securities Trade Act] 1994, § 13, ¶ 2 (F.R.G.).

§ 126 Sufficiently concrete information

In order to qualify as "insider information", the information must be sufficiently concrete. The question of "concreteness" often arises with respect to future events. For example, if an AG is conducting negotiations with another company about a possible merger, the question is whether the conduct of negotiations in and by itself or the potential future merger constitutes insider information. With respect to the conduct of negotiations, the test is whether a reasonable investor would take the fact that negotiations are taking place into account in making an investment decision. Often, the answer will be "no" because it is unclear whether the negotiations will lead to a result. The potential future merger will only qualify as insider information if and when the occurrence of the merger has become sufficiently likely.

An area that raises similar issues are earnings forecasts (and subsequent changes thereto). In practice, questions relating to the determination whether information is sufficiently concrete to qualify as insider information involve difficult judgments on which reasonable persons can reach different results. It is thus important to seek legal advice at an early stage of an M&A-transaction or a potential change to the board of management, or with respect to other events that can have a material influence on the stock price of the AG.

Difficult questions as to whether information is sufficiently concrete also arise with respect to important corporate actions, such as the issuance of new shares, that require an internal decision-making process involving several steps (*e.g.*, management board decisions requiring supervisory board consent). The BaFin has taken the view that generally the information has become sufficiently concrete once the management board has approved the corporate action even if the management board requires the consent of the supervisory board in order to implement the action.[299] The position of the BaFin can create a dilemma for management boards because the public release of the management board's decision prior to the supervisory board's vote would preempt the supervisory board's decision and thereby undermine the corporate governance structure of the AG. In practice, the solution generally is either to ensure that both the management board and the supervisory board act virtually simultaneously or to take advantage of the possibility to delay the publication (*cf.* below).[300]

Market rumors generally do not trigger an obligation for an AG to publish an ad-hoc notification. The management board of the AG should adopt a strict "no comment"-policy in response to market rumors and related press inquiries. Depending on the degree of truth of the rumor and the source of the rumor, it may, however, be advisable for the AG to publish an ad-hoc notification. For example, if employees of the AG planted the rumor or if the rumor is due to a leak in the corporate organization of the AG, the AG generally must promptly publish an ad-hoc notification if the rumor is sufficiently concrete to qualify as insider information. In such a case, it would not be permissible for the AG to delay the publication based upon the exemption

---

299 Emittentenleitfaden der Bundesanstalt für Finanzdienstleistungsaufsicht 2009, IV.2.2.7.
300 Gesetz über den Wertpapierhandel [WpHG] [Securities Trade Act] 1994, § 15, ¶ 3 (F.R.G.) in conjunction with Wertpapierhandelsanzeige- und Insiderverzeichnisverordnung [WpAIV] [Security Trading Announcement and Insider Register Order] 2004, § 6, no. 2 (F.R.G.).

from the ad-hoc notification obligation.[301] Similarly, if a representative of the AG deliberately or accidentally passed on insider information to a journalist or another third party, the AG can no longer rely on the ad-hoc exemption and must make the insider information public.

§ 127 Non-public nature of information

Information only constitutes insider information if it is not publicly known. Facts or circumstances are regarded as publicly known if an indeterminate number of persons have the opportunity to discover them. It suffices, however, if the information is available to the interested public (e.g., persons using a particular generally accessible website). By contrast, releasing information at events to which only a select group of participants has access, such as seminars, shareholders' meetings, press conferences, meetings with analysts or roadshows, is not sufficient for making the information "public".

§ 128 Influence on price

Non-public information only constitutes insider information if it has the propensity to have a material impact on the price of the shares or other securities. The test is whether a competent investor would take the information into consideration in making an investment decision.[302]

There is no clear standard for determining when an impact on the price of a security would be "material". In particular, it is not possible to apply a strict percentage test based upon the expected percentage change of the price. The management board of the AG must exercise an *ex-ante* judgment as to the expected price impact. The probability that the price of the security will change following publication of the information must be over 50%. Given the judgmental nature of the determination, it is often advisable to publish an ad-hoc notification if there is doubt as to the expected price impact of the information.

§ 129 Direct relationship to the issuer

In order to qualify as insider information, the information also must have a direct relationship to one or more issuers or to listed securities that qualify as "insider securities".[303] There is no doubt with respect to this element of the test if the information relates to circumstances that have occurred in the AG's area of business, *e.g.*, actions taken by the management or acts by other corporate bodies.[304] However, information arising from an external source may also affect the issuer, such as the insolvency of an important customer, a change in the issuer's credit rating, or a decision by a court or a governmental authority concerning the issuer's affairs. Information affecting the issuer only indirectly, such as market statistics, interest rates, studies or legislative proposals, does not trigger an ad-hoc publication obligation.[305]

---

301   *Cf.* § 132 below.
302   Gesetz über den Wertpapierhandel [WpHG] [Securities Trade Act] 1994, § 13, ¶ 1 (F.R.G.).
303   Gesetz über den Wertpapierhandel [WpHG] [Securities Trade Act] 1994, § 15, ¶ 1, sentence 1 (F.R.G.).
304   Gesetz über den Wertpapierhandel [WpHG] [Securities Trade Act] 1994, § 15, ¶ 1, sentence 3 (F.R.G.).
305   Emittentenleitfaden der Bundesanstalt für Finanzdienstleistungsaufsicht 2009, IV.2.2.2.

§ 130 Timing of preliminary notification and publication

Both the preliminary notification to the stock exchange(s) and the BaFin, and the publication must take place promptly after the AG has become aware of the insider information. The duty to publish insider information also applies during weekends and otherwise outside stock exchange hours. The issuer is, however, allowed sufficient time to verify (with the assistance of counsel and other external experts, if necessary) whether the facts or circumstances are such as to call for publication, or whether the prerequisites for an exemption from the ad-hoc obligation are met. The preliminary notification should reach the stock exchange(s) and the BaFin 30 minutes before publication of the information and must include the wording of the intended publication, the scheduling of the publication, and the name and telephone number of the contact person at the AG.[306]

§ 131 Form and content of ad-hoc notification

Ad-hoc notifications should be kept brief. Generally, they should not exceed 10 to 20 lines, and must conform to the requirements prescribed by law.[307] The information must be published in German, although simultaneous publication in English is permitted. The publication must be made via a widely-used electronic publication system (*e.g.*, Bloomberg, Reuters or Vereinigte Wirtschaftsdienste) and on the issuer's Internet site.[308]

§ 132 Exemption from publication obligation and delay of publication

An issuer may delay the publication of insider information by ad-hoc notification for as long as required to protect its legitimate interests, provided that the public is not mislead and the issuer can ensure the confidentiality of the insider information. As soon as any of these requirements for exemption is no longer met, the publication must be made promptly. At the time of the publication, the issuer must inform the BaFin of the grounds for relying on the exemption, giving details of the time when the decision to delay the publication was made.[309]

The BaFin has expressed the view that at least one member of the management board of the AG has to participate in the decision to make use of the exemption from the ad-hoc publication obligation.[310]

---

306 Gesetz über den Wertpapierhandel [WpHG] [Securities Trade Act] 1994, § 15, ¶ 4 (F.R.G.); Wertpapierhandelsanzeige- und Insiderverzeichnisverordnung [WpAIV] [Security Trading Announcement and Insider Register Regulation] 2004, § 8, ¶ 1 (F.R.G.).

307 Wertpapierhandelsanzeige- und Insiderverzeichnisverordnung [WpAIV] [Security Trading Announcement and Insider Register Regulation] 2004, § 4, ¶ 1, sentence 2 (F.R.G.) and Wertpapierhandelsanzeige- und Insiderverzeichnisverordnung [WpAIV] [Security Trading Announcement and Insider Register Regulation] 2004, § 3, ¶ 1 (F.R.G.).

308 Wertpapierhandelsanzeige- und Insiderverzeichnisverordnung [WpAIV] [Security Trading Announcement and Insider Register Regulation] 2004, § 5, ¶ 1, 2 (F.R.G.).

309 Gesetz über den Wertpapierhandel [WpHG] [Securities Trade Act] 1994, § 15, ¶ 3, sentence 2 (F.R.G.).

310 Emittentenleitfaden der Bundesanstalt für Finanzdienstleistungsaufsicht 2009, IV. 3.

§ 133 Protection of legitimate interests

An issuer has a legitimate interest in delaying the publication of insider information if its interests in maintaining the confidentiality of the information outweigh the interests of the capital market in complete and full transparency.[311] Typical examples include the risk that publication could jeopardize the outcome of ongoing negotiations of an M&A-transaction or preempt the decision of the supervisory board on granting its consent for certain actions of the management board.[312]

§ 134 No misleading of the public

The use of the exemption from the publication obligation must not mislead the public. Therefore, during the exemption period, the AG may not provide any information to the press or the capital markets contradicting the insider information. The issuer is also required to ensure the confidentiality of the information during this period, including by taking all necessary measures to ensure that only those persons have access to the information who need the information to fulfill their responsibilities.

§ 135 Keeping of insider lists

The management board must ensure that the AG keep lists of all employees and other persons acting on behalf of the AG (including legal and other advisers) who have access to insider information. It must update these lists promptly and transmit them to the BaFin upon request. In practice, AGs often keep general insider lists for areas that constantly deal with insider information (*e.g.*, the offices of the management board or the supervisory board) and special insider lists for specific projects (*e.g.*, the takeover of another company). The lists must include certain information about the persons listed, and the reason why and time when they were added to the list.[313] The insider list may not be made public and must be retained for six years in an accessible form.[314]

§ 136 Relationship between ad-hoc publication and other publication obligations: Parallel publication duties

In addition to the ad-hoc publication obligation, listed AGs are subject to various other publicity requirements to ensure the efficient and transparent communication with the capital markets. Some of these requirements also apply to unlisted AGs that have securities other than shares admitted and traded on the regulated market of a securities exchange (*e.g.*, bonds). These additional publicity requirements do not override the ad-hoc publication obligation, and consequently it is always necessary to determine whether the specific facts and circumstances result in an ad-hoc publication obligation in addition to other publication duties.[315]

311　Wertpapierhandelsanzeige- und Insiderverzeichnisverordnung [WpAIV] [Security Trading Announcement and Insider Register Regulation] 2004, § 6 (F.R.G.).

312　Wertpapierhandelsanzeige- und Insiderverzeichnisverordnung [WpAIV] [Security Trading Announcement and Insider Register Regulation] 2004, § 6, no. 1, 2 (F.R.G.).

313　Wertpapierhandelsanzeige- und Insiderverzeichnisverordnung [WpAIV] [Security Trading Announcement and Insider Register Regulation] 2004, § 14 (F.R.G.).

314　Wertpapierhandelsanzeige- und Insiderverzeichnisverordnung [WpAIV] [Security Trading Announcement and Insider Register Regulation] 2004, § 16 (F.R.G.).

315　Emittentenleitfaden der Bundesanstalt für Finanzdienstleistungsaufsicht 2009, IV.2.2.9.

For example, the Securities Acquisition and Takeover Act, which regulates public takeovers in Germany, provides for a separate duty of the acquirer to publish its decision to make a public bid for a target.[316] The Securities Trading Act, which is the primary source of ongoing capital markets disclosure obligations, requires a listed AG to publish quarterly interim information.[317] Listed AGs and AGs that have securities other than shares admitted and traded on the regulated market of a securities exchange have to publish semi-annual and annual financial reports.[318] The annual report must be published within four months after the end of a fiscal year, the semi-annual report must be published promptly after the end of the first half of its fiscal year, but in any event not later than two months thereafter, and the quarterly interim information must be published during the period which begins ten weeks after the beginning and six weeks before the end of each semi-annual period.

Listed AGs and AGs that have securities other than shares admitted and traded on the regulated market of a securities exchange must also publish at least once a year a document (the so-called "annual document") including (or incorporating by reference) all information that it published pursuant to the requirements of German and foreign capital markets laws within the past twelve months.[319] A misrepresentation in the annual document may constitute a criminal offence.[320]

VI. Liability

A. General principles of liability

§ 137 Introduction
Members of the management board of an AG are exposed to liability risks in connection with their activities under both civil and criminal law. The Stock Corporation Act is the principal basis for the liability regime applicable to management board members. In the following, the basic principles for liability under civil law are discussed.

§ 138 Liability to the AG
A member of the management board who violates his duties to the AG may be liable for damages to the AG. Liability can also arise if a management board member exploits his influence on the AG to cause other board members or employees to inflict harm upon the AG.

§ 139 D&O insurance (Directors and Officers liability insurance)
In Germany, it has become common practice for AGs to insure their management board members against liability risks arising from the performance of their duties. The insurance covers claims by the AG, by the AG's creditors or other third parties. The management board

---

316 Wertpapierübernahmegesetz [WpÜG] [Securities Acquisition and Takeover Act] 2001, § 10 (F.R.G.).
317 Gesetz über den Wertpapierhandel [WpHG] [Securities Trade Act] 1994, § 37x (F.R.G.).
318 Gesetz über den Wertpapierhandel [WpHG] [Securities Trade Act] 1994, §§ 37v, 37w (F.R.G.).
319 Wertpapierprospektgesetz [WpPG] [Securities Prospectus Act] 2005, § 10, ¶ 1 (F.R.G.).
320 Cf. § 179 below.

members generally do not take out insurance themselves. There is no consensus in the legal literature as to whether the insurance premium paid by the AG should be accounted for as part of the management board's overall compensation and consequently requires approval by the supervisory board. To avoid any violation of the law, the D&O insurance policy should be approved by the supervisory board.[321]

§ 140 Entitlement of the management board to D&O insurance

An AG has no legal obligation to take out D&O insurance for its management board members. Whether such insurance is provided, and on what terms, should be agreed in the service agreement.[322] In connection with the risk management system that an AG is required to put in place, the management board and the supervisory board must, however, consider on a case-by-case basis whether liability insurance is called for in order to ensure that the AG would be able to realize any claims for damages against members of its corporate bodies. If a D&O insurance is provided for the benefit of members of the management board, its terms have to provide for a deductible to be borne by a management board member of at least 10% of the amount of the damages from each individual event up to at least 150% of the management board member's fixed annual compensation.[323]

1.   General liability for violation of duties

§ 141 General principles

Any management board member acting at least negligently in violating his duties is liable to the AG for damages.[324] If several management board members are involved in the violation, they are jointly and severally liable. Accordingly, each member is obligated to compensate the AG for the full amount of the damages, but depending upon the extent of the individual responsibility of the other board members may have a claim for reimbursement or contribution against the other board members.[325] The statutory liability of management board members is mandatory and may not be limited by the articles of association of the AG or the service agreement.

§ 142 Violation of duties

Management board duties may arise from applicable law or the articles of association. All duties incumbent upon the management board due to its status as a representational/managerial body of the AG are generally considered duties that can be the basis for damage claims of the AG.[326] Obligations of the management board to other corporate bodies of the AG also constitute obligations to the AG, and thus, *e.g.*, a violation of reporting duties to the supervisory board also constitutes a basis for liability.

---

321 Aktiengesetz [AktG] [Stock Corporation Act] 1965, § 87, ¶ 1 (F.R.G.).
322 *Cf.* Form of Service Agreement for management board members of the AG attached in Chapter Seven: Annex I.A.
323 Aktiengesetz [AktG] [Stock Corporation Act] 1965, § 93, ¶ 2, sentence 3 (F.R.G.).
324 Aktiengesetz [AktG] [Stock Corporation Act] 1965, § 93, ¶ 2 (F.R.G.).
325 Bürgerliches Gesetzbuch [BGB] [Civil Code] 1896, § 426 (F.R.G.). The reversal of the burden of proof pursuant to Aktiengesetz [AktG] [Stock Corporation Act] 1965, § 93, ¶ 2, sentence 2 (F.R.G.) also applies in a subsequent claim against the remaining management board members.
326 §§ 89 *et seq.* cover the duties of management board members in detail.

§ 143 Violation of the general duties of supervision and oversight

Management board members may also be subject to liability as a result of the joint responsibility of the management board. Thus, an individual management board member may be liable even if he is not directly responsible for the damage because the management board's rules of procedure have assigned the duties in question to another board member. The violation of duties giving rise to liability in such a case would be a violation of the general supervisory duty with respect to the actions of the management board member who is directly responsible for the damage. The scope and requirements of the supervisory duty depend on the individual circumstances. Generally, it is not sufficient for a management board member to rely on information given by other board members at a board meeting. In any event, if there are concrete indications of a management board member failing to perform his obligations, the other board members have a duty to intervene. Liability for a violation of duties may also arise if a management board member is outvoted when adopting a board resolution, but does not attempt to prevent a potentially illegal majority resolution from being implemented.[327] Should the attempt fail, the outvoted board member must appeal to the supervisory board.

§ 144 Negligence

Being held liable for damages to the AG requires that the management board member acted negligently or with intent. A board member who has observed the standard of due care of a diligent and conscientious business manager will not be considered to have acted negligently.[328] Negligence will exist, however, if a management board member does not have the requisite knowledge and skills to perform his tasks. In such a case, he is charged with having taken on the board appointment despite the lack of qualifications. If a board member does not have the professional knowledge to perform a specific task, he is required to seek appropriate advice and assistance. Liability may also arise if a member of the management board delegates tasks that are not permitted to be delegated, or selects employees to perform a specific task who do not have the requisite qualifications. In exceptional cases, an error by a management board member may not amount to negligence if an immediate decision is required and no time is left for obtaining advice. Management board members are, however, required to have procedures in place that enable them to seek appropriate advice and assistance on an expedited basis in case of urgency.

§ 145 Burden of proof

The liability provisions of the Stock Corporation Act require a management board member to prove that he has fulfilled his duties according to the standard of a diligent and conscientious business manager, or that the damages would also have occurred if he had adhered to such standard.[329] In legal proceedings, the AG only has to prove that it has sustained damages that are potentially due to the violation of duties by the management board member. It is unclear whether this reversal of the burden of proof also applies to a former member of the management board who no longer has access to the AG's records and is not in possession of any sources of information for his defense. Should a court apply the reversal of the burden of proof

---

327   Cf. § 175.
328   Aktiengesetz [AktG] [Stock Corporation Act] 1965, § 93, ¶ 1, sentence 1 (F.R.G.); cf. § 90.
329   Aktiengesetz [AktG] [Stock Corporation Act] 1965, § 93, ¶ 2, sentence 2 (F.R.G.).

in such a case as well, the former management board member has a right to inspection of the books and records of the AG to the extent required for his defense.

§ 146 Damages

The AG has sustained damages if the value of its assets following the violation of duties is lower than it would have been in the absence of such violation.[330] Thus, in determining damages direct and indirect monetary consequences, including loss of profits or incurrence of liabilities, are taken into account. With respect to violations of certain specific duties enumerated in Section 93(3) of the Stock Corporation Act (e.g., repayment of capital contributions to shareholders, payment of dividends or interest to shareholders or distribution of corporate assets, in each case in violation of the Stock Corporation Act), damages are determined solely by reference to the funds paid out or the reduction of specific assets of the AG without regard to whether the action in question resulted in corresponding benefits to the AG.[331] A change in the value of the shares of the AG due to the action in question is irrelevant in assessing whether the AG has suffered damages because the shares do not form part of the assets of the AG.

§ 147 Limitations

The AG's claim for damages is subject to the statute of limitations after five years. In case the AG's shares are listed[332] at the time of the violation of duties the statute of limitation is ten years.[333] The limitation period begins on the date on which the claim arises, even if the AG does not become aware of the claim or the occurrence of damages until a later date.[334] The period of limitation may not be extended or shortened by the articles of association of the AG or by contractual agreement. It is, however, permissible for the AG and a board member to agree with respect to a specific event or action that the period of limitation be extended until it has become clear whether the AG will suffer any damages. Such agreements are typical in cases in which the conduct of a member of the board of management has given rise to a claim of a third party against the AG. The five-year limitation period also applies to contractual claims for damages due to a violation of the service agreement. By contrast, claims by the AG based upon tort principles are time-barred three years after the AG learned of the existence of the claim (which may be after the time when the claim arose).[335] As a result of the differences in the point of time when the limitation period begins, damage claims based on the Stock Corporation Act may be time-barred sooner than tort claims despite their longer limitation period.

---

330   Bürgerliches Gesetzbuch [BGB] [Civil Code] 1896, §§ 249 *et seq.* (F.R.G.).

331   Aktiengesetz [AktG] [Stock Corporation Act] 1965, § 93, ¶ 3 (F.R.G.).

332   The term "listed" is defined in Aktiengesetz [AktG][Stock Corporation Act] 1965, § 3, ¶ 2 (F.R.G.) and includes AGs that have their shares admitted to a market that is regulated and supervised by publicly recognized bodies, takes place regularly and is directly or indirectly accessible for the public. This includes all AGs that have their shares admitted to trading on a regulated market including admission to a foreign stock exchange with comparable notification requirements.

333   Aktiengesetz [AktG] [Stock Corporation Act] 1965, § 93, ¶ 6 (F.R.G.) according to the Act for the Restructuring and Orderly Liquidation of Credit Institutions, for the Establishment of a Restructuring Fund for Credit Institutions and for the Extension of the Limited Period of Corporate Law Management Liability (*Restrukturierungsgesetz/* "Bank Restructuring Act"). The same ten year statute of limitations applies for AGs that qualify as banking institutions (*Kreditinstitute*).

334   Bürgerliches Gesetzbuch [BGB] [Civil Code] 1896, § 200 (F.R.G.).

335   Bürgerliches Gesetzbuch [BGB] [Civil Code] 1896, §§ 195, 199 (F.R.G.).

a.   **Exclusion of liability, waiver, settlement**

§ 148 Actions based on a lawful resolution by the shareholders' meeting
The personal liability of a management board member of an AG is unlimited in amount and mandatory under German law.

Liability is excluded if an action is based on a resolution of the shareholders' meeting that is legal (*e.g.*, is neither null and void nor challengeable).[336] The exclusion presumes that the management board has not violated any of its duties in passing the resolution, *e.g.*, by providing incomplete or incorrect information to the shareholders' meeting. The resolution must have been adopted prior to the taking of the action that caused the damage; a subsequent resolution cannot retroactively eliminate the management board's liability. Approval of the action by the supervisory board (whether given prior to or after the taking of the action) does not avoid liability of the management board.

§ 149 Waiver and settlement
An AG may waive claims against its management board members, *e.g.*, in a release agreement between the AG and the management board members,[337] or the parties may settle claims in or out of court.[338] To prevent the supervisory board from disposing over claims before it is clear whether and to what extent the AG has suffered damages, waiver and settlement are only permissible three years after the damage claim has arisen. For this reason, the AG may not give contractual indemnities for the benefit of its board members, unless the indemnity is limited to conduct that was not negligent. For example, it should be permissible for an AG to indemnify the members of its management board against strict liability under foreign securities laws. In practice, it is, however, rare for an AG to provide such an indemnity given the limitation on the permissible scope of the indemnity. A waiver of liability or a settlement with a member of the management board requires the approval of the shareholders' meeting in order to be effective. A shareholder or a group of shareholders holding at least 10% of the share capital of the AG may thwart the waiver or settlement by raising an objection.

A waiver or settlement is permissible even before the expiration of the three-year period if the board member in question is insolvent or the waiver or settlement is necessary in order to avert insolvency proceedings concerning the board member or the obligation to pay damages is set out in an insolvency plan involving the board member.[339]

Waivers, settlements and other actions designed to mitigate liability, whether contained in contracts or the articles of association (including provisions on shortening limitation periods) are invalid beyond the cases specifically provided by statute.

---

336   Aktiengesetz [AktG] [Stock Corporation Act] 1965, § 93, ¶ 4, sentence 1 (F.R.G.).
337   Bürgerliches Gesetzbuch [BGB] [Civil Code] 1896, § 397 (F.R.G.).
338   Bürgerliches Gesetzbuch [BGB] [Civil Code] 1896, § 379 (F.R.G.).
339   Aktiengesetz [AktG] [Stock Corporation Act] 1965, § 93, ¶ 4, sentences 2-4 (F.R.G.).

b.   Enforcing claims for damages

§ 150   Claims made by the supervisory board

When damage claims are to be asserted and enforced against management board members, the AG is represented by its supervisory board.[340] On the basis of its statutory duty to oversee the management board, the supervisory board must examine on its own responsibility whether a damage claim against a management board member has merit and, if so, whether there are countervailing considerations that argue in favor of not pursuing the claim. The supervisory board is generally required to assert and enforce all claims that appear justified. It is, however, possible that there are important interests of the AG, which argue in favor of not pursuing a claim. A typical example involves ordinary negligence by a management board member whom the AG considers crucial for the future management of the AG. The supervisory board decides whether to enforce the claim by bringing an action, and has a certain degree of discretion in this regard. On the other hand, the supervisory board is required to bring a claim for damages if the shareholders' meeting has adopted a resolution to such effect based upon a simple majority of the votes cast.[341] Furthermore, by a simple majority of the votes cast the shareholders' meeting may appoint a special representative to enforce a claim for damages against a board member. Based upon an application by shareholders holding at least 10% of the share capital or a *pro rata* amount of EUR 1 million of the share capital, the court may (but is not required to) replace the person appointed as special representative by the shareholders' meeting.[342]

§ 151   Damage claims filed by shareholders

If neither the supervisory board nor the shareholders' meeting decides to assert claims for damages against a management board member, in certain circumstances the shareholders themselves may enforce such claims. Enforcement by shareholders would be for the benefit of the AG, which would receive payment if the action is successful. Shareholders who wish to enforce a claim for damages for the benefit of the AG must file an application with the regional court of the AG's registered office for the action to be admitted.[343] The application will be granted if the shareholders who filed the application together hold at least 1% of the share capital or a *pro rata* amount of EUR 100,000 of the share capital. The shareholders must also be able to prove that they acquired their shares before learning of the violation of duties in question, that the AG failed to enforce the claim against the management board, that there is reason to suspect that the AG has sustained damages due to a serious violation of duties by one of the members of the management board, and finally that filing the claim would not run counter to any overriding interests of the AG.[344]

Under certain conditions, the AG's creditors also have a right to enforce claims for damages against members of the management board.[345]

---

340   Aktiengesetz [AktG] [Stock Corporation Act] 1965, § 112 (F.R.G.).
341   Aktiengesetz [AktG] [Stock Corporation Act] 1965, § 147, ¶ 1 (F.R.G.).
342   Aktiengesetz [AktG] [Stock Corporation Act] 1965, § 147, ¶ 2 (F.R.G.).
343   Aktiengesetz [AktG] [Stock Corporation Act] 1965, § 148, ¶ 2, sentence 1 (F.R.G.).
344   Aktiengesetz [AktG] [Stock Corporation Act] 1965, § 148, ¶ 1 and 2 (F.R.G.).
345   *Cf.* § 160.

2. Liability due to exerting influence on the AG
§ 152 Criteria for liability

Anyone intentionally using his influence over an AG to prompt a member of the management or supervisory board, or a senior officer of the AG to act to the detriment of the AG will be liable to the AG for any damages that arise as a result thereof.[346] Such liability also applies to a management board member who causes damages to the AG by exerting undue influence over the AG. In practice, members of the management board are, however, rarely held liable for undue exertion of influence over the AG because it is generally easier to find liability based upon the statutory liability provisions applicable to violations of duties by members of the management board, which only require negligence and in part reverse the burden of proof.[347] If a shareholder or another third party is held liable for exerting undue influence over an AG, the members of the management board (and supervisory board) are jointly liable together with the shareholder or the other third party if and to the extent that they have violated their duties.[348] In such a case, the general principles applicable to the statutory liability of board members apply (*e.g.*, negligence is sufficient and the burden of proof is reversed in part).

§ 153 Exclusion of liability

Liability of a board member is excluded if the action taken is based on a lawful resolution of the shareholders' meeting of the AG.[349] Furthermore, liability does not apply if the management or supervisory board member acted in accordance with instructions given by the parent company based upon a control agreement.[350] In such cases, the Stock Corporation Act provides for a special set of provisions protecting the AG and its shareholders against an abuse of the power by the parent company.[351]

B. Liability to shareholders

§ 154 Introduction

Shareholders may support actions for damages by the AG against management board members in a resolution of the shareholders' meeting, or if applicable, file claims in their own name but for the benefit of the AG.[352] In certain cases, shareholders may also be entitled to bring their own claims for damages against the management board.[353]

§ 155 Liability for inaccurate financial reporting

The liability of the management board to shareholders for financial reporting errors is based on tort principles, according to which anyone violating a statutory provision intended to pro-

---

346 Aktiengesetz [AktG] [Stock Corporation Act] 1965, § 117, ¶ 1, sentence 1 (F.R.G.).
347 *Cf.* above § 145.
348 Aktiengesetz [AktG] [Stock Corporation Act] 1965, § 117, ¶ 2 (F.R.G.).
349 Aktiengesetz [AktG] [Stock Corporation Act] 1965, § 117, ¶ 2, sentence 3 (F.R.G.). *Cf.* above § 148.
350 Aktiengesetz [AktG] [Stock Corporation Act] 1965, § 117, ¶ 7, §§ 308, 323 (F.R.G.).
351 Aktiengesetz [AktG] [Stock Corporation Act] 1965, §§ 309, 310 (F.R.G.). *Cf.* § 77.
352 *Cf.* §§ 150 *et seq.*
353 Aktiengesetz [AktG] [Stock Corporation Act] 1965, § 117, ¶ 1, sentence 2 (F.R.G.).

tect another person is liable to that person for the resulting damages.[354] The shareholders in particular are protected by the statutory sanctions imposed by the Stock Corporation Act for furnishing false information and inaccurate reporting by the management or supervisory board, and the criteria for criminal violations of trust (*Untreue*).[355] If any of these statutory provisions has been violated, the member(s) of the management board responsible for such violation is (are) liable to the shareholders for damages.

Members of the management board are liable if they inaccurately report on, or submit inaccurate information about, the assets and liabilities of the AG.[356] Such information includes all materials containing financial information, in particular balance sheet and P & L -information. Liability may arise irrespective of whether the information has been prepared for internal or external use. Accordingly, inaccurate financial information included in an ad-hoc notification to the capital markets[357] can also result in liability.

Damages as a result of inaccurate financial reporting include all losses incurred by a shareholder (or other party entitled to compensation), including, for example, the price paid for buying debt or equity instruments issued by the AG (subject to retransfer of the instruments to the AG) or the loss incurred as a result of the extension of a loan to the AG which will not be repaid in full due to the insolvency of the AG.[358] Alternatively, the party entitled to damages may claim the difference between the purchase price and the market value of the instrument (*e.g.*, the price realized upon disposal).

By contrast, if a shareholder has only suffered "indirect" damages due to the reduction of the value of his shares as a result of damages incurred by the AG, the management board generally is not required to compensate the shareholder for damages.

§ 156 Violation of disclosure requirements under capital markets law
There are many bases for liability of a listed AG to participants in the capital markets. In primary capital markets transactions, such as the issuance of new shares in initial public offerings or capital increases or the issuance of bonds, liability can arise primarily under contractual indemnification provisions in underwriting or placement agreements, or based upon statutory provisions on disclosure in offering or listing prospectuses or similar documents.[359] Individual liability of an issuer's board members or officers is, however, rare in primary capital markets transactions in Germany absent intentional conduct. In particular, there is no statutory provision creating liability of board members directly to investors or intermediaries such as banks.

---

354 Bürgerliches Gesetzbuch [BGB] [Civil Code] 1896, § 823, ¶ 2 (F.R.G.).
355 Aktiengesetz [AktG] [Stock Corporation Act] 1965, §§ 399, 400 (F.R.G.); Strafgesetzbuch [StGB] [Criminal Code] 1871, § 266 (F.R.G.).
356 Bürgerliches Gesetzbuch [BGB] [Civil Code] 1896, § 823, ¶ 2 (F.R.G.) in conjunction with Aktiengesetz [AktG] [Stock Corporation Act] 1965, §§ 399, 400 (F.R.G.).
357 Cf. § 124 above.
358 Creditors also have contractual claims against the AG, which may be able to take recourse against management board members, cf. § 160.
359 E.g., Börsengesetz [BörsG] [Stock Exchange Act] 2007, § 44 (F.R.G.); Gesetz über den Wertpapierhandel [WpHG] [Securities Trade Act] 1994, §§ 37b, 37c (F.R.G.).

An AG that is held liable to market participants may, however, be able to have recourse against its management board based upon the principles discussed above.[360]

German law also provides for statutory liability in connection with the ongoing disclosure obligations of companies whose shares (or in certain cases other types of securities) are listed on a securities exchange. Any violation of the ad-hoc publication obligation may result in a claim for damages of investors against the responsible management board member, if the investors engaged in transactions in the shares of the AG in reliance on the ad-hoc notification of the AG (or the failure to publish an ad-hoc notification).[361] The Securities Trading Act only provides for damage claims by investors against the AG.[362] There has, however, been case law to the effect that violations of ongoing disclosure requirements of an AG to the capital markets may also result in a direct claim of investors against a management board member if the claimant can show "causality" and willful intent of the management board member. Causality means that the inaccurate notice or the failure to publish a notice required to be published by law must have caused the investment decision. The burden of proof rests with the claimant.[363]

Based on court decisions, members of management boards of AGs have been held liable for deliberately furnishing incorrect information to the market or misleading third parties by providing false information. Failing to publish a required ad-hoc notification has resulted in liability only if a member of the management board was aware of insider information, but refrained from publishing the information in order to use the information to his personal benefit, *e.g.*, by buying or selling shares of the AG. Investors may only recover damages due to refraining from the sale of shares (or other securities) if they can prove that they refrained from a definitely intended sale on a particular date because of a violation of a publication requirement. In such a case, the amount of damages is determined based on a hypothetical sales price on the basis of the stock price that would have prevailed on the originally scheduled sales date had the publication requirement been fulfilled.

§ 157 Liability due to exerting undue influence

A management board member who, by exerting undue influence over the AG, intentionally causes another management board member or a member of the supervisory board, or a senior officer of the AG to engage in an act that results in damages to a shareholder of the AG is liable to the shareholder for any damages arising as a result thereof.[364] The shareholder is only compensated for any direct damages suffered. Accordingly, a loss in value of the AG's shares as a result of damages suffered by the AG could not be claimed.

Only damages suffered by the shareholder in his capacity as a shareholder and not as a third-party creditor or counterparty to commercial transactions of the AG may be compensated.

---

360 *Cf.* §§ 150 *et seq.* above.
361 *Cf.* § 124 above.
362 Gesetz über den Wertpapierhandel [WpHG] [Securities Trade Act] 1994, §§ 37b, 37c (F.R.G.).
363 Bürgerliches Gesetzbuch [BGB] [Civil Code] 1896, § 826 (F.R.G.).
364 Aktiengesetz [AktG] [Stock Corporation Act] 1965, § 117, ¶ 1, sentence 2 (F.R.G.); *cf.* § 152 with respect to liability to the AG.

However, if the status as a shareholder was the reason for the extension of the loan (or another corporate transaction), damages suffered as creditor are also recoverable.

If a third party is liable for exerting undue influence over the AG according to the above principles, the law provides for joint and several liability of the members of the management board (and the supervisory board) to the extent that they have violated their duties.[365] If shareholders are entitled to be compensated for damages caused by the exertion of undue influence over the AG by a third party, the management board is not only liable to the AG, but also to the shareholders for violating its duties. Under certain circumstances, liability for exerting undue influence over the AG is excluded.[366]

§ 158 Liability in takeover situations

In the event of a takeover offer for the shares of an AG, the management board of the AG is generally required by law to refrain from taking any measures that may thwart the takeover (defensive measures).[367] If the Securities Acquisition and Takeover Act applies to the takeover offer (which would not be the case if the only listing of the AG's shares was on the OTC market (*Freiverkehr*) in Germany or on a third-country securities exchange outside the European Economic Area, such as the New York Stock Exchange), the management board of the AG is also required to issue and publish a detailed opinion on the takeover offer.[368] The management board would be liable to the AG for any violation of the duty to refrain from taking defensive measures or for disseminating inaccurate or misleading information through the opinion. Thus far, there has been no case holding the management board also liable to the shareholders in such a case, but some commentators argue that such liability exists.[369]

C.   Liability to creditors of the AG

§ 159 Introduction

As a general matter, management board members are liable to the AG's creditors on the same basis and to the same extent as to other third parties, including, in particular, on the basis of tort principles. Nonetheless, the management board has specific duties to creditors of the AG, and there are circumstances in which special liability to creditors of the AG can arise.

§ 160 Rights of the creditors of the AG to enforce claims of the AG

Generally, creditors of an AG who claim that management has violated its duties are generally required to obtain a judgment against the AG. Such a judgment could be enforced, among other things, by attaching the recourse claims of the AG against the management board members.[370]

---

365 Aktiengesetz [AktG] [Stock Corporation Act] 1965, § 117, ¶ 2 (F.R.G.).
366 *Cf.* § 153 above.
367 Wertpapierübernahmegesetz [WpÜG] [Securities Acquisition and Takeover Act] 2001, § 33 (F.R.G.).
368 Wertpapierübernahmegesetz [WpÜG] [Securities Acquisition and Takeover Act] 2001, § 27 (F.R.G.).
369 Potential liability pursuant to Bürgerliches Gesetzbuch [BGB] [Civil Code] 1896, § 823, ¶ 2 (F.R.G.) in conjunction with Wertpapierübernahmegesetz [WpÜG] [Securities Acquisition and Takeover Act] 2001, § 27 (F.R.G.).
370 Zivilprozessordnung [ZPO] [Civil procedure statute] 1950, §§ 829, 835 (F.R.G.).

In certain cases, the Stock Corporation Act entitles creditors of an AG to file their claims for compensation from the AG directly against management board members.[371] In such a case, creditors may demand the payment of damages from the board members to themselves.

Such direct actions against board members are, however, only permissible if a creditor has a monetary claim against the AG (irrespective of the legal basis) and is unable to obtain compensation from the AG itself. This criterion is met if the AG is unable to pay; an unsuccessful attempt at enforcement is not necessary. Another requirement for a direct action against a board member is that the AG has a claim against the board member. If the creditor's claim against the AG arose from a violation of duties by the management board member, the right of the AG's creditors to enforce such claim requires a grossly negligent act by the management board member, unless the board member has violated one of the duties specifically enumerated in the Stock Corporation Act (in which case simple negligence is sufficient for giving creditors the right of direct enforcement).[372]

Assuming these requirements are met, the AG's creditors are entitled to claim compensation from the management board member in question in the amount in which their claims against the AG have not been paid. It should be noted, however, that during an insolvency proceeding of the AG only the receiver is entitled to file claims of the AG's creditors; the AG's creditors are not permitted to proceed directly against management board members during such time.[373]

A waiver or settlement between the AG and the liable management board member does not relieve the board member from his obligation to compensate the AG's creditors.[374]

§ 161 Liability for concluding contracts

The members of the management board, as the legal representatives of the AG, also represent the AG when entering into contracts, although in practice contracts are often executed by holders of a commercial power of attorney or Prokuristen. Generally, the AG is responsible if a member of the management board or an employee violates any pre-contractual duties of disclosure or information *vis-à-vis* the counterparty in the context of contractual negotiations.[375] A management board member may be held personally liable to the counterparty only in exceptional cases, in particular, if the counterparty places special trust in the board member as a representative of the AG (*e.g.*, the board member offers a personal guarantee for the fulfillment of the contract), or if the board member pursues his own economic interests in concluding the contract.[376] Special professional knowledge of the acting management board member does not in and by itself form the basis for a relationship of special trust; there must be additional circumstances, such as a statement that the board member assumes personal responsibility for

---

371 Aktiengesetz [AktG] [Stock Corporation Act] 1965, § 93, ¶ 5, sentence 1, § 117, ¶ 5 (F.R.G.).
372 Aktiengesetz [AktG] [Stock Corporation Act] 1965, § 93, ¶ 5, sentence 2, ¶ 3 (F.R.G.).
373 Aktiengesetz [AktG] [Stock Corporation Act] 1965, § 93, ¶ 5, sentence 4 (F.R.G.).
374 Aktiengesetz [AktG] [Stock Corporation Act] 1965, § 93, ¶ 5, sentence 3 (F.R.G.).
375 Bürgerliches Gesetzbuch [BGB] [Civil Code] 1896, § 311, ¶ 2, § 241, ¶ 2, § 280, ¶ 1, § 31 (F.R.G.).
376 Haftung der Gesellschaft aus Bürgerliches Gesetzbuch [BGB] [Civil Code] 1896, § 311, ¶ 2, § 241, ¶ 2, § 280, ¶ 1 (F.R.G.).

the orderly performance of the contract by the AG. Ownership of the AG or a substantial stake in the AG is not sufficient to create liability on the theory that the board member has an economic interest in the contract.

§ 162 Disclosure requirements in a crisis

Management board members have a duty to inform potential business partners when negotiating contracts that the AG is on the verge of insolvency if it is foreseeable that the AG will be insolvent when the contractual liability becomes due. Any member of the management board violating this duty or providing incorrect information about the AG's financial condition may accordingly be held personally liable for damages to the business partner.

§ 163 Liability due to delay in filing for insolvency

Management board members have a statutory duty to file for insolvency if the AG becomes insolvent or overindebted. Any intentional or negligent violation of this duty may serve as grounds for the AG's creditors to claim damages directly from the management board.[377] However, a distinction must be drawn in regard to the type of damages that may be claimed: Old creditors, e.g., creditors whose claims existed at the time when the board violated the duty to file for insolvency, are only entitled to so-called "damage quotas". Damage quotas mean the amount by which the insolvent estate was further reduced due to the delay in applying for insolvency. On the other hand, new creditors, e.g., creditors whose claims came into existence only after the violation of the duty to file for insolvency, are entitled to the full damages caused by the violation. Such damages include, among others, damages sustained by new creditors due to the AG's inability to pay for services rendered or goods delivered.

§ 164 Liability in respect of financing arrangements

Creditors who have extended financing to the AG by way of loans or delivery of goods, or granted a voluntary payment deferral to the AG without being aware of its financial crisis, may claim damages from a management board member if the board member was aware of the financial crisis of the AG at the time of negotiating the financing or the payment deferral and at least tacitly accepted that the creditors' claims could not be met when due.[378]

D.   Liability to other third parties

§ 165 Introduction

With respect to third parties that are not contractual parties of the AG or in the process of negotiating a contractual agreement with the AG, members of the management board can only be liable based upon principles of tort liability due to the lack of a contractual relationship. There are two categories of tort liability that have particular relevance in practice: Organizational faults and violation of laws that are intended to protect the interests of third parties.

---

377   Bürgerliches Gesetzbuch [BGB] [Civil Code] 1896, § 823, ¶ 2 (F.R.G.) in conjunction with Aktiengesetz [AktG] [Stock Corporation Act] 1965, § 92, ¶ 2 (F.R.G.).

378   Haftung aus Bürgerliches Gesetzbuch [BGB] [Civil Code] 1896, § 826 (F.R.G.).

§ 166 General liability for tort

Liability of management board members on the basis of general tort principles arises if a board member intentionally or negligently injures the life, body, health, liberty, property or another right of another individual.[379] Anyone who intentionally or negligently violates a law is also liable, if the law is intended to protect the persons who, as a result of such violation, suffer harm.[380] Examples of laws intended to protect other persons are regulations of the Federal Act against Harmful Emissions into the Environment, the Food Act or various criminal statutes. The key test for determining whether the violation of a particular law can result in civil liability is whether the purpose of the law is to protect the injured party (as opposed to the interest of the general public). Most laws in the capital markets area (*e.g.*, insider trading prohibitions, market manipulation prohibitions or ownership notification obligations) are intended to ensure the integrity of the market rather than the protection of individual market participants. Accordingly, the violation of such laws does not result in civil liability on the basis of general tort principles.

In addition to the management board member who committed the tortuous act, the AG is also liable for any harm inflicted.[381] The AG and the board member are subject to joint and several liability,[382] but, *inter partes*, the allocation of the damages depends on the degree of individual fault, the contractual arrangements between the AG and the board member, and other factors.

§ 167 Liability for violation of organizational duties

As the legal representative body of the AG, the management board also has certain organizational duties associated with running a business. Court decisions have held management board members liable to third parties for violations of such organizational duties. Such liability may result from insufficient supervision of persons charged by the management board with specific assignments or delegation of tasks to employees who lack the necessary qualifications. Moreover, the management board has to establish a risk management system for internal control and supervision. Employees also must be given periodic training if they work in a fast-changing area. These organizational duties are established by law and court rulings and vary from case to case.

§ 168 Tax liabilities

The members of the management board are responsible for carrying out the AG's tax-related duties, in particular for filing tax returns and paying taxes on time.[383] If they violate any tax-related duties intentionally or due to gross negligence and such violation results in tax liabilities of the AG not being determined or not being determined on a timely basis, or taxes are not paid or paid late or refunds being granted without legal foundation, the management board

---

379   Bürgerliches Gesetzbuch [BGB] [Civil Code] 1896, § 823, ¶ 1 (F.R.G.).
380   Bürgerliches Gesetzbuch [BGB] [Civil Code] 1896, § 823, ¶ 2 (F.R.G.).
381   Bürgerliches Gesetzbuch [BGB] [Civil Code] 1896, § 823, ¶ 1, 2, § 31 (F.R.G.).
382   Bürgerliches Gesetzbuch [BGB] [Civil Code] 1896, § 830, ¶ 1, sentence 1 (F.R.G.).
383   Abgabenordnung [AO] [General Tax Code] 1976, §§ 34, 149 *et seq.* (F.R.G.).

members are personally liable.[384] If a management board member relies on the information furnished by a carefully selected and supervised tax consultant and there was no reason to doubt the accuracy of the contents of the tax return prepared by the tax consultant, generally no personal liability should arise. Generally, only the management board member responsible for tax matters is subject to liability. Joint liability of the remaining management board members can, however, arise if they failed to act despite indications that the responsible board member did not duly fulfill his duties.

The fiscal authorities have the right to enforce claims (against the AG as well as against individual members of the management board) by way of issuing administrative orders, which are immediately enforceable. There is no need for the fiscal authorities to obtain a judgment in court prior to commencing enforcement proceedings.

§ 169 Failure to withhold wage taxes
The risk of failing to pay tax liabilities on a timely basis is particularly high if the AG is in a financial crisis. If available funds do not suffice to pay the net salaries of employees, including the wage tax to be withheld by the employer, personal liability of the management board can arise quickly. Wage tax must be transferred by the employer to the tax office at the latest on the tenth day of the following month.[385] This obligation is considered common knowledge and therefore any failure of the management board to comply with this obligation is presumed to have been intentional or at least grossly negligent. To avoid being held personally liable, the principle of satisfying employees and tax authorities on an equal basis must be observed, even if there are insufficient funds to pay employees in full. This means that the salaries have to be reduced to an extent such that the AG is able to pay salaries and wage taxes on the same pro-rata basis.

§ 170 Liability for social security contributions
The management board may also be held liable for failing to pay social security contributions (*e.g.*, health insurance, nursing care insurance, accident insurance). The management board is required by law to transfer social security contributions when due.[386] Any failure to do so in violation of statutory regulations results in personal liability to the social security agencies.[387] Personal liability only applies to the employee's share and not to the employer's share of the social security contributions.

With regard to the joint liability of the management board, the same principles as discussed above apply.[388]

---

384 Abgabenordnung [AO] [General Tax Code] 1976, § 69 (F.R.G.).
385 Einkommensteuergesetz [EStG] [Income Tax Act] 1934, § 41a (F.R.G.).
386 Exact timing *cf.* Sozialgesetzbuch IV [SGB IV] [Social Code IV] 1976, § 23 (F.R.G.).
387 Bürgerliches Gesetzbuch [BGB] [Civil Code] 1896, § 823, ¶ 2 (F.R.G.) in conjunction with Strafgesetzbuch [StGB] [Criminal Code] 1871, § 266a, ¶ 2, § 263 (F.R.G.).
388 *Cf.* § 168.

§ 171 Liability for defective products

German product liability law is comprised of the Product Liability Act (*Produkthaftungsgesetz/ ProdHaftG*) and principles of manufacturer's liability that have been developed over time and are reflected in a large body of case law. The liability anchored in the Product Liability Act exclusively applies to the AG and not to its board members, officers or employees. Management board members may, however, be subject to manufacturer's liability; under such liability, anyone marketing a product must take due care to prevent the product from injuring third parties.

Manufacturer's liability can arise upon the introduction of a defective product to the market. The defect may be due to faulty design, improper manufacture or missing product information (warning notices, instructions for use). In order to be subject to personal liability, the management board must have been aware (or, assuming diligent management of the AG, should have been aware) of the defectiveness of the product when it was introduced to the market. Given the difficulty of purchasers and users of products to prove negligence or intent, the courts have developed a concept of presumption of culpability. If the management board member cannot prove that the AG had organizational measures in place generally ensuring the early recognition and avoidance of product defects, there is a presumption that the management board member was aware that the product was defective.

If the defect of the product was initially unknown and imperceptible, but later becomes apparent, the entire management board is liable if it fails to publish a warning notice, or, if necessary, to protect users by initiating a product recall. Each management board member is required to do everything in his power in such a case to bring about a decision by the entire management board concerning the required notice or recall after the product defect became apparent.

E.   Criminal offenses

§ 172 Introduction

In recent years, the risk of criminal liability of members of the management boards of AGs has significantly increased. Stricter laws, public prosecutors with greater expertise in white collar crime, and increased awareness of shareholders and the general public have contributed to a wave of prosecutions of board members and other senior corporate executives in Germany.

In practice, criminal liability does not only arise as a result of specific conduct of a board member. Failure to act or simply the attribution of responsibility for the behavior of colleagues or employees of the AG can be a basis for criminal liability of a board member. However, criminal responsibility can only apply if the person or persons involved have violated statutory obligations or prohibitions. Therefore, the economic failure of a managerial measure, in and by itself, does not result in criminal responsibility on the part of the decision makers. However, a risky business decision that turns out to be incorrect may provide sufficient indication for an initial suspicion of a criminal act and thus cause a public prosecutor to initiate an investigation.

§ 173 Only natural persons can be held criminally liable

German criminal law does not provide for sanctions against AGs, but only against natural persons. Some penal provisions of the Stock Corporation Act apply directly to anyone acting on behalf of the AG, *i.e.*, generally the members of the management or supervisory board.[389] Other provisions only apply to members of the management or supervisory board, founders, auditors, or liquidators of the AG.

§ 174 Liability for administrative offenses also applies to the AG

A fine of up to EUR 500,000 may be imposed on the AG itself as a penalty for an administrative offense if it has been established that a member of the management board or another person entitled to represent the AG or responsible for the management of the AG has committed a criminal or administrative offense by violating duties applicable to the AG, or by causing (or attempting) enrichment of the AG.[390] Instead of imposing a fine, the court may order payment of a sum of money up to the value of the benefits realized through the administrative offense (which may exceed EUR 500,000).[391] Duties applicable to the AG include, in particular, supervisory measures such as the selection of appropriate staff and the exercise of adequate oversight.

§ 175 Responsibility arising from overall, departmental and general responsibility: Responsibility for decisions conforming to the principles of unanimous and majority voting

In general, the AG is managed and represented by its management board, with responsibility resting with the board as a whole.[392] If the board acts as a body and if a unanimous decision violates a criminal statute, each management board member is considered to be criminally liable as an accomplice.[393] If a decision taken by vote was not supported by all the management board members, only those members who voted for the decision are criminally liable. The other members are neither accomplices nor otherwise parties to the criminal offense. However, according to case law, each member who has doubts about the consequences of a particular decision is obligated to do everything reasonably possible, both before and during the adoption of the resolution, to prevent its adoption. This obligation includes activities such as participating in the discussion preceding the vote in an attempt to persuade the other board members to vote against it. Furthermore, the outvoted board members should document their efforts to prevent the resolution from passing as precisely as possible to be able to prove their role should this become necessary later.[394]

---

389 Aktiengesetz [AktG] [Stock Corporation Act] 1965, §§ 399–404 (F.R.G.).
390 Gesetz über Ordnungswidrigkeiten [OWiG] [Administrative Offence Act] 1968, § 30 (F.R.G.).
391 Gesetz über Ordnungswidrigkeiten [OWiG] [Administrative Offence Act] 1968, § 29a (F.R.G.).
392 Aktiengesetz [AktG] [Stock Corporation Act] 1965, § 76, ¶ 1, § 77, ¶ 1, § 78, ¶ 1, (F.R.G.).
393 Strafgesetzbuch [StGB] [Criminal Code] 1871, § 25, ¶ 2 (F.R.G.).
394 *Cf.* § 145 above.

§ 176 Liability in case of allocation of duties to individual board members

The AG's articles of association or rules of procedure may allocate certain tasks to individual management board members (allocation of duties).[395] For purposes of civil liability, this means that liability for decisions within the area of responsibility assigned to another board member is limited to the responsibility to oversee that board member. However, this principle has limited application to criminal responsibility, because in situations affecting the AG as a whole, which include decisions in critical situations or with far-reaching consequences, the entire management board is responsible. In such a situation, every board member has a duty to avoid inflicting harm on the AG. In such a case, every board member must determine how the decision will affect his area of responsibility. The management board as a whole also bears responsibility for entrepreneurial decisions regarding crisis management when the AG faces financial difficulties. In such a case, there are heightened requirements in terms of having the organizational systems and tools in place for fulfilling tax-related duties, paying social security contributions and filing a timely application for insolvency. The entire board also has shared responsibility if there is doubt whether the responsible board member is fulfilling his tasks properly.

§ 177 Introduction to criteria for liability

The degree of risk of criminal liability for a management board member depends on a number of factors. For example, the AG's area of activity may play a major role if the products manufactured are potentially harmful to health, or the type and method of production harbor hazards for the environment. The liability risk also increases significantly if the AG is in an economic crisis. Below, an overview is provided of the situations that typically present a risk of criminal liability for management board members.

§ 178 Misrepresentation on formation of AG or capital increase

A number of the statutory provisions on criminal liability contained in the Stock Corporation Act concern misrepresentations by the management board in connection with the establishment of the AG or the issue of new shares in a capital increase. Misrepresentations that can give rise to criminal liability relate to information to be submitted to the commercial register for the purpose of entering the AG in the commercial register (*e.g.*, information on the subscription of shares, the capital contribution on shares, the use of paid-in amounts, the issue price, special benefits granted to a subscriber, formation expenses or contributions in kind), information to be included in various reports that have to be prepared in connection with the establishment of the AG and certain transactions effected thereafter, information to be submitted to the commercial register for the purpose of registering an increase in share capital (*e.g.*, information on the contribution of existing capital or the subscription or contribution of new capital, the issue price or contributions in kind). Non-disclosure of material circumstances is treated in the same way as misrepresentation. Any such misrepresentation may be penalized with up to three years' imprisonment. Furthermore, when applying for the AG to be registered in the commercial register, and whenever a change in the composition of the management board is registered, the (new) management board members have to provide written certifications that no circumstances exist that conflict with their appointment as board members.

---

395   *Cf.* § 71 above.

Making false statements, or failing to disclose material conflicting circumstances, results in criminal responsibility.[396]

§ 179 Misrepresentation in financial statements

A member of the management or supervisory board who misrepresents or distorts the financial situation of the AG in the opening balance sheet, the annual financial statements, the annual report or an interim report can be subject to up to three years' imprisonment.[397] A management board member can also be subject to criminal prosecution if he misrepresents or distorts the AG's financial situation in presentations, or in reports containing an overview of the AG's assets and liabilities, in statements or information given to the shareholders' meeting, or in explanations or documentation that must be submitted to an auditor of the AG or one of its affiliates.[398]

Disregarding the legal requirements applicable to the issuance of shares[399] or the acquisition of shares by the AG (treasury stock) are considered administrative offenses, punishable with a fine of up to EUR 25,000, if committed by a management board member.[400]

The Commercial Code requires the management board to keep accounting records that are complete, accurate and prepared on a timely and orderly basis.[401] Under certain circumstances, violating this duty may also be sanctioned under criminal law. A management board member can be subject to criminal prosecution if he fails to keep books of accounts or keeps or alters books of accounts such that an overview of the AG's net assets is made more difficult. Liability can also arise if the management board member disposes of, hides, destroys or damages books of accounts or other documentation before the expiry of statutory retention periods and thereby makes an overview of the AG's net assets more difficult. Moreover, a board member can be held criminally liable, when drawing up balance sheets in such a way that an overview of the AG's net assets is made more difficult; or fails to draw up a balance sheet or inventory within the prescribed time.[402] Negligent violation of duties to keep proper accounts is also punishable.

§ 180 Violation of the duty of confidentiality

Violating the duty of confidentiality by management or supervisory board members is also punishable under criminal law. Unauthorized disclosure or use of a business secret that a board member in this capacity came to know is punishable with up to three years' imprisonment.[403]

---

396 Aktiengesetz [AktG] [Stock Corporation Act] 1965, § 399, ¶ 1, no. 6 (F.R.G.).
397 Handelsgesetzbuch [HGB] [Commercial Code] 1897, § 331, no. 1 (F.R.G.) or for group accounts Handelsgesetzbuch [HGB] [Commercial Code] 1897, § 331, no. 2, 3 (F.R.G.).
398 Handelsgesetzbuch [HGB] [Commercial Code] 1897, § 331, no. 1, 1 a), 4 (F.R.G.) or Aktiengesetz [AktG] [Stock Corporation Act] 1965, § 400, ¶ 1, no. 1, 2 (F.R.G.) subsidiarily.
399 Aktiengesetz [AktG] [Stock Corporation Act] 1965, § 405, ¶ 1, nos. 1–3 (F.R.G.).
400 Aktiengesetz [AktG] [Stock Corporation Act] 1965, § 405, ¶ 1, no. 4, § 71, ¶ 1, nos. 1–4 (F.R.G.).
401 Handelsgesetzbuch [HGB] [Commercial Code] 1897, § 239, ¶ 2 (F.R.G.). § 108 deals with the scope of the duty to keep accounts.
402 Strafgesetzbuch [StGB] [Criminal Code] 1871, § 283b (F.R.G.).
403 Aktiengesetz [AktG] [Stock Corporation Act] 1965, § 404, ¶ 1 and 2 (F.R.G.); Gesetz gegen den unlauteren Wettbewerb [UWG] [Act against Unfair Competition] 2004, § 17 (F.R.G.).

§ 181 Tax evasion

Various tax laws require the AG, and therefore its management board as its authorized representative body, to submit all required tax returns and make all required tax declarations. If a management board member intentionally submits incorrect or incomplete information to the tax authorities, or in violation of applicable duties intentionally neglects to disclose facts of material importance for taxation, thus evading taxes or achieving unjustified tax benefits, he may face up to ten years' imprisonment.[404] Even delayed submission of tax returns may constitute tax evasion under criminal law. If the management board member later realizes that a tax declaration to the tax office was incorrect or incomplete, or that in violation of duties he has neglected to submit a declaration,[405] he is obligated to notify the tax office promptly and to make appropriate corrections.[406] Liability under criminal law applies only to those management board members who contribute to the incorrect or incomplete tax declaration, irrespective of the allocation of tasks under the rules of procedure or the articles of association.

§ 182 Subsidy fraud

A risk that management board members may be criminally liable also exists when state subsidies are granted. For example, it is a criminal offense to provide governmental authorities that administer subsidies with material incorrect information resulting in the grant of the subsidy or not to inform the governmental authorities of material facts.[407] Using funds obtained in violation of restrictions imposed by the law on subsidies also constitutes a criminal offense.[408]

§ 183 Withholding social security contributions

Furthermore, board members may be subject to criminal liability with up to five years' imprisonment for failing to transfer employee's social security contributions.[409] The duty to transfer social security contributions often becomes a significant liability risk for board members when the AG faces financial difficulties. Precautions should be taken if existing funds are insufficient to pay the employer's and employee's contributions, by stating when payment is made that the contributions should be used first to cover the employee's contributions.

Failure to pay employees' social security contributions only renders a management board member criminally liable if he acted with intent: The board member must have been aware of the liquidity problems and at least accepted that due to the lack of precautionary measures it might be impossible to pay the employees' contributions at a later time.

There is no criminal liability if the payment of contributions is impossible for legal or factual reasons, *e.g.*, following sequestration of assets ordered by an insolvency court or due to the AG's insolvency. However, case law has found criminal liability if the AG is in fact insolvent

---

404   Abgabenordnung [AO] [General Tax Code] 1976, § 370 (F.R.G.).
405   Abgabenordnung [AO] [General Tax Code] 1976, § 149 (F.R.G.).
406   Abgabenordnung [AO] [General Tax Code] 1976, § 153 (F.R.G.), Abgabenordnung [AO] [General Tax Code] 1976, § 370, ¶ 1, no. 2 (F.R.G.).
407   Strafgesetzbuch [StGB] [Criminal Code] 1871, § 264, ¶ 1, no. 1, 3 (F.R.G.).
408   Strafgesetzbuch [StGB] [Criminal Code] 1871, § 264, ¶ 1, no. 2 (F.R.G.).
409   Strafgesetzbuch [StGB] [Criminal Code] 1871, §§ 266a, 14, ¶ 1, no. 1, 2 (F.R.G.); for civil liability *cf.* § 170 above.

at the time when the contributions are due, but the management board caused the insolvency by a prior action in violation of duties.

In certain cases, in particular, if paying the contributions in full would jeopardize the existence of the AG, the management board may avoid criminal liability by making adequate disclosure to the authorities.[410] Adequate disclosure requires the board to inform the Federal Labor Office of Germany at the latest when the contributions become due or promptly afterwards, explaining why the AG cannot make the payments on time, despite making a genuine effort to do so.

§ 184 Bankruptcy

A management board member may become criminally liable in connection with the bankruptcy of the AG if he misappropriates, conceals or destroys parts of the corporate assets or, through loss-making and speculative operations contrary to the requirements of regular business, spends excessive sums of money, or engages in some other act of bankruptcy specified in the law.[411] Criminal liability will only arise, however, if at the time of any such action the AG is either overindebted or insolvent, or is threatened by insolvency. These criteria are very difficult to apply in practice. Thus, often it is not possible to prove that all elements are present.[412] Violation of the duty to keep accounts is therefore often used as the basis for imposing criminal liability on members of the management board under such circumstances.

§ 185 Violation of the duty to convene a shareholders' meeting and applying for insolvency

If there are indications based upon an annual balance sheet or an interim balance sheet, or if it becomes apparent from other sources of information, that the AG has incurred a loss equal to half of its share capital, the management board is required to convene a shareholders' meeting immediately and to inform the shareholders of the situation. If the AG is insolvent or overindebted, the management board is required to apply for the opening of insolvency proceedings, without undue delay and at the latest three weeks after the insolvency or overindebtedness has occurred. Violations of these duties may result in up to three years' imprisonment.[413]

§ 186 Waste of corporate funds: Sponsoring, risky transactions and bribes

In many cases, it is difficult to distinguish between poor entrepreneurial decisions and criminal actions. One such case is the waste of corporate funds. The board of management of an AG acts as the trustee of the assets of the AG. A violation of the trust obligation associated with this role can result in criminal liability. The issue often arises with respect to whether and to what extent the management board may decide that the AG will provide gifts or engage in sponsoring to support the arts, science, social projects or sports. Other cases of potential waste of corporate funds involve transactions that pose a high degree of risk, such as the extension of leveraged loans by financial institutions or speculative trading or investment activities.

---

410 Strafgesetzbuch [StGB] [Criminal Code] 1871, § 266a, ¶ 6 (F.R.G.).
411 Strafgesetzbuch [StGB] [Criminal Code] 1871, § 283, ¶ 1 (F.R.G.).
412 § 116 deals with the duties in the event of overindebtedness or insolvency.
413 Aktiengesetz [AktG] [Stock Corporation Act] 1965, § 92, ¶ 1, 2, § 401 (F.R.G.). § 116 deals with the duties in the event of overindebtedness or insolvency.

Criminal liability can arise for the abuse of an authorization of disposal or the incurrence of a liability, or the violation of the duty to manage the AG's assets. A violation of corporate duties constituting a waste of corporate funds occurs only if the management board's decision has clearly gone beyond its discretionary powers in managing the business.

According to case law, not every violation of corporate duties constitutes a violation of the management board's trust obligation that may result in criminal liability. Instead, the violation of duties must be serious. Important aspects in such cases include lack of a connection to the business of the AG, inappropriateness in relation to the AG's revenues and assets, a lack of internal transparency and the presence of motives contrary to the corporate interest, *e.g.*, purely personal preferences. For instance, sponsoring does not constitute a violation of the trust obligation if the amount in question is appropriate for the AG's financial situation, if there is a connection with the corporate interest through advertising or image effects, or if there are advantages from social involvement, and internal corporate transparency and responsibility are maintained.

Entering into transactions that involve a high risk of loss may also result in a violation of the trust obligation. Generally, the management board may engage in business activities that might result in a loss, because any entrepreneurial decision potentially involves this risk. As long as the board does not deliberately accept a high risk that very likely will result in a loss and would not have been accepted by a diligent and conscientious management board, the decision should not result in criminal liability. By contrast, decisions that clearly extend beyond entrepreneurial discretion are inadmissible and constitute a violation of the trust obligation. Indications for acting in violation of the trust obligation include neglecting notification duties, actions going beyond the decision-making powers, being taken in a board member's own interest or exceeding maximum credit limits, concealment or misrepresentation *vis-à-vis* persons sharing responsibility or to supervisory bodies.

Using corporate funds for paying bribes may also lead to criminal liability for waste of corporate funds irrespective of whether paying the bribe serves a corporate purpose or indeed helps secure benefits for the AG.

§ 187 Crimes against physical integrity

According to case law, management board members have a duty to ensure compliance with safety regulations and may therefore be held liable for all occupational accidents caused by non-compliance with such regulations. Furthermore, board members have a duty to protect consumers against risks arising from the AG's products. These duties include the obligation to exercise adequate oversight over development and production of products, to issue warnings and, if necessary, to recall products. Even in the absence of specific indications, the management board is required to find out whether consumers could suffer harm from the products marketed by the AG. If the board neglects these duties and, as a result, consumers suffer harm to their health, the management board may have to answer a criminal charge of negligent or intentional bodily harm.

§ 188 Laws regarding environmental crimes

Management board members may be held criminally liable under environmental law because the board is also responsible for avoiding hazards to the environment arising from corporate operations. Pollution of water, soil or air, causing noise, unlawfully handling hazardous waste or operating equipment and endangering environmentally protected areas can result in criminal penalties for management board members.[414]

§ 189 Prohibition of insider trading

German law prohibits trading in securities on the basis of insider information, inducing others to engage in such trading, and passing on insider information or making insider information available to others. Insider information includes facts concerning the AG or the AG's shares or other securities that are new, unpublicized und potentially relevant to the price of the AG's shares or other securities.[415]

Persons intentionally or recklessly acquiring or selling insider securities using insider information for their own account or that of others, or for another party, may be held criminally liable.[416] A management board member may therefore be criminally liable if he negligently fails to recognize that the information he is using is not in the public domain and is relevant to the AG's share price, thus constituting insider information, or if he negligently fails to recognize that he is dealing in insider securities. Even an attempt to do so is punishable.[417] Furthermore, an intentional violation by a board member of the prohibition of inducement and passing on information, or an attempt to do so, is also punishable.[418] By contrast, anyone who recklessly makes insider information available to another person, or recommends acquiring insider securities to anyone else on the basis of insider information, or induces someone to do so, only commits an administrative offense.[419]

§ 190 Violation of disclosure duties

In certain cases, the management board is required to disclose to the public or to the BaFin hitherto unpublished facts about the AG that are relevant to its share price (insider facts) or about director's dealings (ad-hoc notification obligation).[420] Intentional or reckless violations of such duties represent an administrative offense punishable by a fine of up to EUR 1 million.[421] A duty to inform or disclose is violated if the publication or notification is not made, or is made incorrectly, or incompletely, or not on a timely basis. If the violation of these duties has had an effect on the price of the financial instrument concerned on the stock exchange or

---

414   Strafgesetzbuch [StGB] [Criminal Code] 1871, §§ 324–329 (F.R.G.).
415   Cf. § 117 and §§ 124 et seq. above.
416   Gesetz über den Wertpapierhandel [WpHG] [Securities Trade Act] 1994, § 38, ¶ 1, no. 1, ¶ 4, § 14, ¶ 1, no. 1 (F.R.G.).
417   Gesetz über den Wertpapierhandel [WpHG] [Securities Trade Act] 1994, § 38, ¶ 3 (F.R.G.).
418   Gesetz über den Wertpapierhandel [WpHG] [Securities Trade Act] 1994, § 38, ¶ 1, no. 2, ¶ 4, § 14, ¶ 1, no. 2, § 39, ¶ 2, nos. 3, 4, § 38, ¶ 3 (F.R.G.).
419   Gesetz über den Wertpapierhandel [WpHG] [Securities Trade Act] 1994, § 14, ¶ 1, nos. 1, 2, 3, § 39, ¶ 2, nos. 3, 4 (F.R.G.).
420   § 124 deals with the duty to make ad-hoc notifications.
421   Gesetz über den Wertpapierhandel [WpHG] [Securities Trade Act] 1994, § 39, ¶ 2, no. 5 a) b), ¶ 4, (F.R.G.).

the market, and if the violation was intentional, it is punishable with imprisonment of up to five years or by a monetary fine.[422]

§ 191 Violation of duty to keep an insider list

Violating the duty to keep an insider list and transmit such list to the BaFin upon request is an administrative offense punishable with a fine of up to EUR 50,000.

§ 192 Impacts of the criminal trial

A criminal trial is a lengthy and costly process, which may result in significant negative public attention (even in case of acquittal), as court hearings in Germany are generally open to the public. The indicted management board member is obliged to participate in the court hearings under German criminal law.[423] Prior to the court hearings the management board member has to submit to interrogation by the police or the public prosecutor.[424] However, under German criminal law the accused has the right to remain silent during the criminal process. This right is accompanied with the right to choose a criminal defense lawyer.

Searches of the property of the AG as well as the private property of management board members are permissible by the public prosecutor for the purpose of securing evidence. Files, emails, correspondence or other objects discovered in a search can be impounded or secured if they may have relevance as evidence for the investigation. This includes pieces of evidence that are the property of the AG.[425]

Imprisonment on remand may be ordered against a management board member if he is strongly suspected of the offense and if on the basis of certain facts there is a risk that the board member will evade the criminal proceedings or his conduct gives rise to the strong suspicion that he will destroy, alter, remove, suppress, or falsify evidence or improperly influence witnesses.[426]

§ 193 Consequences of a conviction under criminal law

Apart from imprisonment or the imposition of a monetary fine, a criminal conviction may lead to further consequences, such as an order prohibiting the exercise of the profession and the disqualification from serving as a management board member.

An order prohibiting the exercise of the profession will be imposed on a management board member if the unlawful act is committed during the course of his profession or trade or in gross violation of the duties associated therewith. The maximum period of the prohibition is five years. Furthermore, as long as the prohibition is in effect the management board member may not engage in the profession or trade on behalf of another. He also may not have a person

---

422   Gesetz über den Wertpapierhandel [WpHG] [Securities Trade Act] 1994, § 38, ¶ 2, § 39, ¶ 2, no. 11, § 20a,
        ¶ 1, sentence 1, no. 1 (F.R.G.).
423   Strafprozessordnung [StPO] [Criminal Procedure Code] 1987, § 231 (F.R.G.).
424   Strafprozessordnung [StPO] [Criminal Procedure Code] 1987, § 136 (F.R.G.).
425   Strafprozessordnung [StPO] [Criminal Procedure Code] 1987, §§ 94, 102 (F.R.G.).
426   Strafprozessordnung [StPO] [Criminal Procedure Code] 1987, § 112 (F.R.G.).

who is subject to his instructions engage in his profession or trade on his behalf.[427] A person convicted of certain crimes may be disbarred from serving as a management board member under the Stock Corporation Act.[428] When the judgment becomes final, the management board member automatically loses his position in the AG without a need for revocation.

Moreover, the supervisory board may revoke the appointment of a management board member or the appointment as chairman of the management board in case of a criminal conviction, even if the criminal act does not have a close connection to the management board member's duties within the AG.[429]

---

427   Strafgesetzbuch [StGB] [Criminal Code] 1871, § 70, ¶ 1 (F.R.G.).
428   Aktiengesetz [AktG] [Stock Corporation Act] 1965, § 76, ¶ 3, sentence 2, nos. 2 and 3 (F.R.G.).
429   Aktiengesetz [AktG] [Stock Corporation Act] 1965, § 84, ¶ 3 (F.R.G.).

CHAPTER THREE
SUPERVISORY BOARD OF
THE GERMAN AG

I. Introduction and overview

§ 194 Two-tiered management of the AG

Under German law, management of the AG is two-tiered.[430] The management board is responsible for managing the company, while the task of overseeing and advising management is assigned to the supervisory board. Oversight in this sense relates not only to the legality, but also to the appropriateness of the management of the company by the management board. This does not mean, however, that the supervisory board is entitled to extensive co-participation rights. Indeed, the supervisory board may not directly engage in the management of the company.[431] Rather, it exercises its control largely through the selection of the members of the management board, ongoing discussions with the management regarding the development of the business (including strategy) and consent rights with respect to important decisions of the management board.

The supervisory board must observe the rules of the Stock Corporation Act, the articles of association of the company and principles that have evolved from case law. Listed companies regularly follow the recommendations of the Corporate Governance Code, which are in parts stricter than the rules found in the Stock Corporation Act.[432] Unless the Corporate Governance Code is incorporated into the articles of association, it does not represent mandatory law; however, even though they are not required to follow the Corporate Governance Code, listed companies must annually disclose the extent to which they do not comply with the Corporate Governance Code.[433]

II. Composition and size of the supervisory board

§ 195 Introduction

AGs are required to form a supervisory board. The number of its members and its composition depends on the size of the company's workforce and, to a lesser extent, on the nominal share capital of the company. As a rule of thumb, German companies with more than 500 employees

---

430 *Cf.* § 7.
431 *Cf.* Aktiengesetz [AktG] [Stock Corporation Act] 1965, § 111, ¶ 4, sentence 1 (F.R.G.).
432 *Cf.* § 119.
433 Aktiengesetz [AktG] [Stock Corporation Act] 1965, § 161, ¶ 1, sentence 1 (F.R.G.).

are co-determined and their supervisory boards include representatives of the workforce pursuant to various co-determination rules. Companies below this threshold only have to observe the Stock Corporation Act with its requirements for ordinary supervisory boards. Special rules apply to companies in the coal, iron and steel industries.[434]

A. Ordinary supervisory board

§ 196 Size and composition

A supervisory board must have at least three members, though an AG's articles of association may stipulate a larger board of up to 21 members. In any case, at companies having up to 2,000 employees, the number of members of the supervisory board must be divisible by three. In addition, the number may not exceed certain limits dictated by the amount of the company's nominal share capital. Supervisory boards are limited to nine members at companies with a nominal share capital of up to EUR 1.5 million. For a nominal share capital between EUR 1.5 million and EUR 10 million, the number of members may not exceed 15, and if the nominal share capital exceeds EUR 10 million, a maximum of 21 supervisory board members may be appointed.

If the company is not subject to co-determination rules, every member of the supervisory board is a shareholder representative.

B. Co-determined supervisory boards

§ 197 Supervisory board under the One-Third Participation Act

Pursuant to the One-Third Participation Act[435], the supervisory board of certain companies, including German AGs and GmbHs, must generally include employee representatives if such companies have more than 500, but less than 2,001 employees.[436] Due to grandfathering rules, AGs that have been incorporated prior to August 10, 1994 and are not family-owned are subject to the One-Third Participation Act even if they have 500 or fewer employees.

As the name of the One-Third Participation Act indicates, employee representatives must make up one-third of the supervisory board. Otherwise, the size of the supervisory board is governed by the general rules set forth above.[437]

---

434   Due to their limited practical relevance, the rules set forth in the Montan-Mitbestimmungsgesetz [Montan-MitbestG] [Coal and Steel-Co-Determination Act] 1951 (F.R.G.) and the Mitbestimmungsergänzungsgesetz [MitbestErgG] [Co-Determination Amendment Act] 1956 (F.R.G.) will not be addressed herein in more detail.

435   Drittelbeteiligungsgesetz [DrittelbG] [One-Third Participation Act] 2004 (F.R.G.).

436   Employees of group companies are considered if there is either a domination agreement between the company and the group company or the group company is integrated into the company pursuant to Aktiengesetz [AktG] [Stock Corporation Act] 1965, §§ 319 et seq. (F.R.G.).

437   Cf. § 196.

§ 198 Supervisory board under the Co-Determination Act

If the company regularly has over 2,000 employees, half of the supervisory board must be employee representatives pursuant to the Co-Determination Act.[438] In such case, the supervisory board must consist of six employee representatives and six representatives of the shareholders. This number rises to eight representatives for each group of representatives if the company has over 10,000 employees. Finally, at a company regularly employing over 20,000 employees, both the shareholders and the employees appoint ten supervisory board members. Co-determined companies may require a supervisory board of 16 or 20 members in their articles of association despite failing to reach the respective threshold of more than 10,000 or 20,000 employees.[439]

Despite the same number of supervisory board members representing shareholders and employees under the Co-Determination Act, there is no genuine parity on the supervisory board. The shareholders always appoint the chairman of the supervisory board, who has two votes in stalemate situations. In the event of a conflict, shareholder representatives are thus in a position to pass resolutions over the opposition of employee representatives. Such confrontations, however, remain the exception rather than the rule. They are potentially damaging to the atmosphere and counterproductive to the cooperative aspirations of the supervisory board. Consequently, the German co-determination system virtually forces the parties to reach a compromise in advance of a controversial vote. Sometimes the chairman of the supervisory board may even push through decisions with the help of the votes cast by the employee representatives over the wishes of other shareholder representatives.

§ 199 Procedure to identify appropriate co-determination rules

Special rules apply if increases or decreases of the workforce of an AG require an adjustment of the supervisory board's composition due to a change in the applicable co-determination regime.

If the management board believes that the composition of the supervisory board no longer complies with the applicable co-determination rules, it must immediately make this public in the units (*Betriebe*) of the company and its subsidiaries as well as in the publications designated for the notices of the company, *e.g.*, at least in the electronic version of the Federal Gazette (*elektronischer Bundesanzeiger*). If the management board's assessment of the applicable co-determination rules is not challenged within one month, these rules will apply for the future. If, however, its assessment is challenged, *e.g.*, by the company's works council, the German local court situated where the company has its registered office will determine the applicable co-determination rules with binding effect. In addition, the management board, shareholders, supervisory board members, a certain percentage of employees and certain representative bodies of the employees (*e.g.*, works councils, trade unions) may directly apply to the court to determine the applicable co-determination rules.

---

438 Employees of (German) companies controlled by the stock corporation are considered pursuant to special rules.
439 Mitbestimmungsgesetz [MitbestG] [Co-Determination Act] 1976, § 7, ¶ 1 (F.R.G.).

Necessary changes of the articles of association due to a change of the applicable co-determination rules and the appointment of new supervisory board members must occur at the next shareholders' meeting following the binding determination of such rules. The current supervisory board members lose their offices after this next shareholders' meeting or six months after the binding determination of the composition of the supervisory board if the shareholders have not adjusted the supervisory board composition until then.

III. Commencement, duration and termination of supervisory board membership

§ 200 Introduction
The Stock Corporation Act includes comprehensive provisions addressing the qualifications for membership in the supervisory board of a German AG, how members are appointed, their term of office and the termination of their memberships.

A. Prerequisites for membership

§ 201 Introduction
The main prerequisites to supervisory board membership are stipulated in the Stock Corporation Act. In particular, it dictates the maximum number of supervisory board memberships an individual can have. It also restricts multiple board seats in certain situations, which could result in potential for conflicts of interest. In addition, the articles of association may include provisions limiting eligibility for membership on the supervisory board.

1.   Basic personal requirements
§ 202 Principle of unrestricted legal competency
Any natural person who is legally competent and of sound mind may become a member of a supervisory board.[440] In Germany, legal competency is presumed upon a person's 18th birthday.[441]

§ 203 No nationality or participation requirement
There is no requirement that a candidate be a shareholder or a German national in order to take up a position on a supervisory board. Furthermore, no domicile or residence requirements apply under German law.

§ 204 Maximum number of supervisory board positions
Under the Stock Corporation Act, the number of supervisory board positions an individual may have is generally limited to ten.[442] This calculation is made at the beginning of the respec-

---

440   Aktiengesetz [AktG] [Stock Corporation Act] 1965, § 100, ¶ 1 (F.R.G.).
441   Bürgerliches Gesetzbuch [BGB] [Civil Code] 1896, §§ 2, 106 (F.R.G.).
442   Aktiengesetz [AktG] [Stock Corporation Act] 1965, § 100, ¶ 2, sentence 1, no. 1 (F.R.G.).

tive supervisory board member's term of office[443] rather than on the date of his election by the shareholders' meeting. Additionally, any supervisory board posts count twice against the limit if the member is the chairman of the respective supervisory board.[444] This is intended to take into account the increased workload associated with the chair.

Some supervisory board posts, however, do not count against the total. First, only those seats at companies with a statutory obligation to form a supervisory board are included. Thus, mandates on the supervisory board of a GmbH having less than 500 employees are not taken into account. In addition, supervisory board posts at non-German companies, supervisory seats in cooperatives, foundations, and mutual insurance companies are excluded from the total. Second, under certain circumstances, up to five intra-group supervisory board posts are not counted if the legal representative of a controlling company sits on supervisory boards of subordinated companies of the group.[445] Members of the management board and general managers (in the event the controlling company is a GmbH) are considered legal representatives for this purpose, but supervisory board members of the parent company are not.

In credit institutions, financial services institutions, financial holding companies, insurance companies, pension funds and insurance holding companies, a candidate may not be appointed to the supervisory board if he already holds five supervisory memberships in (financial and insurance) undertakings supervised by the BaFin.[446] For calculating this threshold, memberships in supervisory boards of companies being part of the same guarantee shemes (*institutionsbezogene Sicherungssysteme*) are regarded as one membership.

Even stricter, the Corporate Governance Code generally recommends for management board members of listed companies not to hold more than three supervisory board posts outside the management board member's group of companies.[447]

§ 205 No representatives of controlled companies
A legal representative of a company controlled by the AG may not become a member of the supervisory board of the controlling AG.[448] Members of the management board and general managers of the subsidiary company are considered legal representatives for this purpose.

In contrast to the rules regarding the maximum permissible number of supervisory board posts one may have,[449] the restriction on the legal representatives also applies to non-German controlled companies; however, it is limited to individuals who have similar powers as management board members. This includes individuals who, *e.g.*, are "executive directors." By contrast, "non-executive directors" are entitled to take a seat on the German supervisory board of

---

443   *Cf.* Aktiengesetz [AktG] [Stock Corporation Act] 1965, § 250, ¶ 1, no. 4 (F.R.G.).
444   Aktiengesetz [AktG] [Stock Corporation Act] 1965, § 100, ¶ 2, sentence 3 (F.R.G.).
445   Aktiengesetz [AktG] [Stock Corporation Act] 1965, § 100, ¶ 2, sentence 2 (F.R.G.).
446   Kreditwesengesetz [KWG] [Banking Act] 1961, § 36, ¶ 3, sentence 6 (F.R.G.); Versicherungsaufsichtsgesetz [VAG] [Insurance Company Supervision Act] 1901, § 7a, ¶ 4, sentence 4 (F.R.G.).
447   Deutscher Corporate Governance Kodex [DCGK] [German Corporate Governance Code] 2010, 5.4.5 (F.R.G.).
448   Aktiengesetz [AktG] [Stock Corporation Act] 1965, § 100, ¶ 2, sentence 1, no. 2 (F.R.G.).
449   § 204 deals with the maximum permissible number of supervisory board positions.

the controlling company if their activities in the non-German controlled company are limited to duties comparable to those of a German supervisory board member.

§ 206 Prohibition of interlocking supervisory posts

A member of an unaffiliated company's management board may not become a member of the supervisory board if a member of the unaffiliated company's supervisory board happens to sit on the management board of the company in question (interlocking posts).[450] It is not established whether this restriction also applies if the supervisory board of the respective company is not mandatory or such company is a non-German entity. As a result, it is advisable to avoid, whenever possible, interlocking supervisory posts in these ambiguous cases as a matter of precaution.

§ 207 Restrictions for former management board members

In listed AGs, a person is not eligible for the supervisory board if he has been a member of the company's management board during the previous two years. This restriction does not apply, however, if the relevant person has been proposed for the supervisory board by shareholders holding more than 25% of the voting rights in the company.[451] This two-year "cooling off" period shall serve to foster the independence of the supervisory board; in particular the supervisory board shall be put in a position to review the performance of management board members without being restrained by the fact that members of the management board now moved into the supervisory board. In non-listed corporations, such rules are not applicable since the legislator does not assume a comparable control deficit as a consequence of the membership of a former management board member in the supervisory board.

Stricter rules apply to credit institutions, financial services institutions, financial holding companies, insurance companies, pension funds and insurance holding companies. Here, former members of the management board may not become supervisory board members if already two former management board members sit on the supervisory board.

§ 208 No dual membership in management and supervisory board

A member of the management board may not become a member of the supervisory board of the same company.[452] This prohibition also applies to Prokuristen[453] and holders of a commercial power of attorney.[454] These two proxies are special forms of representation pursuant to German commercial law with broad powers of representation *vis-à-vis* third parties.

In companies subject to the Co-Determination Act, however, Prokuristen may become employee representatives on the supervisory board, provided that the Prokuristen do not directly report to the management board and their power of attorney does not extend to cover all company business.[455]

---

450   Aktiengesetz [AktG] [Stock Corporation Act] 1965, § 100, ¶ 2, sentence 1, no. 3 (F.R.G.).
451   Aktiengesetz [AktG] [Stock Corporation Act] 1965, § 100, ¶ 2, sentence 1, no. 4 (F.R.G.).
452   Aktiengesetz [AktG] [Stock Corporation Act] 1965, § 105, ¶ 1 (F.R.G.).
453   An authorized signatory with a general commercial power of attorney defined by law.
454   Handelsgesetzbuch [HGB] [Commercial Code] 1897, §§ 48 *et seq.*, 54 (F.R.G.).
455   Mitbestimmungsgesetz [MitbestG] [Co-Determination Act] 1976, § 6, ¶ 2, sentence 1 (F.R.G.).

§ 209 Recommendation of sufficient independent members

In connection with the nomination process, the Corporate Governance Code recommends that the supervisory board has a sufficient number of independent members. The Corporate Governance Code describes as independent member one without any relation, either business-related or personal, to the company or its management board potentially capable of giving rise to conflicts of interest.[456] The Corporate Governance Code also recommends that the membership of the supervisory board is diverse (e.g., comprising persons with different backgrounds and knowledge to cover all aspects of the company's operations) and that the objectives for the composition of the supervisory board shall include an appropriate quota of female members.[457] Further, the Corporate Governance Code recommends not more than two former members of the management board should belong to the supervisory board and that supervisory board members shall not exercise directorships or similar positions or advisory tasks for important competitors.[458]

§ 210 Permissible grounds for lack of qualifications under the articles of association

An AG's articles of association may provide additional grounds for board members lacking the required qualifications; however, exclusionary grounds anchored in the articles of association of co-determined AGs are generally only effective if they are limited to shareholder representatives on the board. An example of a permissible restriction is a specific age limitation. The articles of association may also impose conditions upon the qualification of supervisory board members with respect to their nationality, membership in a certain profession, or – but this is disputed – a certain family background. While the articles of association may specify such characteristics, the right of the shareholders' meeting to freely elect supervisory board members must remain essentially undiminished, e.g., the specifications may not be of such detail that they in fact determine whom to appoint.

2.   Professional qualification
§ 211 Professional aptitude as requirement?

Only in certain special types of businesses, e.g., in credit institutions, financial services institutions, financial holding companies, insurance companies, pension funds, insurance holding companies or capital investment companies, professional qualifications are explicitly required for supervisory board members. Typically, in these companies supervisory board members must have the personal reliability and professional expertise required for such businesses.

Apart from such explicit legal requirements or stipulations in the company's articles of association, supervisory board members must also have a minimum level of professional aptitude regardless of whether they are employee representatives or representatives of the shareholders. While the absence of such professional aptitude is not grounds for challenging a candidate's

---

456   Deutscher Corporate Governance Kodex [DCGK] [German Corporate Governance Code] 2010, 5.4.2, sentence 2 (F.R.G.).

457   Deutscher Corporate Governance Kodex [DCGK] [German Corporate Governance Code] 2010, 5.4.1, sentence 3 (F.R.G.).

458   Deutscher Corporate Governance Kodex [DCGK] [German Corporate Governance Code] 2010, 5.4.2, sentence 3 (F.R.G.).

election, a lack of professional qualification might result in the supervisory board member being held liable for damages.[459] Therefore, it is advisable that members meet basic professional requirements. Candidates are only qualified if they are in a position to understand and properly assess the "normal business activities of the company without external assistance." Thus, at a minimum, all supervisory board members must be able to independently carry out the tasks that the supervisory board is not permitted to delegate. They must have the necessary skills to supervise a commercial enterprise. These skills include the ability to make personnel decisions, a certain amount of organizational talent, and a basic knowledge of economics. Conscientious supervisory board members must also have a basic knowledge of bookkeeping and accounting. The Corporate Governance Code imposes similar requirements.[460]

German language capabilities may facilitate the work on a supervisory board but are not legally required. Many of the larger companies conduct the meetings in English and/or provide translation services.

§ 212 Accounting expert

In listed AGs[461], at least one member of the supervisory board must be independent and have expert knowledge in the fields of accounting and/or auditing.[462] In order to be considered competent, such supervisory board member must be professionally engaged with accounting or auditing matters, e.g., as a CFO, auditor, controller or other expert in these fields. The required level of independence is taken for granted if there is no professional or personal relationship between the board member and the company or its management board that may raise concerns of a conflict of interest.

3.   Additional requirements for employee representatives
§ 213 Employees and trade union representatives

In addition to the rules set forth above, the employee representatives in co-determined supervisory boards must also meet certain qualifications to be eligible.

On supervisory boards consisting of three or six members within the scope of the One-Third Participation Act, all employee representatives must come from within the company.[463] In other words, the employee representative must work for either the company itself or a controlled company within the group. In supervisory boards with more than six members, only two of the employee representatives must come from within the company while the additional employee representatives may come from outside (e.g., from trade unions).

At companies with 12 or 16 supervisory board members, e.g., companies co-determined on a parity basis, two of the respective six or eight employee seats are allocated to representatives

---

459   §§ 326 et seq. deal with the liability of supervisory board members.
460   Deutscher Corporate Governance Kodex [DCGK] [German Corporate Governance Code] 2010, 5.4.1 (F.R.G.).
461   In this case the term "listed AG" includes AGs that have other securities outstanding which are admitted to and traded on a regulated market within Germany or another country within the European Economic Area.
462   Aktiengesetz [AktG] [Stock Corporation Act] 1965, § 100, ¶ 5 (F.R.G.).
463   Drittelbeteiligungsgesetz [DrittelbG] [One-Third Participation Act] 2004, § 4, ¶ 2 (F.R.G.).

of trade unions. Similarly, on a supervisory board with 20 members, trade union representatives fill three of the ten employee seats. This statutory membership requirement can lead to conflicts of interest. For example, top-level trade union officers may call upon the company's workforce to strike in order to support certain collective bargaining demands. Such a recommendation can conflict with their roles as supervisory board members obligated to act exclusively in the interest of the company. Finally, one of the employee representatives is allocated to managerial employees (*leitende Angestellte*).

B. Appointment

§ 214 Introduction
There are several methods available for "ordinary" appointments. In addition to the election by the shareholders' meeting, certain shareholders may also be granted a delegation right affording them the right to appoint certain members.[464] If the company is co-determined, special rules apply to the appointment of employee representatives on the supervisory board. In exceptional cases, a court may be called upon to appoint supervisory board members (both employee and shareholder representatives).

Different rules apply to the appointment of the first supervisory board following incorporation in comparison to subsequent "ordinary" appointments.

1. Appointments for the first supervisory board
§ 215 Appointment by founders
The founders of the company must appoint the first supervisory board and the appointment must be recorded by a notary.[465] Even if the number of employees in the company actually requires the appointment of employee representatives to the supervisory board, the initial supervisory board is exempt from this requirement and only includes representatives elected by the shareholders. The term of office for the initial supervisory board ends at the conclusion of the first ordinary shareholders' meeting. This ordinary shareholders' meeting must take place within the first eight months after the end of the first (rump) financial year of the company.

Special rules apply if the company is incorporated by the contribution of a business or a part thereof as a contribution in kind. Here, the founders may only appoint as many supervisory board members as the shareholders will be authorized to appoint under the co-determination rules that apply once the company is incorporated; the employee representatives will be added once the company has been incorporated.

---

464   Aktiengesetz [AktG] [Stock Corporation Act] 1965, § 101, ¶ 1, sentence 1 (F.R.G.).
465   Aktiengesetz [AktG] [Stock Corporation Act] 1965, § 30, ¶ 1 (F.R.G.).

§ 216 Formation of company by transformation

Special rules apply to AGs created by transformation. If the original company had a supervisory board, it may continue to exist if its composition remains unchanged.[466] If, however, the applicable rules for the composition of the supervisory board change or the original company did not have a supervisory board, then the first supervisory board of the new AG following transformation must contain employee representatives pursuant to the applicable co-determination rules.

2.   Election by the shareholders' meeting
§ 217 Nomination of candidates

The usual way of becoming a member of the (regular) supervisory board is to be elected by the shareholders' meeting.

The supervisory board generally has to nominate candidates to the shareholders' meeting.[467] A nomination should contain the candidate's name, current occupation and place of residence. In listed AGs, the nomination also has to contain supervisory board posts in other mandatory German supervisory boards and shall disclose memberships in other supervisory bodies of German and foreign companies. There should be as many nominations as there are vacant posts to fill. In a co-determined supervisory board, only the shareholders' representatives have the right to decide which candidates will be proposed by it for election by the shareholders' meeting.[468] Employee representatives, however, are entitled to participate in any debate on the nominations.

Shareholders may also suggest alternative nominees for election to the supervisory board. If a proposal is duly filed with the company at least fourteen days prior to the shareholders' meeting, the company must inform the other shareholders of the nominees immediately in order to give the shareholders enough time to consider the counterproposal.[469]

Furthermore, shareholders holding at least a combined nominal capital of EUR 500,000 or 5% of the company's nominal share capital are entitled to put the election of new supervisory board members on the agenda of the next shareholders' meeting.[470] This request must be filed with the company 24 days before the shareholders' meeting, in listed AGs 30 days before such meeting. In addition, minority shareholders holding a participation of at least 5% in the company have the right to request that an extraordinary shareholders' meeting be called and the election of new supervisory board members be put on the agenda of such meeting.[471]

---

466   Umwandlungsgesetz [UmwG] [Merger and Reorganization Act] 1994, § 203 (F.R.G.).
467   Aktiengesetz [AktG] [Stock Corporation Act] 1965, § 124, ¶ 3, sentence 1 (F.R.G.).
468   Aktiengesetz [AktG] [Stock Corporation Act] 1965, § 124, ¶ 3, sentence 5 (F.R.G.).
469   Aktiengesetz [AktG] [Stock Corporation Act] 1965, § 127, § 126 (F.R.G.).
470   Aktiengesetz [AktG] [Stock Corporation Act] 1965, § 122, ¶ 2 (F.R.G.).
471   Aktiengesetz [AktG] [Stock Corporation Act] 1965, § 122, ¶ 1 (F.R.G.).

§ 218 Calling the shareholders' meeting

The election of supervisory board members is only considered due and proper if it meets various conditions. The invitation to the shareholders' meeting must announce the agenda, including the contemplated election of new supervisory board members. The announcement must be made in any publications designated for notices of the company, *i.e.*, at least in the electronic version of the Federal Gazette and, depending on the provisions of the articles of association, in other media as well.[472] Listed companies must also make available the invitation on their website.[473] The announcement must also set forth the relevant statutory regulations which govern the composition of the supervisory board.[474] Furthermore, the supervisory board must propose nominees in the agenda.[475]

§ 219 Procedure at the shareholders' meeting

A simple majority of the votes cast generally suffices to elect a candidate to the supervisory board at the shareholders' meeting.[476] A majority shareholder therefore has the power to determine all supervisory board members except the employee representatives. It is quite common, however, to offer shareholders with significant stakes like 10% or more a seat on the supervisory board. Stricter requirements on the required majorities to elect supervisory board members may, however, be stipulated in the articles of association.[477]

If a shareholder properly suggests alternative nominees for election to the supervisory board and gains the support of 10% of the nominal share capital represented, a vote must first be held on the shareholder's nominees before voting on the nominations by the supervisory board can occur.[478]

It is possible to permit block voting in the election of supervisory board members, *e.g.*, all vacant seats are then up for simultaneous election. If a shareholder does not agree to this procedure and requests individual elections, the chairman of the shareholders' meeting calls for a vote to determine whether such individual elections should take place. If the chairman fails to take notice of such objection by a shareholder, the resolution on the election of supervisory board members may be challenged. Moreover, before a block vote, the chairman should inform the shareholders' meeting that any shareholder who disapproves of any of the individual candidates on the list must vote against the complete list, and that individual elections will then be held if the complete list is rejected.

---

472   Aktiengesetz [AktG] [Stock Corporation Act] 1965, § 121, ¶ 4, sentence 1, § 25, sentence 1 (F.R.G.).
473   Aktiengesetz [AktG] [Stock Corporation Act] 1965, § 124 a, sentence 1, no. 1 (F.R.G.).
474   Aktiengesetz [AktG] [Stock Corporation Act] 1965, § 124, ¶ 2, 3, sentence 1 (F.R.G.).
475   Aktiengesetz [AktG] [Stock Corporation Act] 1965, § 124, ¶ 3, sentence 1 (F.R.G.).
476   Aktiengesetz [AktG] [Stock Corporation Act] 1965, § 133, ¶ 1 (F.R.G.).
477   Aktiengesetz [AktG] [Stock Corporation Act] 1965, § 133, ¶ 2 (F.R.G.).
478   Aktiengesetz [AktG] [Stock Corporation Act] 1965, § 137 (F.R.G.).

Even though block voting is permitted under German law, the Corporate Governance Code recommends holding individual elections to the supervisory board.[479] In recent years, German companies have also tended to move towards individual elections.

§ 220 Acceptance of election

Candidates must accept their election to the supervisory board to become effective. Acceptance can be made by an express declaration or, alternatively, is deemed to have occured if the candidate begins performing supervisory board tasks. Nominees can also explicitly declare their acceptance to the shareholders' meeting even before the meeting begins.

3.   Election of employee representatives
§ 221 Workforce specific procedures

The election of employee representatives in co-determined companies must follow special appointment procedures depending, *inter alia*, upon the size of the company's workforce.

In companies with more than 8,000 employees, as a first step the workforce must nominate candidates to fill their supervisory board posts except for the posts reserved for trade unions. Each nomination requires approval of at least one-fifth or 100 of the employees eligible to vote in the election,[480] while each nomination for the (single) representative of the managerial employees in the supervisory board requires one-twentieth or 50 of the votes of the managerial employees eligible to vote. The candidates for the supervisory board posts reserved for trade unions are nominated by the trade unions active in the respective group of companies.[481]

Afterwards, the employees in each unit of the company elect delegates by secret ballot based on the principles of proportional representation.[482] These delegates then elect the employee representatives for the supervisory board among the nominees on behalf of all employees.[483] Alternatively, employees may opt to directly elect their representatives for the supervisory board.

If the company has 8,000 or less, but more than 2,000 employees, the employee representatives are usually not elected by delegates but by the employees directly. The workforce may, however, opt for an election process with delegates.

In companies with up to 2,000 employees, the employees directly elect their representatives by secret ballot.[484] The members of the works council and the employees may nominate candidates for the election. Employee nominations must be signed by at least 100 persons eligible to vote in the election or one-tenth of all eligible voters in the election.[485]

---

479   Deutscher Corporate Governance Kodex [DCGK] [German Corporate Governance Code] 2010, 5.4.3, sentence 1 (F.R.G.).
480   Mitbestimmungsgesetz [MitbestG] [Co-Determination Act] 1976, § 15, ¶ 2, no. 1 (F.R.G.).
481   Mitbestimmungsgesetz [MitbestG] [Co-Determination Act] 1976, § 16, ¶ 2, sentence 1 (F.R.G.).
482   Mitbestimmungsgesetz [MitbestG] [Co-Determination Act] 1976, § 9, ¶ 1 (F.R.G.).
483   Mitbestimmungsgesetz [MitbestG] [Co-Determination Act] 1976, § 15, ¶ 1 (F.R.G.).
484   Drittelbeteiligungsgesetz [DrittelbG] [One-Third Participation Act] 2004, § 5, ¶ 1 (F.R.G.).
485   Drittelbeteiligungsgesetz [DrittelbG] [One-Third Participation Act] 2004, § 6 (F.R.G.).

4. Delegation of supervisory board members
§ 222 Scope and process

A company's articles of association may afford certain shareholders the right to appoint repre-sentatives to the supervisory board without election.[486] The number of delegated representa-tives may not exceed one-third of the total number of seats of shareholder representatives on the supervisory board. The articles may grant the delegation right as a non-transferable right to certain individual shareholders, in which case these shareholders must be identified by name. A delegation right may also be granted to unspecified shareholders holding specified registered shares with transfer restrictions (*vinkulierte Namensaktien*).

The holder of a delegation right can exercise such right by declaration to the management board. German law does not require this declaration to conform to any particular form. Once exercised, the representative concerned has to accept the delegation as in the event of an elec-tion of a representative by the shareholders' meeting.[487]

5. Appointment by court
§ 223 Scope

If the supervisory board lacks a quorum or is not complete, the German local court situated where the company has its registered office may appoint new member(s). The court has an ob-ligation to appoint new members to meet the quorum requirement and, upon request, it has to fill one or more other vacancies in urgent situations. If, however, the quorum is met and there is no case of urgency, the court can only fill open posts in the supervisory board if the board has been incomplete for more than three months. In supervisory boards co-determined on a parity basis, the law assumes that there is a case of urgency, if not all supervisory board posts are filled. In practice, the court often appoints new supervisory board members in post-takeover sce-narios where some or all of the shareholder representatives on the supervisory board resign.

§ 224 Process

The request to appoint supervisory board members may be submitted to the court by either the management board (in the "normal" case), any member of the supervisory board or a shareholder. The management board has a statutory duty to submit the request to the court if the quorum of the supervisory board is not met and the necessary seats are not expected to be filled before the next supervisory board meeting.[488] If there are employee representatives on the supervisory board, various bodies representing the employees, *e.g.*, the company's works council, are also entitled to submit such a request.[489]

The court is not subject to any statutory requirements with respect to its decision on the appointments. Although it is common to propose specific candidates in the request for the appointment, the court is not bound to follow these suggestions. Certainly, the court will not appoint the proposed candidate if the member's nomination would violate statutory provisions

---

486   Aktiengesetz [AktG] [Stock Corporation Act] 1965, § 101, ¶ 2 (F.R.G.).
487   *Cf.* § 220.
488   Aktiengesetz [AktG] [Stock Corporation Act] 1965, § 104, ¶ 1, sentence 2 (F.R.G.).
489   Aktiengesetz [AktG] [Stock Corporation Act] 1965, § 104, ¶ 1, sentence 3 (F.R.G.).

governing personal requirements, the composition of the supervisory board, or any other requirements under the articles of association.[490]

§ 225 Status of appointee

A court-appointed member of the supervisory board assumes a provisional role only. As soon as a regular member of the supervisory board is appointed by election or delegation, the court-appointed member's mandate expires.[491]

C. Substitute members

§ 226 Overview

German law allows the appointment of substitute supervisory board members.[492] A substitute member only joins the board when a supervisory board member vacates his post prematurely. The substitute member then automatically fills the position previously held by the departing member until the previous member's term expires.[493] It is also possible to appoint several substitute members provided that the order in which they are to fill vacated seats is clear.

The substitute member must be appointed at the same time as the regular members of the supervisory board they shall replace. One substitute member may be appointed as the potential replacement for several members, provided that these supervisory board members all belong to the same group of representatives. Thus, a given substitute member may only fill a seat for either the shareholders or for the employees, regardless of whether an elected or delegated representative is replaced.[494]

As a rule, accepting election as a substitute member is regarded as an acceptance of the future mandate. The substitute member must issue a separate declaration of acceptance only if such a declaration was not made upon the initial election.

D. Term of office

§ 227 Commencement of office

The term of office begins once the candidate accepts his appointment to the supervisory board, unless the date specified in the shareholders' resolution or the delegation is subsequent to the candidate's acceptance.

---

490   §§ 202 et seq. deal with the personal requirements under statutory law.
491   Aktiengesetz [AktG] [Stock Corporation Act] 1965, § 104, ¶ 5 (F.R.G.).
492   Aktiengesetz [AktG] [Stock Corporation Act] 1965, § 101, ¶ 3, sentence 2 (F.R.G.).
493   Aktiengesetz [AktG] [Stock Corporation Act] 1965, § 102, ¶ 2 (F.R.G.).
494   To avoid any legal ambiguity, it is advisable to explicitly stipulate in the articles of association or in the resolution appointing the substitute member that he can replace any member of a group of representatives.

§ 228 Maximum term

The articles of association or the appointment resolution may specify the length of the office of the individual members of the supervisory board. The terms can differ among the supervisory board members. German law limits the appointment to a maximum term of about five years which also reflects the usual term of office of supervisory board members.[495]

In concrete terms, any individual board member's term of office must end no later than the conclusion of the shareholders' meeting which resolves on the discharge of the acts of the supervisory board for the fourth financial year after the relevant board member's term of office began. This does not include the financial year in which the term of office started. If the shareholders' meeting fails to pass either a discharge resolution discharging the relevant member of the supervisory board for the fourth financial year, the supervisory board member's term of office still ends at the time when such a resolution should have been passed.

§ 229 Term for employee representatives or delegated members

No special rules apply to the term of office of employee representatives. Of particular relevance is the fact that the term of office for employee representatives ends if they no longer meet personal requirements. This means any employee representatives required to be company employees will automatically cease to be supervisory board members when they are no longer employees of the company.[496]

The term of office of a delegated member corresponds to the term of office of elected members. Therefore, as long as it is within the maximum term of office provided by statute, shareholders holding delegation rights are free to determine their representatives' terms of office. They may also remove the representatives from office at any time and replace them.[497]

With respect to the term of office of a company's first supervisory board, cf. § 215.

§ 230 Reappointment

It is possible to reappoint members of the supervisory board, but early reappointment is not permitted if the shareholders' meeting wishes to extend the term of office for another full term following a maximum term. By contrast, early reappointment is permitted if the appointment does not exceed the statutory maximum period taking into account the remaining time in the supervisory board member's current term.

---

495   Aktiengesetz [AktG] [Stock Corporation Act] 1965, § 102, ¶ 1 (F.R.G.).
496   Mitbestimmungsgesetz [MitbestG] [Co-Determination Act] 1976, § 24, ¶ 1 (F.R.G.).
497   Aktiengesetz [AktG] [Stock Corporation Act] 1965, § 103, ¶ 2, sentence 1 (F.R.G.).

E.   Termination of membership

§ 231 Expiration of office

Unless reelected, supervisory board members leave the board once the period for which they were appointed ends. In addition to this automatic termination, the term of office of a member of the supervisory board may end prematurely in certain circumstances.

§ 232 Removal from office by shareholder(s)

At their discretion, shareholders with delegation rights may remove a delegated member from office at any time. The removal of an elected member, by contrast, always requires a resolution by the shareholders' meeting;[498] the articles of association will often specify the requirements for this resolution. For example, many public companies provide in their articles of association that a simple majority decision suffices for the removal. If the articles do not include any requirements, the resolution to remove a supervisory board member from office requires at least three-quarters of the votes cast.

Employee representatives in co-determined supervisory boards cannot be removed from their office by the shareholders' meeting, but only (directly or indirectly) by the employees pursuant to the applicable co-determination rules.

§ 233 Removal from office by court order

A member can also be removed from office by a ruling of the local court where the company has its registered office.[499] This process requires due cause. The supervisory board is entitled to file a motion for removal based on a decision made by a simple majority of the votes cast.[500] If the member concerned is a delegated member, shareholders, who together hold at least 10% of the nominal share capital or nominal share capital amounting to EUR 1 million, are also entitled to file such a motion.[501]

Due cause always exists in cases of a gross conflict of interest between the supervisory board member's conduct and the interests of the company, or in cases where it is plainly untenable that the board member continues to hold office. Sitting on the supervisory board of a competitor does not usually suffice from a perspective of mandatory rules under the Stock Corporation Act; however, such a conflict may lead to a violation of the rules of the Corporate Governance Code which call for the removal of a supervisory board member in the event of significant conflicts of interest with long-term effects.[502]

---

498   Aktiengesetz [AktG] [Stock Corporation Act] 1965, § 103 (F.R.G.).
499   Aktiengesetz [AktG] [Stock Corporation Act] 1965, § 103, ¶ 3 (F.R.G.) and Gesetz über das Verfahren in Familiensachen und in den Angelegenheiten der freiwilligen Gerichtsbarkeit [FamFG] [Act on Proceedings in Family Law and on Matters of Non-contentious Jurisdiction], 2008, § 375, no. 3, § 376, ¶ 1 (F.R.G.).
500   Aktiengesetz [AktG] [Stock Corporation Act] 1965, § 103 ¶ 3, sentence 2 (F.R.G.).
501   Aktiengesetz [AktG] [Stock Corporation Act] 1965, § 103, ¶ 3, sentence 3 (F.R.G.).
502   Deutscher Corporate Governance Kodex [DCGK] [German Corporate Governance Code] 2010, 5.5.3, sentence 2 (F.R.G.).

Additionally, a gross violation of duty or mandatory legal provisions will constitute due cause, for instance, any violation of insider trading regulations. Additionally, certain actions of a supervisory board member that conflict with the authority of the management board may also reach the threshold for a gross violation of duties. For example, if a supervisory board member contacts business partners of the company without the management board's knowledge or otherwise interferes with the management board's authority to manage the company, he may be removed from office for due cause. The same applies to grossly disloyal conduct. However, simple violations of duty, such as missing a board meeting or minor violations of the duty of confidentiality without any material consequences, would generally not constitute due cause justifying removal from office.

§ 234 Resignation

Supervisory board members may resign from office before the end of their regular term. Resignation is effective once declared to the management board. The declaration requires neither a particular form nor due cause for effectiveness.

The board members should avoid resigning at an untimely juncture, *e.g.*, if the company is experiencing a severe economic crisis during which the expertise of the board member would be of great value to the AG. Nevertheless, a board member's untimely resignation is still effective upon declaration to the management board; however, should the resignation cause damages to the AG, there may be a claim for compensation against the departing supervisory board member.

There are special circumstances that may give rise to a supervisory board member's duty to resign. For example, the Corporate Governance Code suggests that in cases where there is a major conflict of interest, members must resign from the supervisory board.[503] A duty to resign from office may be assumed in a competitive situation affecting the company's core area of activity that would lead to a lasting serious conflict in performing the duties of the supervisory board member's office.

§ 235 Non-fulfillment of personal requirements

By law, without any formal resignation, a supervisory board member's position on the board expires if he ceases to meet any of the personal requirements mandated by German law.[504] If personal requirements stipulated in the articles of association are no longer met, there is no automatic expiration. In such cases, however, removal from office by a court for due cause may be considered.[505]

§ 236 Influence by governmental agencies

In sensitive businesses, *e.g.*, in credit institutions, financial services institutions, financial holding companies, insurance companies, pension funds and insurance holding companies,

---

503 Deutscher Corporate Governance Kodex [DCGK] [German Corporate Governance Code] 2010, 5.5.3, sentence 2 (F.R.G.).

504 §§ 202 *et seq.* deal with the personal requirements under statutory law.

505 *Cf.* § 233.

the BaFin as responsible supervisory agency may order the company to dismiss certain of its supervisory board members, if the latter fail to meet the professional qualifications required for such business. In addition, such an order may also be made, if a supervisory board member negligently fails either to recognize violations of sound business practices by the management board or to address and remedy violations in spite of warnings by the supervisory agencies. If the company does not comply with such an order to remove the supervisory board member, the BaFin is entitled to apply to the court to dismiss such member.

§ 237 Reduction of the supervisory board's size?

The size of the supervisory board may be reduced only if the resulting board has at least the required minimum of three members and any applicable co-determination rules are met. Consequently, a reduction in size of the supervisory board is only feasible in a few situations. It is possible to reduce the size of a board which is not co-determined or where the board is larger than required by the applicable co-determination rules. Additionally, a reduction is possible if the company's share capital declines. All of these cases, however, require the excess members to be removed from office. Under these circumstances, no member automatically loses his position. Apart from that, the supervisory board can be reduced under certain circumstances in connection with the transformation of the AG into an SE.[506]

F.   Disclosure of membership

§ 238 List of supervisory board members

The management board must promptly notify the commercial register of any changes to the membership of the supervisory board and provide the commercial register with a list containing the names, the profession and the residence of all supervisory board members.[507] The commercial register announces in the joint electronic register of the German commercial registers the receipt of an updated supervisory board list.

In addition, the Corporate Governance Code recommends that the company also announces changes to the membership of its supervisory board by posting a list of the current members on the company's website.

IV. Powers, internal rules, committees

§ 239 Overview

After describing the responsibilities of the supervisory board, its internal organization and the supervisory board meetings and resolutions are dealt with in further detail. At the end of this section certain aspects relating to supervisory board committees are discussed.

---

506   § 383 deals with the number of members of the supervisory body in the SE.
507   Aktiengesetz [AktG] [Stock Corporation Act] 1965, § 106 (F.R.G.).

A. Responsibilities of the supervisory board

§ 240 Introduction

Among other things, the supervisory board is responsible for appointing and removing members of the management board, executing service agreements with management board members and supervising the management board. The following sections deal with these and further material duties of the supervisory board.

1. Appointment and removal of management board members

§ 241 Authority to select management board members

The supervisory board is responsible for the appointment and removal of members of the management board.[508] The board cannot transfer these duties to a committee.[509] While individual supervisory board members or the personnel committee may review and prepare personnel decisions, the full supervisory board must make all final decisions. The supervisory board has sole authority and may exercise wide-ranging discretion when making management board appointment and removal decisions within the limits of the law. The articles of association, therefore, may not grant the management board the power to nominate new management board members. Contractual obligations restricting the supervisory board's discretion are also not enforceable. The supervisory board also decides on the number of management board members unless the articles of association address this topic specifically.

§ 242 Process

In a company not subject to the co-determination rules on a parity basis, the election as well as the removal of a management board member by the supervisory board require a simple majority of the votes cast. In addition, the revocation of a membership in the management board requires due cause.[510]

As set out above, a company subject to the co-determination rules based on parity must fill half its supervisory board seats with employee representatives.[511] As a consequence, these companies must follow a special procedure when electing and removing management board members.[512] At the outset, the supervisory board votes on the candidate. Management board candidates require a two-thirds majority of all supervisory board members in order to get elected. In the absence of such a majority, the so-called permanent mediation committee is engaged (comprised of four supervisory board members, two from each of the employee and the shareholder representative groups) which must nominate candidates within one month. The supervisory board then votes again. In the second ballot, a candidate is elected with a simple majority of the votes cast and the supervisory board is not bound solely to the nomination of the mediation committee. If, however, the simple majority of the votes cast is not achieved on the second ballot, a third ballot is held and the chairman of the supervisory board, who is

---

508 Aktiengesetz [AktG] [Stock Corporation Act] 1965, § 84, ¶ 1, sentence 1, ¶ 3, sentence 1 (F.R.G.).
509 Aktiengesetz [AktG] [Stock Corporation Act] 1965, § 107, ¶ 3, sentence 2 (F.R.G.).
510 Details of the appointment and revocation procedure are set forth in §§ 22 et seq. and §§ 30 et seq.
511 Mitbestimmungsgesetz [MitbestG] [Co-Determination Act] 1976, § 1, ¶ 1, § 7 (F.R.G.).
512 Cf. Mitbestimmungsgesetz [MitbestG] [Co-Determination Act] 1976, § 31, ¶ 2–4 (F.R.G.).

a representative of the shareholders, has two votes. These rules apply *mutatis mutandis* for the removal of management board members in companies co-determined on a parity basis.

§ 243 Appointment of supervisory board members to management board

If the management board has fewer members than required by either law or the articles of association, the supervisory board must find replacement(s). These replacements may be provisional if necessary. The replacement may be a supervisory board member if an existing management board member cannot perform his duties, *e.g.*, in cases of prolonged illness or incapacitation.[513] A supervisory board member may only act in this capacity on the management board for a maximum term of one year. At the outset, the supervisory board must determine the exact length of this provisional term but thereafter, the supervisory board member may be repeatedly appointed and have his term of office extended; however, the maximum period of one year may not be exceeded under any circumstances. Given that there is a debate about whether the provisional appointment of a supervisory board member for the management board may be delegated to a committee, it is advisable to proceed on the same principles as those for the appointment of a regular management board member and refrain from delegating the task to a committee. Special rules apply in co-determined companies.

2.   Execution of service agreements with management

§ 244 Introduction

The act of being appointed serves as the sole basis for the management board member's authority under corporate law. German law, however, distinguishes between the corporate authority on the one hand and the contractual relationship on the other hand. The corporate authority bestows the power to represent the company and to act on its behalf upon the members of the management board. The contractual relationship on the other hand, relates to the internal relationship between the member of the management board and the company and governs matters relating to employment law (*e.g.*, compensation issues).

§ 245 Authority of supervisory board

The supervisory board bears the sole responsibility for entering into service agreements with management board members and represents the company in any matters related to the contract (and other legal acts *vis-à-vis* the management board members), both in and out of court.[514] The supervisory board may, in contrast to the appointment resolution, delegate various tasks associated with the service agreement to a committee. The compensation of the management board members, however, must be determined by the plenum. In this context, due care must be exercised that the overall compensation is in a fair relation to the duties and performance of the individual management board member as well as the company's situation and that the overall compensation does not exceed the customary level of compensation without specific reasons.[515]

---

513 Aktiengesetz [AktG] [Stock Corporation Act] 1965, § 105, ¶ 2, sentence 1 (F.R.G.).

514 Aktiengesetz [AktG] [Stock Corporation Act] 1965, § 112 (F.R.G.).

515 §§ 44 *et seq.* deal with the compensation of management board members. §§ 57 *et seq.* deal with the appropriateness of compensation.

The chairman of the supervisory board, who is responsible for actually signing the service agreement with the individual management board member, will execute the contract on behalf of the entire board. His authorization in this context is quite restricted. In fact, the chairman has the right to negotiate certain contractual details, but it must be ensured that the entire supervisory board approves the contract's main features.

Consideration should be given to the fact that entering into a service agreement prematurely may constitute an illegal intervention in the powers of the company's supervisory board to make the appointment. In order to avoid such a situation, parties will often make the supervisory board appointment a condition precedent in the service agreement to prevent it from becoming binding too soon.

§ 246 Reduction of compensation

The supervisory board shall reduce the compensation of the management board members to an adequate (lower) level if the company's situation materially worsens and the agreed compensation proves to be unreasonable.[516] If the compensation is reduced, the management board member has an extraordinary termination right to the end of the next quarter of a calendar year.

§ 247 Termination of the service agreement

In general, the same rules as for the execution of the employment relationship apply to its termination. In particular, a premature termination of the contract must not interfere with the supervisory board's right to decide on the removal of a management board member. In companies with a supervisory board co-determined on a parity basis, notice of the termination of the service agreement must also consider the special process regarding the removal of management board members.[517] In these cases, the removal process must be completed before notice of termination of the service agreement can be given.

3.   Supervision of management
§ 248 Subject, scope and standards of supervision

As German law mandates, the supervisory board has a duty to oversee the management of the company.[518] This duty only relates to the management board and its members. Managers and other company employees who are not on the management board do not fall under the supervisory board's umbrella; rather, the management board is solely responsible for the supervision of those other individuals. That being said, the supervisory board must ensure that the management board fulfills its supervisory duties *vis-à-vis* lower management levels properly. In addition, the supervisory board also plays an important advisory role, which is closely associated with its supervisory duties.

---

516   For the compensation of management board members *cf.* §§ 44 *et seq.*

517   *Cf.* §§ 30 *et seq.* for the revocation of management board members by supervisory board resolution and §§ 96 *et seq.* for the reporting duty of the management board members.

518   Aktiengesetz [AktG] [Stock Corporation Act] 1965, § 111, ¶ 1 (F.R.G.).

The purpose of supervision is to oversee management decisions and to ensure that the management board fully performs its managerial duties. The supervisory board must establish a wide scope of oversight. In addition to reviewing the legality of the management board's activities, the supervisory board must review their appropriateness and profitability. First and foremost this entails *ex post* reviews of the management board's activities. In addition to examining the annual financial statements and the annual report,[519] the supervisory board also has to diligently review the management and business reports that are presented to it by the management board on a regular basis;[520] close examination is especially required when the company reports poor results. The requisite intensity of supervision is dictated not only by the company's economic success but also by factors such as size, market situation and any internal issues at the company. The board must ensure that the management board properly organizes the company, and establishes an adequate risk monitoring system under which any developments which could put the future existence of the company at risk, can be recognized early. In the case of a corporate group, the supervisory board only needs to review the reports of the parent's management board and not those of the management boards of companies it controls. Nevertheless, oversight of the management board of the parent company entails control of its actions in the subordinated companies and supervisory boards must be mindful of important decisions being made at all levels of the group. The supervisory board must aim to supervise the future business policy of the management board as well, *e.g.*, by thoroughly discussing business plans and projections with the management and by providing that significant business transactions may only be carried out with its prior approval.

The members of the supervisory board can generally assume that the legal regulations regarding the minimum number of supervisory board meetings mandated by law suffice to warrant an appropriate level of supervision, provided that the members are well-prepared and the company is not facing an extraordinary situation. At a minimum, the law requires at least two meetings every six months, although the supervisory board of a non-listed company may resolve to meet only once every six months.[521] More frequent supervisory board meetings may be necessary, *e.g.*, in times of crisis or special scenarios such as a hostile takeover bid.

§ 249 Examination of current reports
The quality of the supervisory board's oversight depends heavily on the management board providing the relevant information. The management board must furnish the supervisory board with complete information about important events at regular intervals. This information aids the supervisory board in assessing the condition of the company. Often, the supervisory board specifies in detail the information and report obligations of the management board in a separate information manual (*Informationsordnung*) or in the management board's rules of procedure.

---

519   Aktiengesetz [AktG] [Stock Corporation Act] 1965, § 171, ¶ 1, sentence 1 (F.R.G.).
520   Aktiengesetz [AktG] [Stock Corporation Act] 1965, § 90 (F.R.G.) sets forth a comprehensive reporting obligation for the management board.
521   Aktiengesetz [AktG] [Stock Corporation Act] 1965, § 110, ¶ 3 (F.R.G.).

The management board must regularly submit reports to the supervisory board on a variety of topics, including the company's intended business policy and planning, profitability, business development, revenues, material transactions, and general condition.[522] In corporate groups, the management board reports of the parent company must also refer to subsidiaries and joint ventures, as they also constitute part of the company's assets.[523]

In the event of any development that could materially affect the company (especially its profitability or liquidity), the management board must submit an additional report to the supervisory board chairman as soon as possible.[524] These developments include, in particular, external events that may potentially have an adverse effect, *e.g.*, considerable tax deficiencies, requirements imposed by authorities, product liability cases, major litigation, labor conflicts, default on material claims, or liquidity bottlenecks arising from withdrawal of credit lines. This duty also arises if a company associated with the AG is affected. Depending on the relevance of the issue, the chairman has to decide whether he calls an extraordinary supervisory board meeting, forwards the report to all other supervisory board members or only addresses the matter at the next ordinary supervisory board meeting.

The supervisory board can also require the management board to submit additional reports on corporate matters at any time. This right can be exercised by the entire supervisory board or by any of its members, but the reports must always be provided to the entire supervisory board.

§ 250 Additional supervision instruments

The supervisory board is entitled to perform special audits in the company at its discretion as long as it has a specific reason to do so. In such a scenario, the audit right relates to all company documents and assets. Only the supervisory board as a whole has the right to perform an audit; however, it may adopt a resolution calling on individual members to exercise the right to engage the audit committee directly, or to commission an audit by outside experts.[525] If outside experts are called in, the resolution must specify the individual matter or matters which are to be audited, *e.g.*, the acquisition of a loss-making company.

Furthermore, the law aims to achieve close cooperation between the supervisory board and the auditor of the company. Under German law, the auditor of the company's financial statements audits the annual and group financial statements for the supervisory board. While the shareholders' meeting appoints the auditor,[526] the supervisory board is responsible for issuing the auditing mandate to the auditor (including negotiation of the terms of the engagement).[527] The board may also decide the focal points for the audit and agree on fees with the auditor. The auditor is obliged to attend the supervisory board meeting at which the financial statements

---

522 Aktiengesetz [AktG] [Stock Corporation Act] 1965, § 90, ¶ 1, sentence 1 (F.R.G.).
523 Aktiengesetz [AktG] [Stock Corporation Act] 1965, § 90, ¶ 1, sentence 2 (F.R.G.).
524 Aktiengesetz [AktG] [Stock Corporation Act] 1965, § 90, ¶ 1, sentence 3 (F.R.G.).
525 Aktiengesetz [AktG] [Stock Corporation Act] 1965, § 111, ¶ 2, sentence 2 (F.R.G.).
526 Handelsgesetzbuch [HGB] [Commercial Code] 1897, § 318, ¶ 1, sentence 1 (F.R.G.); Aktiengesetz [AktG] [Stock Corporation Act] 1965, § 119, ¶ 1, no. 4 (F.R.G.).
527 Aktiengesetz [AktG] [Stock Corporation Act] 1965, § 111, ¶ 2, sentence 3 (F.R.G.).

are discussed and to personally report on the results of his audit. In a group of companies, the supervisory board of the parent company bears the sole responsibility for engaging an auditor for the group audit.

The supervisory board is also permitted to call a special shareholders' meeting if the shareholders' meeting has the power to decide the matter at issue and a shareholders' decision is necessary to preserve the company's interests. For example, the supervisory board may request the shareholders' meeting to adopt a no confidence resolution against management board members in order to revoke their appointments for due cause.

§ 251 Right to withhold consent

While the supervisory board may not involve itself in the actual management of the company, the articles of association or a supervisory board resolution must specify certain types of business transactions that may only be carried out with the consent of the supervisory board.[528] This allows supervisory board involvement in shaping corporate policy via its right to veto major management measures.

The supervisory board must use its commercial discretion when deciding whether to withhold its consent. It should at least exert its influence in transactions that have material consequences on the financial situation or profitability of the company. When exercising discretion, it must allow the management board enough flexibility to manage the company. In some cases, however, discretion is "reduced to zero." If, *e.g.*, the supervisory board can prevent illegal behavior by the management board only by withholding consent, the supervisory board must ensure that its consent for the measure in question will be required. Once consent is sought, the supervisory board must then refuse to consent. However, this scenario is extremely rare and should be considered an exception to the rule.

The Corporate Governance Code recommends a catalogue of material business measures that should be made subject to the consent of the supervisory board comprising at least basic decisions or measures that would cause fundamental changes to the company's assets, financial condition or results of operations.[529]

While the supervisory board cannot transfer its consent right to a committee, it may delegate the actual exercise of pre-established consent rights to a committee.[530] If the committee, or the company's supervisory board, does not approve of a proposed business transaction, the management board may call for the shareholders' meeting to approve the transaction.[531] The resolution of the shareholders' meeting must be passed with a majority of three-quarters of the votes cast.[532]

---

528   Aktiengesetz [AktG] [Stock Corporation Act] 1965, § 111, ¶ 4, sentence 2 (F.R.G.).
529   Deutscher Corporate Governance Kodex [DCGK] [German Corporate Governance Code] 2010, 3.3 (F.R.G.).
530   *Cf.* Aktiengesetz [AktG] [Stock Corporation Act] 1965, § 107, ¶ 3, sentence 3 (F.R.G.).
531   Aktiengesetz [AktG] [Stock Corporation Act] 1965, § 111, ¶ 4, sentence 3 (F.R.G.).
532   Aktiengesetz [AktG] [Stock Corporation Act] 1965, § 111, ¶ 4, sentence 4 (F.R.G.).

§ 252 Regulation of the management board's rules of procedure

The management board is responsible for the management of the company and, as a result can generally set out its own rules of procedure. This power, however, is considered a subsidiary power and is superseded in any case where the supervisory board passes rules of procedure for the management board.[533] If the rules of procedure set forth by the supervisory board are incomplete, the management board is entitled to supplement them within the framework permitted by the supervisory board. The rules of procedure passed by the supervisory board may go into great detail; however, the supervisory board should typically allow the management board some organizational flexibility unless special circumstances demand otherwise.

4.   Sanctions against the management board

§ 253 Possible sanctions following failure to furnish information

Various options are available to the supervisory board and its members if the management board violates any of its duties to furnish information. While drastic measures are not always appropriate, in some situations the supervisory board must implement stringent measures in order to avoid incurring liability itself.

If the management board fails to fulfill its duty to provide information, the supervisory board's first option is to initiate an informal procedure. Before exercising any of its more severe statutory powers, e.g., dismissing a management board member or amending the management board's rules of procedure, the supervisory board may choose to discuss the matter initially with the chief executive officer or spokesman of the management board (or, if such a position does not exist) other management board members, who may be able to ensure compliance with the information furnishing requirement.

If this approach does not have the desired effect, the supervisory board may apply to the competent court to enforce its rights to information. The entire supervisory board may choose to do so in a concerted effort, but individual members are also entitled to assert information rights.

§ 254 Actions to prevent mismanagement

The management board has wide-ranging discretion in its management decisions.[534] Mismanagement can therefore only be said to occur if a decision is no longer acceptable, even considering this flexibility, e.g., because the decision is unlawful. If the supervisory board considers a contemplated decision by the management board unlawful, it must inform the management board accordingly. Should the management board nonetheless continue to pursue the matter or is it foreseeable from the outset that the management board will simply ignore the supervisory board's advice, the supervisory board is required to take immediate action by withholding its consent, if consent is required under the existing rules, or impose a consent requirement on an ad-hoc basis.

---

533   Aktiengesetz [AktG] [Stock Corporation Act] 1965, § 77, ¶ 2 (F.R.G.).
534   Cf. §§ 66 et seq.

It is important to note that a violation of any such consent requirement does not render an agreement with a third party invalid that has already been executed by the management board. Thus, although the management board may violate its obligations, the consent requirement as such does not prevent the management board from conducting valid business with third parties. As a result, it may be appropriate to take action against the management board before the courts, if there is a risk that the management board will fail to comply with applicable consent requirements. In such a case, the court action can only be brought by the supervisory board as a representative body.

Another, more drastic option for the supervisory board to prevent mismanagement is the dismissal of the management board member.[535]

§ 255 Asserting claims for damages *vis-à-vis* management

In addition to preventing actions harmful to the company, the supervisory board must investigate past actions that potentially harmed the company. Certain circumstances call for investigating damage claims against management board members and filing of such claims where appropriate. Past court decisions have set out a three-step investigation precedent for the supervisory board to follow in these instances.

The first step includes an analysis of whether damage claims exist at all. The supervisory board has no discretion in this respect and must investigate the relevant factual and legal issues. In the second step, the supervisory board must assess the risk of litigation as well as its likelihood of success. If, following a diligent analysis, the board considers the risk of failure too great, it may decide not to file for damages. On the other hand, if it comes to the conclusion that the risks of litigation are reasonable, the board is required to file a complaint. Finally, in exceptional cases, the supervisory board is permitted to refrain from pursuing such claims, for instance, if the benefits outweigh the negative effects of a litigation scenario or the pursuit of the claim is out of proportion to the benefit gained; this is only applicable in exceptional cases.

5.   Annual financial statements, annual report and appropriation of profits
§ 256 Introduction

The management board must submit the annual financial statements, the annual report and a proposal for the appropriation of profits or losses to the supervisory board for the attention of the supervisory board chairman as soon as they have been prepared.[536] This is usually done by forwarding a copy of the annual financial statements to the supervisory board. The act of forwarding also constitutes the management board's acceptance of the annual financial statements. The supervisory board must then review and approve or disapprove the financial statements and the other submitted reports. The supervisory board must report to the shareholders' meeting on the results of its review and the proposed appropriation of profit or loss.[537]

---

535   *Cf.* §§ 30 *et seq.*
536   Aktiengesetz [AktG] [Stock Corporation Act] 1965, § 170, ¶ 1, 2 (F.R.G.).
537   *Cf.* §263.

§ 257 Approval of annual financial statements

In general, the supervisory board is destined to approve the financial statements after its review. Once the supervisory board passes and approves the annual financial statements they become binding and the discretionary decisions regarding financial policy proposed by the management board in the financial statements become effective. A supervisory board committee may perform a preliminary review of the annual financial statements, but even if such a review takes place, only the supervisory board plenum can resolve to pass the statements.[538] The auditor of the financial statements must attend any preparatory committee meetings and the supervisory board's balance-sheet meeting, so that the supervisory board receives first-hand information on the financial auditor's audit.[539]

Once the supervisory board approves the financial statements, it can no longer unilaterally withdraw its acceptance. It is possible, however, to jointly resolve to amend the annual financial statements together with the management board. The boards may only act in this regard until the annual ordinary shareholders' meeting convenes.

In basically two special situations, however, the shareholders' meeting instead of the company's administrative bodies approves the financial statements. First, the management and supervisory boards, despite passing the financial statements, may resolve to leave the approval up to the shareholders' meeting.[540] Second, the shareholders' meeting is responsible to approve the annual financial statements if the supervisory board refuses to do so.[541]

§ 258 Resolution on annual report and appropriation of profits

As mentioned, the management board must also forward the annual report to the supervisory board and make a proposal for the appropriation of profits. However, only the shareholders' meeting but not the supervisory board is assigned the task of deciding on the appropriation of profits.[542] The delivery of the management board's proposal on the appropriation of profits and the annual report to the supervisory board shall therefore – first and foremost – provide the latter with additional information to enable it to properly oversee the management board. Consequently, the supervisory board has no decisive vote on these items but only has to resolve whether it supports the management board's proposal for the shareholders' meeting.

§ 259 Special rules for corporate groups

Special rules apply to corporate groups with respect to the resolution on annual reports. The supervisory board of the parent company must receive consolidated financial statements and the group annual report.[543] However, in contrast to the annual financial statements for the parent company, the consolidated financial statements are not automatically approved when

---

538 *Cf.* Aktiengesetz [AktG] [Stock Corporation Act] 1965, § 107, ¶ 3 (F.R.G.).
539 Aktiengesetz [AktG] [Stock Corporation Act] 1965, § 171, ¶ 1, sentence 2 (F.R.G.).
540 Aktiengesetz [AktG] [Stock Corporation Act] 1965, § 172, sentence 1, § 173, ¶ 1 (F.R.G.).
541 Aktiengesetz [AktG] [Stock Corporation Act] 1965, § 173, ¶ 1, sentence 1 (F.R.G.).
542 Aktiengesetz [AktG] [Stock Corporation Act] 1965, § 174, ¶ 2 (F.R.G.).
543 Aktiengesetz [AktG] [Stock Corporation Act] 1965, § 170, ¶ 1, sentence 2 (F.R.G.). § 263 deals with the audit report to the shareholders' meeting.

passed by the supervisory board. Approval is always limited to the individual company financial statements because only they serve as the basis for the appropriation of profits. If the supervisory board does not pass the consolidated financial statements for any reason, the company must announce the failure in the electronic version of the Federal Gazette.

6.   Rights and duties at shareholders' meetings
§ 260 Calling the shareholders' meeting
The supervisory board also has extensive duties in connection with the shareholders' meeting.

While the management board generally calls the shareholders' meeting, in certain cases it may become necessary for the supervisory board to call a special meeting. This is permitted only if the shareholders' meeting has the power to decide the matter at issue and a shareholders' decision is necessary to preserve the company's interests.[544] For instance, the shareholders' meeting may need to adopt a resolution of no confidence against management board members in order to revoke their appointments for due cause. A simple majority of supervisory board votes cast is sufficient to call a special shareholders' meeting. The decision cannot be delegated to a supervisory board committee.[545]

There are unresolved questions about the authority of the supervisory board to call a special shareholders' meeting to discuss management issues. In any event, past court decisions permit calling a shareholders' meeting to discuss management measures if a decision by the shareholders' meeting is a prerequisite to management board action. Caution is advised if a shareholders' meeting is called solely to discuss management issues as to which the management board does not require shareholders' approval. While there are good reasons to allow discussion of management matters by the shareholders' meeting in some situations where no approval is necessary, case law to date does not give the shareholders such power.

§ 261 Attendance of shareholders' meeting
Supervisory board members have both the right and the duty to participate in shareholders' meetings.[546] Members violating this duty may be liable for damages. A company's articles of association may allow supervisory board members to participate by video link under certain circumstances.[547] The video link must provide two-way communication of both images and sound and also enable remote participants to follow, and participate in the discussions of, the shareholders' meeting. Additionally, the conditions under which a video link is permitted must be specified in more detail in the articles of association. The company has to make all technical arrangements and bear the accompanying costs.

---

544   Aktiengesetz [AktG] [Stock Corporation Act] 1965, § 111, ¶ 3 (F.R.G.).
545   Aktiengesetz [AktG] [Stock Corporation Act] 1965, § 107, ¶ 3, sentence 3 (F.R.G.).
546   Aktiengesetz [AktG] [Stock Corporation Act] 1965, § 118, ¶ 3, sentence 1 (F.R.G.).
547   Aktiengesetz [AktG] [Stock Corporation Act] 1965, § 118, ¶ 3, sentence 2 (F.R.G.).

§ 262 Proposal for resolutions

The management board and the supervisory board are each required to submit their own proposals on every item on the agenda of the shareholders' meeting.[548] This is still the case even if the supervisory board agrees with the management board's proposals. The two boards may also submit different proposals on the same agenda item. Furthermore, it is possible for them to propose alternate or secondary motions. Proposals may also be amended if new facts come to light, provided that the amendment does not represent a substantial change to the existing proposal.

Certain exceptions to the general requirements set out above apply in the two following cases: First, neither the management board nor the supervisory board is required to submit proposals if shareholders owning at least 5% or an amount of EUR 500,000 of the company's nominal capital have put the relevant item on the agenda.[549] In this respect, it does not matter who called the shareholders' meeting. Nonetheless, the board has the right to give an opinion on the item proposed by the minority.

Second, only the supervisory board (but not the management board) may submit proposals on agenda items relating to the election of supervisory board members and auditors.[550] This prevents the management board from unlawfully influencing the composition of the board overseeing it.

§ 263 Supervisory board report

The supervisory board must report to the shareholders' meeting on the results of its review of the annual financial statements, the annual report and the proposed appropriation of profits including potential dividends.[551] If applicable, the board must also report on the consolidated financial statements and group annual report. It is required that the audit report is adopted by the entire supervisory board; a delegation to a supervisory board committee is not permitted.[552] The supervisory board chairman must sign the written report and forward it to the management board, which must make it available to the shareholders along with the invitation to the shareholders' meeting.[553]

The audit report must be true and complete. It must clearly demonstrate the discrepancies, if any, between the assessments of the management board and those of the supervisory board. If discrepancies exist, the report must have the appropriate level of detail for the shareholders' meeting to gain a clear picture of the situation. Otherwise, the report may be much shorter. The report must also contain information about the supervisory board's monitoring activities

---

548   Aktiengesetz [AktG] [Stock Corporation Act] 1965, § 124, ¶ 3 (F.R.G.).
549   Aktiengesetz [AktG] [Stock Corporation Act] 1965, § 122, ¶ 2 (F.R.G.).
550   "Auditors" is understood in this context to include both auditors for the financial statement (cf. Handelsgesetz-buch [HGB] [Commercial Code] 1897, § 318 (F.R.G.)) and special auditors (Sonderprüfer) for other than ordinary cases (cf. Aktiengesetz [AktG] [Stock Corporation Act] 1965, § 142 (F.R.G.)).
551   Aktiengesetz [AktG] [Stock Corporation Act] 1965, § 171, ¶ 2, sentence 1 (F.R.G.).
552   Aktiengesetz [AktG] [Stock Corporation Act] 1965, § 107, ¶ 3, sentence 3 (F.R.G.).
553   Aktiengesetz [AktG] [Stock Corporation Act] 1965, § 171, ¶ 3, sentence 1, § 175, ¶ 2 (F.R.G.); Handelsgesetz-buch [HGB] [Commercial Code] 1897, § 325 (F.R.G.).

during the previous financial year.[554] It is also useful to inform the shareholders' meeting about the work of the supervisory board in the report in as much detail as possible, even if it is often set forth in very general terms.

At listed companies, the audit report must contain information about any supervisory board committees and their areas of responsibility.[555]

In its audit report, the supervisory board must also deliver an opinion on the result of the audit by the company's auditor.[556] The company's auditor may, following its review, provide either a certificate, which can be unqualified or qualified, or a refusal to issue the certificate; the supervisory board must then express its opinion on the result. If the auditor has not provided an unqualified certificate or the supervisory board has objections, the supervisory board must comment on these items in the audit report in detail to provide the shareholders' meeting with sufficient basis of information on this subject.

The supervisory board's audit report must conclude with a final declaration or summary.[557] If there are no concerns about whether the annual financial statements are correct, the declaration may just state that the supervisory board has no objections and that it approves the financial statements.

In connection with the consolidated financial statements of a group of companies, the supervisory board basically has the same duties relating to the audit of the consolidated financial statements by the company's auditor and also has to opine on such auditor's results.[558]

§ 264 Report regarding relationships with associated companies

The supervisory board must also comment and deliver its opinion on the management board's report regarding the company's relationships with associated companies if the company is a controlled company and no domination agreement exists (*de facto* group).[559] In general, the rules applicable to other reports also apply here and the supervisory board has to add its comments in this context also to its report to the shareholders' meeting described above.

7.   Utilization of authorized capital

§ 265 Approval by supervisory board

The supervisory board has to approve the issuance of new shares out of authorized capital by the management board and the terms of issuance, if the shareholders' meeting created authorized capital. If the envisaged capital increase provides for an exclusion of the shareholders'

---

554   Aktiengesetz [AktG] [Stock Corporation Act] 1965, § 171, ¶ 2, sentence 2 (F.R.G.).
555   Aktiengesetz [AktG] [Stock Corporation Act] 1965, § 171, ¶ 2, sentence 2, 2. part (F.R.G.).
556   Aktiengesetz [AktG] [Stock Corporation Act] 1965, § 171, ¶ 2, sentence 3 (F.R.G.).
557   Aktiengesetz [AktG] [Stock Corporation Act] 1965, § 171, ¶ 2, sentence 4 (F.R.G.).
558   Aktiengesetz [AktG] [Stock Corporation Act] 1965, § 171, ¶ 2, sentence 5 (F.R.G.).
559   Aktiengesetz [AktG] [Stock Corporation Act] 1965, § 314 (F.R.G.).

subscription rights, the supervisory board also has to review whether the exclusion is legal and reasonable and approve it.[560]

8.   Extending loans
§ 266 Extension of loans to members of management board

In some exceptional cases, the supervisory board must take an active role in managing the company. Certain business transactions may harbor a particular potential for misuse if undertaken by the management board. In these situations, the supervisory board is required to act to preserve the interests of shareholders and other investors. One such case is when loans are extended to management board members.

A company may only extend loans to its management board members if the supervisory board approves the loan by resolution.[561] The supervisory board may delegate this authority to a committee. The resolution must specify the amount of the loan, the applicable interest rate and the terms of repayment, and may not be passed more than three months in advance.

The term "loan" does not only refer to cash payments. It also includes other benefits, such as credit facilities, deferments of payment, securities and withdrawals. It does not include benefits with a value of less than one month's salary of the relevant management board member. If a loan is extended without obtaining the proper supervisory board approval, the recipient must repay it immediately and the company must release any security held against the loan. Alternatively, the supervisory board may approve a loan after the fact.

§ 267 Loans to recipients other than management board members

To prevent abuse, loans to certain other groups of persons require supervisory board consent. This includes anyone close to the management board in the company hierarchy and any individuals closely associated with people in the respective group in order to prevent circumvention of this rule.

Supervisory board consent to grant loans is therefore also required for Prokuristen or holders of a commercial power of attorney.[562] Consent is also required for loans to Prokuristen of controlled companies.[563] If the AG itself is controlled, this also applies to Prokuristen of the controlling company.

Furthermore, loans to spouses or children of any person in a recipient group and loans to persons acting for the account of any person in a recipient group need the consent of the supervisory board.[564] The same applies to other legal entities and business partnerships with a representative or supervisory board member belonging to a recipient group; however, exceptions apply to legal entities and business partnerships which are associated with or sell goods

---

560   Aktiengesetz [AktG] [Stock Corporation Act] 1965, § 204, ¶ 1 (F.R.G.).
561   Aktiengesetz [AktG] [Stock Corporation Act] 1965, § 89, ¶ 1, sentence 1, ¶ 2, sentence 1 (F.R.G.).
562   Aktiengesetz [AktG] [Stock Corporation Act] 1965, § 89, ¶ 2, sentence 1 (F.R.G.).
563   Aktiengesetz [AktG] [Stock Corporation Act] 1965, § 89, ¶ 2, sentence 2 (F.R.G.).
564   Aktiengesetz [AktG] [Stock Corporation Act] 1965, § 89, ¶ 3, sentence 1 (F.R.G.).

to the company.[565] Special regulations also apply to banks and institutions providing financial services.[566]

Whenever the supervisory board votes on extending a loan to one of its members or a closely associated person, the member concerned is not permitted to vote.

9.   Participation rights in co-determined subsidiaries
§ 268 Transfer of participation rights of subsidiary's supervisory board

In companies co-determined on a parity basis holding 25% or more of the shares in another company which is also co-determined on a parity basis, special rules apply to the exercise of certain shareholder rights in other companies by the management board.[567] In such a case, the supervisory board of the parent company must adopt resolutions on the exercise of these participation rights which have binding effect on the management board. The Co-Determination Act contains an exhaustive list of participation rights subject to this rule, for example with respect to the appointment, revocation of appointment and discharge of the acts of administrative bodies. The list further includes resolutions on associated companies in connection with a dissolution or transformation, entering into company agreements (*Unternehmensvertrag*) and the transfer of assets.

In the parent's supervisory board resolution on these topics only the shareholder representatives have the right to vote while the employee representatives are only allowed to advise. Therefore, the supervisory board has a voting quorum when half of the shareholder representatives are present. The resolution is passed by a majority of the shareholder representatives present. The supervisory board may delegate these rights to a committee. In that case, the employee representatives have the right to participate in the committee meetings but voting on the resolution is still limited to the shareholder representatives on the committee.

10.   Declaration of compliance concerning the Corporate Governance Code
§ 269 Duty to prepare and issue declaration of compliance

Every year, both the management board and the supervisory board of listed[568] German AGs are required to disclose to which extent the company has followed the recommendations set forth in the Corporate Governance Code.[569]

The supervisory board and the management board each resolve independently on issuing the declaration. They may issue differing declarations, but this is not advisable from a business perspective. The supervisory board can prevent the management board from acting contrary

---

565   Aktiengesetz [AktG] [Stock Corporation Act] 1965, § 89, ¶ 4, sentence 2 (F.R.G.).
566   Aktiengesetz [AktG] [Stock Corporation Act] 1965, § 89, ¶ 6 (F.R.G.).
567   Cf. Mitbestimmungsgesetz [MitbestG] [Co-Determination Act] 1976, § 32 (F.R.G.).
568   This obligation also applies to companies whose shares are traded on a multilateral trading facility
       (*i.e.*, OTC markets) provided that the company has issued securities other than shares in a regulated market
       within Germany or another country within the European Economic Area.
569   Aktiengesetz [AktG] [Stock Corporation Act] 1965, § 161 (F.R.G.); cf. § 119.

to the Corporate Governance Code, *e.g.*, by incorporating compliance with it into the service agreement.

The task of issuing the declaration may not be assigned to a committee and must be made in the annual financial statements and consolidated financial statements[570] and submitted to the commercial register.[571] The Corporate Governance Code also recommends publishing the declaration in the annual report.[572] The declaration must be made available to the shareholders on the website of the company on a permanent basis.

The declaration of compliance must be updated if it becomes false in the course of the year between the regular issuance of such declaration, because the company changes its position *vis-à-vis* a Corporate Governance Code recommendation. Pursuant to recent case law a failure to do so may otherwise make the discharge of the acts of the supervisory board in the ordinary shareholders' meeting challengeable.

11. Editorial amendments of the articles of association
§ 270 Scope

The shareholders' meeting may authorize the supervisory board (as a whole) to amend the articles of association if it is solely a technical alteration of the wording of the articles.[573] This is understood to include amendments, which affect only the wording of the articles. If there is any chance an amendment will have a substantive effect, the supervisory board should refrain from implementing it.

B. Internal organization

§ 271 Introduction

The Stock Corporation Act addresses the internal organization of the supervisory board only to a certain extent and leaves the board some discretion on how to organize its duties and responsibilities. While most supervisory boards of larger AGs have established rules of procedure and formed committees, there is no legal obligation to do so.[574] All supervisory boards must elect a chairman and at least one deputy chairman.

1. Rules of procedure
§ 272 Certain level of autonomy

The supervisory board may choose to set out rules of procedure for itself but it is not required to do so. Rules of procedure must be compatible with the articles of association and statutory regulations. For example, statutory law regulates the form and content of the minutes and

---

570 Handelsgesetzbuch [HGB] [Commercial Code] 1897, §§ 285, 314, ¶ 1, no. 8 (F.R.G.).
571 Handelsgesetzbuch [HGB] [Commercial Code] 1897, § 325 (F.R.G.).
572 Deutscher Corporate Governance Kodex [DCGK] [German Corporate Governance Code] 2010, 3.10 (F.R.G.).
573 Aktiengesetz [AktG] [Stock Corporation Act] 1965, § 179, ¶ 1, sentence 2 (F.R.G.).
574 For committees *cf.* §§ 297 *et seq.* below.

how supervisory board meetings are called.[575] By contrast, the supervisory board is free, within certain limits, to form committees and fill the posts of the supervisory board chairman and deputy chairman.[576]

The supervisory board passes its rules of procedure by simple majority of the votes cast with an ordinary supervisory board resolution. As a result, the supervisory board can in specific cases overrule individual provisions of its rules of procedure provided it has the appropriate majority. The rules of procedure remain in force until the supervisory board rescinds or amends them by a simple majority of the votes cast. They do not become invalid when the term of office of supervisory board members expires.

2.   Chairman and deputy chairman
§ 273 Introduction
The supervisory board has to elect a chairman and at least one deputy chairman.[577] The following sections elaborate on the role of the supervisory board chairman, in particular on the appointment, term of office, duties and powers, as well as the role of the deputy chairman.

§ 274 Appointment
The articles of association may set forth a specific election procedure for the chairman of the supervisory board. If the articles are silent, the general rules for passing resolutions apply to electing a chairman. This usually requires a simple majority of the votes cast, but the articles may permit election by a qualified majority or call for a larger quorum. Every member of the supervisory board is eligible for election as chairman and all members may vote, including candidates. Any provisions of the articles of association stipulating that only certain members of the supervisory board are eligible for chairman are invalid. Additionally, the Corporate Governance Code recommends that shareholders be informed of nominations.[578] The appointment as chairman becomes effective when the successful candidate accepts his election.

While no special rules apply to co-determined companies where one-third of the supervisory board members are employee representatives, a special election procedure is mandated in companies with a supervisory board composed of equal numbers of shareholders and employee representatives.[579] This procedure ensures that the shareholders have an advantage when electing the chairman. Hereunder, a two-thirds majority is required to elect both the chairman and the deputy chairman on the first ballot. These two elections may be combined on one ballot or conducted separately. If one or both of these votes fail to produce the requisite majority, a second ballot is held on which the shareholder representatives elect the chairman and the employee representatives elect the deputy chairman independently of one another. A simple majority of the votes cast suffices on the second ballot. Before proceeding to the second ballot,

---

575   Aktiengesetz [AktG] [Stock Corporation Act] 1965, § 107, ¶ 2, § 110 (F.R.G.).
576   Aktiengesetz [AktG] [Stock Corporation Act] 1965, § 107, ¶ 1, 3 (F.R.G.).
577   Aktiengesetz [AktG] [Stock Corporation Act] 1965, § 107, ¶ 1 (F.R.G.).
578   Deutscher Corporate Governance Kodex [DCGK] [German Corporate Governance Code] 2010, 5.4.3, sentence 3 (F.R.G.).
579   Mitbestimmungsgesetz [MitbestG] [Co-Determination Act] 1976, § 27 (F.R.G.).

the supervisory board may repeat the first ballot any number of times, subject to the consent of all supervisory board members.

§ 275 Term

The chairman is appointed for the same period he is elected to the supervisory board, unless the articles of association, rules of procedure or the election resolution stipulate otherwise. If the chairman is reelected as a supervisory board member, his term of office as chairman must be extended in order to continue such office. If the chairman ceases to be a member of the supervisory board, he automatically relinquishes the chairman position. The terms of office of the chairman and deputy chairman must be identical in a supervisory board co-determined on a parity basis.

Appointments as chairman or deputy chairman may be terminated in the same way as the appointment itself. It is possible to revoke an appointment, the conditions for which may be specified in the articles of association or rules of procedure for the supervisory board. The chairman may also resign at his option, except at an untimely moment. Untimely resignation is effective, but it may lead to liability for damages.

§ 276 Duties and powers

The chairman coordinates and manages the supervisory board's activities with all the powers usually attributed to a chairman of a board or committee, including preparing for, calling and chairing the supervisory board meetings. The chairman also represents the supervisory board in dealings with the management board. The chairman receives the management board's reports on important developments[580] and must then take any necessary steps to provide other supervisory board members with the information before the next supervisory board meeting. As a general matter, all members of the supervisory board must have access to all information, written and oral, to be provided to the chairman of the supervisory board by the management of the company.

Whenever the company's capital is increased or reduced, the company must notify the commercial register of the relevant resolutions and capital measures. This is the responsibility of the management board together with the supervisory board chairman.[581]

Generally, the articles of association also stipulate that the chairman chairs the general meetings of the shareholders.

§ 277 Deputy chairman

The deputy chairman carries out the duties and exercises the powers of the chairman whenever the latter is unable to fulfill his duties in a timely manner. In situations requiring urgent action, the deputy chairman is authorized to act *in lieu* of the chairman if the latter is unavailable to

---

580 *Cf.* Aktiengesetz [AktG] [Stock Corporation Act] 1965, § 90, ¶ 1, sentence 3, 1. part (F.R.G.); §§ 96 *et seq.* deal with the reporting duty of the management board to the supervisory board.

581 *Cf.* Aktiengesetz [AktG] [Stock Corporation Act] 1965, § 184, ¶ 1, § 188 ¶ 1, § 195 ¶ 1, § 207 ¶ 2, §§ 223, 229, ¶ 3, § 237, ¶ 2 (F.R.G.).

take action. If there are multiple deputy chairmen, the articles of association or rules of procedure should specify the order in which they are entitled to act.

In co-determined companies on a parity basis where the first ballot fails to result in a two-thirds
majority,[582] the deputy chairman elected by the employee representatives is always the deputy
chairman. In a stalemate situation in the supervisory board, he does not have two votes (other
than the chairman).[583]

§ 278 Registration in the commercial register
The commercial register must be notified of the name and address of the supervisory board
chairman and deputy chairmen.[584] The supervisory board chairman must also be named in the
company's business letters, fax messages and emails.

C.   Supervisory board meetings and resolutions

§ 279 Introduction
There are many regulations that need to be observed in calling and holding a supervisory board
meeting. Supervisory board resolutions are usually passed in actual meetings.

1.   Relevance of supervisory board meetings
§ 280 Minimum number
Generally, the supervisory board must meet at least four times a year,[585] although the articles
of association may require additional meetings. The supervisory board of non-listed companies may resolve to meet only two times each year by a simple majority of the plenum. These
ordinary meetings should preferably not be held by telephone or videoconference. While telephone and videoconferences are permissible, the supervisory board must make sure that such
meetings without the physical presence of all supervisory board members guarantee a due and
proper supervision of the AG.[586]

2.   Calling supervisory board meetings
§ 281 General responsibility of supervisory board chairman
The supervisory board chairman is responsible for calling supervisory board meetings.[587] If he
cannot do so, the task falls to the deputy chairman. If there is no chairman or deputy chairman,
any supervisory board member may call a meeting. The supervisory board chairman may decide
to call a supervisory board meeting on his own initiative and is required to do so if the interests
of the company require that the supervisory board convenes.

---

582   Cf. § 274.
583   Cf. § 198, § 291.
584   Aktiengesetz [AktG] [Stock Corporation Act] 1965, § 107, ¶ 1, sentence 2 (F.R.G.).
585   Cf. Aktiengesetz [AktG] [Stock Corporation Act] 1965, § 110, ¶ 3 (F.R.G.).
586   It is therefore advisable to hold at least one physical meeting semiannually.
587   Cf. Aktiengesetz [AktG] [Stock Corporation Act] 1965, § 110, ¶ 1 (F.R.G.).

In addition, any member of the supervisory board or the management board may require the chairman to call a supervisory board meeting.[588] Individual management board members, however, generally do not have this right individually, so management board members who want to call a supervisory board meeting must first convince the entire management board to do so. Additionally, the purpose and the grounds for the meeting must be indicated ahead of time. A proposed agenda, which details the reasons for calling the meeting at the time in question, is sufficient for describing the purpose.

If there are grounds for a meeting, the chairman must call the supervisory board meeting promptly and the meeting must be held within two weeks of issuing notice.[589] The chairman may only refuse to call a meeting if the demand is abusive, in particular if an unlawful purpose is being pursued or there are no apparent reasonable grounds for it. If the motion has little chance of being successful or the chairman considers the demand unfounded, this does not constitute abuse per se.

§ 282 Calling by other persons
If the supervisory board chairman denies a request to call a meeting, a supervisory board member or the management board may call the supervisory board meeting itself.[590] This is only possible, however, if the chairman fails to honor a valid request to call a meeting or the meeting fails to address the items on the agenda.

If the supervisory board member or the management board calls the meeting, it should also take place within two weeks after giving notice for the meeting. The notification must comply with the usual formalities[591] and indicate the reasons for calling the meeting. The costs of calling the meeting are borne by the company; in the absence of grounds for calling the meeting, however, the company may request reimbursement from the person calling the meeting.

§ 283 Formal requirements
The notice for the meeting may be issued in any form, e.g., orally, by telephone, or by email. Written notice is sufficient if properly sent; it does not need to be received. The articles of association or rules of procedure may impose special form requirements, including that the notice must be sent out by registered mail. The notice must clearly state who called the meeting and the company's name. It must also include the items on the agenda, the venue, date and time of the meeting. The supervisory board chairman determines what items are on the agenda. In due time before the meeting, the supervisory board members should receive the documentation that is necessary for a careful preparation with respect to the items on the agenda.

The meeting should not harbor any surprises for the members of the supervisory board. Prior to the meeting, supervisory board members may propose amendments or additions to the agenda. Motions are also permitted before the meeting, provided that there is sufficient time for the su-

---

588   Aktiengesetz [AktG] [Stock Corporation Act] 1965, § 110, ¶ 1, sentence 1 (F.R.G.).
589   Aktiengesetz [AktG] [Stock Corporation Act] 1965, § 110, ¶ 1, sentence 2 (F.R.G.).
590   Aktiengesetz [AktG] [Stock Corporation Act] 1965, § 110, ¶ 2 (F.R.G.).
591   § 283 deals with the formal requirements of the notification.

pervisory board members to prepare for any changes. The agenda may not be amended during the meeting, unless an exceptional case requires an urgent decision. Management board members have no right to receive copies of the agenda for meetings of the supervisory board. The management board may, however, request that certain items be placed on the agenda of the supervisory board.

§ 284 Deficiencies in calling the meeting

As a rule, deficiencies in calling the meeting lead to the resolutions passed at the meeting being null and void. This can only be avoided if despite the deficiency, all supervisory board members attend and a full plenary assembly is held. If the deficiency only affects certain supervisory board members, they are expected to report the deficiency.[592]

3.   Formalities of supervisory board and committee meetings
§ 285 Attendees

Supervisory board members are both entitled and required to attend meetings of the supervisory board and the committees they belong to. The right to attend a meeting includes the right to inspect documents associated with the meeting. The chairman may exclude a member from a meeting only if otherwise it cannot be warranted that the meeting can be held without disruption. Furthermore, in exceptional cases, the full board may exclude a member if the member's presence threatens the interests of the company, *e.g.*, a secret might be divulged.

All supervisory board members may also attend meetings of the committees of which they are not members.[593] The supervisory board chairman may, however, use due discretion to prohibit members from attending individual committee meetings. Generally, persons who do not belong to the supervisory board are not allowed to attend meetings of the supervisory board or its committees.[594] There are three common exceptions: management board members, Prokuristen, and experts frequently attend meetings of the supervisory board (or parts thereof) upon invitation of the chairman.

If a supervisory board member cannot attend a board or committee meeting, the articles of association may allow another person to attend the meeting in the member's place.[595] Those proxies have no meeting rights of their own, but may deliver the declarations, motions and written votes[596] of the absent supervisory board member. The absent member must authorize the proxy or messenger accordingly in writing, by email or fax, for only one specific meeting.

In some instances, experts, or other persons providing information to the supervisory board, may take part in individual topic discussions at supervisory board meetings.[597] The chairman

---

592   § 295 deals with deficient resolutions.
593   Aktiengesetz [AktG] [Stock Corporation Act] 1965, § 109, ¶ 2 (F.R.G.).
594   Aktiengesetz [AktG] [Stock Corporation Act] 1965, § 109, ¶ 1, sentence 1 (F.R.G.).
595   Aktiengesetz [AktG] [Stock Corporation Act] 1965, § 109, ¶ 3 (F.R.G.).
596   § 294 deals with written votes.
597   *Cf.* Aktiengesetz [AktG] [Stock Corporation Act] 1965, § 109, ¶ 1, sentence 2 (F.R.G.).

decides whether to allow such individuals to be present; however, the plenum may resolve to override this decision. An expert is any person with special knowledge related to the matter under discussion. In accounting meetings, the auditor of the financial statements is an expert and must attend.[598] It is also possible to invite others to provide information, such as managerial employees and former members of the supervisory board. Finally, auxiliary persons may be invited to attend, including interpreters, secretaries and persons taking the minutes.

§ 286 Language
Supervisory board meetings do not have to be conducted in the German language. The supervisory board's rules of procedure may specify a different language for the meetings. Regardless of which language is chosen, any supervisory board member unable to communicate in the language of the meeting is entitled to simultaneous translation.

§ 287 Postponement of agenda items
The articles of association or rules of procedure may authorize the supervisory board chairman to postpone one or more items on the agenda. The full plenary may, however, prevent the chairman's postponement. The supervisory board has also the right to postpone an item by a majority vote. Under certain circumstances, a company with co-determination based on parity may have articles of association provisions that govern postponement. An example of a permissible postponement provision is one granting the supervisory board chairman the ability to postpone matters or resolutions if an unequal number of shareholder and employee representatives are present.

§ 288 Minutes
Minutes must be taken at each supervisory board meeting and signed by the chairman.[599] The minutes must include the meeting's venue, date, participants, agenda items, resolutions, and material contents of the discussions. Motions and resolutions must be recorded verbatim. The minutes must provide the outcome of meeting votes, including the number of yes-votes, no-votes and abstentions. The description of discussions must include the matters presented by the management board and the main arguments of the supervisory board members. This also applies to any resolution passed outside of a physical meeting.

The chairman of the meeting is responsible for the minutes, even if another person prepares them. All supervisory board members are entitled to a copy of the minutes. If a member objects to the written minutes, the member may request a correction at the next meeting. The chairman of the supervisory board will decide whether to accept these requests.

A deficiency regarding the minutes does not diminish the validity of resolutions approved at the meeting.

---

598   Aktiengesetz [AktG] [Stock Corporation Act] 1965, § 171, ¶ 1, sentence 2 (F.R.G.).
599   Aktiengesetz [AktG] [Stock Corporation Act] 1965, § 107, ¶ 2 (F.R.G.).

4.   Adoption of resolutions

There are differences between the rules for adopting resolutions in supervisory boards that are co-determined on a parity basis and those that are not. There are also special forms of adopting resolutions. The basic distinction in this regard is whether the resolutions are adopted in or outside a supervisory board meeting.

§ 289 Quorum

A majority of the supervisory board members constitute a quorum for any supervisory board meeting provided that at least three members participate.[600] If one of the supervisory board members present is precluded from voting and abstains, *e.g.*, since he is conflicted, such member generally will be considered in establishing the quorum. The articles of association may set forth another quorum requirement, provided, however, that, for companies not co-determined on a parity basis, the articles of association can only stipulate a higher quorum.

§ 290 Resolutions of boards not co-determined on a parity basis

Supervisory board decisions are made by voting on resolutions.[601] Resolutions must be formulated explicitly. A majority of the votes cast is sufficient to adopt a resolution, unless a special rule applies.[602] Abstentions do not count as votes cast, but must be counted when the board determines whether a quorum is present. The articles of association may specify that in the event of a tie vote, the supervisory board chairman (or if absent, the deputy chairman) or the chairman of the meeting has a right to a casting vote. The chairman may not be granted the right to veto a resolution.

All supervisory board members must have the same rights; therefore, the articles of association and rules of procedure may not prohibit members from voting. A supervisory board member is only prohibited from voting on a resolution which concerns a legal transaction, including the initiation or settlement of a legal dispute, with such member.[603] In contrast, members are entitled to vote in their own board position election.

§ 291 Resolutions of boards co-determined on a parity basis

Supervisory boards co-determined on a parity basis must abide by special rules when adopting resolutions that deviate to a certain extent from the general rules set forth above. For example, in a co-determined supervisory board on a parity basis, the supervisory board chairman can cast a vote in the event of a tie vote, assuming the resolution only requires a simple majority.[604] This casting vote cannot be modified or eliminated by the articles of association or rules of procedure. By contrast, the deputy chairman is not entitled to a casting vote if he chairs a meeting in the absence of the chairman.

---

600   Aktiengesetz [AktG] [Stock Corporation Act] 1965, § 108, ¶ 2 (F.R.G.).
601   Aktiengesetz [AktG] [Stock Corporation Act] 1965, § 108, ¶ 1 (F.R.G.).
602   *Cf.* Aktiengesetz [AktG] [Stock Corporation Act] 1965, § 133, ¶ 1 (F.R.G.).
603   Bürgerliches Gesetzbuch [BGB] [Civil Code] 1896, § 34 (F.R.G.); GmbH-Gesetz [GmbHG]
        [Limited Liability Companies Act] 1892, § 47, ¶ 4 (F.R.G.) analogously.
604   Mitbestimmungsgesetz [MitbestG] [Co-Determination Act] 1976, § 29, ¶ 2, § 31, ¶ 4 (F.R.G.).

Special rules also exist for the election of the supervisory board chairman and the deputy chairman and for removing or appointing management board members.[605]

§ 292 Adopting resolutions outside board meetings

The supervisory board can adopt resolutions without holding a meeting unless the articles of association or rules of procedure prohibit it.[606] Any supervisory board member, however, may oppose the adoption of resolutions outside of meetings, unless the articles of association or rules of procedure allow resolutions to be adopted outside meetings unconditionally. However, as this is disputed among legal commentators, it should be ensured that every supervisory board member approves the adoption of a resolution outside a supervisory board meeting to avoid any legal uncertainty.

The supervisory board chairman must initiate the process of adopting a resolution outside a meeting by asking all members to cast their votes on a motion within a certain timeframe. When setting the voting schedule, the chairman is not required to observe deadlines that apply to ordinary meetings; however, adequate time must be allotted for objections. No special requirements of form apply, but the chairman must abide by any rules set forth in the articles of association or rules of procedure governing the adoption of resolutions outside a meeting.

§ 293 "Mixed Vote"

An absent supervisory board member may take part in adopting a resolution in a supervisory board meeting. If there are no objections from other members, the supervisory board may hold a so-called "mixed vote" on a resolution. During a mixed vote some members vote in the meeting, while others submit votes in a different form. It is not entirely clear if this type of mixed voting is legally permitted if the articles of association do not explicitly approve it. Thus, it is advisable that a corresponding clause allowing "mixed voting" is included in the articles of association.

§ 294 No representation of absent supervisory board members

Supervisory board members absent in a supervisory board meeting cannot be represented by other persons. If a meeting is held using a video link or telephone conferencing, members using this technology are not absent and may therefore vote as usual.

Members unable to attend a meeting may only appoint a messenger to cast their votes for them.[607] The messenger may be any other supervisory board member. The appointment of messengers who are not supervisory board members is only possible if explicitly permitted by the articles of association. Messengers are not permitted to exercise their own discretion in voting. The specific motions should therefore be circulated to the supervisory board members as early as possible, so that absent members are in a position to issue adequately specific voting instructions to their messengers.

---

605   §§ 241 *et seq.* deal with the appointment and removal of management board members.
606   Aktiengesetz [AktG] [Stock Corporation Act] 1965, § 108, ¶ 4 (F.R.G.).
607   Aktiengesetz [AktG] [Stock Corporation Act] 1965, § 108, ¶ 3 (F.R.G.).

In order to vote, absent supervisory board members must provide messengers with a written, signed ballot; oral instructions by telephone are not permitted. As it is unclear whether votes may be accepted via telefax, telex, telegram or digitally signed email, the member should give the messenger a signed ballot to ensure that the requirement for the written form is fulfilled in any case.

§ 295 Deficient resolutions

A resolution by the supervisory board is deficient if the procedures for its adoption are not followed or if the resolution violates either the law or the articles of association. A deficient resolution is always null and void. Any supervisory board member and the management board may motion to pronounce the nullity of a resolution through a declaratory action by the competent local court. To the extent the invalidity of the resolution influences membership rights of shareholders (e.g., if the supervisory board approves the issuance of new shares from authorized capital), the shareholders also have an interest to seek a declaratory judgment.

However, case law assumes that in certain circumstances the right to claim that a resolution is null and void may expire if not asserted in due time. This can occur if the resolution is null and void due to a minor defect only. Examples are a violation of the two-week period to call a supervisory board meeting, the discussion of items that have not been on the meeting's agenda or the attendance of persons at the supervisory board meeting that are not allowed to do so. In such cases of less serious faults, any aggrieved person must therefore assert that a resolution is null and void within an adequate period of time. Typically, the objection should be submitted to the supervisory board chairman within one month after the following supervisory board meeting. Any actions against the company should be filed before the expiration of this deadline.

If the resolution has a serious fault, supervisory board members and other aggrieved persons never lose the right to challenge its validity. Examples that always allow claiming the nullity of the resolution include a failure to invite individual supervisory board members without valid reason or to adopt resolutions without a quorum. In such cases the validity of the resolution may be challenged without being subject to a time limit and an action may be filed to have the resolution declared null and void.

Resolutions of a supervisory board co-determined on a parity basis are always null and void if passed in violation of the provisions of the Co-Determination Act. This also applies to resolutions passed in a meeting held without invitation or violating either laws or the articles of association. Resolutions may also be null and void if the board passed the resolution in gross violation of their duty to provide information regarding the resolution to employee representatives and allow adequate time for consideration of the measure.

Certain minor violations do not make a resolution deficient. For example, failing to keep minutes is immaterial.[608] The same is true if only individual votes have been cast improperly

---

608   Aktiengesetz [AktG] [Stock Corporation Act] 1965, § 107, ¶ 2, sentence 3 (F.R.G.).

or only votes of individual supervisory board members are deficient, provided the outcome of voting could not be influenced. However, if the outcome is influenced, the resolution is not adopted.

§ 296 Execution of resolutions

The supervisory board chairman is responsible for any measures necessary to implement a resolution and the articles of association or rules of procedure of the AG should explicitly stipulate such authority of the chairman, *e.g.*, to issue legal declarations on behalf of the supervisory board. However, as no one is authorized to make decisions in place of the supervisory board, the chairman may not exercise any discretion while implementing a resolution.

D.   Committees

§ 297 Introduction

Supervisory board committees are intended to relieve the workload of the full supervisory board and increase efficiency. The Corporate Governance Code recommends the formation of committees with specific areas of expertise (*e.g.*, audit committee, nomination committee).[609] Generally, the supervisory board is not required to establish committees.[610] Neither the articles of association nor the general shareholders' meeting may require the supervisory board to form committees. Nonetheless, it is common practice to have supervisory board committees, especially in larger AGs.

1.   Types of committees
§ 298 Overview

The supervisory board may form different types of committees such as committees for preparing the discussions and resolutions of the full board (preparatory committees), committees that oversee the management board (oversight committees), and committees that make decisions in place of the plenum (decision-making committees).

One customary committee is the personnel committee, which decides issues related to the conclusion, amendment and termination of service agreements with management board members. The Corporate Governance Code recommends forming an audit committee[611] to examine accounting and risk management issues, evaluate the independence of the financial statement auditors and their fee agreements, and determine focal areas for audits. The German legislator has also acknowledged the importance of the audit committee by implementing special rules for the composition of this committee.[612] Frequently, boards form a presiding committee with a wide range of tasks, in particular to maintain contact with the management board between the supervisory board meetings. The presiding committee usually also performs the above mentioned functions of the personnel committee. A presiding committee, like all other commit-

---

609   Deutscher Corporate Governance Kodex [DCGK] [German Corporate Governance Code] 2010, 5.3 (F.R.G.).
610   Note that a company co-determined on parity basis has to form a mediation committee, *cf.* § 298.
611   Deutscher Corporate Governance Kodex [DCGK] [German Corporate Governance Code] 2010, 5.3.2 (F.R.G.).
612   *Cf.* § 300 below.

tees that make decisions *in lieu* of the full board, requires the supervisory board to delegate its powers to the committee.

Companies co-determined on a parity basis must form a mediation committee.[613] The sole task of the mediation committee is to submit proposals to the full board for appointing or removing management board members if the required two-thirds majority was not achieved in the initial vote.[614]

§ 299 Relationship with plenum

The entire supervisory board must oversee the work of the committees.[615] For example, even though the audit committee has the same rights to information as the supervisory board, forming a committee can never relieve the board of its supervisory duties. There is no special form of reporting, but the committees must regularly report their work to the full board, which may request disclosure of comprehensive information from the committee at any time.

§ 300 Audit committee

Although the Stock Corporation Act does not require the formation of particular committees, it does nonetheless prominently address the competences of the audit committee in case such a body is formed. In this respect, the Stock Corporation Act sets forth obligatory (minimum) tasks and duties. An audit committee must supervise the company's accounting process, the effectiveness of its internal control systems, risk management and internal auditing system, as well as supervise its year end-audit. Furthermore, the audit committee must propose to the supervisory board plenum a suitable auditor as candidate for the following year's year-end audit. As regards its composition, the audit committee must include one independent accounting expert.[616]

2.   Scope of delegation
§ 301 Limitations

There are certain powers that the supervisory board cannot delegate to committees. For example, the board cannot delegate control of the organizational form and working methods of the supervisory board. Other non-delegable tasks include:[617] appointing and removing management board members and the management board chairmen, deciding on the compensation of management board members, issuing rules of procedure for the management board, consenting to the payment of an interim dividend, approving and reviewing the annual financial statements and consolidated financial statements (including the annual report, business report and proposal for the appropriation of profits), review of the dependency report[618], electing and removing the supervisory board chairman and their deputies, calling a general shareholders'

---

613   Mitbestimmungsgesetz [MitbestG] [Co-Determination Act] 1976, § 27, ¶ 3 (F.R.G.).
614   *Cf.* § 242 and § 247.
615   *Cf.* Aktiengesetz [AktG] [Stock Corporation Act] 1965, § 107, ¶ 3, sentence 4 (F.R.G.).
616   *Cf.* § 212.
617   *Cf.* Aktiengesetz [AktG] [Stock Corporation Act] 1965, § 107, ¶ 3, sentence 3 (F.R.G.).
618   Aktiengesetz [AktG] [Stock Corporation Act] 1965, § 314 (F.R.G.) requires the management board to submit a report on the company's dealings with affiliated companies.

meeting, deciding on matters that require the consent of the supervisory board as specified in the articles of association and adopting resolutions on the supervisory board report and its submission to the management board.

§ 302 Revocation of delegations

The full board may decide to revoke powers delegated to committees at any time. This revocation may apply generally or to one particular matter.

3. Formation of committees

§ 303 Setup

On the formation of committees, a distinction should be drawn between the setup and their composition. Committees are formed and dissolved by resolution of a simple majority of the supervisory board plenum. Committees cannot dissolve themselves.

§ 304 Composition

The supervisory board has wide-ranging discretion concerning the number and identity of members appointed to a committee. A committee requires at least two members. A decision-making committee must have at least three members. The number of members does not need to be divisible by three.

The supervisory board does not need to name committee members at the time the committee is formed. After forming a committee, the board may reserve the selection of committee members for a later meeting.

All supervisory board members are eligible for election to a committee; they are not required to be representatives of the shareholders or the employees. The composition of committees may only be regulated by the supervisory board's rules of procedure. The supervisory board may override these provisions by a simple majority resolution.

Committee members should be selected according to their abilities. Even on co-determined supervisory boards, the employee representatives do not have per se a right to representation in the committees. They are not permitted to demand the election of an employee representative as long as there is an objective reason for not choosing such a representative. On the other hand, it is not permissible to deny employee representatives participation in committees in a discriminatory manner. In supervisory boards co-determined on a parity basis, the committees should as a rule contain employee representatives.

Currently, the mediation and audit committees are the only committees regulated by mandatory composition provisions under German law. The mediation committee must include the supervisory board chairman, deputy chairman, one shareholder representative and one employee representative. [619] These are statutory requirements that cannot be amended by the supervisory board. Shareholders and employees elect their representatives separately. Further,

---

619   Mitbestimmungsgesetz [MitbestG] [Co-Determination Act] 1976, § 27, ¶ 3 (F.R.G.).

the audit committee of listed AGs must include at least one supervisory board member that is independent and competent in accounting and/or auditing matters.[620]

§ 305 Departure of individual members

Removing committee members from office is possible by resolution of the supervisory board. Supervisory board members who lose their supervisory board mandate automatically cease to be a committee member. This is particularly important for decision-making committees because a three-member decision-making committee can no longer make decisions if a member departs. Substitute members replacing former members do not automatically take the place of departing committee members on the committee.

Committee members may also resign from their posts. Untimely resignation may constitute a violation of duty prompting damage claims of the company under certain circumstances.

4.   Internal committee rules
§ 306 Introduction

The internal committee rules are generally similar to those of the supervisory board.

§ 307 Legal sources

The procedural rules for committees have multiple sources. The articles of association may regulate individual procedural issues for the committees. Unless the articles or the law specifies otherwise, the supervisory board's rules of procedure may establish committee rules of procedure as well. The committee may issue its own rules of procedure if there are no other procedural rule sources. The supervisory board can intervene in a committee's procedural issues at any time.

§ 308 Term of committees

If a committee is formed to address a specific task (*e.g.*, determine the supervisory board's position in a hostile takeover situation), then the committee dissolves upon the completion of its task. The supervisory board has the right to dissolve a committee early, *e.g.*, if it becomes apparent the committee is not able to perform the task for which it was created.

§ 309 Committee chairman

There is generally no legal requirement for committees to have a chairman. The mediation committee is an exception. By law, this committee must have a chairman,[621] unless the mediation committee itself decides otherwise. The supervisory board may determine that a committee should have a chairman and can appoint a chairman when forming a committee. If the board does not pass any specific regulations, then the committee itself may elect its chairman and deputy chairman by a simple majority.

---

620   Aktiengesetz [AktG] [Stock Corporation Act] 1965, § 107, ¶ 4 (F.R.G.).
621   Mitbestimmungsgesetz [MitbestG] [Co-Determination Act] 1976, § 27, ¶ 3 (F.R.G.).

§ 310 Committee meetings

The rules for committee meetings and supervisory board meetings are similar.

Committee invitation rules are the same as those for supervisory board meetings,[622] *e.g.*, the chairman of the committee is usually responsible for invitations. The chairman also ensures that all relevant documents and the agenda are forwarded to the committee members before the meetings so that they are able to prepare with sufficient time. In exceptional cases, an individual committee member is entitled, or even obligated, to call a meeting of the committee if the meeting is necessary for the committee to continue its work in the proper manner.

Given that every supervisory board member has the right to attend committee meetings, unless the chairman of the supervisory board determines otherwise, all supervisory board members must be notified of the dates of the committee meetings. Upon request, the agenda must also be made available to any supervisory board members who are not on the committee. If the supervisory board chairman prohibits supervisory board members who are not on a committee from attending a particular meeting of that committee, notice of the meeting and its agenda need to be given only to committee members.[623]

The committee chairman chairs committee meetings. In the chairman's absence, the deputy chairman chairs the meeting. In the event of a tie vote, the committee chairman may be granted a second vote. Granting such a right in the articles of association or rules of procedure is advisable because it allows resolutions to be passed in spite of a stalemate.

§ 311 Attendees

Generally, all supervisory board members may attend committee meetings, but cannot vote unless they are members of the committee. This right of attendance should only be exercised in exceptional cases to avoid unduly complicating the committee's work.

Only the supervisory board chairman has the power to exclude individual supervisory board members from attending committee meetings.[624] Even though this right cannot be set aside, the supervisory board chairman may not arbitrarily exclude supervisory board members, *e.g.*, only the employee representatives, from participating at committee meetings. The chairman must base each exclusion on appropriate grounds and should limit an exclusion to individual cases.

A committee may demand that members of the management board attend its meetings. The committee chairman should issue the invitation. Other persons permitted to attend supervisory board meetings may also attend committee meetings, *e.g.*, experts, special auditors and persons taking minutes. If the articles of association permit, committee members prevented from attending may appoint a third person to read out their declarations and motions. Proxies may also take part in adopting resolutions on behalf of the absent committee member by

---

622 *Cf.* §§ 279 *et seq.*
623 Aktiengesetz [AktG] [Stock Corporation Act] 1965, § 109, ¶ 2 (F.R.G.) analogously.
624 Aktiengesetz [AktG] [Stock Corporation Act] 1965, § 109, ¶ 2 (F.R.G.).

submitting the latter's vote in writing.[625]

§ 312 Committee resolutions

Only committees with three or more members may make a decision in place of the full board. In order to adopt a resolution, at least three members must participate in the vote, including abstentions. The articles of association and the supervisory board's rules of procedure may contain more detailed regulations regarding committee quorums, *e.g.*, a minimum number of members present or a qualified majority. If such regulations do not exist, at least half of the committee members should be present to adopt resolutions.

The articles or the rules of procedure may stipulate the level of majority required to adopt a resolution. The supervisory board's rules of procedure should specify the required majority when the committee is formed or earlier. If neither the articles nor the rules of procedure specify a required majority, a simple majority suffices.

§ 313 Minutes of meetings

Minutes must be kept of committee meetings, including information about all resolutions. All supervisory board members have the right to inspect the minutes of committee meetings. Supervisory board members only lose this right if the supervisory board chairman excludes them from participating in a committee meeting.

V. Rights and responsibilities of supervisory board members

§ 314 Introduction

The basic competences of the supervisory board are attributed to the board as a whole. Each supervisory board member has both a right and a duty to actively and diligently participate in supervisory board matters. Supervisory board members have various enforcement rights to preserve their participation rights. Supervisory board members that fail to perform their duties may become liable to the company. In some circumstances, supervisory board members may even face criminal liability.

A. Rights and responsibilities

§ 315 Equal rights

Generally, all members of the supervisory board have the same rights and duties. In particular, all members have a duty to act in the best interest of the company, irrespective of who elected or appointed them. All members have also the same rights to information and participation. Supervisory board decisions cannot discriminate against employee representatives in any form, particularly when filling committee seats. Finally, the vote of each supervisory board member is generally equal.

---

625   Aktiengesetz [AktG] [Stock Corporation Act] 1965, § 108, ¶ 3, sentence 1 (F.R.G.).

Only the supervisory board chairman has certain additional rights and duties. The chairman receives important reports from the management board[626] and forwards them to the other supervisory board members. The chairman may, at his discretion, prohibit a supervisory board member from attending a committee meeting. The supervisory board chairman may also cast a tie-breaking vote in supervisory boards co-determined on a parity basis or if the articles of association provide the chairman with such right.

§ 316 Duty to participate
All supervisory board members must participate and engage in the undertakings of the supervisory board. Most notably, they must attend supervisory board meetings regularly. In advance of meetings, board members must meticulously study any information provided by the company and must, if necessary, request additional information to understand upcoming agenda items. Supervisory board members also have an obligation to cooperate with each other whenever necessary, *e.g.*, providing full and timely notice to other members of any relevant news they became aware of.

§ 317 Independent mandate
The supervisory board members are independent representatives committed to the company's best interest. All supervisory board members are free to make their own decisions and cannot be instructed how to decide. Even if a majority shareholder is in a position to appoint all shareholder representatives, those representatives must vote in the company's interest, not in the interest of the majority shareholder. In particular, supervisory board members violate their obligations if they benefit certain shareholder groups to the detriment of the company's interest.

§ 318 Prohibition of deputizing in the supervisory board
Further, supervisory board members must carry out their duties in person. Deputies cannot represent them. If board members cannot attend a meeting, they may send a messenger but such messengers cannot participate in any decision-making.[627] Supervisory board members may only engage external consultants if neither the supervisory nor the management board can resolve the relevant issue.

§ 319 Duty of loyalty
Each member of the supervisory board owes the company a duty of loyalty. This duty requires members to safeguard the interests and welfare of the company. The supervisory board member may not use the supervisory board position to pursue either personal or third party interests to the detriment of the company.

This duty is particularly relevant with respect to conflicts of interest. Conflicted board members must pursue all actions in the company's best interest when acting as a supervisory board member. The supervisory board member with a conflict of interest must avoid a violation of the duty of loyalty by refraining from participating in decisions, voting, or otherwise influencing

---

626 *Cf.* §§ 96 *et seq.* for the reporting duty of the management board.
627 *Cf.* § 294.

supervisory board actions relating to the issue which conflicts the member. The appropriate scope of a supervisory board member's restraint depends on the details of the actual conflict. If the conflict of interest is lasting and impairs the board member's ability to perform any requisite duties on a long-term basis, the member must resign from the board. In any case, a supervisory board member must disclose a potential conflict of interest to the supervisory board early on so that the board is aware of this situation. The Corporate Governance Code also requires the supervisory board to disclose any past or ongoing conflict of interest in its annual report to the shareholders.[628]

Supervisory board members typically exercise their position on the supervisory board as additional office, so the scope of their fiduciary duties is somewhat limited if they are acting outside their role as a supervisory board member. In such a scenario, a supervisory board member is not always obliged to give preference to the AG's interests, although he should still avoid harming the AG. In any case, actions of supervisory board members outside their supervisory board posts are inappropriate if they use confidential information from the AG or their influence within the AG to accomplish the acts.

B.   In particular: Confidentiality

§ 320 Overview
Supervisory board members receive confidential information from the management board, *e.g.*, confidential reports and advice. All supervisory board members have a duty to maintain the confidentiality of this information.[629] This duty not only prohibits disclosure of confidential information, but also bars any conduct that may enable third parties to acquire the information. The articles of association or rules of procedure cannot modify this duty.

§ 321 Scope and duration
The duty of confidentiality is particularly important with regard to operating and business secrets. Operating and business secrets include all information unknown to outsiders and that the company intends to remain unknown. The duty of confidentiality also applies to information about voting behavior, the outcome of notes on resolutions, and the discussions, positions and statements of individual persons attending supervisory board meetings. If the announcement of the subject of advice includes confidential information, the announcement itself must also be kept confidential. Supervisory board members must also observe strict confidentiality when the rights of third parties are concerned, particularly during discussions regarding personnel decisions.

The duty of confidentiality does not end when the supervisory board member's term of office expires unless the interests of the company no longer require secrecy. Often the rules of procedure require a supervisory board member to return confidential documents to the company

---

628   Deutscher Corporate Governance Kodex [DCGK] [German Corporate Governance Code] 2010, 5.5.3 (F.R.G.).
629   Aktiengesetz [AktG] [Stock Corporation Act] 1965, § 116, sentence 2 (F.R.G.).

upon expiration of the term of office. Otherwise, members leaving the supervisory board have to destroy confidential documents using any suitable means.

§ 322 Special rules for corporate groups

The duty of confidentiality for corporate groups extends to the secrets and confidential information of affiliated companies because it is also in the interest of the parent company to keep internal issues of subsidiaries confidential. Members of the supervisory board of a subsidiary also must treat internal issues of the parent company as confidential.

§ 323 Consequences of violating the duty of confidentiality

Supervisory board members violating their duty of confidentiality may be liable to the company for damages.[630] The law does not allow supervisory board members any discretion in judging whether certain information should be kept confidential; this is assessed solely on the basis of objective corporate interests. Members are advised to exercise caution if they have any doubts about disclosing corporate information, as a violation of confidentiality is also punishable by criminal law.[631] Criminal sentences are generally a fine, up to two years imprisonment for violations in connection with a listed company, or up to one year imprisonment for violations in connection with a non-listed company. One year is added to the maximum sentence if the perpetrator was paid to divulge the information, sought personal enrichment, or intended to damage the company. The offense is only prosecuted if so requested by the management board.

C. Additional responsibilities for board members in listed companies

§ 324 Prohibition of insider trading

In addition to the confidentiality obligations set forth above, supervisory board members must abide by the insider trading rules. This obviously applies to supervisory board members of listed companies, but in other companies the supervisory board members may also receive confidential insider information (e.g., information regarding a listed subsidiary). The Securities Trading Act prohibits trading in insider securities that utilizes insider information, inciting others to do so, and passing on insider information or making it available to another party.[632] In this context, supervisory board members often face problems if they plan to pass on information to third persons. Passing on insider information to persons like secretaries, personal assistants or legal advisers that are consulted by the supervisory board member in the ordinary course is generally permissible. Providing information to other persons is however generally prohibited. For example, an employee representative is not permitted to disclose insider information to the works council or trade union representatives. Similarly, a supervisory board member who has been appointed at the request of a large shareholder may not pass on insider information to the management or other representatives of such shareholder.

---

630   Cf. Aktiengesetz [AktG] [Stock Corporation Act] 1965, § 93, ¶ 1, sentence 2, § 116 (F.R.G.).
631   Aktiengesetz [AktG] [Stock Corporation Act] 1965, § 404 (F.R.G.).
632   For details with respect to "insider information" cf. also §§ 125 et seq. and § 189.

§ 325 Dealings in shares of the company

Supervisory board members generally must disclose to the AG and to the BaFin any personal dealings and dealings of closely related persons in the AG's shares or related financial instruments within five business days. The company must then publish this information. Intentional or reckless violation of this duty constitutes an administrative offense punishable by a fine of up to EUR 1 million.[633] The duty is violated if the publication or notification is not made, or is made incorrectly, or incompletely, or is not made on a timely basis. If the violation was intentional and affects the price of the financial instrument, then it is punishable by a criminal fine or a prison sentence of up to five years.[634]

D. Consequences of a violation of duties

§ 326 Overview

If a supervisory board member violates his duties, this may entail various consequences. Apart from corporate law consequences like the denial by the shareholders to discharge the act of the respective supervisory board member in the next ordinary shareholders' meeting or his removal from office, supervisory board members may also become liable for damages to the company.[635]

Theoretically, in special circumstances, supervisory board members may also be held liable by third parties under tort law.[636] Thus far, such claims generally have not been successful, as the burden of proof makes it difficult to enforce such claims; however, claims may be more likely to succeed if the wrongdoing also triggers criminal investigations whose findings may be used in a subsequent civil trial for damages. It is quite common for the public prosecutor to allow the company and its legal advisors access to the prosecution files in preparation for civil damages claims.

Finally, the supervisory board member may face other legal consequences, such as criminal liability or administrative fines, for illegal actions. The most significant criminal charges are embezzlement (*Untreue*) and a violation of insider trading rules.[637]

1. Corporate law consequences
§ 327 No discharge of the acts of supervisory board member

Part of the agenda of the annual shareholders' meeting is the motion to discharge the acts of the supervisory board members for the last financial year. Although the wording may suggest otherwise, a discharge of acts does not preclude the company from asserting claims against

---

633   Gesetz über den Wertpapierhandel [WpHG] [Securities Trading Act], 1994, § 39, ¶ 2, nos. 5 a), b), ¶ 4 (F.R.G.).

634   Gesetz über den Wertpapierhandel [WpHG] [Securities Trading Act], 1994, § 38, ¶ 2, § 39, ¶ 2, no. 11, § 20a, ¶ 1, no. 1 (F.R.G.).

635   Aktiengesetz [AktG] [Stock Corporation Act] 1965, §§ 116, 93, ¶ 2 (F.R.G.).

636   Aktiengesetz [AktG] [Stock Corporation Act] 1965, § 117, ¶ 2, sentence 1, § 317, ¶ 2, 1, sentence 1 (F.R.G.); Bürgerliches Gesetzbuch [BGB] [Civil Code] 1896, § 823 (F.R.G.).

637   *Cf.* § 189 for the management board.

the supervisory board member for violations of duty in the past. Rather, the resolution is an indication of confidence in the supervisory board members by the shareholders.[638] If a supervisory board member has violated his duties the shareholders may refrain from approving his discharge of acts, thereby indicating disapproval with such supervisory board member. Other direct consequences do not result from the refusal.

§ 328 Removal from office

As a more serious consequence of violations, the supervisory board member may be removed from office by shareholders' resolution or by the court.[639]

2. Liability to the company
§ 329 Overview

Supervisory board members have a duty to fulfill all their responsibilities with the care of a diligent and prudent supervisory board member. Board members are liable to the company for damages resulting from a culpable failure to meet this standard of care.[640] Members of the supervisory board who violate their obligations are jointly and severally liable to the company. In the past, damage claims were rarely brought against supervisory board members unless the company became insolvent. Today, supervisory board members face a considerably higher risk that the company will enforce damage claims.

§ 330 Standard of care

Liability for damages to the AG presumes culpability, e.g., intent or negligence, of the supervisory board member. Board members who observe the standard of due care of a diligent and prudent supervisory board member are not culpable. However, in the event of a dispute as to whether a member of the supervisory board observed the required standard of care, the burden of proof to show diligence and no fault is on the member of the supervisory board.[641]

In order to meet the standard, supervisory board members must have the requisite qualifications necessary to understand and assess the ordinary business transactions of the company without external assistance.[642] If an individual accepts a position on the supervisory board without this minimum professional aptitude, the member may be liable for damages. Once a person has accepted to become supervisory board member, he has to comprehensively inform himself about the company, its capital and organizational structure, its business and its corporate planning.

Further, each supervisory board member must diligently participate in supervisory board tasks and ensure that the board fulfills its duties properly. Thus, supervisory board members must prepare themselves for board meetings thoroughly. For example, they should diligently study the reports provided by the management and any other information necessary to participate in meetings or exercise adequate supervision. If a supervisory board member becomes aware of

---

638 Aktiengesetz [AktG] [Stock Corporation Act] 1965, § 120, ¶ 2 (F.R.G.).
639 Cf. §§ 232 et seq.
640 Aktiengesetz [AktG] [Stock Corporation Act] 1965, §§ 116, 93, ¶ 2 (F.R.G.).
641 Aktiengesetz [AktG] [Stock Corporation Act] 1965, §§ 116, 93, ¶ 2 (F.R.G.).
642 Cf. § 211.

information material to the supervisory board's decisions, the member must provide the information to the other board members. The level of involvement expected of supervisory board members increases if the company's circumstances require heightened attention (*e.g.*, during times of financial difficulties).

To the extent the supervisory board takes a forward-looking business decision, *e.g.*, approving a transaction that is subject to its consent or appointing a new management board member, it may rely on the business judgment rule. Hereunder, the supervisory board does not violate its duties if it reasonably believed to act in the company's best interest, provided that its decision is based on adequate information and not motivated by personal interests. In order to be able to successfully assert the business judgment rule, the supervisory board should diligently document its information-gathering and consideration process.

§ 331 Individual shortcoming

Liability for a supervisory board member can only arise in the event of an individual shortcoming of such member. As a result, the individual's knowledge or expertise is relevant when determining if a supervisory board member violated the duty of care.

If the supervisory board as a whole violates its duties, it is necessary that an individual board member failed to meet his individual obligations on the board in order to become liable. Consequently, board members must actively challenge any illegal or invalid opinion, resolution, or other action of the board. For example, if a supervisory board member believes a resolution to be invalid, merely abstaining from the vote is insufficient. Board members must actively raise their concerns and vote against proposals they oppose. Supervisory board members can reduce the risk of liability by ensuring that any concerns are reflected in the minutes of the meeting. In certain situations, the supervisory board member may even be required to challenge a resolution in court; however, this is reserved to extraordinary situations that could lead to material negative consequences for the company because public discussion of supervisory board disputes should generally be avoided.

If the violation of duty occurred in a supervisory board committee, all the members of that committee may be held responsible. Actions by a preparatory committee may result in liability for non-committee members as well, unless it was reasonable for non-committee members to rely on the findings of the committee. If the committee is a resolving committee, non-committee members may only be held liable if indications of shortcomings existed or the committee's work lacked proper supervision.

By statute, the burden of proof is on the supervisory board member being sued to prove either that all duties were fulfilled with the care of a diligent and prudent supervisory board member, or that the damages would also have occurred even if the duties were fulfilled. As mentioned above, to the extent a decision of the supervisory board is a business decision, the supervisory board may also rely on the business judgment rule.[643]

---

643   *Cf.* § 330.

§ 332 Limitation, liability exclusion, waiver, settlement

The statute of limitations and the rules regarding mitigation or waiver of liability are identical to those applicable to claims against the management board, *e.g.*, the right to claim damages expires after five years and any limitation on a supervisory board member's liability in the articles of association or by separate agreement is not permissible. The company can generally only waive claims three years after the violation of duty and if the waiver is approved by a shareholders' resolution with at least 90% approval.[644]

The company may purchase D&O insurance for its supervisory board members. The Corporate Governance Code recommends a deductible of at least 10% of the damage which might be capped but not below one and a half times the yearly compensation.[645] By contrast, a 10% deductible is mandatory for members of the management board under the Stock Coporation Act.[646]

§ 333 Enforcement of claims against supervisory board member

If a supervisory board member violates his duties, the management board generally must pursue damage claims on behalf of the company. To overcome potential reluctance of the management board to pursue such claims, German law provides for several instruments by which shareholders may either compel the management board to act or appoint a special representative to pursue damage claims against supervisory board members. Additionally, under certain circumstances, shareholders may themselves file damage claims on behalf of the company, if the latter fails to enforce damage claims against the supervisory board.[647]

E.   Enforcement of rights

§ 334 Protection of individual rights

As mentioned previously, individual supervisory board members have the right and the obligation to participate in the work of the supervisory board. Consequently, supervisory board members have the right to file claims against the company to safeguard and enforce their participation rights. For example, if the chairman of the supervisory board prohibits a member from attending a committee meeting, withholds information on personnel committee resolutions, or fails to forward a management board report, then the aggrieved member may file an action against the company as a last resort.

In addition, individual supervisory board members have certain rights *vis-à-vis* the management board and the shareholders. Individual supervisory board members may demand that the

---

644 *Cf.* identical rules for management board members under § 148 *et seq.* regarding the statute of limitations for the liability.

645 Deutscher Corporate Governance Kodex [DCGK] [German Corporate Governance Code] 2010, 3.8, ¶ 2 (F.R.G.).

646 *Cf.* Aktiengesetz [AktG] [Stock Corporation Act] 1965, § 93, ¶ 2, sentence 3 (F.R.G.).

647 For details of these various instruments that also apply for claims against management board members *cf.* §§ 150 *et seq.*

management board supply reports on corporate matters to the supervisory board.[648] Supervisory board members have the right and the duty to attend shareholders' meetings.[649] Members may also enforce these rights against the company.

The law also explicitly provides each individual supervisory board member with certain statutory rights to file certain actions or applications, namely to ensure that the supervisory board or management board is properly composed or to determine whether a shareholders' resolution is void. Individual supervisory board members may also file actions for avoidance and annulment of the annual financial statements. Under certain additional conditions also other shareholders' resolutions can be challenged by any member of the supervisory board by means of an action for avoidance and annulment.[650]

In addition, a member of the supervisory board may also challenge the validity of the board's own resolutions by an action for declaratory judgment. This action has to be filed against the company.

§ 335 Protection of rights of the supervisory board as a whole

Supervisory board members are generally not entitled to file actions on behalf of the supervisory board as a whole. If there are disputes between supervisory board members on whether a claim should be filed, it must be discussed and decided internally within the supervisory board. Individual board members may not externalize such conflict by filing an individual claim on behalf of the supervisory board.

§ 336 Protection of personal rights

Finally, supervisory board members have certain personal entitlements that are not directly associated with exercising their competencies as members of the supervisory board, most notably the right for compensation and reimbursement of their expenses. The supervisory board members may bring actions against the company, represented by the management board, to enforce these rights.

F.   Compensation

§ 337 Introduction

Different rules apply for setting the compensation of the first supervisory board following the incorporation of the AG and for all supervisory boards thereafter.

---

648   Cf. Aktiengesetz [AktG] [Stock Corporation Act] 1965, § 90, ¶ 3, sentence 2 (F.R.G.).
649   Cf. § 261.
650   Aktiengesetz [AktG] [Stock Corporation Act] 1965, § 245, no. 5 (F.R.G.).

1.   Compensation in existing companies

§ 338 Supervisory board compensation

Supervisory board members have a right to claim compensation for their activities only if provided by the articles of association or approved by the shareholders.[651] Otherwise, the members may only demand reimbursement of expenses considered necessary in light of the circumstances.[652] Neither the management board nor the supervisory board has the authority to award compensation to supervisory board members.

If attendance fees are reimbursed in excess of the costs associated with attendance, they count as compensation. These fees accordingly either have to be provided for by the articles of association or approved by the shareholders' meeting. Shareholder approval is not needed for the payment of premiums for the supervisory board's D&O insurance because the insurance is considered a company benefit and not compensation.

§ 339 Level of compensation

The compensation authorized by the articles of association or the shareholders may be either specific to individual supervisory board members or an overall lump sum to be divided by the supervisory board among its members. The latter option is only permitted if the articles explicitly allow it. The Corporate Governance Code recommends individualizing and itemizing the amounts of payments made to supervisory board members.[653] The shareholders may decide by a simple majority to reduce the supervisory board compensation.[654]

The level of compensation should be appropriate considering the members' tasks and the financial situation of the company.[655] The Corporate Governance Code specifies similar requirements.[656] The Code also recommends adjusting the compensation according to whether the members serve on any committees and whether they chair any committees. Differentiating between compensation levels for shareholder and employee representatives is not permitted.

Fixed annual compensation becomes due at the end of the financial year, unless provided otherwise. Members who serve on the board for less than a year may only claim compensation *pro rata* for the time they have served as members.

§ 340 Bonus payments

The articles of association or a shareholders' meeting resolution may tie a portion of the compensation to the company's profits. Such variable bonus payments are governed by mandatory rules for calculating the bonus payments and prohibiting other arrangements.[657] In such a case,

---

651   *Cf.* Aktiengesetz [AktG] [Stock Corporation Act] 1965, § 113, ¶ 1, sentence 2 (F.R.G.).
652   Bürgerliches Gesetzbuch [BGB] [Civil Code] 1896, §§ 670, 675 (F.R.G.) analogously.
653   Deutscher Corporate Governance Kodex [DCGK] [German Corporate Governance Code] 2010, 5.4.6, ¶ 3, sentence 1 (F.R.G.).
654   Aktiengesetz [AktG] [Stock Corporation Act] 1965, § 113, ¶ 1, sentence 4 (F.R.G.).
655   Aktiengesetz [AktG] [Stock Corporation Act] 1965, § 113, ¶ 1, sentence 3 (F.R.G.).
656   Deutscher Corporate Governance Kodex [DCGK] [German Corporate Governance Code] 2010, 5.4.6, ¶ 1 (F.R.G.).
657   Aktiengesetz [AktG] [Stock Corporation Act] 1965, § 113, ¶ 3 (F.R.G.).

the bonus payments are determined on the basis of balance sheet profits, which are calculated according to the profit for the year, increased by the profit carried forward and withdrawals from retained earnings and reduced by the loss carry-forward or allocations to retained earnings. The balance sheet profits must be reduced by at least 4% of the amount paid in respect of the par value of the shares. The calculation depends on the nominal value of the shares or percentage of the company's nominal share capital, excluding a possible agio. This calculation method should also be used for any other form of performance-based compensation of the supervisory board, *e.g.*, payments linked to earnings before taxes or before interest and taxes, cash flow, or profits per share.

As an alternative, it is also possible to tie the bonus payment to other parameters, *e.g.*, to the dividend paid to the company's shareholders.

§ 341 Impermissible forms of compensation

Stock options may not be granted to supervisory board members as compensation because neither conditional capital nor treasury shares may be utilized to deliver shares upon exercise of such options and supervisory board members are excluded by law from receiving convertible bonds and bonds with warrants as compensation.[658]

Furthermore, supervisory board members cannot receive bonus payments based on the market value of the company's shares, such as phantom stocks and stock appreciation rights, despite the fact that these do not impinge on shareholder subscription rights. This is due to the boards' monitoring responsibilities. The rationale behind this is that if the compensation depends on the value of the company's stock, there may be a risk that the supervisory board will concentrate too much on maintaining high share prices in the short term in order to receive higher compensation payments. The supervisory board's primary task is to ensure the long-term success of the company, which is not always compatible with keeping the share price high in the short term.

§ 342 Reimbursement of expenses

German law provides for the reimbursement of expenses of members of the supervisory board.[659] These reimbursements do not constitute compensation and therefore, no special provisions in the articles of association or resolutions by the shareholders are necessary. The company is only required to reimburse expenses that prudent supervisory board members would consider necessary under the circumstances. The standard for necessary expenses depends on the individual member's usual activities and company practice.

Expenses eligible for reimbursement include accommodation and board, travel costs, telephone charges, postage, and similar out of pocket expenses. The cost of attending separate preparatory meetings for employee and shareholder representatives should also be reimbursed. Reimbursement may be made as a lump sum.

---

658   Aktiengesetz [AktG] [Stock Corporation Act] 1965, § 71, ¶ 2, no. 2, § 192, ¶ 2, no. 3 (F.R.G.).
659   *Cf.* Bürgerliches Gesetzbuch [BGB] [Civil Code] 1896, §§ 670, 675 (F.R.G.) analogously.

Personnel costs, *e.g.*, for secretarial services or a personal assistant, are not normally reimbursed. The same applies to the costs of attending seminars and training courses covering knowledge needed for supervisory board members to fulfill their duties. The law assumes that all supervisory board members already have all requisite knowledge. Exceptions may be made where specialized knowledge or skills are acquired.

2.   Compensation of the first supervisory board
§ 343 Overview

The articles of association cannot set in advance the compensation levels of the first supervisory board. The shareholders must therefore resolve on the compensation of the members of the first supervisory board after the discharge of the acts of the supervisory board.[660] If the AG is a newly founded company, any resolutions on supervisory board compensation passed before the discharge of its acts are void. If the AG is formed by a change in corporate form and a supervisory board existed in the previous form, then the existing compensation rules remain in force.[661]

3.   Taxation of compensation
§ 344 Taxation of supervisory board members

A supervisory board member's compensation is subject to German taxation (*e.g.*, personal income tax, a solidarity surcharge thereon and, if applicable, church tax) irrespective of the place of residence of the supervisory board member.[662] Taxable income generally includes all payments in kind and monetary payments. Personal income tax is an annual tax. The compensation is taxed in the calendar year in which it is received by the supervisory board member.

A supervisory board member being resident in Germany will generally be required to make quarterly tax pre-payments that correspond to the estimated annual tax liability. Such payments will be applied against the income tax liability of the respective supervisory board member at year-end. The combined progressive tax rates range from approximately 14.77% up to approximately 50%.

A supervisory board member not having his residence or habitual abode in Germany is subject to a special flat tax of 30%. [663] In this case the tax is withheld by the AG and directly remitted to the tax authorities.[664] Travel costs paid by the AG to the supervisory board member only constitute taxable income if the reimbursement exceeds the actual costs incurred (this applies to costs regarding traveling and accomodation) or the lump sum provided by the Income Tax Act (this applies to food costs).[665] Such lump sums generally range between EUR 6 and EUR 24 per calendar day, depending on the duration of the travel.[666]

---

660   Aktiengesetz [AktG] [Stock Corporation Act] 1965, § 113, ¶ 2 (F.R.G.).
661   Umwandlungsgesetz [UmwG] [Merger and Reorganization Act], 1994, § 197, sentence 2, § 203 (F.R.G.).
662   *Cf.* Einkommensteuergesetz [EStG] [Income Tax Act] 1934, § 18, ¶ 1, no. 3, § 49, ¶ 1, no. 3, (F.R.G.).
663   Einkommensteuergesetz [EStG] [Income Tax Act] 1934, § 50a, ¶ 2, sentence 1 (F.R.G.).
664   Einkommensteuergesetz [EStG] [Income Tax Act] 1934, § 50a, ¶ 5 (F.R.G.).
665   Einkommensteuergesetz [EStG] [Income Tax Act] 1934, § 50a, ¶ 2, sentence 2 (F.R.G.).
666   Einkommensteuergesetz [EStG] [Income Tax Act] 1934, § 4, ¶ 5, sentence 1, no. 5, (F.R.G.).

As the income tax on compensation for non-resident supervisory board members is withheld at source by the AG, the respective supervisory board member cannot apply any income-related expenses against the compensation in order to reduce the tax base. However, there are exceptions for supervisory board members who are EU citizens or citizens of the European Economic Area and are resident or have their habitual abode within the territory of one of these countries: If the supervisory board member duly documents income-related expenses or if such expenses were reimbursed by the AG, the AG may offset such expenses when withholding the tax.[667] Alternatively, supervisory board members who are EU citizens or citizens of the European Economic Area and who are resident or have their habitual abode within the territory of one of these countries may opt for a tax assessment at year-end and may declare their income-related expenses within the assessment procedure.

For supervisory board members who are neither EU citizens nor citizens of the European Economic Area or who are not resident or have not a habitual abode within the territory of one of these countries the 30% withholding tax is final and not subject to further assessment. Applicable double tax treaties may, however, provide for special rules.

Without going into details of international tax law, it has to be noted that potentially Germany and the home state of the supervisory board member (based on criteria such as citizenship or residence) may both claim the right to tax the supervisory board member's compensation. Such double taxation is in practice often mitigated by the application of double tax treaties that Germany has concluded with many countries. In many cases, both countries (e.g., Germany and the state of residence) will levy tax on the board member's compensation but the state of residence will deduct the tax withheld in Germany from the board member's foreign tax liability.

Both resident and non-resident supervisory board members generally qualify as entrepreneurs for German value added tax purposes. In consequence, the compensation is subject to VAT that must be remitted by the supervisory board member to the tax authorities. VAT generally is borne by the AG who may be able to deduct such VAT paid under the input VAT regime. To avoid doubts the payment of VAT should be addressed in connection with the appointment of the supervisory board member.

§ 345 Taxation of the German AG

As a general rule only, half of the compensation paid by the AG to the supervisory board member may be deducted as operating expenses by the AG and offsets the AG's taxable profit.[668] Separately reimbursed expenses may generally be deducted from profits in full.

---

667   Einkommensteuergesetz [EStG] [Income Tax Act] 1934, § 50a, ¶ 3 (F.R.G.).
668   Körperschaftsteuergesetz [KStG] [Corporate Income Tax Act], 1976, § 10, no. 4 (F.R.G.).

VI. Contracts between the AG and its supervisory board members

§ 346 Introduction

Subject to certain restrictions, AGs can enter into contracts of any kind with their supervisory board members. Service agreements, however, are not valid without approval by the full supervisory board.[669] Service agreements are agreements that require one party to render services without being bound to specific instructions and establish a payment obligation for the other party in exchange. Consulting and advisory agreements are typical examples of service agreements with supervisory board members. Employment agreements (*e.g.*, of the employee representatives on the supervisory board), however, do not require such approval.[670] Contracts granting compensation to supervisory board members for activities that are part of the range of duties owed as a member of the supervisory board, however, will be considered a "hidden compensation" and be void, irrespective of an approval by the full supervisory board.

§ 347 Avoidance of "hidden compensation"

The supervisory board must therefore examine whether the activity in question is actually a supervisory board activity. As a rule, the services owed to the company by the supervisory board member are fully reimbursed by the member's compensation unless the shareholders or articles of association provide otherwise. A separate service agreement must therefore govern an activity not included within the area of supervisory board tasks.

In some cases, it may be difficult to distinguish between supervisory board activity and activities to be rendered pursuant to a consulting contract. The extent to which the service is time-consuming or complicated is not relevant. Even highly intensive forward-looking consulting services rendered for the management board are part of the supervisory board's responsibility as a form of preventive oversight. The distinction is therefore drawn on the basis of the nature of the activity. Separately compensated activities to be performed by a supervisory board member must be related to a specialized area outside the supervisory board's area of oversight, *e.g.* activities relating to day-to-day business decisions.

The above principles also apply to consulting services rendered by supervisory board members for companies controlled by the AG. In addition, the courts have expanded the scope of these rules to advisory firms in which a supervisory board member holds a significant equity interest.

§ 348 Supervisory board approval

The supervisory board approval requirement for service agreements between a supervisory board member and the company aims to prevent unduly high payments and inappropriately influencing supervisory board members. An agreement that has not been approved by the supervisory board is null and void. Such approval should be obtained before the agreement is executed as it is unclear whether an approval after execution will suffice. The supervisory board approves

---

669   Aktiengesetz [AktG] [Stock Corporation Act] 1965, § 114, ¶ 1 (F.R.G.).
670   *Cf.* Aktiengesetz [AktG] [Stock Corporation Act] 1965, § 114, ¶ 1 (F.R.G.).

an agreement by resolution. The resolution should specify the amount of the compensation or at least the approximate range or basis for the calculation of compensation. The supervisory board member involved in the agreement is not permitted to vote. The decision regarding approval may be delegated to a committee. In order to be valid, the supervisory board (or any committee granting the approval) must have received accurate and complete information on the agreement, generally by way of submission of a copy of the entire agreement.

§ 349 Consequences of inappropriately granted compensation

The company must be paid back any compensation for services not validly approved by the supervisory board.[671] Depending upon the specific circumstances, the supervisory board member may be able to claim some compensation based upon the principles of unjust enrichment if the company has received a financial benefit from the services.[672] If the supervisory board member was aware that the contract would or could not be approved, he cannot demand any payment from the company.[673] Offsetting his claims based upon unjust enrichment against the company's claim for repayment of the compensation is also not permitted.[674]

Management board members granting compensation to a supervisory board member without the requisite approval may be liable to the company for damages. For example, if the company's claim is worthless due to the supervisory board member's lack of solvency, the members of the management board of the company may be obliged to take the responsibility for the shortfall.

---

671   Aktiengesetz [AktG] [Stock Corporation Act] 1965, § 114, ¶ 2 (F.R.G.).
672   Bürgerliches Gesetzbuch [BGB] [Civil Code] 1896, §§ 812 *et seq.* (F.R.G.).
673   Bürgerliches Gesetzbuch [BGB] [Civil Code] 1896, § 812 (F.R.G.).
674   Aktiengesetz [AktG] [Stock Corporation Act] 1965, § 114, ¶ 2, sentence 2, 2. part (F.R.G.).

CHAPTER FOUR
BOARD MEMBERS
IN THE GERMAN SE

I. Introduction

§ 350 Societas Europaea

The Societas Europaea ("SE") is a European public limited company with a nominal share capital of at least EUR 120,000. The SE has been created by the European Union in an effort to facilitate the cooperation, combination and transfer of domicile of companies across the borders of individual European Union Member States by providing a uniform legal form of stock corporation throughout the European Union.

Although, the SE is a creature of European Union legislation, it still requires registration according to the national law of an European Union Member State. A German SE thus must be registered in the commercial register in Germany to come into existence.

Due to the hybrid status of an SE as an entity created by European legislation but registered under national law, an SE is governed by a combination of European Union legislation (Council Regulation (EC) No. 2157/2001 (the "SE-Regulation")) and national laws, as well as its articles of association. The national laws include the national SE implementation legislation,[675] and the provisions of the national corporate law of the country where the SE has its registered office, which in Germany is the Stock Corporation Act. As a result of this SE regime, SEs incorporated in different European Union Member States are subject to different legal rules. Notwithstanding its supranational origin, a German SE thus still is a German company.

Unlike an AG, an SE can only be formed if certain prerequisites are met. The formation of an SE typically requires an international aspect: The shareholders are located in different European Union Member States,[676] the SE is created by way of a merger of companies located in different European Union jurisdictions, the SE is the result of the conversion of an AG which has had one or more foreign subsidiaries for at least two years, or there are specific other cross-border elements. In practice, however, meeting the prerequisites for forming an SE rarely poses an obstacle if a company wishes to convert to an SE or a group of investors wish to form an SE. It is even possible today to acquire an "off-the-shelf" SE from a service provider, which can reduce the time otherwise necessary to form a new SE.

---

675 SE-Ausführungsgesetz [SEAG] [SE Implementation Act] 2004 (F.R.G.).
676 Including members of the European Economic Area, *e.g.*, Iceland, Liechtenstein and Norway.

The key differences between an SE and an AG relate to corporate governance. By contrast, the capital regime of the SE, including the structure of the share capital, the rights of shareholders, and the requirements for issuing new shares or reducing the share capital, is virtually identical to the capital regime of the AG.

From a tax perspective, an SE is generally treated as an AG. Differences in taxation can, however, arise in the international context, such as the transfer of the SE's registered office to another member state.

§ 351 Employee co-determination

An additional layer of complexity with respect to the formation of an SE is added by employee co-determination. Unlike AGs that meet certain size criteria,[677] German SEs are not subject to the statutory co-determination regime in Germany. To ensure adequate employee participation in the administration of an SE, the founders of the SE have to conduct a specifically regulated, complex and time-consuming negotiation process with representatives of the employees of the companies participating in the formation of the SE (including the employees of subsidiaries of the (future) SE) to determine the employee co-determination regime applicable to the SE.[678] If these negotiations are successful, a specific tailor-made co-determination system is created for the SE *in lieu* of the statutory provisions on co-determination. If, however, the negotiations on the future co-determination system fail within the period prescribed by law, the applicable national co-determination rules, in the case of conversion, to the entity being converted into an SE or, in other cases, to the companies participating in the formation of the SE will – subject to certain modifications – generally apply to the SE to safeguard the rights of the employees.[679]

Irrespective of whether a negotiated or statutory co-determination regime will apply to an SE, the SE will have to install a works' council. If the negotiated co-determination system so provides or if the statutory requirements for applying the German co-determination legislation are met,[680] employee representatives will become members of the supervisory board of the SE (or the administrative board of the SE in case of a one-tier SE).

§ 352 One-tier and two-tier system of corporate governance

The corporate laws of the Member States of the European Union provide for two basic corporate governance models for (national) stock corporations: The one-tier system and the two-tier system. In Germany, under the Stock Corporation Act, an AG must have a two-tier system. Thus, each AG must have a supervisory board in addition to the management board.[681] By contrast, the SE legislation gives an SE the option of choosing between the one-tier system and

---

677 *Cf.* §§ 197 *et seq.*

678 The rules applicable to the SE's co-determination are set forth in SE-Beteiligungsgesetz [SEBG] [SE Participation Act] 2004 (F.R.G.).

679 In the event that the employees' negotiating body resolves not to initiate negotiations on the co-determination rules applicable to the SE or to terminate such negotiations, the SE will generally not be subject to co-determination.

680 *Cf.* §§ 197 *et seq.*

681 *Cf.* § 4, § 7 and § 194.

the two-tier system. Thus, using the form of an SE makes it possible for a German corporate entity to adopt a board structure similar to stock corporations in the United States and other Anglo-Saxon jurisdictions.

In the one-tier system, also referred to as a unified system or board system, management and oversight functions are concentrated within one and the same body. On the one hand, not having a separate supervisory board can reduce costs and increase efficiency due to the smaller number of board members and the reduced administrative effort associated with operating only one corporate body. On the other hand, the one-tier system presents the challenge of integrating management and oversight functions into a single body. In addition, if the SE is subject to co-determination (whether by way of application of the statutory fallback rules or as a result of the co-determination negotiations), a one-tier system results in much more direct participation of the employees in the administration of the company. Whereas in an AG or a two-tier SE, the employees are only represented on the supervisory board, which has no responsibility for setting the corporate strategy and running the day-to-day business, in a one-tier SE, the employees are also represented on the administrative board (*Verwaltungsrat*) and thus are directly involved in the management of the company.

In practice, the two models have converged considerably. In the one-tier model, the task of managing the company on a day-to-day basis is regularly allocated to certain executive members of the administrative board who are overseen by, and with respect to important decisions require the consent of, the non-executive members of the administrative board. On the other hand, in the two-tier model, oversight and consent rights are exercised by the supervisory body, which is composed only of non-executive members.

Most large listed AGs, which have converted to an SE (including Allianz SE, BASF SE, GfK SE, MAN SE, Porsche Automobil Holding SE, Q-Cells SE and SGL Carbon SE), have retained the two-tier board structure. Several smaller companies that have changed their corporate form to an SE and some newly-formed SEs have, however, adopted the one-tier system (*e.g.*, Deichmann SE, Elster Group SE and Conrad Electronic SE). The one-tier system presents novel legal questions with respect to how the provisions of the Stock Corporation Act, which apply to SEs in addition to the special SE legislation, are to be interpreted with respect to a company that has only a single board. For large listed corporations with sizable boards, retaining the conventional two-tier structure thus generally means more legal certainty and less risk of creating conflicts with traditional corporate governance principles.

§ 353 Potential benefits and drawbacks of an SE

The legal form of an SE has several advantages compared to an AG. In particular, the SE offers more flexibility in structuring the corporate governance system of the company. First of all, the transformation into an SE provides an option to choose between the one-tier and the two-tier system of corporate governance. Furthermore, the rigid regime of the Co-Determination Act does not apply to an SE, and in a two-tier system the size of the supervisory body can be substantially reduced. In addition, the position of the CEO can be strengthened and the CEO can be given a veto right and/or a casting vote. Finally, there is no need to appoint a labor director on the management board of an SE. A non-legal benefit of operating as an SE is the enhancement of the European and international image of the company. An SE may also offer more flexibility for cross-border mergers and a change of domicile from one European Union Member State to another.

However, there are also certain drawbacks. Most notably, the formation of an SE involves a complex and lengthy transformation procedure, mainly due to the co-determination negotiation process. In addition, the legal foundations of an SE with its overlapping European and German legal provisions are complex, especially for the one-tier SE which is conceptually new to German law.

II. Corporate governance of the SE

§ 354 Introduction
The founders of an SE are free to choose either a one-tier or a two-tier system of corporate governance. Given the prevalence of the two-tier system among SEs in Germany, the following chapters focus on the two-tier system but will also highlight the principal differences of the one-tier system.

§ 355 One-tier system
Prior to the adoption of the SE legislation, the one-tier system of corporate governance in a stock corporation had no precedent under German law. Consequently, in conjunction with the creation of the SE regime, Germany was required to adopt a new set of provisions for SEs specifically addressing the one-tier system. While this has been accomplished in part by way of adopting the SE Implementation Act, the interplay between that law and the Stock Corporation Act results in a number of interpretive questions with respect to one-tier SEs.

In the one-tier structure, the administrative board is the governing body of the company. The administrative board directs the business, establishes the corporate strategy and supervises its implementation.[682] While the administrative board generally carries out its responsibilities as a body, the allocation of specific management tasks to certain members is possible (and customary).

To run the day-to-day operations, a one-tier SE has to appoint at least one managing director (*geschäftsführender Direktor*).[683] The managing directors represent the SE *vis-à-vis* third parties. In general, the position of a managing director is more readily comparable to that of a general manager of a German GmbH than that of a member of the management board of an AG. For example, in contrast to management board members of an AG, who are not subject to instructions by the supervisory board with respect to strategy or day-to-day management, the managing directors of an SE are obligated to follow the instructions issued by the administrative

---

682   SE-Ausführungsgesetz [SEAG] [SE Implementation Act] 2004, § 22, ¶ 1 (F.R.G.).
683   SE-Ausführungsgesetz [SEAG] [SE Implementation Act] 2004, § 40 (F.R.G.).

board on any and all matters relating to the company. Furthermore, they can also be dismissed at any time, even without cause.

§ 356 Two-tier system
The structure and rules of a two-tier SE largely correspond to those of an AG. In essence, the role of the management body of an SE corresponds to that of the management board of an AG. Similarly, the supervisory body of an SE oversees management and can therefore be compared to the supervisory board of an AG.

As the Stock Corporation Act contains an elaborate set of provisions for the two-tier system of AGs, the German legislator has not adopted specific provisions for the two-tier system of the SE. Rather, the few provisions on two-tier SEs contained in the German SE implementation legislation aim to ensure equivalency between SEs and AGs.

As a consequence, the differences between the two-tier systems of the SE and the AG, respectively, are minor. Instead of providing a detailed discussion of the corporate governance system of the SE, the following sections therefore concentrate on the major differences between the SE and the AG. For further information, reference is made to the discussion of the management and supervisory boards of AGs.[684]

III. General rules for one-tier and two-tier SEs

§ 357 Introduction
The SE-Regulation, in a general section, sets forth a limited number of rules that are applicable for all SE administrative bodies, irrespective of whether the SE has adopted the two-tier or one-tier model. Consequently, in a two-tier model, these rules apply to both the management and the supervisory bodies. The rules contained in the SE-Regulation do not establish a comprehensive system of corporate governance, but only address certain specific topics such as the quorum in SE bodies or the maximum term of office. If and to the extent that the SE-Regulation is silent, the provisions of the Stock Corporation Act apply.

A. Adoption of resolutions by SE bodies

§ 358 Quorum and decision-making
Pursuant to the SE-Regulation, an SE body is competent to adopt a resolution if at least half of its members are present or represented. For a resolution to be adopted, the majority of the members present or represented must vote in favor. Abstentions and invalid votes are therefore regarded as votes against a resolution. In the event of a tie vote, the chairman of the body has a casting vote. The articles of association may deviate from these provisions, but the casting vote

---

684   For the management board refer to §§ 66 *et seq*. For the supervisory board refer to §§ 240 *et seq*.

of the chairman is mandatory in order to safeguard the decisive influence of the shareholders, if the SE is subject to co-determination on a parity basis between the shareholders and the employees.

The foregoing rules apply equally to committees to which responsibilities of a corporate body have been delegated, such as audit or compensation committees.

§ 359 Representation when adopting resolutions

The SE-Regulation allows board members to be represented by other persons in board meetings.[685] The representatives need not be board members themselves unless the articles of association provide otherwise. This contrasts with the Stock Corporation Act, which does not permit members of the management or supervisory board to send representatives to board meetings to participate in the decision-making process.[686]

B. Term of office in SE bodies

§ 360 Maximum term of office

In contrast to the Stock Corporation Act, the maximum term for a member of a corporate body of an SE is six years. The articles of association of an SE may provide for a shorter term. Re-appointment is possible unless the articles of association provide otherwise.[687]

C. Duty of confidentiality

§ 361 Duty of confidentiality

The members of SE bodies owe a duty of confidentiality to the company similar to the duty of the management and supervisory boards of an AG.[688] In contrast to the Stock Corporation Act, however, the SE-Regulation addresses certain points explicitly. For example, it provides that the duty of secrecy is not limited to a board member's term of office, but terminates at the earliest when the release of the confidential information can no longer harm the company. Furthermore, the SE-Regulation does not expressly limit the confidentiality obligation to information that is obtained through the activity as a member of a corporate body of an SE. Instead, the SE-Regulation broadly prohibits the disclosure of any information concerning the SE, which might be prejudicial to its interests, except where such disclosure is legally required or permitted or is in the public interest. In substance, there is, however, no material difference between the scope of the duty of confidentiality of board members of the two types of corporations.

---

685   SE-Ausführungsgesetz [SEAG] [SE Implementation Act] 2004, § 50, ¶ 1 (F.R.G.).
686   Cf. § 285 for the supervisory board and §§ 78 et seq. for the management board.
687   SE-Verordnung [SE-VO] [SE Regulation] 2001, Art. 46.
688   SE-Verordnung [SE-VO] [SE Regulation] 2001, Art. 49.

The consequences of a breach of the duty of confidentiality are not stipulated in the SE-Regulation. Rather, the same consequences apply as for members of the management and supervisory boards of an AG.[689]

D. Requirement of consent by supervisory body for business transactions

§ 362 Specification of transactions requiring consent in the articles of association

A technical difference compared to an AG is that the articles of association of an SE must subject certain types of business transactions to the consent of the supervisory body.[690] In addition, the articles of association may authorize the supervisory body of the SE to impose further consent requirements, and the supervisory body may do so even in the absence of specific authorization in the articles of association. By contrast, an AG need not include any consent requirements in its articles of association. All consent requirements for management decisions of an AG may be provided in the management board's rules of procedure or imposed by the supervisory board in a resolution (for general purposes or on an ad-hoc basis).

§ 363 Types of business transactions requiring consent

As is the case for an AG, consent requirements are generally required for material transactions outside the ordinary course of business. They serve as a preventive control mechanism of the management. The term "business transactions" refers not only to legal transactions, but also to all entrepreneurial measures, such as investment decisions and corporate planning.[691]

§ 364 Consent requirements imposed by resolution

If the articles of association of an SE do not specify otherwise, a simple majority of the members of the supervisory body present or represented is sufficient in order to impose a requirement of consent.[692]

§ 365 Refusing consent

If, in a two-tier system, the supervisory body of an SE refuses to approve a transaction requiring consent, the management body may demand that the general shareholders' meeting overrules this decision.[693] The shareholders' resolution then requires a majority of at least three-quarters of the votes cast. The articles of association may not specify a different majority or additional requirements in this respect.

---

689   Cf. § 94, §§ 180 et seq. for the management board and §§ 320 et seq. for the supervisory board.
690   SE-Verordnung [SE-VO] [SE Regulation] 2001, Art. 48, ¶ 1.
691   Cf. § 251.
692   Cf. details for the AG in § 78 and §§ 289 et seq.
693   SE-Verordnung [SE-VO] [SE Regulation] 2001, Art. 9, ¶ 1 c) (ii) in conjunction with Aktiengesetz [AktG]
      [Stock Corporation Act] 1965, § 111, ¶ 4, sentence 3 (F.R.G.)

§ 366 Effect of consent required
It should be noted that due to the unlimited power of the management body *vis-à-vis* third parties, a legal transaction with a third party would be effective even if the management body had failed to obtain any supervisory body consent required by the articles of association (or otherwise). Such failure only has legal consequences for the internal relationship between the two bodies of the SE and the liability of the members of the management body.

E.   Requirement of consent by general shareholders' meeting

§ 367 Legal transactions calling for referral to the general shareholders' meeting
Although there is no case law with respect to an SE, it is likely that the principles requiring the management board of an AG to present matters that affect the core competences of the general shareholders' meeting to the shareholders for their approval also apply to an SE. According to these principles, the shareholders have an unwritten right (which is not expressly provided by statute) to vote on a restructuring measure proposed by the management body if such measure would result in changes that are similar to those that can only be achieved by amending the articles of association (called the "Holzmüller/Gelatine principles"). These principles, which have been developed by the German courts, serve first and foremost to protect the company's minority shareholders.

Apart from this very special concept, the consent of the general shareholders' meeting of an SE is required only in the circumstances provided by law (SE-Regulation, SE-Implementation Act and Stock Corporation Act). These circumstances are essentially the same as those requiring the consent of the shareholders of an AG.

IV. Corporate governance in the two-tier SE

A.   Management body

§ 368 Basic principles
There are no functional differences between the management body of an SE and the management board of an AG. Like the management board of an AG, the management body of an SE is responsible for both representing the SE and managing the SE's business.

1.   Size and composition
§ 369 Size and composition
The management body of an SE consists of one or more natural persons and must have at least two members if the nominal share capital of the SE exceeds EUR 3 million, unless the articles of association stipulate otherwise.[694] Frequently, the articles only specify a minimum number of

---

694   SE-Ausführungsgesetz [SEAG] [SE Implementation Act] 2004, § 16 (F.R.G.).

management body members and leave the decision on the precise number to the supervisory body.

If the founders of the SE have not agreed on a co-determination model, the management body has to consist of at least two members, one of whom is then responsible for labor and social affairs.[695]

§ 370 Chairman

The SE-Regulation does not explicitly address the election or appointment of a chairman of the management body. By contrast, these matters are specifically regulated in the SE-Regulation for the supervisory body. Therefore, national corporate law governs the question whether to appoint a chairman of the management body at all, and if so his election and tasks.

An AG need not have a chairman of the management board, such as a CEO. If the articles of association or the rules of procedure for the management board provide for the appointment of a chairman, the Stock Corporation Act gives the supervisory board authority to make the appointment. The same principles apply to an SE. The chairman chairs the meetings of the management body and coordinates its work. As discussed above, the chairmen of the corporate bodies of SEs have a casting vote in the event of a tie and, consequently, the chairman of the management body also has such authority unless the articles of association provide otherwise.

Instead of a chairman (which would have to be appointed by the supervisory body), an SE may have a speaker of the management body, who is appointed by the members of the management board and whose functions generally are set out in the rules of procedure. The position of the speaker of the management body is weaker than that of a chairman.[696]

§ 371 Incompatibilities

Similarly to the Stock Corporation Act, the SE-Regulation explicitly prohibits simultaneous membership in the management and supervisory bodies.[697] Violation of this prohibition renders the later appointment null and void. By contrast, if the second appointment is made in anticipation of the resignation of the person concerned from one office in order to take up the other office, the second appointment remains provisionally invalid pending such resignation.

Furthermore, a member of the management body of an SE must fulfill the personal requirements that apply under German law to management board members of an AG.[698]

§ 372 Temporary appointment of a supervisory board member to management body

A member of the SE supervisory body may temporarily assume the responsibilities of a management body member.[699] This is, however, only permitted if the management body does not

---

695 SE-Beteiligungsgesetz [SEBG] [SE Participation Act] 2004, § 38, ¶ 2 (F.R.G.).

696 Cf. § 9.

697 SE-Verordnung [SE-VO] [SE Regulation] 2001, Art. 39, ¶ 3, sentence 1.

698 Cf. §§ 14 et seq.

699 SE-Verordnung [SE-VO] [SE Regulation] 2001, Art. 39, ¶ 3, sentence 2.

have a full complement of members, *i.e.*, the number of its members falls short of that provided by law, the articles of incorporation or its rules of procedure. Secondment to the management body is therefore possible in cases such as the death, resignation or revocation of the appointment of a member of the management body; secondment is not permitted if a member of the management body is only temporarily indisposed, *e.g.*, due to illness or vacation.

The secondment is made by resolution of the supervisory body, followed by the acceptance of the person that is to become a temporary member of the management body. A secondment may last for a maximum period of one year. While renewal is possible, a supervisory body member may generally not serve on the management body for an aggregate period exceeding one year.[700] During the secondment, the office of the supervisory body member is suspended.[701]

2.   Appointment and Dismissal
§ 373 Introduction
The members of the SE management body are appointed and dismissed by the supervisory body.[702] The option available under the SE-Regulation to transfer appointment and dismissal authority to the general shareholders' meeting has not been exercised by the German legislator. This result is consistent with the provisions of the Stock Corporation Act, which as a general principle do not authorize the shareholders (but the supervisory board only) to appoint the management board.

If the composition of the management body does not comply with the requirements of law or the articles of association and such failure affects the ability of the management body to function properly, the court situated where the SE has its registered office is authorized to appoint member(s) of the management body upon request by the management or supervisory body or another person who has a legitimate interest in ensuring the appropriate composition of the management body.[703]

§ 374 Appointment by the supervisory body
The plenum of the supervisory body has to resolve on the appointment (and dismissal) of a member of the management body; a transfer of this authority to a committee is not permissible. Although the Stock Corporation Act provides for a simple majority to appoint a management board member, it is possible to require a larger majority in the articles of association of an SE. Accordingly, if the articles of association are silent, the appointment requires a simple majority.

The cumbersome appointment procedure set forth in the Co-Determination Act for management board members of co-determined AGs does not apply to a co-determined SE. The chair-

---

700   SE-Ausführungsgesetz [SEAG] [SE Implementation Act] 2004, § 15, sentence 2 (F.R.G.).
701   SE-Verordnung [SE-VO] [SE Regulation] 2001, Art. 39, ¶ 3, sentence 2.
702   SE-Verordnung [SE-VO] [SE-Regulation] 2001, Art. 39, ¶ 2.
703   *Cf.* § 23.

man of the SE supervisory body will therefore have a decisive second vote in case of a tie in the first ballot.[704]

§ 375 Dismissal

The SE-Regulation neither defines the situations in which the supervisory body may dismiss management body members nor the grounds required for such dismissal, although these questions are key factors for assessing the actual influence of the supervisory body in the company's corporate governance system. If the management body can be dismissed at any time, the position of the supervisory body is considerably strengthened. Although there are different views among commentators, the general approach of the SE-Regulation – referring to national law instead of providing for exhaustive details in the SE-Regulation itself – supports the view that the national law should govern the requirements for dismissal. This means that cause is required for the dismissal of a member of the management body.

Whether cause for dismissal exists, depends on the specific facts, applying the same standards as in the case of an AG. In particular, the supervisory body is entitled to dismiss a member of the management body, if the general shareholders' meeting has passed a resolution of no confidence in relation to such member.[705]

§ 376 Other grounds for termination

Other grounds for terminating membership in the management body include expiration of the term of appointment, death and the dissolution or transformation of an SE into another legal form. Members of the management body may also resign from their office at any time. Resignation does not require cause.

3. Service agreement
§ 377 Overview

As is the case for an AG, the contractual relationship between a member of the management body and the company is set forth in a separate service agreement.[706]

In executing the service agreement, the SE is represented by the supervisory body, which may delegate preparatory work (including negotiations) to a committee, but has to decide on the final content of the service agreement as well as all remuneration aspects in the plenum.[707] The maximum term of the service agreement is six years, which is the same maximum period as for appointments. Extensions are possible. The service agreement may also stipulate that it remains in force if the appointment to the board is renewed.

---

704 Cf. § 22.
705 For details cf. § 34.
706 Cf. § 36.
707 Cf. § 245.

4.   Responsibilities of the management body
§ 378 Management of the SE

The duties of the management body of an SE are comparable to those of the management board of an AG. It is responsible for independently managing the SE[708] and representing it in and out of court.[709] If the management body is composed of more than one member, all members manage and represent the company jointly. However, with respect to management, the articles of association or the rules of procedure may provide otherwise – subject to certain limitations.[710] Typically, specific responsibilities are allocated to individual members of the management body.[711] Similarly, authority to represent the SE can be given to individual board members or two board members acting jointly by the articles of association, or, if permitted by the articles of association, by the supervisory body.[712]

In fulfilling its responsibilities, the management body is obliged to act in the SE's best interests with a view to the creation of sustainable value of the company.

§ 379 Position of the management body in a group of companies

The responsibility of the management body to manage the SE independently generally is restricted if the SE is a controlled company under a control agreement.[713]

B.   Supervisory body

§ 380 Introduction

The duties and organization of the SE supervisory body are set forth in Art. 40 of the SE-Regulation. The main task of the supervisory body is to oversee the management body, which also is the primary role of the supervisory board of an AG. The supervisory body of an SE thus essentially has the same role as the supervisory board of an AG.[714]

1.   Relationship of the supervisory body to other SE bodies
§ 381 Relationship to the general shareholders' meeting

The relationship between the supervisory body and the general shareholders' meeting of an SE is identical to the relationship of these bodies in an AG. The shareholder representatives on the supervisory body are elected by the general shareholders' meeting, but as is the case for supervisory board members of an AG they are not bound by instructions of a majority shareholder.[715]

---

708   For details cf. §§ 66 et seq.
709   For details cf. §§ 81 et seq.
710   Cf. §§ 68 et seq.
711   Cf. § 71.
712   Cf. §§ 81 et seq.
713   Cf. § 74 and § 77.
714   Cf. §§ 248 et seq.
715   Cf. §§ 317 et seq.

§ 382 Relationship to the management body

In addition to appointing and dismissing the members of the management body, the supervisory body has first and foremost the task of overseeing the activities of the management body. For this reason, simultaneous membership in both the management and supervisory body is prohibited, as is the execution of management tasks by the supervisory body. Aside from this explicit restriction in the SE-Regulation, the members of the supervisory body of an SE must also comply with the requirements for supervisory board members of an AG. [716]

The supervisory body represents the SE *vis-à-vis* the members of the management body. This authority is not explicitly set forth in the SE-Regulation. The absence of a specific provision does not, however, mean that the management body's general power of representation extends to dealings with its members. A corporate body's power of representation is limited to the extent that there is a conflict of interests. This principle is recognized in all European legal systems and also applies to AGs and SEs. It is therefore generally accepted that the supervisory body represents the SE in all dealings with the management body, in particular in negotiating and executing service agreements.[717]

2. Composition and size of the supervisory body

§ 383 Number of members

The size of the supervisory body is laid down in the articles of association of an SE. The SE-Regulation, however, has empowered the national legislators to provide for the exact or maximum and/or minimum number of members in local law. Germany has used this power to provide for the same maximum and minimum number as applies to an AG. The minimum number is three members, but the articles of association may prescribe a larger number, which must, however, be divisible by three. Moreover, the SE Implementation Act sets maximum sizes for the supervisory body scaled according to the nominal share capital of the company (up to EUR 1,500,000 – nine, over EUR 1,500,000 – 15, and over EUR 10,000,000 – 21).[718]

§ 384 Composition of co-determined supervisory body

Unlike a co-determined AG, an SE that is subject to co-determination as a result of negotiations with the employees is not subject to any statutory requirements with respect to the composition of its supervisory body. The result of the negotiations, however, includes an agreement on the size and the composition of the supervisory body.

If the negotiating parties cannot agree on a tailored co-determination regime, the mandatory fallback regime will apply, which is generally the national co-determination regime of the participating companies with the most extensive co-determination rules. If such rules – as is the case for the Co-Determination Act – provide for specific numbers of supervisory board members,[719] the shareholders of the SE have to reflect these numbers in the SE's articles of association. It is also widely accepted among legal commentators that the articles of associa-

---

716 *Cf.* §§ 204 *et seq.*
717 *Cf.* § 377.
718 SE-Ausführungsgesetz [SEAG] [SE Implementation Act] 2004, § 17, ¶ 1 (F.R.G.).
719 *Cf.* § 198.

tion must reflect the number of employee representatives set forth in the agreement on the SE co-determination.

§ 385 Flexibility of rules on supervisory body composition make SE attractive for German companies

The rules with respect to the composition of a co-determined SE supervisory body have been one of the principal reasons why a significant number of German companies have converted their corporate form to that of an SE.

First, German companies that are subject to the Co-Determination Act may achieve a reduction of the size of the supervisory body in the co-determination negotiation process. This result is particularly attractive for German companies with more than 20,000 employees, as their supervisory board would otherwise generally have to consist of 20 members – ten shareholder representatives and ten employee representatives. To increase the efficiency of their supervisory body, several large listed AGs have reduced the size of their supervisory body in connection with their change to the legal form of an SE from 20 to 12 members.[720] It should be noted, however, that if the SE is incorporated by conversion from an AG some legal commentators question whether a reduction of the size of the supervisory body is legally permissible. While in case of incorporation of an SE by way of a statutory merger or otherwise, the only requirement is that the number of supervisory body members be allocated based on the highest percentage of employee representatives in the entities being merged, in case of a conversion of an AG into an SE, the SE Participation Act provides that the co-determination rules which existed prior to the change shall remain in force. Nonetheless, a considerable number of legal commentators convincingly argue that this requirement means only that the quality of co-determination (*i.e.*, the ratio between shareholder representatives and employee representatives) must remain the same, whereas the actual number of representatives is a matter that the shareholders have the power to decide. In practice, several large listed AGs have used the conversion to an SE in order to reduce the size of their supervisory body. Thus far, there is no case law suggesting that the courts consider such a reduction impermissible.

Second, the co-determination status of an SE is generally "frozen" when the SE is incorporated. In particular, expanding the workforce generally does not result in an extension of the scope of the co-determination of the SE, as would be the case for an AG under the statutory co-determination regime.[721] This feature is particularly attractive for German companies that are not yet subject to co-determination on a parity basis (generally companies with fewer than 2,000 employees), because conversion to an SE enables them to maintain their co-determination status at the lower employee participation threshold of one third versus fifty percent.

---

720 For example Allianz SE, BASF SE, MAN SE.
721 Structural changes of the SE, however, may result in a new round of negotiations with the employees with respect to its co-determination regime.

Finally, the legal form of an SE enables the internationalization of the representation of the company's workforce on its supervisory body. Consequently, the SE allows a more balanced and fair representation of the employees of an international corporate group.

§ 386 Personal requirements for membership

The restrictions and requirements for membership in the supervisory body of an SE are not addressed in the SE-Regulation. Consequently, the national rules, *i.e.*, the provisions of the Stock Corporation Act, apply.[722]

3.   Membership in the supervisory body
§ 387 Appointment

Under the SE-Regulation, the members of the supervisory body are appointed by the general shareholders' meeting. If the SE is co-determined, the appointment of the employee representatives follows the provisions set forth in the co-determination agreement. If no co-determination agreement has been concluded, the employee representatives are generally nominated by special employee representative bodies (alternatively, by the SE works council) and elected by the general shareholders' meeting without any room for discretion. The members of the first supervisory body of a new SE are appointed by designating them as supervisory body members in the articles of association.

In addition, the SE's articles of association may give certain shareholders the right to appoint representatives to the supervisory body without election.[723]

§ 388 Termination of membership

The SE-Regulation lacks provisions for terminating membership or removing members from the supervisory body. A draft of the SE-Regulation contained such provisions, but they were not included in the final text. The European legislator thus intended to leave flexibility for national corporate laws. For Germany, this means that members of the supervisory body elected by the shareholders can be removed at any time by a resolution of the general shareholders' meeting.[724] While in case of an AG a majority of three-quarter of the votes cast is required for such a resolution, unless the articles of association provide for a lower majority, in the SE a dismissal is possible with a simple majority of the votes cast. In addition, the courts may remove a supervisory board member in the same circumstances as supervisory board members of an AG can be removed.[725]

Special rules apply to the termination of the membership of employee representatives in a co-determined SE to ensure that the employees have a say in such termination.

---

722 *Cf.* §§ 201 *et seq.*
723 *Cf.* § 222.
724 SE-Verordnung [SE-VO] [SE-Regulation] 2001, Art. 52, sentence 2 in conjunction with Aktiengesetz [AktG] [Stock Corporation Act] 1965, § 103 (F.R.G.).
725 *Cf.* §§ 231 *et seq.* for other reasons by which a membership in the supervisory board can terminate.

4.   Internal organization
§ 389 Overview
The internal organization of the supervisory body, including the formation of committees[726] and the election of chairmen, generally follows the rules with respect to the supervisory board of AGs.

§ 390 Chairman of the supervisory body
The supervisory body must elect one of its members as chairman. The SE-Regulation provides that if half of the members of the supervisory body are appointed by the employees (*i.e.*, the SE is subject to co-determination on a parity basis),[727] the chairman has to be a member appointed by the general shareholders' meeting. This is a consequence of the chairman's casting vote in order to safeguard the decisive vote for the shareholders[728] in a supervisory body made up of equal numbers of employee and shareholder representatives.

At least one deputy chairman is to be elected in addition to the chairman. Since the deputy chairman takes the place of the chairman with all his legal powers if the chairman is indisposed (including the right of a casting vote), the deputy must also be a shareholder representative in an SE that is co-determined on a parity basis. If several deputy chairmen are appointed, the articles of association must ensure that only deputies that are representatives of the shareholders have a casting vote.

The SE-Regulation does not address the procedure to be applied if the election of the chairman ends in stalemate. In this situation, the chairman of the supervisory body[729] cannot cast a decisive vote because there is as yet no chairman at the constituent meeting of the first supervisory body of the SE. If the supervisory body cannot agree on a candidate, as a last resort it is proposed by some authors that the local court shall appoint the chairman.

5.   Responsibilities of the supervisory body
§ 391 Supervision of management
The principal task of the supervisory body is to oversee the management body. This consists of a review of past activities and events, most notably of the lawfulness of the management activities, but also a strategic role by advising the management body in relation to future business policy.[730] The supervisory body is prohibited, however, from conducting the management of the company. Notwithstanding this clear division of powers between the management and supervisory bodies, the articles of association of an SE must provide that certain fundamental transactions require the approval of the supervisory body as part of the supervisory body's preventive supervision.[731]

---

726   For the details on committees, *cf.* §§ 297 *et seq.*
727   SE-Verordnung [SE-VO] [SE-Regulation] 2001, Art. 42, sentence 2.
728   SE-Verordnung [SE-VO] [SE-Regulation] 2001, Art. 50, ¶ 2.
729   SE-Verordnung [SE-VO] [SE-Regulation] 2001, Art. 50, ¶ 2.
730   For further details *cf.* §§ 248 *et seq.*
731   *Cf.* § 362.

§ 392 Subject and standards for oversight

In performing its oversight, the supervisory body has to assess the activities of the management body regarding lawfulness, appropriateness and efficiency. The work of the members of the supervisory body always revolves around the interests of the SE.[732] Each member of the supervisory body must perform his responsibilities with the prudence of a diligent member of a supervisory body.[733]

The supervisory body has no obligation to supervise the management in every detail of its activity. Instead, the focus of the oversight is on matters, which the management body of an SE must notify to the supervisory body under its statutory reporting duties. Further, the supervisory body only supervises the management body, but not lower levels of management of the SE. In this respect, its task is to ensure that the management body itself properly oversees the employees of the SE. Members of the supervisory body thus generally should not directly communicate with the employees of the SE (*e.g.*, by requesting information from them), unless such communication takes place in coordination and with the consent of the member of the management body to whom the employee reports.

§ 393 Means of oversight

The SE supervisory body is vested with certain powers enabling it to carry out its oversight function properly. These powers are covered in detail in the SE-Regulation. Therefore, the Stock Corporation Act is not applicable.[734] In practice, there is, however, no appreciable difference between an SE and an AG as regards the manner in which the supervisory body and the management body interact.

First of all, under the SE-Regulation the management body is required to inform the supervisory body every three months of progress in the company's business and its expected development.[735] In contrast to the Stock Corporation Act,[736] the SE-Regulation does not list in detail the items about which the supervisory body is to be specifically informed. Furthermore, the management body is also required to inform the supervisory body fully and promptly at all times of events "likely to have an appreciable effect on the SE."[737]

In addition, the supervisory body may demand from the management body any information required for its tasks. On the basis of the authorization in the SE-Regulation,[738] each member of the supervisory body of an SE is also entitled to demand such information. The information is always to be supplied to the supervisory body in its entirety.

---

732   *Cf.* § 319.
733   *Cf.* § 330.
734   SE-Verordnung [SE-VO] [SE-Regulation] 2001, Art. 41 in conjunction with Aktiengesetz [AktG] [Stock Corporation Act] 1965, § 90 (F.R.G.).
735   SE-Verordnung [SE-VO] [SE-Regulation] 2001, Art. 41, ¶ 1.
736   Aktiengesetz [AktG] [Stock Corporation Act] 1965, § 90 (F.R.G.).
737   SE-Verordnung [SE-VO] [SE-Regulation] 2001, Art. 41, ¶ 2.
738   SE-Verordnung [SE-VO] [SE-Regulation] 2001, Art. 41, ¶ 3, sentence 2.

The supervisory body may, in addition to exercising its right to information, undertake such verifications as it deems necessary to perform its tasks.[739] The supervisory body may assume that the facts notified by management are correct and only has to undertake further investigation of its own if there is serious doubt as to the accuracy of the facts available to the supervisory body.

Consent requirements for certain transactions represent another important means of exercising supervision by the supervisory body. Some consent requirements are provided by law. For example, the supervisory body must be involved in the decision on issuing new shares from authorized capital. Contracts between individual members of the supervisory body and the SE are also subject to a statutory requirement of consent by the full body. The articles of association may, and generally do, provide for additional requirements of consent. Finally, the supervisory body may, by resolution, subject certain types of transactions of the SE to its consent.

§ 394 Additional competences of the supervisory body

The supervisory body is responsible for appointing and dismissing, as well as entering into service agreements with, the members of the management body. The authority to represent the SE *vis-à-vis* the members of the management body lies exclusively with the supervisory body. Such authority does not only apply to all matters relating to appointment, dismissal, compensation and conclusion of the service agreement; it also extends to the assertion of claims of the SE against members of the management body for breach of duties or decisions on granting loans to members of the management body or their relatives.[740]

The supervisory body must issue the mandate for the audit of the annual financial statements and consolidated financial statements of the SE. Thus, in this exceptional situation, the supervisory body represents the SE in relation to third parties. Furthermore, the supervisory body must review the annual financial statements, the annual report and the proposal for the distribution of profits prepared by the management body.[741]

V. Corporate governance in the one-tier SE

A. Structure

§ 395 Basic principles

In a one-tier SE, the administrative board is responsible for the duties and obligations assigned to the management and supervisory bodies in a two-tier structure. Administration and management of the SE as well as supervisory functions are concentrated at this single corporate body. For the operation of its day-to-day business, however, the administrative board of a one-tier SE must appoint one or several managing directors who have responsibilities comparable to those of officers in US companies.

---

739 SE-Verordnung [SE-VO] [SE-Regulation] 2001, Art. 41, ¶ 4.
740 *Cf.* § 255 and §§ 266 *et seq.*
741 *Cf.* §§ 256 *et seq.*

§ 396 Size and composition of the administrative board

The administrative board consists of at least three natural persons unless the articles of association provide otherwise. The articles of association may not reduce the minimum number below three if the nominal share capital of the SE exceeds EUR 3 million or the SE is co-determined. Furthermore, there are limitations on the maximum number of board members in the administrative board of an SE ranging from nine to 21 members depending on the nominal share capital of the SE. These limitations are identical to those for the supervisory board of an AG.[742]

The size and the composition of the administrative board may also be affected by the co-determination regime negotiated between the SE and its workforce. If no such regime has been agreed on, the applicable national co-determination rules – with certain modifications – will apply.[743]

B. Administrative board

1.   Appointment and dismissal
§ 397 Appointment

Administrative board members are appointed and dismissed by resolution of the general share-holders' meeting unless individual shareholders have the right to appoint administrative board members under the SE's articles of association.[744] If the SE is co-determined, administrative board members may also be elected by the workforce subject to the SE's co-determination regime.[745] Finally, in urgent situations, the German local court situated where the SE has its registered office is authorized to appoint member(s) of the administrative board upon application.[746]

Administrative board members must fulfill certain personal requirements, which are largely identical to those applicable to supervisory board members of an AG.[747] The managing directors of an SE may at the same time serve as administrative board members provided that the majority of the members of the administrative board at all times consists of persons who are not managing directors. The general shareholders' meeting may appoint substitute members (*Ersatzmitglieder*) for the administrative board to replace regular members in the event a person ceases to be an administrative board member prior to the expiration of his term.

---

742   *Cf.* § 196.
743   SE-Beteiligungsgesetz [SEBG] [SE-Participation Act] 2004, §§ 34 *et seq.*, *cf.* §§ 197 *et seq.*
744   *Cf.* § 222.
745   This depends on the SE's specific employee co-determination regime. If no such regime has been agreed on with the SE's workforce, national co-determination rules will apply. For the German co-determination rules, *cf.* §§ 197 *et seq.*
746   *Cf.* §§ 223 *et seq.*
747   *Cf.* §§ 202 *et seq.*

§ 398 Dismissal and other grounds for termination

The general shareholders' meeting of an SE may dismiss administrative board members appointed by it at any time without cause by adopting a resolution with a three-quarter majority of the votes cast unless the articles of association provide for another majority.

Other grounds for termination of membership in the administrative board that do not require cause include the expiration of the term of appointment, the withdrawal of an administrative board member by the shareholder having board delegation rights, death, resignation, loss of unrestricted legal competency, dissolution of the SE or conversion of the SE into another legal form.

2.   Compensation

§ 399 Overview

The general shareholders' meeting determines the compensation of administrative board members, either by setting forth the details of the compensation in the articles of association or by resolving on the compensation by individual resolution. In principle, the compensation for administrative board members must comply with the rules applicable for members of the management board of an AG.[748] It should be permissible for an SE to grant shares of the company as part of the compensation package to its administrative board members.

3.   Responsibilities of the administrative board

§ 400 Management of the SE

The administrative board is responsible for the management of the company. It must direct the business conducted by the SE, establish the general principles for its activities and supervise their implementation. Consequently, the duties of the administrative board of an SE combine the duties attributed to the management and supervisory boards of an AG or a two-tier SE. Only a limited number of responsibilities – generally closely related to the day-to-day operation of the SE – are explicitly assigned to the managing directors of the SE;[749] the ultimate responsibility with respect to the administration of the SE is always with the administrative board. Notwithstanding such responsibility, in practice the corporate governance of a one-tier SE can be rather flexible. Depending on the envisaged role of the administrative board in the day-to-day operations of the SE, the administrative board can closely manage the daily operations or it can focus on the supervision of the daily operations by the managing directors and only establish the general principles of the SE's business. In order to be able to fulfill its responsibilities, each administrative board member has access to all information available to the administrative board.

§ 401 Representation of the SE *vis-à-vis* third persons

In addition to appointing and dismissing managing directors, the administrative board represents the SE *vis-à-vis* the managing directors, in particular in negotiating and executing the managing directors' service agreements. The administrative board is also responsible for engag-

---

748 Cf. §§ 44 *et seq.*
749 Cf. § 411.

ing the auditors for the purpose of auditing the annual financial statements of the company and the group.

§ 402 Liability

In fulfilling their responsibilities, the administrative board members are obliged to act in the SE's best interests and with a view towards increasing the sustainable value of the company. If the administrative board members breach their duties *vis-à-vis* the company, they may be held liable pursuant to the same rules applying for members of the management board of an AG or a two-tier SE.[750] Furthermore, the liability of the administrative board *vis-à-vis* other persons is similar to that of the management board of an AG.[751]

4.   Internal Organization
§ 403 Procedures of the administrative board

The administrative board must convene meetings as often as the business of the company requires, but at least once every three months. The chairman calls administrative board meetings by timely notifying the board members of the date, time, place and preliminary agenda for such meeting. The administrative board is flexible in organizing its procedures and may adopt its own rules of procedure. While the administrative board generally carries out its responsibilities as a body, the delegation of specific management tasks to certain members is possible.

§ 404 Chairman

The administrative board is required to elect a chairman and a deputy chairman from among its members. The chairman or, if he is prevented from doing so, the deputy chairman chairs the meetings and coordinates the work of the board. As mentioned above, chairmen in administrative bodies of SEs generally have a casting vote in the event of a tie. In an administrative board that includes members elected by the employees, both the chairman and the deputy chairman must be members appointed by the shareholders. In addition, the SE Implementation Act provides that the chairman has a second vote if another board member who at the same time is a managing director is prohibited from exercising his voting right due to a conflict of interest.

§ 405 Committees

The administrative board may establish committees from among its members to consider particular matters and to supervise the implementation of its resolutions. Customary committees are the audit, personnel and compensation committees. Certain matters of particular importance must always be adopted by the whole administrative board and may not be decided by committees, in particular the appointment of managing directors as well as the decision on their compensation, the review and approval of the annual financial statements, the calling of a shareholders' general meeting and the overall supervision of the SE's accounting and controlling systems. All committees must regularly report to the whole administrative board about their activities.

---

750   *Cf.* §§ 137 *et seq.*
751   *Cf.* §§ 154 *et seq.*

C. Managing directors

1.   Structure and organisation
§ 406 Overview
The basic responsibility of the managing directors of an SE entails the management of the day-to-day business of the company and the representation of the SE in and out of court. Managing directors are appointed and dismissed by the administrative board and must comply with instructions given by the administrative board unless such instructions are evidently illegal.

§ 407 Size and composition
The SE must have at least one, or in a co-determined SE under certain circumstances, at least two managing directors, one of whom must have responsibility for labor and social affairs. The exact number of managing directors may be set forth in the articles of association or by resolution of the administrative board. Managing directors must fulfill the same personal requirements applicable to members of the management board of an AG.[752]

§ 408 Appointment and dismissal
Managing directors are appointed and dismissed by resolution of the administrative board. A dismissal does not require cause and can be adopted at any time and with immediate effect.

§ 409 Compensation
In addition to their appointment, the SE typically executes a service agreement with its managing directors addressing the contractual relationship between the company and a managing director, in particular his compensation. The compensation for managing directors must comply with the rules that apply for members of the management board of an AG.[753]

§ 410 Internal organization
Unless the SE's articles of association or a resolution of the administrative body provides otherwise, managing directors manage the business of the company acting jointly, and resolutions of the managing directors are adopted by a majority of the votes cast. The managing directors may adopt their own rules of procedures unless the administrative body adopts such rules for them.

2.   Responsibilities and liability
§ 411 Responsibilities
Apart from managing the daily operations of the SE, certain additional matters are explicitly referred to the managing directors, in particular all filings with the German commercial register, preparation of the unconsolidated and consolidated financial statements as well as the annual report (*Lagebericht*) and group annual report (*Konzernlagebericht*) and the preparation of the dependency report[754] for the company, if required. The managing directors also have the obligation to provide the administrative board with regular, prompt and comprehensive

---

752   *Cf.* §§ 14 *et seq.*
753   *Cf.* §§ 44 *et seq.*
754   SE-Ausführungsgesetz [SEAG] [SE Implementation Act] 2004, §§ 41, ¶ 1, 46, 47, ¶ 1, 49 (F.R.G.).

updates of all material developments, including strategy, planning, business development, and risk management as these arise in the course of the company's operations. The managing directors must also inform the administrative board immediately if the SE becomes insolvent or overindebted or if it appears that the SE has incurred a loss equal to one half of its share capital.

In addition, the managing directors represent the company *vis-à-vis* third parties. Unless the articles of association provide otherwise, *i.e.*, for individual representation or representation by one managing director acting together with a *Prokurist*[755], the managing directors represent the company jointly.

§ 412 Liability

Managing directors are liable to the SE for a breach of their duties under the same rules that apply for members of the management board of an AG or a two-tier SE.[756] If, however, a managing director acts on the basis of a binding instruction of the administrative board, such managing director generally will have no liability.[757]

---

755 An authorized signatory with a general commercial power of attorney defined by law.
756 *Cf.* §§ 137 *et seq.* and § 361.
757 *Cf.* § 355 and § 406.

CHAPTER FIVE
INTRODUCTION TO
THE GERMAN GMBH

I. General

§ 413 "Regular" GmbH and Unternehmergesellschaft (*haftungsbeschränkt*)

The German limited liability company is a legal entity under German law. It is governed by the Limited Liability Companies Act (*GmbH-Gesetz*). The GmbH is by far the most popular legal form in Germany at least by numbers, showing the high significance of the GmbH for the German economy. Because the GmbH is considered to be a "private" entity due to its usually small number of shareholders and the fact that its shares (*Geschäftsanteile*) may not be publicly traded on a stock exchange, it is sometimes seen as a "small business corporation" when compared to its counterparts, the AG and the SE.[758] However, also very large German enterprises have chosen the form of the GmbH.

One of the many reasons why the GmbH is favored by entrepreneurs in Germany is the benefit of limited liability for the GmbH shareholder, at least in principle, as opposed to personal liability, *e.g.*, in partnerships. The GmbH also provides a high degree of flexibility with regard to structuring the company and keeps the costs of founding, operating and liquidating the company on a relatively moderate level. Hence, the GmbH is often more attractive to many small and medium-sized businesses, the so-called "*Mittelstand*", than the AG, which is subject to stricter rules.

By the GmbH reform implemented in late 2008,[759] the German legislator newly introduced a second type of GmbH, the so-called entrepreneurial company with limited liability (*Unternehmergesellschaft (haftungsbeschränkt)*/"UG"). With its implementation, it was mainly intended to simplify the formation of a GmbH for small businesses in light of the international competition of corporate forms, and, in particular, as a reaction to the success of the UK-style *limited* in Germany. This being said, the UG is subject to (most) of the statutory provisions applicable to a "regular" GmbH.

---

758 *Cf.* for the AG §§ 1 *et seq.* and for the SE §§ 350 *et seq.*
759 *Cf.* § 414.

§ 414 Reform of the Limited Liability Company Law implemented in 2008

The legal rules applying to the GmbH underwent fundamental changes as a result of the Act on Modernizing Limited Liability Company Law and Fighting Abuses (*Gesetz zur Modernisierung des GmbH-Rechts und zur Bekämpfung von Missbräuchen*/"MoMiG"), which entered into force on November 1, 2008. These changes primarily relate to the corporate rules governing the GmbH's financial constitution, but they also affect the position of the company's general managers. The MoMiG is intended, *inter alia*, to expedite the establishment of GmbHs and to increase the attractiveness and prevent abuses of this corporate form.

II. Basic features of the GmbH

§ 415 Principle of limited liability

The GmbH is a legal entity that is separate and distinct from its shareholders. The GmbH itself can thus be subject to rights and obligations arising out of the legal relationships it has entered into or that came into existence with its formation. In particular, it may hold property, including real estate, may appear before a court, file suit or be sued in its own name. Furthermore, the GmbH's existence as a legal entity is not affected by changes among its shareholders, *e.g.*, by way of share transfers.

§ 416 Registration with the commercial register

The company needs to register with the commercial register maintained at the competent local court in order to validly come into existence as a GmbH. Prior to registration, the company merely exists as a so-called "pre-GmbH" (*Vor-GmbH*). Generally, following registration only the GmbH, and not its shareholders, is liable for the performance of its obligations. However, the shareholders may incur personal liability under certain circumstances.

III. Corporate governance of the GmbH

§ 417 Corporate bodies

The GmbH is usually vested with two corporate bodies: its shareholders and one or more general managers (*Geschäftsführer*). In certain cases, the GmbH may also have a supervisory board or advisory council (*Beirat*).

§ 418 Shareholders

As a matter of principle, the decision-making power of the shareholders is unlimited. Although they usually only vote on general business matters, they may as well give binding instructions to the general managers on specific issues relating to the company's day-to-day business. The right to give instructions to management is one of the principal distinguishing features of a GmbH as compared to an AG. Decisions of the shareholders of an GmbH are made in the shareholders' meeting and generally require a majority of the votes cast.

Unless otherwise stipulated in the company's articles of association (*e.g.*, one vote per share-holder), the voting rights of the shareholders are proportionate to their interests in the company's nominal share capital. Except for fundamental decisions (*e.g.*, amendments of the articles of association, liquidation of the GmbH), the shareholders may transfer the power to make decisions on behalf of the GmbH to the general managers or to a supervisory board, as the case may be.

§ 419 General managers and Prokuristen

The position of a general manager of a GmbH is essentially twofold. First, general managers assume an executive position within the company due to their appointment. This executive position comprises both the (internal) authority to manage the company's business and the (external) authority to represent the company *vis-à-vis* third parties. As a general rule, however, general managers do not assume any liability *vis-à-vis* third parties.[760] Second, in most cases, general managers also render services to the GmbH on the basis of a contractual service relationship.[761]

The statutory principle of joint power of representation by all general managers may be changed into sole power of representation or otherwise modified. In conducting the daily business of the GmbH, the general managers are formally under an obligation to act only within the company's business purpose and, under certain circumstances, have to seek shareholders' authorization before taking action. In addition, they have to act in accordance with the instructions issued by the shareholders. Furthermore, the shareholders may revoke their appointment at any time.

As a separate function, general managers assume the responsibilities of the employer on behalf of the GmbH *vis-à-vis* the company's workforce. They also carry out the "entrepreneurial function" on behalf of the company.

Most limited liability companies also have one or several Prokuristen.[762] Such Prokuristen are generally employees of the company who are given the power of representation for the purpose of conducting all business undertaken by the company on a regular basis. Such power may also be revoked at any time, although the dismissal of an employee who no longer is a Prokurist must comply with German employment laws.

General managers, as a matter of law, have unlimited power of representation. The power of representation of Prokuristen, however, is limited to transactions that fall within the regular operation of a business, and they need special authorization regarding certain real estate transactions.

---

760 *Cf.* §§ 603 *et seq.*, below (outlining possible exceptions to the general rule that general managers do not assume any liability *vis-à-vis* third parties), *e.g.*, liability as a result of a specific relationship to the company's creditors, culpable breaches of fiduciary duties or liability based on principles of reliance or tort law.

761 Bürgerliches Gesetzbuch [BGB] [Civil Code] 1896, §§ 611 *et seq.* (F.R.G.); *cf.* §§ 464 *et seq.*, below (addressing the particularities of the underlying service agreement).

762 An authorized signatory with a general commercial power of attorney defined by law.

The explanations in Chapter Five below apply to general managers of both limited liability companies and limited partnerships whose general partner is a GmbH ("GmbH & Co. KG"). The form of the GmbH & Co. KG is used frequently in Germany, and certain of its special characteristics will be highlighted in the liability context below.[763] In particular, due to the dual structure of a GmbH & Co. KG, the general managers act on behalf of both the GmbH and the KG.

§ 420 Supervisory board/advisory council

The establishment of additional corporate bodies, in particular a supervisory board or advisory council is generally permitted. The shareholders' meeting may, *e.g.*, delegate certain powers to such corporate bodies.

As a matter of principle, the installation of a supervisory board or advisory council is optional for a German GmbH. Only if the GmbH has more than 500 employees on a regular basis, it is obliged to form a supervisory board, which must provide, as a matter of co-determination law, for a certain quota (thirty percent or one half), depending on the total number of employees, of members appointed by the shareholders and members appointed by the company's employees. [764]

IV. Articles of association

§ 421 Formal requirements

The articles of association constitute the legal framework of the GmbH. They are adopted by unanimous vote of the shareholders, must be signed by all shareholders and require notarization. Amendments to the articles generally require approval of three-quarters of the votes cast.

§ 422 Content of the articles

The articles of association must contain at least provisions regarding name and registered office of the company, the registered nominal share capital and the initial contribution of each shareholder, and designate a corporate purpose. Any place in Germany may be chosen as the registered office of the GmbH, and any lawful purpose is eligible as its corporate purpose. If the corporate purpose includes regulated banking or insurance activities, the formation of the GmbH can only be completed with the approval of the BaFin, the German banking and insurance regulator.

The articles of association may contain further arrangements, such as an obligation for shareholders to make additional contributions, provisions regarding the distribution of profits, provisions regarding liquidation and the like. It is also possible to restrict the free transferability of shares.

---

763   *Cf.* §§ 622 *et seq.*
764   *Cf.* §§ 197 *et seq.* above for the supervisory board of a German AG.

§ 423 Sample protocol

Together with the UG, the possibility to execute a so-called sample protocol was introduced to the Limited Liability Companies Act. The sample protocol combines three documents (articles of association, shareholders' resolution to appoint a general manager and a list of shareholders) into one single document with only a few blanks left to complete. The sample protocol may be used for the formation of a regular GmbH as well as a UG having up to three shareholders and one general manager. The sample protocol is therefore a suitable option for small businesses. Its use is rewarded by lower incorporation costs. However, it does not allow for much flexibility, as it may not be modified in any way. For example, it does not provide for contributions in kind.

V. Registered nominal share capital

§ 424 General rule and particularities in the case of an UG

As a matter of principle, the minimum registered nominal share capital to set up a "regular" GmbH is EUR 25,000. It is to be divided into one or more shares. In deviation from the general rule, the UG may be incorporated with a registered nominal share capital as low as EUR 1. During the period in which the registered nominal share capital of the UG remains below EUR 25,000, the UG is obliged to contribute one quarter of its annual net profits to a special mandatory reserve that may only be released for certain specified purposes. Once the UG increases its registered capital to EUR 25,000 or above, it matures to a "regular" GmbH and may change the suffix to its corporate name to GmbH.

CHAPTER SIX
GENERAL MANAGERS
OF THE GMBH

I.   Composition and number of general managers

§ 425 Introduction

The GmbH must have at least one general manager to conduct the GmbH's business and represent the GmbH *vis-à-vis* third parties. The company cannot be released from the statutory requirement of having a general manager, *e.g.*, by a provision to this effect in the articles of association, as such release would render the company incapable of acting. The appointment of a shareholder to the position of a general manager (so-called *Gesellschafter-Geschäftsführer*) is permitted. However, shareholder status is not a prerequisite for the appointment as a general manager. The following sections elaborate on the number as well as on the particular types of general managers.

A.   Number of general managers

§ 426 General managers as an essential corporate body

Because only general managers are entitled to apply for the registration of a company as a GmbH with the commercial register (*Handelsregister*), at least one general manager must already be in office prior to that registration.[765] Should an existing GmbH lose its sole general manager, *e.g.*, due to death, removal or resignation from office, it is no longer capable of acting.[766] In such a case, although Prokuristen[767] or holders of a commercial power of attorney may temporarily continue conducting the business of the company, new general managers must be appointed without undue delay.[768] By comparison, where a GmbH loses only one of several general managers, a new general manager must be appointed only if no other general manager with authorization to represent the company is available, or if a specific number of general managers is required under applicable law (*e.g.*, for financial institutions pursuant to the Banking Act) or under the company's articles of association.

Where declarations are made *vis-à-vis* the GmbH or legal documents (including submissions in legal proceedings) are served on the company during a period without a general manager in

---

765 GmbH-Gesetz [GmbHG] [Limited Liability Companies Act] 1892, § 6, ¶ 1, § 78 (F.R.G.).
766 GmbH-Gesetz [GmbHG] [Limited Liability Companies Act] 1892, § 6, ¶ 1, § 35, ¶ 1 (F.R.G.).
767 An authorized signatory with a general commercial power of attorney defined by law.
768 *Cf.* §§ 432 *et seq.*, below (discussing the appointment of general managers).

place, each shareholder functions as an authorized recipient (*Empfangsvertreter*) with regard to such communication on behalf of the company.

§ 427 Determination by the company of the number of general managers

As a general principle, each GmbH is entitled to determine, at its discretion, the number of general managers to be appointed. However, in the case of a "co-determined"[769] GmbH (*e.g.*, a company required to install a supervisory board with the mandate that half of its members are employee representatives), in addition to the regular general managers a so-called labor director must also be appointed to the position of general manager.[770] Thus, co-determined limited liability companies must have at least two general managers. If a GmbH's articles of association do not contain any provisions regarding the number of general managers to be appointed, the shareholders' meeting may determine such number by way of a simple majority vote.

B.   Types of general managers

§ 428 Chairman

Where a GmbH has several general managers, the shareholders may appoint one of them as chairman on the basis of a provision in the articles of association, the rules of procedure, or a shareholders' resolution. To the extent not stipulated otherwise by any of such acts, the general managers may appoint a chairman on their own. In the case of co-determined companies,[771] the supervisory board is the sole competent body to appoint a chairman.[772] An appointment for chairman may be revoked at any time.

The chairman usually assumes responsibilities pertaining to business coordination and the representation of the company, and is often also granted sole (internal) management power. Depending on the agreed structure of the position, the chairman may also have the right to exercise veto rights regarding resolutions of the other general managers. In a co-determined company, the chairman can never have a general veto right, because this would compromise the equal weight of the position of the labor director.

As an alternative to appointing a chairman, the shareholders or general managers of a GmbH may instead choose to appoint a spokesperson for the executive board who will then assume responsibilities pertaining to business coordination and the representation of the company similar to a chairperson.

---

769 *Cf.* §§ 197 *et seq.*, above for the supervisory board of a German AG.
770 Mitbestimmungsgesetz [MitbestG] [Co-Determination Act] 1976, § 33 (F.R.G.); Montan-Mitbestimmungsgesetz [MontanMitbestG] [Coal and Steel-Co-Determination Act] 1951, § 13 (F.R.G.); Mitbestimmungsergänzungs-gesetz [MitbestErgG] [Co-Determination Amendment Act] 1956, § 13 (F.R.G.). *Cf.* § 11 above and § 429 below.
771 *Cf.* § 427.
772 Mitbestimmungsgesetz [MitbestG] [Co-Determination Act] 1976, § 30; Aktiengesetz [AktG] [Stock Corporation Act] 1965, § 84, ¶ 2 (F.R.G.).

§ 429 Labor director

As mentioned above, in co-determined companies, a member of the management who is of equal standing to the other members is to be appointed as labor director.[773] The labor director is responsible for personnel and social issues, but may also be assigned additional responsibilities as specified in the rules of procedure of the general managers.[774] Like all general managers, the labor director is required to comply with the instructions of the shareholders.[775]

§ 430 Deputy general managers

Deputy general managers may be appointed in accordance with the same requirements that apply with respect to the appointment of regular general managers.[776]

Deputy general managers enjoy the same status as regular general managers *vis-à-vis* third parties, including, in particular, the power of representation. Thus, where the general managers of the company have joint power of representation, any deputy general managers also have to participate in order to make the transaction or other legal action binding on the company. Similarly, applications for registration with the commercial register, which must be executed by all general managers, must also be signed by any deputy general managers.[777]

As a general rule, deputy general managers also have unlimited internal authority with respect to conducting the company's business. However, the specific powers of deputy general managers may be limited in the articles of association or the rules of procedure of the management board. For example, the internal management powers of deputy general managers may be limited such that they are only authorized to participate in the management of the company where one of the regular general managers is unable to do so.

II. Appointment and service relationship of general managers

§ 431 Relationship between appointment and service agreement

As mentioned above, two distinct legal relationships exist between the company and each general manager: On the one hand, the general manager, through his appointment, is installed as a member of a corporate body (*i.e.*, the executive board) of the company. His appointment gives rise to the right and obligation to assume the management and representation of the company as well as additional executive obligations. On the other hand, the company usually concludes a service agreement with the general manager, which governs their contractual relations.

---

773   Mitbestimmungsgesetz [MitbestG] [Co-Determination Act] 1976, § 33 (F.R.G.); Montan-Mitbestimmungsgesetz [MontanMitbestG] [Coal and Steel-Co-Determination Act] 1951, § 13; Mitbestimmungsergänzungsgesetz [MitbestErgG] [Co-Determination Amendment Act] 1956, § 13 (F.R.G.). *Cf.* § 11 above.
774   Mitbestimmungsgesetz [MitbestG] [Co-Determination Act] 1976, § 33, ¶ 2, sentence 2 (F.R.G.).
775   GmbH-Gesetz [GmbHG] [Limited Liability Companies Act] 1892, § 37, ¶ 1 (F.R.G.).
776   GmbH-Gesetz [GmbHG] [Limited Liability Companies Act] 1892, § 44 (F.R.G.).
777   *E.g.*, GmbH-Gesetz [GmbHG] [Limited Liability Companies Act] 1892, § 78 (F.R.G.).

The appointment as general manager and the service agreement are each subject to different requirements in respect of their validity and termination, and the legal status of one is generally not dependent on the legal status of the other. For example, the termination of the service agreement does not affect the appointment as general manager. Where a dismissal from the executive position is desired as a consequence of the termination of the service agreement, this must be explicitly decided by the shareholders' meeting.

A. Requirements, commencement and termination of the appointment of a general manager

§ 432 Registration with the commercial register
Both the appointment and the removal from office of a general manager must be registered with the competent commercial register. While such registration is not a prerequisite for the validity of the appointment or removal from office, it is necessary in order to release the company from liability on the basis of principles of reliance (*Vertrauenshaftung*) that may otherwise be incurred.[778]

1. Eligibility requirements
§ 433 Introduction
A candidate for general manager must fulfill certain statutory eligibility requirements. In addition, the shareholders of the company may stipulate further requirements in the articles of association and have considerable discretion in this regard within the boundaries of public policy.

§ 434 Unlimited legal capacity
Both shareholders and third parties with no connection to the company may be appointed as general managers. General managers must be natural persons with unlimited legal capacity.[779] Therefore, persons who do not have full legal capacity, as well as legal entities, are not eligible for the position of general manager. Should a general manager lose his full legal capacity, he will *ipso facto* lose his status as general manager, *e.g.*, without any need for further action to be taken in this regard.

§ 435 General managers residing abroad
As a general principle, foreign citizens may be appointed as general managers of a German GmbH. The Limited Liability Companies Act does not impose any particular requirements in this case. According to the prevailing view, foreign citizens who are appointed as general managers are not required to have a place of residence in Germany or a permanent residence, work or trading permit. However, various courts have required general managers residing abroad to have a reliable means of entering the country legally. Recent court decisions have demon-

---

778   Handelsgesetzbuch [HGB] [Commercial Code] 1897, § 15, ¶ 1 (F.R.G.).
779   GmbH-Gesetz [GmbHG] [Limited Liability Companies Act] 1892, § 6, ¶ 1 (F.R.G.).

strated more flexibility in this respect in light of the new rules according to which the administrative office of a GmbH can be located outside of Germany.[780]

§ 436 No convictions or suspensions

Any person who has been convicted of an insolvency offense may not become a general manager of a GmbH for a period of five years from the date when such conviction became final.[781]

Moreover, a person who has been barred by a court or public authority from carrying out a particular profession or business, or from being active in a particular industry, may not, for the duration of the period of suspension, become a general manager of a company whose business is, entirely or partially, the same as the profession or business which is the subject matter of the suspension.[782]

In the application for the registration of his appointment with the commercial register the general manager to be appointed must affirm that neither a conviction for an insolvency offense nor any pertinent suspension from the practice of his occupation or operation of a business poses an obstacle to his appointment, and that he has been informed of his obligation to provide all relevant information to the court.[783]

As a result of the MoMiG, the grounds for ineligibility of general managers were recently expanded and now also include, *inter alia*, convictions for delay of initiating insolvency proceedings, provision of false information and misrepresentation, as well as convictions for offenses with a corporate connection.[784] This also applies in respect of convictions for comparable offenses abroad.

§ 437 Instruction of appointee

A person who is to be appointed as general manager must be given various instructions – orally or in writing – by a German notary. In the case of a foreign appointee, such instructions are intended to provide information about the personal prerequisites of a general manager under German law and, in particular, the obligation to fully disclose any relevant information to the commercial register. If the appointee is domiciled abroad, instruction by a foreign notary, a representative of a comparable profession (in particular attorneys) or a consular officer is also permissible. The instruction may be provided in writing in a language other than German, to be acknowledged by the appointee through his signature. In the interest of legal certainty, it is advisable to coordinate the concrete steps to be taken in this respect with the competent commercial register.

---

780   GmbH-Gesetz [GmbHG] [Limited Liability Companies Act] 1892, § 4a (F.R.G.).
781   GmbH-Gesetz [GmbHG] [Limited Liability Companies Act] 1892, § 6, ¶ 2, sentence 2, no. 3 b) (F.R.G.);
        Strafgesetzbuch [StGB] [Criminal Code] 1871, §§ 283-283d (F.R.G.).
782   GmbH-Gesetz [GmbHG] [Limited Liability Companies Act] 1892, § 6, ¶ 2, no. 2 (F.R.G.).
783   GmbH-Gesetz [GmbHG] [Limited Liability Companies Act] 1892, § 8, ¶ 3, sentence 1 (F.R.G.).
784   GmbH-Gesetz [GmbHG] [Limited Liability Companies Act] 1892, § 6, ¶ 2 (F.R.G.).

§ 438 Special requirements for general managers of certain types of limited liability companies

Certain statutes and professional laws stipulate special additional requirements for general managers. For example, specific reliability and professional qualification requirements apply to general managers of financial institutions and insurance companies. Furthermore, the general managers of a tax consultancy GmbH must, as a basic principle, be qualified tax consultants. In addition, at least one general manager must have his place of residence at the location of the company's registered office or at least in its vicinity. Similar requirements apply to auditing and accountancy GmbHs[785] as well as law firms organized as a GmbH.

§ 439 Specification of eligibility requirements in the articles of association

The GmbH's articles of association may contain additional requirements with regard to the personal qualifications of general managers. For example, it is possible to stipulate that general managers may not be older than a certain age at the time of their appointment or that they have certain professional qualifications.

Furthermore, it may be stipulated that only shareholders can be appointed as general managers. A shareholder may also be granted an irrevocable right to participate in the management of the company by virtue of the articles of association.

Special restrictions apply to provisions regarding the eligibility requirements of general managers in the articles of co-determined limited liability companies.[786]

§ 440 Non-fulfillment of a statutory eligibility requirement

Where a statutory eligibility requirement is not met at the time of the appointment of the general manager, the appointment is null and void from the outset. This is true even if the situation is later remedied, *e.g.*, if the appointee's suspension from the practice of his occupation expires.

If a general manager ceases to meet one of the eligibility requirements at a later point in time, his term of office will automatically terminate by operation of law, and the corresponding entry in the commercial register must be deleted *ex officio*. Under certain circumstances, the prior dealings of such terminated general managers are considered to be valid in accordance with the so-called principles of irregular appointments under German law, and the appointment may be declared invalid only with effect for the future.

Notably, in the case of an appointment that is null and void, the company may become liable *vis-à-vis* third parties in accordance with the principles of reliance if the general manager remains registered with the commercial register.

---

785 Wirtschaftsprüferordnung [WPO] [Auditors' Regulations] 1961, §§ 28, 130, ¶ 2 (F.R.G.).
786 According to a differing opinion, no additional stipulations regarding eligibility requirements for general managers are permissible in the articles of a co-determined GmbH.

§ 441 Non-fulfillment of an eligibility requirement stipulated in the articles of association
Where an eligibility requirement stipulated in the GmbH's articles of association is not observed in the appointment of a general manager, the appointment can be challenged, *e.g.*, by
minority shareholders. If a general manager no longer meets a stipulated eligibility requirement at a later point in time, this will constitute due cause for the general manager's removal
from office and may even give rise to an obligation of the shareholders to remove the general
manager from office.

§ 442 Members of the supervisory board
A GmbH may have an optional supervisory board or advisory council. In case of a co-determined GmbH, the company must have a supervisory board as a matter of law.[787] Because the
function of the supervisory board or advisory council is to supervise the management of the
company, it is not permissible to appoint a member of the supervisory board or advisory council
as a general manager on a permanent basis.[788] However, it is permissible to appoint members of
these bodies as temporary substitutes for absent or incapacitated general managers for a finite
period with a maximum of one year. This is an exceptional measure that is generally only used
in cases of emergency.

§ 443 Non-compete obligation
As a matter of principle, general managers of a German GmbH are subject to a non-compete
obligation. Specifically, general managers are not permitted to use their position to harm the
company by exploiting its business opportunities in their own interest or to operate a competing business. Therefore, a company may be entitled to claim damages from a general manager
not complying with the non-compete obligation.

It is controversial among commentators (absent a clear indication from the courts) whether
general managers are allowed to assume dual or multiple mandates according to Section 88(1)
of the Stock Corporation Act,[789] which would then apply *mutatis mutandis* to limited liability
companies. If dual or multiple mandates are allowed at all, they would only be permissible with
the consent of the company's shareholders' meeting or, in the case of a co-determined GmbH,
the consent of the company's supervisory board. Thus, it is in any event advisable for a general
manager to obtain the consent of the competent corporate body prior to assuming a corporate
position with another company.[790]

2.   Act of appointment
§ 444 Introduction
An appointment of a member of the executive board may be effected in the articles of association, by a resolution of the shareholders' meeting or the supervisory board, as the case may be,
by a shareholder who has been given the right to appoint one ore more general managers, and,

---

787   *Cf.* § 427 above.
788   Aktiengesetz [AktG] [Stock Corporation Act] 1965, § 105, ¶ 2 sentence 1; GmbH-Gesetz [GmbHG] [Limited
      Liability Companies Act] 1892, § 52, ¶ 1 (F.R.G.).
789   *Cf.* § 93 above.
790   For further discussion on the non-compete obligation in the context of a general manager's duty of loyalty, *cf.* § 513.

in urgent, exceptional cases, also by a court of law.[791] The effectiveness of the appointment is always contingent upon its acceptance by the designated general manager.

The subsequent sections deal with the different options for regular appointments and the legal consequences of an irregular appointment.

§ 445 Requirements for an appointment in the articles of association

The appointment of a general manager may be effected by the GmbH's articles of association.[792] In practice, the general manager is usually appointed during the start-up phase of the company, because the GmbH must already have a general manager in office prior to its registration with the commercial register. A shareholder is eligible to be appointed as general manager at this early stage.

As a basic principle, an appointment in the articles of association implies an appointment on the occasion of the adoption of the articles. However, the rules for the amendment of the articles generally do not have to be observed in the case of a removal from office or re-appointment of a general manager.

In the case of a co-determined GmbH, an appointment of a general manager in the articles of association is not permissible due to the special role of the mandatory supervisory board.[793]

§ 446 Requirements for an appointment by the shareholders' meeting

Where the appointment of general managers has not already been effected in the articles of association and has not been assigned to another corporate body (or a shareholder) in the articles or by statute, the shareholders' meeting is generally competent to appoint the general managers of the company. In fact, appointment by the shareholders' meeting is the usual case.

The shareholders' meeting appoints general managers by way of a resolution with a majority vote.[794] Shareholders may generally vote on a resolution regarding their own appointment, even where their remuneration is to be determined in the same resolution. The written minutes of the shareholders' meeting or a transcript thereof must be submitted to the competent commercial register, which will examine whether the resolution appointing the general manager was duly adopted.

§ 447 Requirements for an appointment by the supervisory board

The appointment of a general manager may also be assigned to the supervisory board or in

---

791   It is subject to controversy whether also third parties and public authorities may be authorized to appoint a general manager.

792   GmbH-Gesetz [GmbHG] [Limited Liability Companies Act] 1892, § 6, ¶ 3, sentence 2 (F.R.G.).

793   Mitbestimmungsgesetz [MitbestG] [Co-Determination Act] 1976, § 31 (F.R.G.); Montan-Mitbestimmungsgesetz [MontanMitbestG] [Coal and Steel-Co-Determination Act] 1951, § 12 (F.R.G.); Mitbestimmungsergänzungsgesetz [MitbestErgG] [Co-Determination Amendment Act] 1956, § 13 (F.R.G.) in conjunction with Aktiengesetz [AktG] [Stock Corporation Act] 1965, § 84 (F.R.G.).

794   GmbH-Gesetz [GmbHG] [Limited Liability Companies Act] 1892, § 46, no. 1, § 47, ¶ 1 (F.R.G.).

case the company is not co-determined, the optional supervisory board, to the chairman or a committee thereof.

Except in the case of co-determined companies, an assignment of the appointment authority to the supervisory board must be based on a provision in the articles of association to that effect. Unless the articles of association, the applicable rules of procedure or the applicable co-determination statute stipulate otherwise, a resolution passed with a simple majority of the votes cast suffices for an appointment of a general manager by the supervisory board.

§ 448 Requirements for an appointment by an authorized shareholder or public authorities

Except in the case of co-determined companies, the articles of association may authorize a shareholder to nominate a general manager directly.[795] In this case, it is also possible for the authorized individual to nominate himself as general manager. A specific shareholder group, e.g., a family, may also be afforded the right to appoint a general manager. Such an appointment must not follow a particular form, but should be recorded in writing, because proof of the appointment must be provided for purposes of its registration with the commercial register.[796]

§ 449 Requirements and proceedings for an appointment by the court

If, for whatever reason, the position of general manager is vacant, the local court at the location of the company's registered office has, in urgent cases, the right to appoint a so-called emergency general manager (*Notgeschäftsführer*). Such appointment is only carried out upon application. All shareholders and members of other corporate bodies of the company are entitled to apply for the appointment of an emergency general manager. An application for an emergency appointment may also be submitted by any third party who is unable to enforce its rights *vis-à-vis* the company, because the company is not validly represented. The application may include a specific nomination. While the court, in selecting the general manager, is bound only by the legal and statutory eligibility criteria, it will usually be inclined to appoint the nominee.

The position of general manager is considered vacant where the company no longer has any general managers at all, or where the existing general managers are unable to perform the duties of their office for legal or *de facto* reasons. In this context, a legal obstacle exists, *e.g.*, where there is no longer the requisite number of general managers required for the purposes of representing the company, or where a general manager, in acting for the company, would contravene the restrictions on self-dealing imposed by Section 181 of the Civil Code. A *de facto* obstacle exists, *e.g.*, where a general manager is unable to perform the duties of his office on a permanent basis due to illness.

---

795 It is controversial among commentators whether the articles of association may also assign the right to appoint a general manager to a public authority or another third party. Pertinent case law does not exist with regard to this issue.

796 GmbH-Gesetz [GmbHG] [Limited Liability Companies Act] 1892, § 39; §§ 39, 8, ¶ 1, no. 2 (F.R.G.).

The court may only appoint a general manager in urgent cases where it is not possible for another authorized person or body to make the appointment without delay, or where the company in question would suffer considerable damage unless an emergency appointment is effected. An emergency appointment is invalid where the consequences of the lack of a general manager could be dealt with through less drastic measures. The shareholders' inability to reach an agreement regarding the regular appointment of a general manager does not provide the requisite element of urgency for an appointment by the court.

In connection with the appointment, the court specifies the degree of power of representation conferred upon the emergency general manager. In addition, the court must restrict the management power of the emergency general manager to only those actions and transactions that are absolutely necessary.

§ 450 Legal consequences of inadequate appointments of general managers

Where the appointment of a general manager is irregular on the ground that the statutory requirements have not been properly fulfilled or the general manager has not accepted the appointment, it will be null and void. In such a case, however, the so-called principles of irregular appointments may apply, *e.g.*, the company might still be bound by the actions of such persons. If an individual acts as a general manager with the consent of the shareholders, but absent any formal appointment, such an individual is referred to as a "*de facto* general manager". The actions of a *de facto* general manager on behalf of the company may in part be effective.

It should also be noted that upon the registration of the general manager with the commercial register, his actions may give rise to obligations on the part of the company based on the principles of reliance, even where the resolution appointing the general manager was inadequate or no formal appointment occurred. In this case, third parties are under certain conditions entitled to rely on the accuracy of the commercial register.

3. Termination of the mandate
§ 451 General principle

As a matter of principle, the corporate body responsible for the appointment of a general manager is also responsible for his removal from office.

§ 452 Authority for the removal

According to the applicable statutory provisions, the removal from office of a general manager generally falls within the authority of the shareholders' meeting.[797] Such authority may be transferred, however, by the company's articles of association to other corporate bodies.[798] Where this responsibility has been transferred to another corporate body, the shareholders' meeting nonetheless retains secondary competence in case the corporate body so empowered should prove unable to carry out that responsibility. If the right of removal from office is grant-

---

797 GmbH-Gesetz [GmbHG] [Limited Liability Companies Act] 1892, § 33; § 46 no. 5 (F.R.G.).

798 It is controversial among commentators whether such authority may also be transferred to third parties, such as dominant entities in the corporate group, silent partners or public authorities.

ed to an individual or to a group of shareholders, a corporate body of the company must still retain the right of removal for due cause.

In the case of a co-determined GmbH,[799] the mandatory supervisory board is the solely responsible corporate body for the removal from office of general managers.[800]

In a GmbH & Co. KG,[801] the removal of a general manager of the GmbH (with the GmbH being the general partner of the company) also requires the approval of the limited partners. Such approval is required because the removal constitutes a fundamental measure with regard to the KG due to the GmbH's position as general partner managing the KG.

§ 453 Requirements for a removal resolution

As a general principle, the shareholders' resolution for the removal from office of a general manager requires a simple majority of the votes cast. The articles of association may provide different majority requirements. The general manager to be removed from office is entitled to vote on the resolution if he is a shareholder, except in the case of a removal from office for due cause.

The agenda for the shareholders' meeting in question must be sufficiently specific, *e.g.*, it must enable the shareholders to discern that it relates to a removal of a general manager from office. However, it is not necessary to specify the reason for the removal in the agenda.

§ 454 Removal from office possible at any time

As a general principle, the general managers of a GmbH may be removed from office at any time and without reason.[802]

However, a removal from office effected on evidently improper grounds is invalid.[803] For example, a removal from office, which is only effected in order to enable the general manager to be called as a witness, constitutes an abuse of a legal right. Moreover, in the case of a shareholder acting as a general manager, there must always be proper grounds for a removal from office because of the fiduciary duty that shareholders owe to one another under corporate law. Conversely, this mutually owed fiduciary duty obligates the shareholders to consent to the removal from office of one of their fellow shareholders, where significant reasons exist that would make it unreasonable for him to retain such position.

A removal for due cause must always remain within the power of the shareholders and be accomplished through a resolution by way of a simple majority vote, except where the right of removal falls within the competence of the supervisory board or another corporate body.

---

799 *Cf.* § 427, above (discussing the principles of co-determination).
800 Mitbestimmungsgesetz [MitbestG] [Co-Determination Act] 1976, § 31 (F.R.G.); Montan-Mitbestimmungsgesetz [MontanMitbestG] [Coal and Steel-Co-Determination Act] 1951, § 12 (F.R.G.); Mitbestimmungsergänzungsgesetz [MitbestErgG] [Co-Determination Amendment Act] 1956, § 13 in conjunction with Aktiengesetz [AktG] [Stock Corporation Act] 1965, § 84, ¶ 3 (F.R.G.).
801 *Cf.* § 622, below (explaining the particularities of a GmbH & Co. KG from a liability perspective).
802 GmbH-Gesetz [GmbHG] [Limited Liability Companies Act] 1892, § 38, ¶ 1 (F.R.G.).
803 Bürgerliches Gesetzbuch [BGB] [Civil Code] 1896, §§ 226 and 826 (F.R.G.).

A removal from office remains possible even in cases where the company will be incapable of acting as a consequence of such removal. However, the company must appoint a new general manager without delay in such a case.

§ 455 Stipulations regarding removals from office in the GmbH's articles of association

The possibility of a removal from office at any time and with immediate effect for due cause must always be preserved and may not be excluded by the terms of the articles of association. Thus, while the articles of association of a GmbH may provide that the appointment of a general manager can only be revoked for due cause,[804] any stipulation excluding an objective due cause as a reason for a revocation of the general manager's appointment would be invalid. Where the position of general manager is conferred "irrevocably" or "for life" in the articles of association, this clause is usually interpreted as permitting a removal from office only for due cause.

Other limitations on the right of removal are also possible. For example, the articles of association may stipulate that a general manager can only be removed from office for a reason other than due cause if a specified period of notice is provided.

§ 456 Removal from office for due cause

Due cause is present where, upon consideration of the conflicting interests involved, it would be unacceptable for the GmbH and its shareholders to keep the general manager in office.

The Limited Liability Companies Act identifies gross breaches of duty or an inability to assume the proper management of the company as due cause for the removal from office of a general manager.[805] Further grounds that have been recognized as constituting due cause include gross breaches of confidence, inadequate keeping of accounts, use of company assets for personal purposes, participation in dubious transactions, breach of the duty to maintain confidentiality, acceptance of bribes, persistent illness or discord among the general managers. However, where the articles of association provide that the appointment of a general manager may be revoked for due cause, a mere withdrawal of confidence by the shareholders' meeting will not be sufficient to justify such a revocation.

The articles of association can stipulate further reasons that shall qualify as due cause, even though they do not constitute due causes from an objective perspective (*e.g.*, age limits, relocation of domicile, assumption of political functions etc.).

The right of removal for due cause may be forfeited if the company was aware of the circumstances constituting the due cause for a considerable period of time, yet did not act upon this knowledge by revoking the appointment, and the general manager in question could thus, on reasonable grounds and in good faith, assume that the company would not rely on those circumstances as a basis for a revocation of his appointment. However, there is no clear-cut time period for the forfeiture.

---

804   GmbH-Gesetz [GmbHG] [Limited Liability Companies Act] 1892, § 38, ¶ 2 (F.R.G.).
805   GmbH-Gesetz [GmbHG] [Limited Liability Companies Act] 1892, § 38, ¶ 2, no. 2 (F.R.G.).

§ 457 Management position as a shareholder's right

Where the right to participate in the management of a company was granted to a shareholder in the form of an irrevocable right of membership, the removal from office of the general manager who is also a shareholder may only be effected with the latter's agreement, unless there is due cause for the removal from office.

§ 458 Legal effects of a revocation from office

A valid revocation from office terminates the general manager's executive position, thus entailing the termination of his statutory management competences and power of representation.

The revocation does not, however, automatically lead to the termination of the general manager's service agreement with the company.[806] Furthermore, according to pertinent case law, a revocation for due cause as such does not entitle the general manager to claim damages for breach of the service agreement.

§ 459 Termination of office by way of expiration of term

In addition to a possible removal or resignation, the appointment of a general manager can also terminate by expiration of the term of office.

Whether a general manager is to be appointed for an indefinite term or for a fixed term and, in the latter case, the duration for which he is to be appointed, is fundamentally within the discretion of the shareholders. In the case of co-determined companies, the duration of the appointment is limited to a maximum of five years, although re-appointment is possible.[807]

§ 460 Termination by way of resignation

Provided that the GmbH's articles of association do not stipulate otherwise, a general manager may, as a rule, resign from office at any time, even without due cause, by a simple notice of resignation.

The resignation notice does not have to take any particular form. It must be submitted to the corporate body that appointed the general manager in question. A confirmation of the competent body's receipt of the resignation notice must be submitted to the commercial register together with an application for registration of the resignation from office.

A resignation from office is invalid only in exceptional cases, namely when it is inappropriate as to its timing or otherwise declared in an abusive manner. For example, a resignation may be deemed invalid where the sole general manager wishes to step down in the absence of due cause and without nominating a successor to his office.

---

806   *Cf.* §§ 464 *et seq.* (dealing with specific aspects of the service agreement).
807   Aktiengesetz [AktG] [Stock Corporation Act] 1965, § 84, ¶ 1 (F.R.G.) in conjunction with Mitbestimmungsgesetz [MitbestG] [Co-Determination Act] 1976, § 31 (F.R.G.); Montan-Mitbestimmungsgesetz [Montan-MitbestG] [Coal and Steel-Co-Determination Act] 1951, § 12 (F.R.G.); Mitbestimmungsergänzungsgesetz [MitbestErgG] [Co-Determination Amendment Act] 1956, § 13 (F.R.G.).

The validity of the resignation from the corporate office of the general manager is independent of the legal relationship under the law of obligations between the general manager and the company, which is usually reflected in the service agreement. However, where the general manager resigns from office without being entitled to do so under the service agreement, this may give rise to a claim for damages by the company.

As an alternative to unilateral resignation from office, a general manager and the company may mutually terminate the appointment by means of a termination agreement (*Aufhebungsvertrag*). Where such a termination agreement is later rescinded or terminated, the general manager does not *ipso facto* assume his former position, but has to be formally reappointed.

§ 461 Termination of the service agreement

It is permissible to stipulate in the service agreement[808] that the term of the appointment shall be dependent upon the persistence of that service agreement. Where the service agreement ends by way of termination or expiration of its term, the appointment would then also terminate automatically without the need for any further resolution in this regard. Even where the appointment and the persistence of the service agreement are not contractually linked, pertinent case law holds that a termination of the service agreement by the company generally entails the simultaneous revocation of the appointment.

§ 462 Death of a general manager, operation of law and dissolution of the company

Where the statutory eligibility criteria (*e.g.*, unlimited legal capacity, no conviction for an insolvency offense, no suspension from the practice of one's occupation or from the operation of a business etc.)[809] cease to be met, the mandate of the general manager will terminate by operation of law, *e.g.*, without the need for any further action. The death of a general manager always results in the termination of his office, and the position will not be transferred to his heir(s).

Moreover, the office of a general manager also terminates upon the dissolution of the company, unless the position of general manager is thereupon automatically converted into that of a liquidator.[810] The general managers will be the liquidators of the company if such function has not been assigned to another person in the company's articles of association, by shareholders' resolution or, in exceptional cases, by court decision.

The former general managers in their capacity as liquidators have the same power of representation as they previously had in their capacity as general managers. However, their authority to manage the company is restricted by the purpose of liquidation.[811] The former general manager's service agreement with the company continues to exist.

---

808 *Cf.* §§ 464 *et seq.*, below (addressing specific aspects of the service agreement).
809 *Cf.* §§ 434 *et seq.*, above (discussing the relevant eligibility criteria).
810 GmbH-Gesetz [GmbHG] [Limited Liability Companies Act] 1892, § 66 (F.R.G.).
811 GmbH-Gesetz [GmbHG] [Limited Liability Companies Act] 1892, § 70 (F.R.G.).

The termination of an appointment may also occur upon the implementation of certain types of corporate reorganizations, *e.g.*, in certain cases of statutory mergers or transformation of the GmbH into another legal form.

§ 463 Termination of the office of an emergency general manager

Special rules apply to a removal from office of an emergency general manager.

As a matter of principle, where an emergency general manager does not resign from office, he may only be removed from office by the court which appointed him. Such removal from office may occur upon application by the shareholders or the management of the company and should also be permissible on an *ex officio* basis. To the extent that the conditions for the appointment of an emergency general manager still persist at the time of the application for removal,[812] the removal from office must be for due cause and the court must contemporaneously appoint another emergency general manager. The office of an emergency general manager automatically terminates once the emergency situation has been resolved, *e.g.*, when a new general manager is appointed by the shareholders' meeting.

B. Service agreement of the general manager

§ 464 Introduction

Much like the articles of association and rules of procedure for the executive board govern the appointment of a general manager, the service agreement governs the relationship between the general manager and the company under the law of obligations.

In particular, the service agreement usually contains provisions regarding the general manager's remuneration, his responsibilities, as well as the term of the service relationship and termination modalities; see Chapter 7: Annexes, item form of service agreement: General manager of a GmbH, contains a sample service agreement.

1. Service agreement and employment relationship
§ 465 Applicability of labor law provisions[813]

As a practical matter, it is crucial to verify whether certain labor law provisions apply, which may serve to provide the general manager with additional rights *vis-à-vis* the company.

The service agreement is considered a service contract (*Dienstvertrag*) in the form of an agency agreement or, where the management function is carried out on a gratuitous basis, as a mandate, and is in each case subject to the relevant statutory provisions.[814] The service agreement generally does not qualify as an employment contract that is governed by all provisions of labor law, because the general manager is vested with general entrepreneurial freedom (within

---

812   *Cf.* § 449, above (discussing the appointment of an emergency general manager).
813   *Cf.* §§ 481 *et seq.*, below (outlining pension-related issues).
814   Bürgerliches Gesetzbuch [BGB] [Civil Code] 1896, § 611, § 675 or, as the case may be, § 662 (F.R.G.).

certain limits) and is not subject to orders by an employer. By contrast, the general manager exercises the function of an employer *vis-à-vis* the employees of the company.

The Employment Protection Act (*Kündigungsschutzgesetz*), the Working Hours Regulation (*Arbeitszeitordnung*), the Federal Leave Act (*Bundesurlaubsgesetz*) and the Industrial Tribunal Act (*Arbeitsgerichtsgesetz*) are the most important labor law statutes that do not apply in respect of general managers – by operation of explicit statutory provisions to this effect.

However, as far as the protection of the general manager's personal and economic existence is concerned, certain provisions and principles of labor law may apply *mutatis mutandis*.[815] Further, certain general principles of labor law may apply in individual cases where the service relationship comes close to an employment relationship in terms of its form and duration. This may be the case where a general manager is *de facto* obligated to observe the instructions of the shareholders, is dependent on and functionally integrated into the work processes of the company, and does not have any decision-making power. Whereas a controlling shareholder serving as general manager or a shareholder with a blocking minority generally does not qualify as employee, an external or non-controlling shareholder acting as general manager may qualify as an employee.

§ 466 Applicability of social security law provisions

A general manager of a GmbH is generally obligated to pay social security contributions, unless he is in a position to exercise significant influence over the company. A general manager is in a position of significant influence if he can act independently of the other general managers, be it for factual or legal reasons. Such significant influence generally involves a shareholder/ general manager with a share in the company of more than 50%. However, depending on the shareholder structure, a shareholder/general manager with a smaller share – *e.g.*, a blocking minority (*Sperrminorität*) – may also enjoy such independence of action.

§ 467 Former employees as general managers

According to case law, where a former employee is appointed as general manager of a GmbH, the former employment relationship is presumed to have terminated. However, in the interest of clarity and to avoid a dispute relating to the applicable formal requirements, the termination of the former employment relationship and the exclusive application of the new service agreement should be explicitly stipulated in writing. Alternatively, the existing employment contract could be suspended for the duration of the appointment.

2. Conclusion of the service agreement
§ 468 Competence

As a general rule, the service agreement is concluded between the relevant general manager and the GmbH. Because the corporate body responsible for the appointment of a general manager is also responsible for the conclusion and termination of his service agreement, the shareholders' meeting generally is the competent body for the conclusion of the service agreement

---

815   *Cf.* § 475, below (providing further details with regard to employee inventions).

on behalf of the company, even if the company has an optional supervisory board. Special provisions apply to co-determined limited liability companies. The articles of association may provide that the authority to conclude the service agreement may be transferred to other corporate bodies of the company, which may in turn delegate that authority to other bodies. The corporate body that is competent for the conclusion of the agreement is generally also responsible for any amendments thereto and the termination thereof.

§ 469 Service agreements with third parties

A general manager may also conclude a service agreement with a third party – *e.g.*, with the parent company or the KG in a GmbH & Co. KG[816] – in the form of a so-called third-party service agreement. However, the general manager's duties arising out of his executive position are owed to the company which appointed him and remain unaffected by any third-party service arrangements.

Against this background, a general manager may generally not be subject to any instructions issued by third parties on the basis of a third-party service agreement, to the extent that such instructions do not comply with statutory provisions governing the GmbH or its articles of association. Therefore, according to the prevailing view among commentators, the shareholders' meeting of the appointing company must consent to the conclusion of any service agreement a general manager enters with a third-party.

§ 470 Form requirements

There is no required form for a service agreement. The agreement may be concluded orally or even tacitly by way of a meeting of the minds inferred from the conduct of the parties. However, for evidentiary purposes, it is advisable to record the service agreement in writing. Such written form is particularly desirable because salary payments may not be treated as operational expenditure where the content of the service agreement cannot be substantiated in its entirety *vis-à-vis* the competent tax office. Case law has established strict standards for this substantiation of the service agreement, particularly as regards general managers who are also shareholders, which has resulted in a *de facto* written form requirement. Where the company does not succeed in substantiating the existence of a service agreement, payments to the shareholder serving as general manager may be treated as a hidden distribution of profits (*verdeckte Gewinnausschüttung*). The *de facto* written form requirement also applies to amendments of the service agreement.

§ 471 Irregular service agreement

A service agreement is irregular where it contains a defect which would, as a matter of principle, result in it being null and void. A defect is present where the agreement was not concluded by the competent corporate body, or where grounds for cancellation exist, such as willfull deceit (*arglistige Täuschung*) by the general manager or the company.

---

816   *Cf.* §§ 622 *et seq.*, below (describing the structure of such legal entity).

Where the general manager has already assumed office despite the presence of a defect and with the knowledge of the corporate body responsible for the conclusion of the service agreement, the service agreement is to be considered valid for the duration of its *de facto* implementation. Either party may claim the invalidity of the contract only in respect of the future and by means of notice to the other party to the effect that the service relationship should be terminated.

3.   Rights arising out of the service agreement
§ 472 Introduction
In addition to the general manager's right to compensation (treated separately below[817]), the service agreement usually provides for certain other rights in his favor.

§ 473 Right to be provided with employment
A general manager is entitled to the position for which his service agreement is concluded. Should a simultaneous appointment to the position of general manager not occur for any reason, he has a right to be employed in a leading managerial position within the GmbH, unless the company has a legitimate interest in not appointing him. In the latter case, the general manager has an extraordinary right to terminate the service agreement and may be entitled to claim damages from the company.

§ 474 Reimbursement of expenses
A general manager has a claim against the company for the reimbursement of any expenses that he is entitled to regard as necessary for the performance of his duties. However, with respect to meal expenses the general manager has a claim for the reimbursement only to the extent that these are tax-deductible. Further, as a basic principle, a general manager has no claim for the reimbursement of illegal payments such as bribes paid by him.

The general manager also generally does not have a claim for the reimbursement of any penalties or fines incurred by him. However, in the event of an acquittal in proceedings relating to actions taken in his capacity as general manager, the general manager has a claim against the company for the reimbursement of the procedural costs in connection therewith. Contractual indemnification and hold harmless arrangements previously agreed between the company and the general manager are only valid in limited circumstances and may generally only be concluded to cover the negligent commitment of administrative offenses (*Ordnungswidrigkeiten*).

§ 475 Employee inventions
The Act on Employee Inventions (*Arbeitnehmererfindungsgesetz*) does not apply to general managers of a company. As a matter of principle, an invention therefore belongs to the general manager, and the company is generally not entitled to claim the transfer of any right of use regarding inventions by general managers.

However, the service agreement may contain specific provisions regarding the use of the general manager's inventions. For example, the service agreement may set forth whether the gen-

---

817   *Cf.* §§ 478 *et seq.*, below (discussing the compensation of general managers).

eral manager is under an obligation to cede any inventions created by him to the company by way of a full transfer of the respective right or an exclusive or non-exclusive license. In particular, it is permissible to stipulate in the service agreement that the provisions of the Act on Employee Inventions shall apply *mutatis mutandis*. If the company makes use of a general manager's invention, the general manager is generally entitled to demand the compensation that was agreed upon or, if there is no explicit agreement, compensation customary for such invention.[818]

Compensation only has to be granted in cases where the invention constitutes an "over-performance" with regard to the general manager's general service obligations. Notably, if one of the general manager's responsibilities pursuant to the service agreement is the performance of research and development activities, then any invention by that general manager merely reflects the results of the services rendered under the agreement and not an over-performance that should be subject to additional compensation.

§ 476 Vacation

Because a general manager generally does not qualify as an employee of the company,[819] the Federal Leave Act (*Bundesurlaubsgesetz*) also does not apply to him. If the service agreement does not contain any provision regarding vacation, the company is obligated, in accordance with its duty to provide social and medical assistance to its general managers, to ensure that the general manager has a right to a reasonable amount of vacation. Where appropriate, the general manager is compensated in monetary terms for any unused vacation allowance. A general manager going on vacation must ensure that sufficient coverage is found to perform his duties for the duration of his absence.

§ 477 Reference

All general managers, including controlling shareholders acting as general managers, have a right to be provided with a qualified reference by the company in connection with the termination of their service relationship.[820] The corporate body authorized to conclude the service agreement with the general manager is also responsible for the preparation of the reference.

4.   Compensation of general managers
§ 478 Introduction

The compensation of the general manager of a German GmbH usually consists of several components. These are usually a fixed base payment and a variety of additional variable elements. However, there are certain limits to the total amount of a general manager's compensation. Special standards apply, *e.g.*, in case the general manager is at the same time a shareholder of the GmbH concerned.

---

818   Bürgerliches Gesetzbuch [BGB] [Civil Code] 1896, § 612, ¶ 2 (F.R.G.).
819   *Cf.* §§ 465 *et seq.*, above.
820   Bürgerliches Gesetzbuch [BGB] [Civil Code] 1896, § 630 (F.R.G.).

§ 479 Fixed and variable components of compensation

The compensation paid to a general manager may be a fixed or a variable amount. In most cases, a combination of fixed and variable compensation is agreed upon. A general manager's compensation may consist of diverse types of performance-related components, such as bonus payments, preference dividends or an increased shareholding in the company. Consideration in kind, such as a company car and pension commitments, also often forms part of the compensation.[821]

§ 480 Bonus payments

One form of performance-related variable compensation is the management bonus. Sales- or earnings-related bonus payments, or discretionary or fixed-amount bonus payments, may be agreed upon. The annual earnings of the GmbH, preferably before taxes but after loss carry-forwards, as reported in the financial statements of the company, are often chosen as the basis for the calculation of bonus payments. Sales-related bonus payments are less common in practice and are generally more appropriate for companies that are in their start-up phase. In the interest of clarity, the basis for the calculation of the bonus payments should be stipulated in the service agreement.[822]

§ 481 Retirement pensions, payments to dependents and other pension benefits

A general manager is typically granted various pension benefits in his service agreement (or in a separate arrangement referenced in the service agreement), such as a retirement pension, disability benefits and provision for his dependents in the event of his death.[823]

A general manager generally has a claim for a retirement pension only where he has reached an agreement with the company to this effect. In most cases, it will not be possible to deduce the existence of any such claim from a business practice or the principle of equal treatment, as the terms of a general manager's service agreement are negotiated on an individual basis. If a retirement pension agreement exists, it is very important that the amount of the payments be precisely determined. The amount of the retirement payments is usually stipulated as a percentage of the last compensation amount or of the compensation at a particular point in time. It is also possible to link the retirement pension to the compensation of other social groups such as civil servants, in which case the relevant benefits for civil servants, including bonus payments, form the basis for the calculation of the general manager's retirement pension.

§ 482 Vesting of future pension benefits

Corporate pension schemes are governed by the provisions of the Improvement of Company Pension Schemes Act (*Gesetz zur Verbesserung der betrieblichen Altersversorgung*). Such Act, *inter alia*, contains labor law provisions regarding the vesting of, and insolvency insurance for, rights to a company pension that may be of particular importance to general managers.

---

821   *Cf.* Form of Service Agreement for the general manager of a GmbH attached in Chapter Seven: Annex I. B.
822   *Cf.* Form of Service Agreement for the general manager of a GmbH attached in Chapter Seven: Annex I. B.
823   *Cf.* Form of Service Agreement for the general manager of a GmbH attached in Chapter Seven: Annex I. B.

It further provides that on-going pension payments must be reviewed on a regular basis and adjusted where appropriate. In addition, the Improvement of Company Pension Schemes Act stipulates the conditions for an early availment of retirement benefits.

The Improvement of Company Pension Schemes Act is generally applicable to general managers to the extent that company pension commitments have been made to them on the basis of their activities for the company. On the other hand, the statutory provisions may not be applicable where the general manager holds a position similar to that of an entrepreneur. Whether such an entrepreneurial position is given is to be determined on a case-by-case basis. If a general manager holds a majority participation in the GmbH or, despite having a smaller shareholding, is able to exercise decisive influence over the company, he is usually considered an entrepreneur.

If the Improvement of Company Pension Schemes Act is not applicable, the parties should agree upon the point in time as of which the general manager's rights to future pension benefits shall vest, also in the event of an early departure from the company. The general manager will then have a generally irrevocable right to *pro rata* benefit payments, even if he leaves the company prematurely. The amount of the benefit payments will depend on the length of the general manager's service with the company.

§ 483 Inflation protection
General managers of a GmbH are usually granted an increase in pension benefits only if such increase is provided for in the service agreement or required by law.

Where the Improvement of Company Pension Schemes Act is applicable,[824] the general manager is entitled to a regular review and adjustment of the amount of his pension benefits.[825] Alternatively, the service agreement may contain inflation protection clauses or adjustment clauses that seek to counterbalance any increase in prices due to inflation. Even where there is no such stable value clause, a general manager may under certain circumstances have a claim for the adjustment of the amount of his pension benefits on the basis of the principle of good faith if the value of the benefits has been eroded to an extent that it no longer meets the purpose behind those benefits. However, the financial situation of the company must also be taken into account.

§ 484 Reduction or refusal of retirement pension commitments
Once a general manager has retired or the right of a general manager to receive a retirement pension vested for other reasons, the company may reduce the amount of the pension, or refuse to pay it altogether, only in very exceptional cases. This is only possible where, upon a consideration of the interests of both parties, the payments are no longer objectively justified and it would be unreasonable to expect the company to continue to make them. Examples

---

824 *Cf.* § 482, above.
825 Gesetz zur Verbesserung der betrieblichen Altersversorgung [BetrAVG] [Improvement of Company Pension Schemes Act] 1974, § 16 (F.R.G.).

of such cases include particularly serious misconduct on the part of the general manager or a deterioration in the company's financial position that threatens its existence. However, the importance of the pension commitments for the general manager must always be considered. A reduction or even cancellation of pension benefits, dependents' benefits or disability benefits is not permissible merely because due cause for the termination of a general manager's service agreement exists.

§ 485 Specified or reasonable amount of compensation

A general manager is generally entitled to payment of the compensation agreed upon in his service agreement. If the amount of compensation is not stipulated in the service agreement, or in the absence of a service agreement, the general manager is entitled, as a matter of principle, to a reasonable amount of compensation.[826] This principle may be overridden only in the exceptional case where the parties have agreed to a gratuitous service relationship, e.g., where the general manager function does not constitute the general manager's primary employment relationship.

§ 486 Limits of the service agreement in respect of compensation

The shareholders may exercise their discretion in setting the compensation of a general manager. However, the contractually owed compensation must represent reasonable compensation for the performance of the function of general manager. The reasonableness of the compensation depends on the type and line of business, the size and results of the company's operations and on the age, qualifications, professional experience and performance of the general manager. The assessment of the reasonableness of the compensation must take into account all constituent elements of the compensation. Although no statutory provisions on reasonableness similar to those under stock corporation law exist,[827] certain special rules apply with regard to shareholders acting as general managers.

§ 487 External general managers

The parties enjoy full contractual freedom with respect to the amount of the compensation of external general managers. Only the corporate fiduciary duty and the prohibition of transactions that are contrary to public policy impose certain limitations in this regard. For example, the stipulation of an amount of compensation which is so excessive as to endanger the existence of the company will be null and void. In addition, the principle of equal treatment under labor law must be observed to the extent general managers have an employee-like status.[828] In such a case, the payment of different amounts of compensation to different general managers must be objectively justified, e.g., on the basis of different responsibilities assigned to them or their respective professional qualifications.

---

826   Bürgerliches Gesetzbuch [BGB] [Civil Code] 1896, § 612, ¶ 2 (F.R.G.).
827   §§ 44 et. seq. deal with the compensation of management board members of a German AG.
828   Cf. § 465, above (discussing the applicability of labor law to general managers).

§ 488 Shareholders acting as general managers

The amount of compensation for a shareholder acting as general manager is reasonable where it is equal to the amount that would be paid to an external general manager. The reasonableness criteria discussed above must also be considered in the context of this evaluation.[829]

The compensation arrangement of a shareholder acting as general manager may be considered in breach of the duty of loyalty if it is unreasonable, *e.g.*, where the amount of the compensation is so large that the residual amount of profits cannot adequately be distributed among the remaining shareholders. A shareholders' resolution in respect of such an unreasonable arrangement is challengeable, and the company generally has a claim for reimbursement against the shareholder/general manager concerned. In addition, an unreasonable or highly unusual payment may be treated as a hidden distribution of profits for tax purposes, *i.e.*, qualified as dividend payment that is not deductible at the level of the GmbH and subject to a different tax regime.

In the determination of the compensation of shareholders who act as general managers, the prohibition against the repayment of capital contributions and the corporate fiduciary duty must also be observed. Pursuant to the prohibition against the repayment of capital contributions, the financial assets necessary for the maintenance of the company's nominal share capital may not be repaid to the shareholders. Where the company's nominal share capital is no longer covered by the value of the company, an unreasonably large amount of compensation constitutes an impermissible repayment of capital contributions.[830] However, a reasonable amount of compensation may be paid to a shareholder acting as general manager even in the case of negative equity, because the general manager may not be placed in a worse position than an external general manager in such a situation.

§ 489 Reduction and increase of compensation

Should the economic position of the company become significantly worse after the conclusion of the service agreement, shareholders acting as general managers are, under certain circumstances, obligated on the basis of their corporate fiduciary duty to accept a reduction of their compensation. However, such general managers have the right to terminate their service agreement. Where, as a result of the crisis situation affecting the GmbH, the assets of the company no longer cover the amount of its nominal share capital, a shareholder acting as general manager may, under certain circumstances, be obligated to repay an excessive amount of compensation that he has received.[831]

Unless otherwise provided for in the service agreement, a general manager has a right to an increase in his compensation only in exceptional cases. For example, an increase may be appropriate in the case of a service agreement with an indefinite term if the commercial basis for the service agreement has changed profoundly due to unexpected growth of the company or a significant change in the allocation of duties among the general managers.

---

829 *Cf.* §§ 485 *et seq.*

830 In respect of the legal consequences hereof, *cf.* GmbH-Gesetz [GmbHG] [Limited Liability Companies Act] 1892, § 31 (F.R.G.).

831 GmbH-Gesetz [GmbHG] [Limited Liability Companies Act] 1892, § 30, ¶ 1 (F.R.G.).

§ 490 Taxation of compensation

The compensation is subject to German tax (*e.g.*, personal income tax, a solidarity surcharge thereon and, if applicable, church tax). Accordingly, a general manager's cash compensation as well as benefits in kind (*e.g.*, the use of company cars) are subject to tax. This is also true if the general manager is at the same time a shareholder of the company. The combined tax rate is progressive and rates vary between approximately 14.77% and 50%.[832]

§ 491 Compensation in an insolvency situation

In insolvency proceedings, a general manager will have a claim for any unpaid compensation that became due before the opening of the insolvency proceedings. If the compensation becomes due after the opening of insolvency proceedings, the general manager has a preferential claim to be served from the liquidation of the company's assets.

If the general manager is deemed an employee,[833] he may be entitled, pursuant to statutory provisions, to receive payments from the insolvency fund of the Federal Employment Office (*Bundesagentur für Arbeit*) in the amount of unpaid compensation for the last three months preceding the opening of the insolvency proceedings.[834] Whether the general manager concerned is entitled to such insolvency payments is determined on a case-by-case basis.

Furthermore, a general manager's pension claims may be subject to special protection in an insolvency situation as well.

5. Duties arising out of the service agreement

The service agreement usually provides for certain rights of the general manager, in particular relating to the payment of compensation, but it may also set forth a variety of duties in addition to those resulting from the appointment or arising under the articles of association or the rules of procedure.

§ 492 Payment of social security contributions

A general manager of a GmbH is generally obligated to pay social security contributions (*Sozialversicherungsbeiträge*), unless he is in a position to exercise considerable influence over the company.[835]

§ 493 Agreement regarding working hours

It is advisable to agree on the general manager's working hours, particularly in the case of external general managers and non-controlling shareholders acting as general managers. Service agreements typically stipulate that general managers are not obligated to work specific hours but must be available at all times and devote their entire professional capacity to the GmbH on a full-time basis.

---

832   The taxation of the general manager's compensation follows the same principles outlined for the taxation of management board members of a German AG, *cf.* §§ 59 *et seq.*

833   *Cf.* §§ 465 *et seq.*, above (discussing the applicability of labor law provisions to general managers).

834   Sozialgesetzbuch III [SGB III] [Social Code III] 1997, § 183, ¶ 1 (F.R.G.).

835   *Cf.* § 466, above (outlining the applicability of social security law provisions to general managers).

6.   Termination of the service agreement
§ 494 Introduction
Where a service agreement is concluded for an unlimited term, either party may terminate the agreement at any time. Where the service agreement is concluded for a fixed term, it may generally only be terminated for due cause. The terminating party must observe any notice periods and any other prerequisites for termination.

Where the company has revoked the appointment of a general manager, such revocation may under certain circumstances be interpreted as a termination of the service agreement. Finally, a mutually agreed termination of the employment relationship by means of a termination agreement is also possible.

§ 495 Relationship between revocation of the appointment and termination of the service agreement
The revocation of the appointment of a general manager does not automatically result in the termination of the service agreement. Where an appointment is revoked, this does not necessarily constitute a notice of termination of the service agreement. A revocation of the appointment for due cause is typically interpreted as a simultaneous termination of the service agreement. Nevertheless, the effectiveness of the revocation and the termination are to be assessed separately.

The service agreement may also link the appointment as general manager to the service relationship. To this end, it may be stipulated in the agreement that any circumstances which justify a revocation from office shall also justify the termination of the contractual relationship for due cause. Furthermore, the imposition of a condition may link the appointment and the service agreement to one another. For example, the service agreement may stipulate that the validity of the service agreement shall be subject to the condition subsequent that the person concerned is and remains a validly appointed general manager.

§ 496 Competence
The corporate body responsible for the appointment of a general manager is also responsible for the conclusion and termination of the service agreement.[836] Thus, the shareholders' meeting is generally responsible for the termination of the service relationship. If the termination of the service agreement of a shareholder/general manager is the subject of a shareholder resolution, the shareholder/general manager is entitled to cast a vote on the resolution, unless the termination is to be declared for due cause.

§ 497 Ordinary termination of the service agreement
An employment relationship with an unlimited term can be terminated with the applicable notice period without giving any reasons. The service agreement will usually stipulate a notice period of three, six or twelve months. In the absence of a contractual notice provision, the statutory notice periods that apply to general employment relationships also apply to a com-

---

836   Cf. § 468, above (dealing with the competence for the conclusion of the service agreement).

pany's termination of a general manager's service agreement, because a general manager usually performs the duties of his office on a full-time basis and earns his living through the compensation of those services. In any event, statutory notice periods certainly apply to external general managers and shareholders acting as general managers who do not have a controlling influence over the company and are thus unable to prevent the termination. While the termination notice does not need to be effected in any particular form, it is advisable to provide the notice in writing or, preferably, by registered mail. The service agreement may indeed provide for a written notice requirement.

§ 498 Extraordinary termination of the service agreement

A company may terminate a general manager's service agreement for due cause at any time, irrespective of whether the agreement provides for an unlimited or fixed term. Termination for due cause cannot be contractually excluded, and may not be *de facto* hampered by the imposition of specific rules that may have the effect of hindering such termination, *e.g.*, clauses providing for a substantial severance payment. Extraordinary termination for due cause and without notice period is generally decided by the shareholders' meeting. Unlike in the case of an ordinary termination, a shareholder serving as a general manager is not entitled to vote on a termination of his service relationship for due cause.

§ 499 Due cause

Like any other long-term contractual relationship,[837] the service agreement may be terminated for due cause by either party if certain circumstances render the continuation of the agreement unacceptable for the terminating party.[838] The terminating party bears the burden of proof with regard to the existence of facts that constitute due cause.

In determining whether due cause for a termination exists, all relevant circumstances and the interests of both parties must be considered. With respect to the general manager, the following factors are taken into account: his conduct to date, his achievements on behalf of the company, and his personal living circumstances such as his age and the social consequences of a termination of his service agreement. With respect to the company, the determination involves an analysis of its interest in a termination without notice period, which greatly depends on the extent of the breach of conduct committed by the general manager.

Misconduct and personal grounds represent important examples of due cause for the termination of an employment relationship. The service agreement may also specify a list of grounds for a termination without notice period. Operational reasons or even insolvency do not, as a general principle, provide sufficient justification for an extraordinary termination of a service agreement, because the employer bears the corporate risk involved in running the company. Even a withdrawal of confidence by the shareholders' meeting does not usually justify a termination for due cause. Furthermore, due cause that would justify the removal from office of a

---

837   Bürgerliches Gesetzbuch [BGB] [Civil Code] 1896, § 314 (F.R.G.).
838   Bürgerliches Gesetzbuch [BGB] [Civil Code] 1896, § 626, ¶ 1 (F.R.G.).

general manager does not necessarily justify the extraordinary termination of the service agreement. The validity of such termination must always be assessed separately.

Conduct-related grounds for termination of the service agreement generally require a gross breach of duty by the general manager. A breach of the duty to manage the company – *e.g.*, in the form of non-compliance with instructions of the shareholders, violation of reporting duties, and non-observance of the internal allocation of duties among the general managers – may constitute sufficient grounds in this respect. Furthermore, a breach of the general manager's fiduciary duty – *e.g.*, an improper use of business opportunities of the company for his own benefit, the acceptance of prohibited secondary employment, the use of resources of the company for personal purposes and a breach of the duty to maintain confidentiality – may constitute due cause for a termination of the service agreement. In addition, a violation of statutory duties, such as the duty to keep accounts or certain duties to act in a crisis situation affecting the company, may also constitute conduct-related due cause for a termination of the service agreement.

§ 500 Termination notice

An extraordinary termination must occur within two weeks of the terminating party becoming aware of the circumstances justifying such termination.[839] Where, as is generally the case, the authority to terminate the agreement lies with the shareholders' meeting, the two-week deadline, according to case law, commences once the shareholders' meeting has been informed of the pertinent circumstances. Where an individual who is entitled to convene the shareholders' meeting becomes aware of those circumstances, the shareholders' meeting must be convened without delay.

§ 501 Prior hearing and warning

The extent to which a general manager must receive a formal warning or be given a hearing prior to his termination will depend on the specific circumstances. Case law suggests that a prior hearing or formal warning is generally not required because general managers require less protection than ordinary employees.

However, a formal warning or hearing may be required in certain cases, depending on the terms of the general manager's service agreement and the specific breach of duty at issue. Further, where a termination is sought based on a strong suspicion that grounds for termination exist, the shareholders' meeting may not decide on the termination without first having attempted to clarify the situation.

A general manager whose service agreement is to be terminated may, in any case, demand that the company inform him of the grounds for the termination. Where the company does not comply with this demand, the general manager may have a claim for damages against the company, although this does not result in the invalidity of the termination as such.

---

839   Bürgerliches Gesetzbuch [BGB] [Civil Code] 1896, § 626, ¶ 2, sentence 1 and 2 (F.R.G.).

§ 502 Protection of the general manager under labor law

As a basic principle, protective provisions under labor law,[840] such as the Law on the Protection of Expectant and Nursing Mothers (*Mutterschutzgesetz*) or the Ninth Social Security Code on Rehabilition and Participation of Disabled Persons (SGB IX – *Rehabilitation und Teilhabe behinderter Menschen*), do not apply to the termination of a general manager's service agreement. If the general manager wishes to challenge his extraordinary termination in court, he is not bound by the three-week cut-off period under the Employment Protection Act (*Kündigungsschutzgesetz*), because the Act generally does not apply to a general manager's service agreement.[841] However, the general manager may forfeit his right to sue if he waits too long to file a complaint.

Where the general manager is a former employee of the company, it is possible that a suspended employment relationship (*ruhendes Arbeitsverhältnis*) coexists with the service agreement. In that case, the suspended employment relationship will be reactivated upon the termination of the service agreement.[842] Where the company terminates the employment relationship and the service agreement simultaneously, the general manager is entitled to challenge the termination of the employment relationship by means of an action for protection against dismissal (*Kündigungsschutzklage*). For such an action, he would be required to observe the then applicable three-week cut-off period under the Employment Protection Act.

§ 503 Ordinary termination of the service agreement

A general manager may generally terminate his service agreement by means of ordinary termination without being required to provide any reasons. Such ordinary termination right is generally excluded, however, if the agreement provides for a fixed term. If the service agreement is silent on the notice period, the general manager, as a basic principle, has to observe a notice period of four weeks to the end of the fifteenth day of a calendar month or to the end of the calendar month. However, notice periods depend on the actual duration of the service relationship.[843] Where the service agreement was concluded for the duration of the general manager's lifetime or for a period of more than five years, the general manager may only terminate the agreement with six months' notice after the expiration of the five-year period. He must submit his notice of termination to one of the other general managers, to one of the shareholders, to a person authorized to receive legal declarations and notifications on behalf of the company, or simply to the registered address of the company. To avoid problems in the event of a dispute, it is advisable to stipulate in the service agreement that the notice of termination has to be submitted in writing.

§ 504 Extraordinary termination of the service agreement

A general manager may terminate his service agreement for due cause without having to observe any period of notice.[844] Due cause may exist where the shareholders' meeting or the

---

840 *Cf.* § 465, above (discussing the applicability of labor law provisions to general managers).
841 Kündigungsschutzgesetz [KSchG] [Employment Protection Act] 1969, § 4 sentence 1 (F.R.G.).
842 *Cf.* § 467, above (dealing with former employees being appointed as general managers of a GmbH).
843 Analogous application of Bürgerliches Gesetzbuch [BGB] [Civil Code] 1896, § 622 (F.R.G.).
844 Bürgerliches Gesetzbuch [BGB] [Civil Code] 1896, § 626 (F.R.G.).

supervisory board requires the general manager to act in a manner that is against the law, where his authority to manage or represent the company is restricted without cause, or where information necessary for the management of the company is systematically withheld from him. Due cause may also relate to the general manager's personal situation, *e.g.*, a difficult and long illness or excessive demands on his time or health.

Where the general manager terminates his service agreement without due cause and notice period, the company may have the right to terminate the agreement for due cause and to claim compensation for any resulting damage it suffered.

Notably, a general manager is under an obligation not to terminate the employment relationship without observing the applicable notice period at an inappropriate time. He is obligated to ensure that the company is able to make arrangements regarding the management of its business on an interim basis. If he fails to do so, the termination is nevertheless valid but the general manager may be liable for any damage suffered by the company as a result of such conduct.

§ 505 Termination of the service agreement by mutual consent

In practice, a general manager's service agreement is most commonly terminated by mutual consent by way of a termination or severance agreement. A termination agreement may (but need not) coincide with the date of termination resulting from a termination notice given by one of the contracting parties. Thus, where a company terminates its contractual relationship with a general manager, it may still conclude a termination agreement with the general manager which secures the general manager's acceptance of the termination and simultaneously governs the rights and obligations of the parties with respect to the ending of the service agreement. A termination by mutual consent may also be reached by means of a court settlement, *e.g.*, in cases where the parties are in dispute as to whether there were sufficient grounds for a termination for due cause.

§ 506 Formal requirements

A termination agreement is concluded between the general manager in question and the GmbH, and the shareholders' meeting or another corporate body responsible for the termination will act on behalf of the company in this regard.[845] Although a termination agreement is not subject to any statutory form requirements, it is generally concluded in writing due to the complexity of the arrangements contained therein. Further, it may be advisable for the general manager to request the notarization of the termination agreement as such deed may, under certain circumstances, serve as a title for immediate enforcement against the company.

§ 507 Content of the termination agreement

A termination agreement should contain provisions dealing with the timing of the general manager's departure as well as any other questions arising out of the termination of the employment relationship, including post-contractual non-compete commitments and a duty of confi-

---

845   *Cf.* § 496, above (dealing with competence for the termination of the service agreement).

dentiality, provisions regarding the company pension scheme, the handing over of documents, compensation for inventions made in the course of employment, resignation from office, and severance payments. The termination agreement may also provide for the waiver by the company of all claims against the general manager.

§ 508 Severance payment

The general manager will be particularly interested in ascertaining whether he receives a severance payment and, if so, in what amount. Whether a severance payment will be paid depends to a great extent on the interest of the GmbH in releasing the general manager at an early stage from a service relationship that has a fixed term or is subject to long termination periods. Severance payments may be subject to a favorable tax regime.

§ 509 Impact of an insolvency situation on the service agreement

The insolvency of the company does not automatically result in the termination of the general manager's service agreement. Thus, the agreement initially remains valid.

Further, as a matter of principle, the insolvency of the company does not constitute a justification for a termination for due cause without notice period. However, the service agreement may be terminated by the insolvency receiver, who will assume the position of the appointing or terminating corporate body with, at most, three months' notice to the end of a calendar month.[846]

Notwithstanding an effective termination of the service agreement, the general manager's corporate position remains unaffected by such termination. Thus, the general manager's information and cooperation obligations under the Insolvency Code (*Insolvenzordnung*) still apply. The general manager may even be obliged, upon order of the competent court, to be at the insolvency receiver's disposal in order to comply with his statutory information and cooperation obligations.

III. Duties and obligations of general managers

§ 510 Overview

Most of the rights and duties of a general manager of a German GmbH arise as a matter of statutory law, namely the duty to conduct the business affairs of the company in a sound manner, but they may also be set forth in a variety of corporate documents.

First, the company's articles of association, the rules of procedure or the service agreement may set forth requirements extending the catalogue of statutory rights and duties of the general manager or further concretize the statutory framework. Stipulations regarding a general manager's rights and duties may also be contained in the shareholders' resolution on the appointment of the general manager or later shareholders' resolutions. Moreover, the service agree-

---

846   Insolvenzordnung [InsO] [Insolvency Code] 1994, § 113, sentence 2 (F.R.G.).

ment may define or expand the general manager's statutory duties and the duties stipulated in the articles of association or the rules of procedure.[847] The service agreement may also restrict the statutory powers of the general manager by, *e.g.*, prohibiting the undertaking of certain transactions or making these subject to the consent of the shareholders' meeting.

Where a general manager's rights and duties are specified in more than one document, the respective provisions must be consistent with one another. Otherwise, the stipulation set forth in the company's articles of association prevails.

Special obligations apply during the foundation phase of the company.

A. General duties and obligations of general managers

§ 511 Introduction
A general manager is subject to certain duties arising from his corporate position. The fulfillment of these duties is part of his general duty to manage the company.

Where a company has several general managers, it is possible to assign to one of them, in the context of the allocation of responsibilities among the general managers, the performance of a statutory duty (*e.g.*, the duty to keep accounts). The remaining general managers would then merely be obligated to monitor the performance of the responsible general manager with respect to this duty.

1. Duty of care, duty of loyalty, and duty to maintain confidentiality
§ 512 Duty of care
In carrying out his responsibilities on behalf of the company, a general manager must exercise the due care of a diligent and conscientious businessperson[848] – that is to say, the diligence of an independent, fiduciary administrator of third-party assets in a position of responsibility.

The most important management task is achieving the GmbH's corporate objective. A general manager must therefore strive to realize the objectives of the GmbH to the greatest possible extent within the bounds set by law, the company's articles of association, and the terms of his service agreement. The general manager must generate profits for the company as effectively as possible. This means that his duty of care comprises, *inter alia*, the preparation and carrying out of favorable transactions while refraining from concluding unfavorable transactions. Under the business judgment rule, general managers have some leeway with regard to these types of business decisions.[849]

---

847 *Cf.* §§ 472 *et seq.* and §§ 492 *et seq.*, above (outlining rights and duties arising out of the service agreement).
848 GmbH-Gesetz [GmbHG] [Limited Liability Companies Act] 1892, § 43, ¶ 1 (F.R.G.).
849 *Cf.* § 583, below (discussing the business judgment rule).

Furthermore, the general manager must shape the corporate policy of the company and advise the shareholders. The duty of care also encompasses compliance with the rules of the company pertaining to competence, including in particular the observance of any instructions given by the shareholders. Thus, a general manager must diligently observe the guidelines regarding corporate policy developed by the shareholders. In respect of social actions with uncertain advertising potential (*e.g.*, charitable donations), the general manager must obtain the consent of the shareholders in order to avoid acting in breach of his duty of care. The general manager is also under an obligation *vis-à-vis* the GmbH to ensure the company's compliance with its statutory obligations.

Personal characteristics of a general manager are irrelevant in this regard, with the result that inadequate capabilities or experience do not result in a lower duty of care standard. However, modifications may be possible under certain special circumstances.

§ 513 Duty of loyalty

A general manager is subject to a general duty of loyalty *vis-à-vis* the company, which places him under an obligation to refrain from all conduct that could cause damage to the company. In particular, the general manager must not let his personal interests prevail over the business interests of the company. Both the non-compete obligation and the duty of confidentiality in respect of trade and business secrets are derived from this fiduciary duty.

§ 514 Non-compete obligation

The Limited Liability Companies Act does not contain any explicit non-compete provisions. However, general managers are, on the basis of their fiduciary duty and their duty of loyalty towards the company, under an obligation not to carry out any transactions for their own purposes or those of third parties in the company's area of business. Given that this non-compete obligation is derived from the general manager's corporate position as such, it only applies for the actual duration of his term of office. Even after the expiration of his term of office, however, a general manager may be in violation of the non-compete obligation if he procures contracts for himself that the company concluded or could have concluded during his term of office.

The non-compete obligation prevents a general manager from using his position for his own benefit. In particular, it prevents him from carrying out any transactions in competition with the company, regardless of whether he is thereby acting in his own name or in the name of a third party, or for his own account or for the account of a third party. Thus, as a matter of principle, a general manager may not act as a board member of another company or as commercial representative of another business, or acquire a controlling stake in another entity, provided in each case that such business or company operates in the same area of business. The precise scope of the non-compete obligation depends upon the company's business purpose as defined in its articles of association, irrespective of whether the company fully realizes such purpose in practice.[850] A general manager may act for his own interest outside of the business purpose of the company, provided that such acting is compatible with his corporate position. To avoid

---

850   GmbH-Gesetz [GmbHG] [Limited Liability Companies Act] 1892, § 3, ¶ 1, no. 2 (F.R.G.).

uncertainties in practice, a general manager's service agreement may grant permission with regard to a particular field of parallel business activity.

A general manager of a parent company within a group of companies is subject to an extended non-compete obligation that covers the areas of operations of companies within that entire group.

Where a general manager is uncertain in a particular case as to the scope of the non-compete obligation, or where the company in question does not have sufficient liquid funds at its disposal to be able to carry out a transaction, the general manager in question should consult the shareholders' meeting before exploiting a business opportunity for his own purposes.

§ 515 Exemption from the non-compete obligation

A general manager may be exempted from the non-compete obligation. Where he is to be exempted from the non-compete obligation on a general basis, the articles of association must contain provisions to this effect or authorize the shareholders' meeting to resolve upon the exemption. Where the exemption from the non-compete obligation relates to a single transaction, a simple shareholders' resolution may be sufficient. An exemption may be revoked at any time.

§ 516 Legal consequences of violating the non-compete obligation

In the event of a violation of the non-compete obligation, the company has the right to require the general manager in question to desist from the infringing activity. The company may also have a claim for damages or, at the company's discretion, for a share of the profits obtained from the infringing activity, as well as a right to disclosure in respect of the transaction in question.

Non-compliance with the non-compete obligation may justify the general manager's removal from office for due cause and the termination of his service agreement without notice period. In the case of gross misconduct on the part of the general manager, the company may even withhold his compensation. From a tax perspective, a violation of the non-compete obligation may constitute a hidden distribution of profits in certain cases, *e.g.*, where the general manager is at the same time a shareholder of the GmbH.

§ 517 Post-contractual non-compete obligation

If a general manager is to be subject to a post-contractual non-compete obligation, such obligation has to be stipulated in the service agreement or in a separate agreement.[851] Although the effectiveness of a post-contractual non-compete obligation is not dependent on a correlating compensation payment, the company may not be able to enforce a non-compete obligation against the general manager without payment of reasonable compensation. Therefore, it is advisable to provide for a reasonable compensation payment for the duration of the non-compete obligation in the service agreement.

---

851   *Cf.* Form of Service Agreement for the general manager of a GmbH attached in Chapter Seven: Annex I. B.

A post-contractual non-compete obligation must serve the purpose of protecting a legitimate interest of the company. Further, the non-compete obligation may not prevent the general manager from engaging in economic activities and practicing his profession through unreasonable provisions regarding geographic scope, time period and subject matter. A time period of two years is generally considered reasonable. Where the contracting parties have agreed to the imposition of a non-compete obligation for a longer period of time, such period may, according to some court decisions, be reduced to a permissible duration in line with the opinion of the competent court (*e.g.*, to a duration of two years). A non-compete obligation without any geographical limitation is generally considered unreasonable and thus null and void.

§ 518 Duty of confidentiality

As part of the duty of loyalty, a general manager is under an obligation to maintain secrecy *vis-à-vis* third parties in respect of confidential information and secrets relating to the GmbH. The duty of confidentiality does not apply *vis-à-vis* shareholders, members of the supervisory board or advisory council, works council (*Betriebsrat*) or economic committee, to the extent that the general manager is under an obligation to provide these corporate or employee representative bodies with information. Information is considered confidential where it is in the interests of the company to keep it secret.

2.   Duty to keep accounts and prepare financial statements
§ 519 Competence of the general managers, delegation

A company's statutory duty to keep accounts and secure an orderly bookkeeping[852] falls within the general managers' field of competence.[853] Where a company has several general managers these duties may, in the context of the allocation of responsibilities among general managers, be assigned to one of the general managers. The remaining general managers are under an obligation to monitor the performance of the accounting and bookkeeping duties by such general manager continually.[854] However, the general managers are certainly not required to perform the required bookkeeping efforts in person but may delegate this duty to employees or third parties, such as accounting professionals or tax consultants. In that case, the general managers are under an obligation to monitor those third parties closely, *e.g.*, by involving internal or external auditors or by asking for regular reports.

§ 520 Content of the duty to keep accounts and prepare financial statements

General managers must ensure that the company's accounting procedures are organized in such a manner as to enable them to obtain an overview of the financial situation of the company at any time. The duty to keep accounts comprises the recording of all business events, the drawing up of an opening balance sheet and the preparation of (consolidated) annual financial statements, including a final balance sheet and a profit and loss account, notes thereto and,

---

852   GmbH-Gesetz [GmbHG] [Limited Liability Companies Act] 1892, § 13, ¶ 3 (F.R.G.); Handelsgesetzbuch [HGB] [Commercial Code] 1897, § 238, ¶ 1 and § 242 (F.R.G.).

853   GmbH-Gesetz [GmbHG] [Limited Liability Companies Act] 1892, § 41 (F.R.G.).

854   *Cf.* § 511, above (noting the possibility of delegating responsibilities in the context of the allocation of duties among the general managers and the residual monitoring obligation).

depending on the size of the company, a (consolidated) annual report.[855] The duty to keep accounts also comprises the duty to retain all relevant documents. There are further obligations to keep accounts and records under tax law.

The Commercial Code (*Handelsgesetzbuch*) divides corporations, including limited liability companies, into one of three size categories: small, mid-size and large corporations.[856] The general managers are subject to varying accounting and publication obligations depending on the size category to which the company belongs. Furthermore, whether or not it is necessary to commission an auditor also depends on the size of the company.[857] General managers are therefore under an obligation to ascertain to which size category the company belongs in order to fulfill their statutory obligations properly.

§ 521 Preparation of the annual financial statements

A company must prepare its annual financial statements and annual report within the first three months following the most recent balance sheet date.[858] Small companies may prepare their annual financial statements within six months of the previous balance sheet date, where this constitutes normal business procedure. Because the obligation to prepare financial statements falls within their field of competence, the general managers may be liable *vis-à-vis* the company if they do not carry out their accounting responsibilities within the relevant deadline.[859]

The following procedures must be observed in connection with the preparation of the company's annual financial statements: The general managers must submit the annual financial statements and annual report to the shareholders for their approval without undue delay following their preparation.[860] The annual financial statements and possibly also the consolidated annual financial statements, where required[861], have to be examined by an auditor prior to their submission to the shareholders. The audit report must then be submitted to the shareholders and to the supervisory board (if the company has one).[862] The shareholders' meeting will then approve the annual financial statements and resolve upon the appropriation of the net income of the company.

The annual financial statements must be signed and dated by all general managers.[863] A general manager must refrain from signing the financial statements where they do not comply with statutory provisions, but he is not obliged to refrain from signing in case of non-compliance with accounting rules set forth in the company's articles of association.

---

855 Handelsgesetzbuch [HGB] [Commercial Code] 1897, §§ 242 and 264 as well as §§ 297 and 315, if applicable (F.R.G.).
856 Handelsgesetzbuch [HGB] [Commercial Code] 1897, § 267 (F.R.G.).
857 Handelsgesetzbuch [HGB] [Commercial Code] 1897, § 316 (F.R.G.).
858 Handelsgesetzbuch [HGB] [Commercial Code] 1897, § 264, ¶ 1, sentence 3 (F.R.G.).
859 GmbH-Gesetz [GmbHG] [Limited Liability Companies Act] 1892, § 43, ¶ 2 (F.R.G.).
860 GmbH-Gesetz [GmbHG] [Limited Liability Companies Act] 1892, § 42a (F.R.G.).
861 For large and mid-size limited liability companies, *cf.* Handelsgesetzbuch [HGB] [Commercial Code] 1897, § 316, ¶ 1 (F.R.G.).
862 GmbH-Gesetz [GmbHG] [Limited Liability Companies Act] 1892, § 43a, ¶ 1 (F.R.G.); Handelsgesetzbuch [HGB] [Commercial Code] 1897, § 316, ¶ 2 (F.R.G.).
863 Handelsgesetzbuch [HGB] [Commercial Code] 1897, § 245 (F.R.G.).

§ 522 Publication of the annual financial statements

General managers are under an obligation to submit the annual financial statements, the annual report (if applicable), and the resolution as to the appropriation of net income, subsequent to their submission to the shareholders, to the operator of the electronic version of the German Federal Gazette for publication within twelve months of the previous balance sheet date. The rules in this regard also vary according to the size category to which the company belongs.[864] Where the general managers do not comply with the duty to publish these reports, the general managers may be subject to an administrative fine.[865]

3.   Duty to convene the shareholders' meeting
§ 523 Convention of the shareholders' meeting

Once a year, the ordinary shareholders' meeting is held, at which the annual financial statements are approved and appropriation of net income is resolved upon. In addition to this ordinary meeting, an extraordinary shareholders' meeting must be convened in certain defined cases set forth by statutory law or where such convention appears to be in the interests of the company.[866] The competent corporate body, e.g., usually the general managers, are responsible for the convention of the meeting and have to observe the formal requirements in this regard. Where these requirements are not followed, any resolutions passed by the shareholders' meeting will be null and void or at least challengeable.

Whether a general manager has a right to attend the shareholders' meeting is the subject of academic controversy. The running of the shareholders' meeting is in fact not one of the original duties of a general manager. He is only under an obligation to appear before the shareholders' meeting if he is summoned to attend by the shareholders. In practice, however, the general managers almost always participate in the shareholders' meeting, as they have to be at the shareholders' disposition to respond to any questions or requests. General managers are, however, generally excluded from any discussions of and decisions that concern management personnel matters.

§ 524 Grounds for a convention of the shareholders' meeting

The shareholders' meeting must be convened in cases set forth by statutory law. In particular, the shareholders' meeting must be convened if it may be derived from the annual or interim balance sheet that the GmbH incurred losses amounting to half of its registered nominal share capital.[867] It is also necessary to convene the shareholders' meeting where, e.g., the general managers wish to resolve upon a particular measure, which falls within the competence of the shareholders. Generally, this holds true for any extraordinary corporate measure such as an amendment to the articles of association or the liquidation of the company. Furthermore, the general managers are under an obligation to convene the shareholders' meeting where this would appear to be necessary in the interests of the company.[868] This may be the case, e.g.,

---

864 Handelsgesetzbuch [HGB] [Commercial Code] 1897, §§ 325 through 327 (F.R.G.).
865 Handelsgesetzbuch [HGB] [Commercial Code] 1897, § 335, ¶ 1, no. 1 (F.R.G.).
866 Cf. § 524, below.
867 GmbH-Gesetz [GmbHG] [Limited Liability Companies Act] 1892, § 49, ¶ 3 (F.R.G.). Cf. § 539 for details.
868 GmbH-Gesetz [GmbHG] [Limited Liability Companies Act] 1892, § 49, ¶ 2 (F.R.G.).

where the general managers wish to take action in a matter for which they could assume that the shareholders would withhold their approval. Such situations may arise, where the general managers intend to conclude a transaction outside of the ordinary course of business, or where they consider it necessary or advantageous that the shareholders' meeting explicitly support a certain contemplated measure with a corresponding resolution.

The convention of a shareholders' meeting involves the dedication of time and expense on the part of the shareholders that can be avoided by requesting a written vote on the issue. Provided that all of the shareholders agree in written or electronic form to the action to be taken, or generally consent to the passing of resolutions in written form, the physical convention of the shareholders' meeting will not be required. Such passing of resolutions in written form may also be expressly permitted in the GmbH's articles of association. However, a written vote is generally not sufficient in a case where half of the company's nominal share capital was lost. In such a case, exhaustive information, consultation and a decision-making process is required.

§ 525 Competence for the convention of the shareholders' meeting

As a rule, the general managers are responsible for calling the shareholders' meeting.[869] Where a company has several general managers, each individual general manager is authorized to convene the shareholders' meeting, irrespective of whether he is vested with sole or joint power of representation in respect of the company.[870] Thus, controversies among the members of the executive board do not prevent the convention of a shareholders' meeting. The authority to convene the shareholders' meeting even vests with general managers whose appointment was irregular, but who are nevertheless registered as general managers with the competent commercial register. Even an emergency general manager[871] is authorized to convene the shareholders' meeting.

The GmbH's articles of association may assign the authority to convene the shareholders' meeting to another corporate body, e.g., an advisory council or a Prokurist. Furthermore, where the authority to convene the shareholders' meeting was delegated to another body within the GmbH, the general managers are under an obligation to inform and encourage the competent corporate body to convene the shareholders' meeting where this is in the best interests of the company. However, where the company incurs losses amounting to half of its nominal share capital, the general managers' authority to convene the shareholders' meeting cannot be delegated.

§ 526 Formal requirements for the convention of the shareholders' meeting

The notice of the convention of the shareholders' meeting must be directed to the shareholders personally and delivered by way of registered mail.[872] Recipients of the invitation should be

---

869 Under certain conditions, shareholders whose shareholdings collectively amount to at least one tenth of the share capital may also convene the shareholders' meeting. In case of a co-determined GmbH, also the supervisory board will be authorized to convene the shareholders' meeting.
870 Cf. § 558, below (discussing the different types of representation of the GmbH).
871 Cf. § 449, above (discussing the appointment of an emergency general manager).
872 GmbH-Gesetz [GmbHG] [Limited Liability Companies Act] 1892, § 51, ¶ 1 (F.R.G.).

able to see that it has been issued by the general managers as the corporate body responsible for the convention of the shareholders' meeting. In the interest of certainty, the general managers should also personally sign the invitation. The articles of association may stipulate that the shareholders' meeting can be convened otherwise (*e.g.*, orally or by email or fax), provided that the shareholders are able to exercise their right of participation and obtain sufficient information as to the agenda for the meeting.

The invitation to the shareholders' meeting must contain details of the venue and time of the shareholders' meeting, which must generally be held at the registered office of the company or in its vicinity.

Subject to specific provisions in the GmbH's articles of association, the shareholders' meeting must generally be convened at least one week prior to the date of the meeting. The time required for the delivery of the notice must also be taken into account.

As a general rule, the agenda for the meeting should be delivered along with the invitation. However, it is sufficient if the issue to be resolved upon is communicated to the shareholders three days prior to the meeting at the latest by way of registered mail (or otherwise in the manner provided in the articles of association). The agenda must be detailed enough to enable the shareholders to adequately prepare for the meeting.

§ 527 Legal consequences of an improper convention of the shareholders' meeting
Depending on the specific defect in the convention of the shareholders' meeting, a resolution passed in the course of such meeting will either be null and void or merely challengeable.

Where the shareholders' meeting is convened by an unauthorized person, where not all of the shareholders have been duly invited to the meeting, or where details as to the venue and time of the meeting are not included in the invitation, any resolutions passed at the meeting will be null and void. This is also the case where the invitation to the shareholders' meeting is not delivered by way of registered mail, absent any provision in the articles of association permitting a different form of notice.

Where the notice period for the invitation to or announcement of the shareholders' meeting is not complied with, or where the requirement of specificity is not observed in the formulation of the agenda and, as a result of the defect in the convention of the meeting not all of the shareholders are present, any resolutions passed at that meeting will not be null and void, but merely challengeable.

Where all shareholders are present (so-called universal meeting), they may mutually agree to waive the formalities in respect of the manner of convening the meeting, with the result that the defects in regard thereof are "cured." If the shareholders do not choose to proceed this way, the resolutions passed will be void or challengeable, as the case may be, unless it is obvious that the resolutions would also have been passed if the formalities in respect of the convention of the meeting had been observed.

4.   Obligation to provide information to the shareholders

§ 528 Scope of the obligation to provide information

Each shareholder is entitled to receive, without undue delay, information from the general managers regarding matters pertaining to the company, and also has the right to access the accounts and documentation of the company.[873] The shareholders' right to information is to be construed broadly and extends to any matter that could form the subject matter of a shareholders' resolution or may be of significance for the economic value of the company and/or the control, financial or proprietary interests of the respective shareholder. The right to information concerns all documents of the company (including books, documentation in written or electronic form, etc.) regardless of where such information is located. Where the company is not in possession of the information in question, it must exert reasonable efforts to request it from a third party. The information to which a shareholder is entitled excludes personal matters of the general managers or other shareholders. Where the company has a supervisory board, the shareholders' right to information and the right of inspection also encompass the activities, documents and meeting minutes of the supervisory board.

Furthermore, the shareholders' right to information encompasses information pertaining to affiliated companies, companies in which the GmbH holds an equity participation, and companies with a shareholding in the GmbH (to the extent that the GmbH has the requested information in possession or is able to obtain it).

§ 529 Right to withhold information

The general managers are entitled to withhold information or prevent access to the company's accounts/documents where a concrete danger exists that the shareholders will use the information obtained for non-company related purposes and cause considerable damage to the company or one of its affiliated companies.[874] Furthermore, a shareholder does not have a right to information where his interest has already been satisfied through the receipt of other information such as quarterly reports, or where questions are posed in an abusive manner.

A general manager's decision to withhold information must be supported by a shareholders' resolution passed with a simple majority of the votes cast.[875] The shareholder concerned is precluded from voting on this resolution.

§ 530 Treatment of the right to information in the articles of association or shareholders' resolutions

A divergence from the statutory provisions regarding the shareholders' right to information is only permissible where it is in favor of the shareholders and may be effected by means of a provision in the articles of association or a shareholders' resolution. In an effort to ensure the proper provision of information, it is advisable to provide the shareholders with information on a regular basis by means of standardized reports and updates as to current developments. In

---

873   GmbH-Gesetz [GmbHG] [Limited Liability Companies Act] 1892, § 51a, ¶ 1 (F.R.G.).

874   GmbH-Gesetz [GmbHG] [Limited Liability Companies Act] 1892, § 51a, ¶ 2 (F.R.G.).

875   GmbH-Gesetz [GmbHG] [Limited Liability Companies Act] 1892, § 51a, ¶ 2, sentence 2 (F.R.G.).

addition, it may be helpful to set up an arrangement by which answers to questions posed by one shareholder are communicated to all other shareholders in order to avoid multiple queries regarding the same matter.

5.   Reporting obligation *vis-à-vis* the supervisory board
§ 531 Reporting obligation

Where the GmbH has a supervisory board (in particular, in cases of co-determination), this corporate body must be adequately informed in order to be able to carry out its supervisory and advisory functions. While, based upon the statutory requirements, the general managers are not obligated to report regularly to the supervisory board, the supervisory board may at any time request information as to matters pertaining to the company and the legal and business relationships of the company with affiliated companies.[876]

As a basic principle, the general managers may not refuse to report to the supervisory board, unless there are justified concerns that individual board members will breach their duty of confidentiality. If there is a possibility of a conflict of interest in respect of individual members of the supervisory board, the requested information may be withheld from those board members.

The articles of association may expand the statutory reporting obligation in favor of the supervisory board. However, limitations on the reporting obligation are only possible in the case of an optional supervisory board, *e.g.*, not in cases where the establishment of a supervisory board is required by law.

6.   Registration and submission obligations
§ 532 Introduction

General managers have certain obligations relating to the registration of specific corporate information with the competent commercial register. Furthermore, they are responsible for the submission of a variety of documents, including lists of shareholders and financial statements.

§ 533 Registration obligations

General managers are responsible for registering certain events pertaining to the company with the competent commercial register.[877] This is generally undertaken by the number of general managers required for an authorized representation of the company. In certain cases, participation of all general managers is required in order to effect the registration (*e.g.*, in connection with the foundation of the company or capital increases).

The registration obligation includes the registration of the company itself, its general managers, amendments to the articles of association and/or rules of representation, capital increases or decreases, and the dissolution of the company.

---

876   GmbH-Gesetz [GmbHG] [Limited Liability Companies Act] 1892, § 52, ¶ 1 (F.R.G.).
877   GmbH-Gesetz [GmbHG] [Limited Liability Companies Act] 1892, § 78 (F.R.G.).

§ 534 Filing obligations

In addition to registration obligations, general managers are also under an obligation to submit certain documents to the commercial register.

In particular, the general managers must submit a current list of shareholders to the commercial register without undue delay upon the occurrence of any changes regarding the shareholders or the amount of their shares (*e.g.*, in cases of share transfers, capital increases or a split-up or consolidation of shares).[878] In certain cases, the obligation to submit the list of shareholders does not rest with the general managers, but with the officiating notary involved in changes to the shareholder structure, *e.g.*, where share transfers are effected on the basis of a notarial deed.[879] The submission of the list of shareholders may be enforced by the imposition of a monetary fine.

A number of substantial modifications to the required form and legal consequences arising from the list of shareholders were introduced by the German legislature in 2008. According to the new rules, such list of shareholders must contain the last name, first name, date of birth and place of residence of the shareholders as well as the nominal amounts and sequential numbers of their shares. Whereas the list of shareholders used to serve only informational purposes, it now serves as a potential basis for *bona fide* acquisition of shares in a GmbH.[880] *Bona fide* acquisitions of GmbH shares had previously not been possible under German law. Furthermore, under the new statutory regime, changes in the shareholder structure of the company are only valid *vis-à-vis* the company if they are reflected in the list of shareholders submitted to the commercial register.[881] This is important with regard to a shareholder's right to a share in the distribution of profits generated by the GmbH, but also with regard to the obligation to pay in the required capital contributions.

The general managers also have to submit a copy of the company's annual financial statements, the annual report (where applicable), and the resolution as to the appropriation of net income of the company to the operator of the electronic version of the German Federal Gazette for publication.[882]

§ 535 Correspondence of the GmbH

In all company correspondence, including email correspondence, the general managers must state the legal form of the company, the location of the registered office, the competent commercial register and the registration number, as well as the surname and at least one first name, in full, of each general manager and, where applicable, the chairman of the supervisory board.

---

878   GmbH-Gesetz [GmbHG] [Limited Liability Companies Act] 1892, § 40, ¶ 1 (F.R.G.).
879   GmbH-Gesetz [GmbHG] [Limited Liability Companies Act] 1892, § 40, ¶ 2 (F.R.G.).
880   GmbH-Gesetz [GmbHG] [Limited Liability Companies Act] 1892, § 16, ¶ 3 (F.R.G.).
881   GmbH-Gesetz [GmbHG] [Limited Liability Companies Act] 1892, § 16, ¶ 1 (F.R.G.).
882   Handelsgesetzbuch [HGB] [Commercial Code] 1897, § 325, ¶ 1 (F.R.G.). *Cf.* §§ 520 *et seq.*, above (discussing the duty to keep accounts and the duty of disclosure).

7.   Obligations relating to tax, labor law, and social security

§ 536 Tax related obligations

General managers are responsible for the fulfillment of the GmbH's tax-related obligations. These duties are comprehensive and comprise all actions necessary for the performance of the company's statutory tax-related obligations. The duties include, in particular, the keeping of accounts and records, the timely submission of the company's tax returns, the provision of certain information to the tax authorities as well as the withholding and remitting of wage taxes (*Lohnsteuer*) for employees and of capital gains tax (*Kapitalertragsteuer*) in connection with the distribution of profits to shareholders as well as timely payment of all taxes to which the GmbH is subject.[883]

In most cases the GmbH will carry out transactions that are subject to German value-added tax (*Umsatzsteuer*). In that case the general managers must timely submit the monthly value added tax advance tax return as well as the annual tax return for value-added tax. Such advance tax returns include a calculation of the value-added tax payment obligation or refund claim for input tax paid by the GmbH for the applicable period and generally must be submitted by the tenth day after the end of each calendar month.

In the event of an intentional or reckless violation of tax-related obligations, the general managers are personally liable for taxes owed by the GmbH (including, *e.g.*, late payment interest or late filing fines) and may also face criminal charges.[884]

§ 537 Labor law and social security related obligations

While the GmbH is the employer of its workforce, the general managers perform the duties of the employer *vis-à-vis* the company's workforce in their capacity as the company's management body. Thus, they must ensure compliance of the company with all of its labor and social law obligations, including pursuant to the Federal Leave Act (*Bundesurlaubsgesetz*) and the Working Hours Act (*Arbeitszeitgesetz*). They must observe all provisions under labor law that protects employees. The general managers also function as a point of contact for the works council and/ or the economic committee.[885]

Furthermore, the general managers are responsible for the performance of the GmbH's obligations under social security law. Social security benefits are generally funded through contributions from both employees and employers. The contributions go towards pension insurance, mandatory health insurance, long-term care insurance, and unemployment insurance.

The employer has a statutory right *vis-à-vis* its employees to deduct the employee's share of the contribution from his compensation. In addition, the employer must pay certain contributions for which he is solely responsible, *e.g.*, contributions towards statutory accident insurance. While these statutory duties are borne by the GmbH and not the general managers personally,

---

883   Abgabenordnung [AO] [General Tax Code] 1976, § 34, ¶ 1 (F.R.G.).
884   *Cf.* §§ 618 *et seq.* (dealing with liability of general managers for taxes payable by the GmbH).
885   *Cf.* § 518.

a delegation of responsibilities, *e.g.*, in the context of the allocation of duties or an outsourcing of responsibilities, is permissible.

The general managers are liable for damages in respect of unpaid social security contributions from paid wages and salaries, irrespective of whether they personally dealt with social security contributions within the company.[886] They may also be liable under criminal law in this respect.

8.   Obligations in crisis situations
§ 538 Introduction
During crisis situations affecting the GmbH, the general managers are subject to particularly extensive requirements as to their appropriate conduct. They should therefore always strive to recognize such situations at an early stage and undertake anticipatory liquidity planning measures. The general managers are under an obligation to monitor the economic situation of the company continually and to obtain an overview of the actual financial situation in the event of any indications of a potential crisis by means of the preparation of an interim balance sheet.

§ 539 Obligations in the event of losses suffered by the company
Where the company has suffered losses leading to a reduction of at least half of its share capital, the general managers must convene the shareholders' meeting in order to give the shareholders the opportunity to resolve upon potential crisis measures, *e.g.*, a capital increase.[887]

As a matter of principle, the shareholders' meeting must be convened without undue delay. The losses suffered by the company must be disclosed in the invitation to the shareholders' meeting.

Where a general manager fails to comply with the obligation to convene the shareholders' meeting, he may be liable *vis-à-vis* the company for damages[888] and also face criminal charges.

§ 540 Obligations in the event of illiquidity or over-indebtedness of the company
In the event of the illiquidity or over-indebtedness of the company, the general managers are under an obligation to file a petition for the commencement of insolvency proceedings.

The general managers may already file for insolvency where illiquidity appears to be imminent.[889] Under favorable circumstances, they may thus swiftly obtain approval for a contemplated insolvency plan and ultimately a recapitalization of the company.

In addition to the obligation to file for insolvency, the general managers are also under an obligation to effect a financial restructuring of the company. This entails carrying out an assess-

---

886 Bürgerliches Gesetzbuch [BGB] [Civil Code] 1896, § 823, ¶ 2, sentence 2 (F.R.G.) in conjunction with Strafgesetzbuch [StGB] [Criminal Code] 1871, § 266a (F.R.G.). *Cf.* §§ 620 *et seq.*
887 GmbH-Gesetz [GmbHG] [Limited Liability Companies Act] 1892, § 49, ¶ 3 (F.R.G.). *Cf.* § 524.
888 GmbH-Gesetz [GmbHG] [Limited Liability Companies Act] 1892, § 43, ¶ 2 (F.R.G.).
889 Insolvenzordnung [InsO] [Insolvency Code] 1994, § 18, ¶ 1 (F.R.G.).

ment of whether the company is even capable of undergoing a financial restructuring. Where this is the case, the general managers must initiate appropriate financial restructuring measures also within the three-week deadline for filing an insolvency petition.[890]

§ 541 Deadline for filing an insolvency petition

The general managers must file the insolvency petition without undue delay, but at the latest within three weeks of the occurrence of the illiquidity or over-indebtedness.[891] According to case law, the general managers' actual knowledge of such situations tends to be viewed as triggering the beginning of the three-week period. It is very difficult to demonstrate that the general managers did not have any knowledge of the company's financial distress, because a state of illiquidity of the company hardly remains unnoticed by the general managers. The strict requirements of the limitation period compel the general managers to continually assess the financial situation of the company.

In order to avoid a filing of an insolvency petition, the grounds for the commencement of insolvency proceedings (*e.g.*, the illiquidity or over-indebtedness of the company) must be eliminated within the three-week notification period. However, this will only be the case if there is a sustained improvement in the company's financial situation that precludes the reoccurrence of a state of illiquidity or over-indebtedness any time soon.

§ 542 Illiquidity

One triggering event for the obligation to file an insolvency petition is the illiquidity of the company. Illiquidity is generally presumed where a debtor ceases to make payments when due.[892] Thus, the due date is decisive for the establishment of illiquidity. A court order prohibiting payments or an inability to meet outstanding delivery obligations is not sufficient to establish a state of illiquidity giving rise to an obligation to file an insolvency petition.

In order to result in an obligation to file an insolvency petition, the illiquidity of the company must last for some period of time. Under no circumstances may the uncertainty as to whether the company is able to meet its obligations persist for more than three weeks. A state of illiquidity lasting for more than two weeks is generally sufficient to establish an obligation on the part of the general managers to apply for the opening of insolvency proceedings. However, mere temporary liquidity shortfalls are not sufficient to constitute a state of illiquidity for purposes of filing for insolvency.

The state of illiquidity terminates upon the reestablishment of liquidity and the resumption of payments by the GmbH.

---

890   *Cf.* § 541, below (specifying the deadline for filing an insolvency petition).
891   Insolvenzordnung [InsO] [Insolvency Code] 1994, § 15a, ¶ 1 (F.R.G.).
892   Insolvenzordnung [InsO] [Insolvency Code] 1994, § 17, ¶ 2, sentence 2 (F.R.G.).

§ 543 Over-indebtedness

The obligation to file an insolvency petition also arises in a situation of over-indebtedness, *e.g.*, where the GmbH's assets are no longer sufficient to meet its liabilities.[893] In order to determine whether the company is over-indebted, the general managers must prepare a special over-indebtedness balance sheet (*Überschuldungsbilanz*). The rules for preparing an over-indebtedness balance sheet are different from those for regular commercial balance sheets in respect of the determination and valuation of the balance sheet items.

The Act on the Implementation of Measures to Stabilize the Financial Market (*Finanzmarkt-stabilisierungsgesetz*), which entered into force on October 18, 2008 as a means of stabilization against the impact of the financial crisis on the German financial market, as amended by subsequent legislation,[894] modified the concept of over-indebtedness at least through December 31, 2013.

The Act amended Section 19(2) of the Insolvency Code in that over-indebtedness no longer requires a company to file for insolvency provided that the continuation of the company's business is deemed highly likely under the circumstances. A positive outlook is not only relevant for the appropriate evaluation method (as it was under the old rules), but it excludes the state of over-indebtedness as such. According to the new rule, even if the assets of the company are no longer sufficient to meet its liabilities, it may continue its business as long as it remains solvent. Notably, this amendment to the Insolvency Code applies to all German companies, not just to financial institutions.

The general managers bear the burden of proof as to the positive outlook if the company ends up failing nevertheless. They must also demonstrate the (subjective) intention of the company to continue its existence and show that the company has the (objective) option of continuing its business. The general manager can show this by drawing up a financial plan including a budget. Because the forecast of the company's continuing existence is decisive for the general managers' liability, it is advisable to seek expert advice in this regard.

§ 544 Responsibility of the general managers

Each general manager is subject to the obligation to file an insolvency petition, regardless of the internal allocation of duties within the management board or the respective powers of representation. This obligation cannot be eliminated by any contrary instructions of the shareholders or by consent of the company's creditors.

Where a general manager wishes to resign from office, he must either file the insolvency petition himself beforehand or induce one of the other general managers, or his successor, to do so. If a resignation from office has the sole purpose of evading the obligation to file an insolvency

---

893   Insolvenzordnung [InsO] [Insolvency Code] 1994, § 19 (F.R.G.).
894   Gesetz zur Erleichterung der Sanierung von Unternehmen [FMStGÄndG] [Act Facilitating the Reorganization of Businesses] 2009.

petition, such resignation would constitute an abuse of right and may be deemed invalid by the competent court.

If the general managers do not comply with their obligation to file an insolvency petition, they may be liable for damages *vis-à-vis* both the company and its creditors.[895] Furthermore, such non-compliance may also entail sanctions under criminal law.

B. Specific duties and obligations during the formation of the GmbH

§ 545 Introduction
General managers are subject to certain special obligations during the formation of a GmbH, *i.e.*, before the articles of association have been notarized and the company has been registered with the competent commercial register. During that initial period, the GmbH exists as a so-called "GmbH in formation" (*GmbH in Gründung*).

§ 546 Application with the commercial register
The general managers are responsible for the application of the company for registration with the competent commercial register. The application must include the articles of association, a list of shareholders,[896] the resolutions containing the appointment of the general managers and details about the representation of the company, information about the contribution of the share capital, a domestic business address, etc. The application has to be signed by all general managers of the company. Their signatures must be certified by a notary.

§ 547 Statement regarding capital contributions
The responsibility for the contribution of the registered share capital lies with the company's shareholders, not its general managers. However, upon the formation of the company, the general managers must declare in the application of the GmbH for registration with the commercial register that the capital contributions have been duly and validly paid and are at the unrestricted disposal of the general managers.[897] The general managers must also state whether and to what extent the capital that was contributed prior to the application will be required to meet corresponding liabilities. The same holds true in case of subsequent capital increases.

Furthermore, according to the new provisions recently introduced by the MoMiG, the initial application to the commercial register must contain a statement as to whether a cash contribution, from an economic perspective, in light of an existing arrangement in connection with the contribution has (at least partially) to be regarded as contribution in kind (so-called "hidden contribution in kind"), *e.g.*, in cases where a shareholder sells an asset to the company shortly after the company's registration with the commercial register against consideration emanating from the cash contribution. Further, if any transaction has been effected or agreed with any of

---

895   *Cf.* §§ 598 *et seq.*, below.
896   *Cf.* § 534, above (dealing with the list of shareholders).
897   The same applies in the case of the application of a capital increase.

the shareholders prior to the cash contribution that, from an economic perspective, constitutes a repayment of such contribution, *e.g.*, in cases where the company has granted an upstream loan to the relevant shareholder, the general mangers must state in the application that the claim against the shareholder is fully recoverable. If no such statement can be made, the shareholder will be deemed not to have fulfilled his obligation to make the cash contribution. The general managers have to assess whether the claim for refund is fully recoverable. Particular problems may arise in connection with cash pooling arrangements to which the company is a party. It remains to be seen how the courts will deal with this additional disclosure requirement and what standard of care will apply with regard to the necessary assessment by the general managers.

Where the general manager's statement is incorrect, the general manager may be personally liable for damages *vis-à-vis* the GmbH.[898] However, he may be entitled to take recourse against the company's shareholders. Such liability usually becomes relevant in the case of an insolvency of the GmbH where the insolvency receiver has the right to assert claims on behalf of the company. Also, criminal charges may be incurred, including an occupational ban for a period of five years.

IV. Executive functions of general managers

§ 548 Overview

The executive board of a German GmbH, which may comprise one or several general managers, constitutes the executive body of the company. In this capacity, the specific role of the members of the executive board is the representation of the company and the management of its business.

It is important to distinguish between general managers' administrative and representative functions. The authority to manage the company's business relates solely to the internal relationship between the general manager(s) and the company. The authority to represent the company relates to the legal authority of a general manager to legally bind the company in relation to third parties. General managers' administrative and representative powers may, but do not necessarily have to, correspond (*e.g.*, a general manager who may take business decisions alone may be authorized to represent the company only jointly with another general manager). However, where the company's articles of association and/or the rules of procedure do not contain specific provisions on the allocation of administrative and representative powers of general managers, the law provides for consistency of the management power and the power of representation of the general managers.

---

898   *Cf.* §§ 576 *et seq.* for further details.

A.   Business management

§ 549 Introduction

The general managers of a GmbH are both entitled and under an obligation to manage the company's business within the limits set forth in the Limited Liability Companies Act, the company's articles of association or as otherwise decided by the shareholders.

As a basic principle, the general managers are vested with comprehensive management powers. Managing a GmbH involves the taking of all measures and decisions necessary for pursuing the company's corporate purpose as set forth in the articles of association. The day-to-day management of the company is one of the primary responsibilities of the general managers. Provided that the shareholders' meeting does not assume responsibility for particular transactions, the general managers are authorized to make decisions regarding on-going company matters independently, *e.g.*, without consulting with the shareholders' meeting. In particular, the general managers can decide about the use and coordination of the company's resources, *e.g.*, the setting of targets for its employees. Those activities that do not relate to the pursuit of the company's corporate objectives are not part of the general manager's functions but pertain to the competence of the shareholders. In particular, shareholders are responsible for the organization of the corporate relationships of the company, *e.g.*, the appointment of general managers, the distribution of profits or the conclusion of subscription agreements in respect of capital increases.

1.   Sole and joint management of the company
§ 550 General principles

Where a GmbH has only one general manager, he is subject to all rights and obligations connected with the management of the company's business. The general manager is thus authorized to manage the company's business acting alone as the sole management power. Where several general managers have been appointed by a GmbH, the principle of joint management power applies[899] unless the shareholders have stipulated otherwise. This means that the general managers must jointly decide on matters pertaining to the company. In order to make such a joint decision, the general managers must pass a unanimous resolution.

Because the exercise of joint management power often proves to be impractical in the day-to-day running of the company, the shareholders are entitled to grant individual general managers sole management power in respect of particular areas of responsibility. The shareholders may also stipulate that joint management power shall only be necessary in respect of certain important decisions. The allocation of specific areas of responsibility and the identification of important transactions requiring the exercise of joint management power is entirely within the shareholders' discretion. Shareholder stipulations regarding management powers are usually set forth in the rules of procedure for the executive board. However, it is also possible to provide for sole management powers in the articles of association, which enables the general managers to allocate the different tasks among themselves.

---

899   *Cf.* GmbH-Gesetz [GmbHG] [Limited Liability Companies Act] 1892, § 35, ¶ 2, sentence 2 (F.R.G.).

In the case of a co-determined GmbH, the labor director[900] must be granted a certain level of autonomy regarding personnel-related matters. However, this does not automatically mean that he must also be granted sole management power in this area.

§ 551 No exemption from joint responsibility

The assignment of a specific area of responsibility to a certain general manager generally means that such general manager has exclusive responsibility over that area. However, such assignment does not release the general manager from the obligation to involve the remaining general managers in important decisions. At the same time, the remaining general managers are obligated to participate and, where appropriate, intervene in the taking of such essential management decisions. In order to enable them to do this, the general manager with sole management power must inform the other general managers in advance of particularly important decisions to be taken. All of the general managers must then confer with each other and resolve upon the issue in question. In this connection, the general managers must also examine whether there are any exceptional measures under consideration that would require the convention of the shareholders' meeting.

2. Limitations of the management power
§ 552 Introduction

Unlike with respect to a German AG,[901] statutory law does not provide for a strict separation of the powers allocated to the company's management and the competences of the shareholders. Although the general managers are vested with comprehensive management powers, the shareholders' meeting – as the highest decision making body within the GmbH – may at its discretion place limitations on the general managers' authority to manage the company's business.[902] However, such limitations are only permissible to the extent that they do not deprive a general manager of his ability to perform his statutory obligations. For example, the general managers must always have unlimited authority to represent the company *vis-à-vis* third parties[903] and to perform the obligations imposed on them by law.

Limitations on the general managers' management power may be stipulated in the articles of association, the rules of procedure for the executive board, a separate service agreement or by individual resolutions and instructions of the shareholders' meeting. The limitations may, *e.g.*, concern transactions intended by management that would have a fundamental impact on the company. The shareholders are even empowered, within certain limits, to influence the company's day-to-day business by the issuance of individual instructions to the executive board. The shareholders may delegate the power to limit the general manager's authorization to the supervisory board or another corporate body, as the case may be.

---

900 §§ 427 *et seq.* deal with co-determination and the concept of labor director.
901 *Cf.* §§ 1 *et seq.* above.
902 GmbH-Gesetz [GmbHG] [Limited Liability Companies Act] 1892, § 37, ¶ 1 (F.R.G.)
903 §§ 559 *et seq.* deal with the representation of the GmbH by its general managers.

§ 553 Limitations resulting from the decision-making competence of the shareholders
In some cases, the Limited Liability Companies Act assigns certain management responsibilities to the shareholders:[904] The approval of the annual financial statements, the implementation of measures for the assessment and monitoring of the management of the company, and the appointment of Prokuristen and holders of a commercial power of attorney.

The GmbH's articles of association may provide for the transfer of certain competences to the executive board, including the approval of the annual financial statements, but not the decision as to the appropriation of the company's profits and the appointment of general managers.

§ 554 Limitations imposed by the articles of association
Limitations on the management power which arise from the articles of association may take many forms. For example, the articles of association may impose an obligation to obtain the consent of the shareholders' meeting in respect of particular transactions. Such a provision in the articles of association should stipulate the concerned transactions as precisely as possible in order to prevent any disputes as to its interpretation.

§ 555 Limitations imposed by means of resolutions and instructions of the shareholders' meeting
As a matter of principle, the same limitations that may be stipulated in the articles of association may also be imposed by way of a shareholders' resolution, as *e.g.*, reflected in the internal rules of procedure for the executive board.[905] A shareholders' resolution limiting the general managers' management authority may not, however, be in conflict with the articles of association. The shareholders may also pass resolutions on concrete issues in individual cases, and then instruct the general managers to take – or desist from – specific actions. Such instructions do not have to observe any particular form. However, they must not lead to a situation that entails the insolvency of the GmbH or that damages the company's creditors.

A shareholders' resolution that violates the company's articles of association is generally not null and void but merely challengeable. This presents a difficult situation for the general managers and requires a nuanced approach since a general manager is obliged to adhere to effective shareholders' resolutions. On the one hand, a general manager is obligated to carry out shareholder instructions given pursuant to a contestable resolution once that resolution – due to the lapse of the respective period – is no longer challengeable. On the other hand, resolutions that have been successfully challenged are not binding upon management. The general manager concerned is in a particularly difficult position where a resolution is still challengeable but has not yet been challenged, in particular if the period for filing an action has not yet expired. Determining what course of action the general manager should take in such a situation is only possible on a case-by-case basis and after balancing the interests at stake. Following such balancing of the interests, the general manager may decide to refuse to follow

---

904   GmbH-Gesetz [GmbHG] [Limited Liability Companies Act] 1892, § 46, no. 1, 6, 7, 8 (F.R.G.).
905   *Cf.* GmbH-Gesetz [GmbHG] [Limited Liability Companies Act] 1892, § 37, ¶ 1 (F.R.G.).

the shareholder instruction provisionally or conclude that the contestable resolution must be complied with.[906]

In exceptional cases, a general manager himself has a right to challenge a shareholders' resolution where implementing the resolution would expose him to liability to pay damages or to criminal prosecution.[907] Challenging a resolution may also be a way to prevent a subsequent claim for damages where there is uncertainty as to whether a resolution will be challenged.

§ 556 Limitations based on the nature of the transaction concerned

The comprehensive management power of the general managers is restricted in case of extraordinary transactions. Extraordinary transactions are transactions outside of the company's corporate purpose as specified in the articles of association, transactions that are in conflict with the business parameters established by the shareholders' meeting, and transactions that qualify as exceptional due to their importance or the entrepreneurial risk attached to them. For example, a sale of the GmbH's business, a spin-off of substantial business units or a strategic realignment of the GmbH's operations generally qualifies as extraordinary. Whenever an extraordinary transaction is contemplated, the general managers are not permitted to take such a step independently but are obligated to submit the matter to the shareholders for their consideration.

Particular standards apply to management decisions that, from the perspective of the general managers, may give rise to objections by the shareholders. If only a minority of shareholders is likely to object, the decision may generally be taken without involving the shareholders. However, in case of doubt, the transaction should be submitted to the shareholders for their consideration and approval.

§ 557 Limitations imposed by the supervisory board, advisory council or individual shareholders

It is possible to stipulate in the articles of association that certain corporate bodies of the GmbH (*e.g.*, the advisory council or the supervisory board) have the right to limit the management power of the general managers. A shareholders' resolution or provisions in the rules of procedure would not be sufficient for this purpose. If the articles of association confer the right to limit the general managers' management authority on a corporate body, such corporate body then has the right to impose binding rules on the general managers or issue instructions to them.

The shareholders always retain a number of core rights of their own, even where the assessment and monitoring of the company's management has been delegated to another corporate body. In addition, the shareholders' meeting can always order that certain management measures be taken, even where this is not explicitly provided for in the articles of association.

---

906   *Cf.* § 527 and § 615.
907   Aktiengesetz [AktG] [Stock Corporation Act] 1965, § 245, no. 5 (F.R.G.) analogously.

Where the GmbH is subject to co-determination rules and has a mandatory supervisory board, the provisions of stock corporation law apply to the legal relationship between the supervisory board and the executive board.[908] Where the supervisory board is optional, it has the functions of a mere advisory council and the shareholders generally have broad discretion in providing for the structure and the responsibilities of such corporate body.

B.   Representation of the company

§ 558 Introduction
A GmbH – as a legal entity – may only enter into legal transactions through natural persons. While the general managers' management power relates to their internal powers within the company, the power of representation relates to their activities *vis-à-vis* third parties.

The general managers may only represent the company acting jointly, unless only one general manager is in place or the articles of association authorize certain general managers to represent the company acting alone.

As an exception to the representation of the company by its general managers, the shareholders are authorized to bring claims for compensation or damages of the company against general managers.[909] They also function as the legal representatives of the company in the context of legal proceedings against the members of the executive board. Shareholders may also act as the legal representatives of the company for the purpose of entering or terminating service agreements with general managers.[910]

1.   The representation of the GmbH by its general managers
§ 559 Entering into transactions through the general managers
The authority of general managers to act with binding effect for the GmbH *vis-à-vis* third parties is unlimited and cannot be restricted, not even in the articles of association.[911] It is only limited by the principles of abuse of power. This rule was established by the legislature for the sake of legal certainty: Every business partner of a GmbH should be able to rely on the ability of general managers to effectively represent the company.

Even where a general manager has not expressly stated the intention to act on behalf of the GmbH, the company will nonetheless be bound if the circumstances surrounding the transaction indicate that the parties intended a legal transaction or physical act being carried out on behalf of the company (so-called company-related transaction (*unternehmensbezogenes Geschäft*)). In the context of written correspondence, the use of the GmbH's letterhead generally suffices to legally bind the company. The general managers, and not the company, become

---

908   §§ 248 *et seq.* above deal with the supervision of management by and specific rights of the supervisory board under stock corporation law.
909   GmbH-Gesetz [GmbHG] [Limited Liability Companies Act] 1892, § 46, no. 8 (F.R.G.).
910   §§ 468 *et seq.* deal with the conclusion of the service agreement.
911   GmbH-Gesetz [GmbHG] [Limited Liability Companies Act] 1892, § 37, ¶ 2 (F.R.G.).

legally bound in the event that there is no indication – not even in the circumstances surrounding the conclusion of the contract – that the general managers intended to legally bind the GmbH by the transaction in question.

§ 560 Scope of the extrajudicial (out of court) representation

General managers' extrajudicial representation of the GmbH encompasses all legal transactions that arise in the ordinary course of business, including the issuance and acceptance of legally relevant declarations. For example, the general managers are authorized to take all legal actions in connection with the employment contracts of the company's employees, to acquire interest in other companies on behalf of the GmbH, to establish subsidiaries, and to exercise the company's participation rights in its subsidiaries.

Where the GmbH has several general managers, these must jointly register the formation of the GmbH[912] and any capital increase with the competent commercial register.[913]

§ 561 Representation requiring the participation of shareholders

With regard to certain transactions, the general managers vested with power of representation may still only legally bind the company on the basis of a valid shareholders' resolution. Transactions requiring such shareholders' resolutions include those that are subject to the Merger and Reorganization Act (*Umwandlungsgesetz*). By contrast, the general managers have the power to bind the company with respect to extraordinary transactions even if the (internal) management power does not encompass entering into any such transaction in the absence of a shareholders' resolution.[914]

In respect of agreements regarding a statutory merger concluded with another GmbH or a German AG, the effectiveness of the agreement depends on the existence of a shareholders' resolution in support thereof.[915] Whether a shareholders' resolution is required for the conclusion of a control and profit transfer agreement depends on the effect of the agreement for the GmbH: Where the GmbH becomes the dependent party as a result of the control and profit transfer agreement, an amendment of the articles of association is required. It is subject to controversy among commentators whether a majority of three-quarters of the shareholders is sufficient in this respect or an unanimous resolution has to be passed.[916] Where the GmbH becomes the controlling entity pursuant to the agreement, there are no doubts that a vote by three-quarters of its shareholdes is required (but sufficient) in support of the resolution.

---

912   GmbH-Gesetz [GmbHG] [Limited Liability Companies Act] 1892, § 7, ¶ 1; § 78 (F.R.G.).
913   GmbH-Gesetz [GmbHG] [Limited Liability Companies Act] 1892, § 57, ¶ 1; § 78 (F.R.G.). §§ 545 *et seq.* deal with specific duties and obligations of general managers in the stage of formation of the GmbH.
914   *Cf.* § 556.
915   Umwandlungsgesetz [UmwG] [Merger and Reorganization Act] 1994, § 13, ¶ 1, § 50 (F.R.G.).
916   *Cf.* GmbH-Gesetz [GmbHG] [Limited Liability Companies Act] 1892, § 54, ¶ 2, sentence 1 (F.R.G.).

§ 562 Representation in respect of transactions with the shareholders

In transactions between the GmbH and its shareholders, the company is represented by its general managers. Thus, the general managers may consent on behalf of the company to the sale of shares where such consent is required under the articles of association.

With respect to any matters related to the service agreements between the GmbH and its general managers, the shareholders' meeting or (in particular in co-determined limited liability companies) the supervisory board is responsible, including for the assertion of damage claims as a result of a violation of the service agreement.

In ordinary legal transactions between a general manager and the GmbH, the latter is represented by one of the other general managers and/or Prokurist, unless the supervisory board is to represent the company *vis-à-vis* the general manager in case of a co-determined GmbH or pursuant to specific provisions of the company's articles of association.

§ 563 The basic principle: Judicial representation through the general managers

As a basic principle, the general managers may represent the GmbH in legal proceedings, irrespective of the court before which these proceedings are held. However, the German law of civil procedure provides that the involvement of an attorney admitted to the bar in Germany is mandatory for matters being heard before a regional court or higher courts.

§ 564 Exception: Legal proceedings involving a general manager and the company

A general manager is not entitled to represent the company in legal proceedings between him and the GmbH. If the company does not have a supervisory board that would assume this role as a matter of law,[917] the representation of the company is generally assumed by the shareholders, at least in those cases where the company would not be duly represented by the other general managers.[918] The shareholders then appoint a legal representative (*Prozessvertreter*) to conduct the action against the incumbent general manager. A formal shareholders' resolution is required where the company seeks to assert a compensation claim against a general manager. In the absence of such shareholders' resolution, the claim will be deemed unfounded on the merits.[919]

2.   Joint power of representation as a general rule

§ 565 Active and passive power of representation

Where the shareholders appoint several general managers, the Limited Liability Companies Act provides for joint power of representation of the GmbH (*e.g.*, the general managers may only represent the company acting jointly), unless the articles of association provide otherwise.[920] Sole power of representation of the company by a general manager is the exception and merely exists where only one general manager has been appointed, where all of the general

---

917   GmbH-Gesetz [GmbHG] [Limited Liability Companies Act] 1892, § 52 (F.R.G.); Aktiengesetz [AktG] [Stock Corporation Act] 1965, § 112 (F.R.G.).
918   GmbH-Gesetz [GmbHG] [Limited Liability Companies Act] 1892, § 46, no. 8 (F.R.G.).
919   GmbH-Gesetz [GmbHG] [Limited Liability Companies Act] 1892, § 46, no. 8 (F.R.G.).
920   GmbH-Gesetz [GmbHG] [Limited Liability Companies Act] 1892, § 35, ¶ 2, sentence 2 (F.R.G.).

managers except one leave the company or where the articles of associates provide for the option of such sole power.

The receipt by one of the joint representatives of legally relevant declarations addressed to the company is sufficient for the effectiveness of service.[921] This also applies in the context of legal proceedings.[922]

§ 566 Collective action in respect of joint power of representation

Where the general managers have joint power of representation, the general managers may execute legally relevant declarations or documents either jointly or individually. Thus, it may also be permissible to execute an agreement or other written document in two separate instruments, unless otherwise provided for under applicable mandatory form requirements. However, the legal transaction at issue is only valid once all of the individual declarations have been executed.

Also, a general manager may conclude an agreement on behalf of the company provided that the other general managers subsequently consent thereto.[923] This consent may be issued on an informal basis.[924] Once the consent has been given, the legal transaction in question becomes valid with retroactive effect.[925]

Alternatively, the joint representatives may authorize a single general manager in advance to conclude a transaction. The granting of such authorization requires the same number of general managers as would be required to represent the company *vis-à-vis* third parties. The authorization may not be granted on a general basis, but must relate to a particular transaction or at least a clearly distinguishable type of transactions. The authorization may be granted orally, and may be withdrawn at any time by any one of the general managers.

3.   Regulation of the power of representation in the articles of association
§ 567 Divergence from statutory provisions

Arrangements which diverge from the statutory provisions regarding the representation of the GmbH can be specified in the articles of association. The articles of association may authorize the shareholders or another corporate body (*e.g.*, the supervisory board or an advisory council) to decide upon the scope of the power of representation (*e.g.*, whether any general manager shall be authorized to represent the company acting alone).

The articles of association may also stipulate types of joint power of representation that diverge from the general rule, *e.g.*, modified joint power of representation and the so-called quasi joint power of representation.

---

921   § 566 deals with the representation of the company in the acceptance of legal declarations.
922   Zivilprozessordnung [ZPO] [Code of Civil Procedure] 1950, § 171, ¶ 3 (F.R.G.).
923   Bürgerliches Gesetzbuch [BGB] [Civil Code] 1896, § 177, ¶ 1, § 182 (F.R.G.).
924   Bürgerliches Gesetzbuch [BGB] [Civil Code] 1896, § 182, ¶ 2 (F.R.G.).
925   Bürgerliches Gesetzbuch [BGB] [Civil Code] 1896, § 184, ¶ 2 (F.R.G.).

§ 568 Modified joint power of representation

Under the model of modified joint power of representation, a specific number of general managers is authorized to represent the GmbH acting jointly without involving all members of the executive board (*e.g.*, where the company has three general managers, two of them may represent the company acting jointly).

It may also be stipulated in the company's articles that whereas one general manager shall be authorized to represent the company acting alone, another general manager shall only be authorized to represent the company together with another general manager.

As in the case of sole power of representation,[926] the modified joint power of representation must apply to all transactions. A restriction on a particular type of transactions is not permissible.

§ 569 Quasi joint power of representation

Under the model of the so-called quasi joint power of representation, a general manager is only entitled to represent the company jointly with a Prokurist. However, a Prokurist may not be granted a veto position in this respect. Quasi joint power of representation is therefore not permissible where the GmbH has only one general manager, as the company would then only be capable of acting with the support of a Prokurist, so that he could *de facto* veto the implementation of management decisions. For the same reason, the quasi joint power of representation cannot constitute the only form of representation where the company has several general managers, but may only exist in addition to other forms of power of (joint) representation.

§ 570 Sole power of representation

As a matter of law, a general manager is vested with sole power of representation where only one general manager is appointed or remains within the GmbH. Where several managers are appointed, all, some or one of them may be granted sole power of representation either in the articles of association or on the basis of a shareholders' resolution (if permitted in the articles). Once it has been granted, a general manager's sole power of representation applies with respect to all transactions involving the GmbH. A limitation of the sole power of representation to a particular type of transactions is not permissible.[927] In certain cases, the general managers must act jointly, *e.g.*, in respect of certain applications for registration with the commercial register.[928]

4. Self-dealing and multiple representation
§ 571 Prohibition of self-dealing

Under German law, transactions concluded by a general manager on behalf of the GmbH with himself, acting in his own name or as representative of a third party, are not permitted due to the apparent conflict of interest.[929]

---

926   § 570 deals with sole power of representation.
927   *Cf.* GmbH-Gesetz [GmbHG] [Limited Liability Companies Act] 1892, § 37, ¶ 2, sentence 1 (F.R.G.).
928   GmbH-Gesetz [GmbHG] [Limited Liability Companies Act] 1892, § 78 (F.R.G.).
929   Bürgerliches Gesetzbuch [BGB] [Civil Code] 1896, § 181 (F.R.G.).

A violation of the prohibition of self-dealing and multiple representation results in the transaction being provisionally invalid (*schwebend unwirksam*).[930] However, the company may subsequently consent to the transaction and thereby validate it retroactively.

§ 572 Permission of self-dealing/multiple representation

Self-dealing and multiple representation may exceptionally be permitted where such acting occurs in connection with the performance of a pre-existing obligation, or where the general manager has been authorized to do so.

For example, the general manager acts in performance of a pre-existing obligation where he transfers his compensation from the company's account to his own account, because the company is obligated to make such payment under the service agreement with himself.

Authorization of self-dealing or multiple representation may be granted subsequently (in the form of retroactive consent) or as a general matter. Subsequent authorization may, *e.g.*, be obtained from other general managers authorized to represent the company or from the shareholders' meeting or by approval of another general manager who may validly represent the company. Self-dealing and multiple representation may also be authorized from the outset by the articles of association, by a shareholders' resolution or by another corporate body empowered to do so, *e.g.*, a supervisory board. Authorization of self-dealing and multiple representation does not have to be explicitly granted but may also be inferred from the conduct of the empowered body or person.

The articles of association may contain an exemption from the prohibition of self-dealing or multi-representation with regard to all or some of the members of the executive board, or may provide for the possibility to authorize the general managers by way of an individual shareholders' resolution. It is subject to controversy whether an authorization may be granted by the shareholders' meeting without a corresponding empowerment in the company's articles of association. It is therefore preferable in practice to expressly provide for such option in the articles of association.

5.   Abuse of the power of representation
§ 573 Introduction

A general manager's power of representation is unlimited and unrestrictable.[931] To the extent the general manager's management power has been limited on an internal level, he has more legal power *vis-à-vis* third parties than he is permitted to exercise in the internal context of the GmbH.[932] Such excess of external authorization may give rise to the potential for an abuse of powers. In some cases, an abuse of the power of representation can result in the invalidity of the transaction at issue, with the consequence that the GmbH is not legally bound by the general manager's actions.

---

930   Bürgerliches Gesetzbuch [BGB] [Civil Code] 1896, § 177, ¶ 1 (F.R.G.).
931   §§ 558 *et seq.* deal with the general principles of the power of representation.
932   GmbH-Gesetz [GmbHG] [Limited Liability Companies Act] 1892, § 37, ¶ 2 (F.R.G.).

§ 574 Collusion and knowledge of an abuse of power
Not every time a general manager exceeds his management power, the relevant legal action or agreement is deemed invalid. In fact, as a general principle, a GmbH is legally bound by the actions of its general managers, even where the transaction is to its disadvantage.

There are, however, two scenarios in which an abuse of a general manager's power of representation could potentially be established:[933]

First, an abuse of power may be established where a general manager deliberately collaborates with a third party to the disadvantage of the company (collusion/*Kollusion*). Second, an abuse of power may be established where a general manager exceeds the boundaries of his management power in a manner which is objectively in breach of his duty and the third party concerned actually knows or should have known (gross negligence) that such a transaction would not normally have been effected on behalf of the GmbH.

Where a general manager colludes with a contracting party with the intent of causing harm to the GmbH, the transaction in question is null and void,[934] and the company is not bound by it. In all other cases of a general manager's abuse of the power of representation, the transaction in question is, according to pertinent case law, not enforceable against the company if the company raises the objection of bad faith. The company, if it is aware of the abuse of the power of representation, may still opt to accept the transaction as binding in an explicit or conclusive manner, *e.g.*, by performing the contractual obligations agreed upon by the general manager and the third party.

V. Liability of general managers

§ 575 Overview
The liability of a general manager under civil law may become relevant in a number of situations. It may arise *vis-à-vis* the company itself (so-called internal liability/*Innenhaftung*), its shareholders or third parties, in particular creditors of the company (so-called external liability/*Außenhaftung*). A general manager may also incur liability in connection with the company's obligations under tax or social security laws. Some of these liability risks may be covered by obtaining so-called D&O insurance (Directors and Officers liability insurance).

A. Liability *vis-à-vis* the company

§ 576 Introduction
Liability of a general manager *vis-à-vis* the company may arise on various grounds. Generally, it is irrelevant whether the action or conduct giving rise to the general manager being liable

---

933 The details are subject to controversy.
934 Pursuant to Bürgerliches Gesetzbuch [BGB] [Civil Code] 1896, § 138, ¶ 1 (F.R.G.).

under statutory law at the same time constitutes a breach of the general manager's obligations under the service agreement.

1.   Liability for breach of the duty of care
§ 577 General prerequisites for liability for breach of the duty of care
The Limited Liability Companies Act imposes liability on a general manager where he does not apply the standard of care of a prudent business person with respect to company matters,[935] where the breach of duty was committed in a culpable manner, and where such breach gave rise to damages.

§ 578 Appointment
A prerequisite for incurring liability is the position as general manager. The general manager must, after his appointment, have assumed office, at which point he is vested with executive functions of the GmbH. Registration of the general manager's appointment with the commercial register is not required to establish liability, as such registration is merely of a declaratory nature. A general manager does not avoid liability merely because the act appointing him as general manager is null and void or the service agreement is invalid.

A general manager of a GmbH whose establishment has been notarized but not yet registered with the commercial register (a so-called "pre-GmbH") is subject to the same liability regime as a general manager of an already registered GmbH.

Liability ceases upon the termination of the position of general manager, *e.g.*, normally by means of the general manager's removal from office.

§ 579 Types of general managers
In addition to the "regular" general managers, the labor director of a co-determined GmbH who qualifies as a general manager may also be held liable *vis-à-vis* the company. An emergency general manager appointed by the court is equally liable. In the event of the dissolution of the company, both the liquidators and the general managers (if not identical with the liquidators) are liable.[936] Where the GmbH has a supervisory board, the supervisory board members may be held liable as well.

§ 580 Introduction
In addition to being liable for the violation of capital maintenance rules,[937] a general manager may be held liable for any and all breaches of duty that he commits in service, provided that he is culpable of such a breach.

---

935 GmbH-Gesetz [GmbHG] [Limited Liability Companies Act] 1892, § 43, ¶ 1 and 2 (F.R.G.).
936 GmbH-Gesetz [GmbHG] [Limited Liability Companies Act] 1892, § 52, ¶ 1 (F.R.G.) in conjunction with Aktiengesetz [AktG] [Stock Corporation Act] 1965, § 116; § 93, ¶ 1 and 2 (F.R.G.).
937 § 585 deals with liability under the capital maintenance rules.

§ 581 Duty of care standard

A general manager must exercise the due careof a prudent business person. He must always remember that he is dealing with assets that are not his own and that he is responsible for the preservation of those assets on a fiduciary basis. The size and the type of the company in question must be taken into account when determining the precise standard of the duty of care.

Although under German labor law the liability of employees towards their employer is subject to certain limitations and employees are, in certain cases, entitled to indemnification regarding their liability resulting from damage caused in the course of the performance of their functions, a general manager of a GmbH can usually not rely on this privileged position. He is generally not considered an employee.[938] However, where the general manager was not performing the typical duties of a general manager when the breach of duty occurred (*e.g.*, in the case of an accident while driving a company car), a mitigation of liability may be possible under certain circumstances.

§ 582 Conduct of general managers in breach of duty

Not every damaging outcome of an action of a general manager justifies the conclusion that a breach of duty has occurred. Rather, in order to establish a general manager's liability for a breach of duty, the breach must be linked to the obligations and duties of a general manager.[939]

The general managers bear the burden of proof that their decisions and actions are in full compliance with their duty of care and other management duties. In the context of legal proceedings, a general manager must establish that he acted with the due care of a prudent business person. The burden of proof in this regard comprises both objective and subjective aspects. This means that the general manager must prove that his decision was reasonable. The company bears the burden of proof that it has suffered damages as a result of the general manager's conduct.

§ 583 The business judgment rule

Management must always act in the best interests of the company. Members of the management and/or the supervisory boards can be held personally liable *vis-à-vis* the company where their decisions or actions are not in the best interests of the company. However, under German law, a company's management generally has discretionary power to make decisions which can reasonably be assumed to be in the best interests of the company,[940] unless the statutory provisions, articles of association or individual instructions by shareholders are binding upon the general managers and require a specific decision or action. This provision provides a "safe harbor" for a company's management similar to the business judgment rule in the United States. Under this provision, management liability is limited to situations where it is evident that the general manager's decision is not in line with the best interests of the company and where the

---

938   § 465 deals with applicability of labor law provisions.
939   §§ 510 *et seq.* deal with the obligations of a general manager arising out of his appointment.
940   Aktiengesetz [AktG] [Stock Corporation Act] 1965, § 93, ¶ 1 sentence 2 (F.R.G.), which applies *mutatis mutandis* to a GmbH.

general manager has taken unreasonable risks. Where a management decision is made after the gathering of all relevant information and the consideration of possible alternatives, it is presumed that management has not breached its duty of care.

Against this background, the conclusion of risky transactions does not *per se* constitute a breach of a general manager's duties towards the company, as long as they have been carefully considered and the inherent risks have been sufficiently weighed against the anticipated benefits. The greater the potential risk for the company, the more carefully the general manager must consider whether or not to enter into the transaction.

§ 584 Fault

A general manager is liable for intentional and negligent conduct. Even the slightest element of negligence may be sufficient to give rise to liability. However, fault may be lacking where, *e.g.*, the general manager causes a violation of law in circumstances where immediate action is required. Fault may also be lacking where the general manager, after careful consideration, implements a challengeable resolution of the shareholders' meeting prior to the expiration of the period for challenges and the resolution is subsequently successfully challenged contrary to his expectations. The same may apply where it was impossible for the general manager to recognize the invalidity of a resolution.[941]

§ 585 Liability under capital maintenance rules

General managers are prohibited from providing financial benefits to the shareholders to the extent that the funds or assets used for this purpose are necessary for the maintenance of the company's nominal share capital.[942] This prohibition seeks to protect the company's creditors. Because generally no individuals within a GmbH are personally liable for a failure of the company, it is important for the creditors that the company's nominal share capital is maintained. Where a general manager nonetheless makes payments out of funds necessary to preserve the nominal share capital in violation of this statutory obligation, he is personally liable[943] and is obligated to replace the amount he has paid out. In that situation, the general manager may have recourse against the recipient shareholder(s) of the payment(s).

The repayment of shareholder loans is, according to the modifications brought about by the MoMiG and implemented into insolvency law,[944] excluded from the pay-out prohibition. According to the amended insolvency provisions, claims for repayment of shareholder loans are always subordinated to creditor claims in an insolvency situation.[945] However, repayments of shareholder loans within one year prior to the company's filing for insolvency may later be challenged by the insolvency receiver.[946] Such a challenge in and by itself generally does not

---

941   § 555 deals with the appropriate conduct of general managers in cases of challengeable shareholder resolutions.
942   GmbH-Gesetz [GmbHG] [Limited Liability Companies Act] 1892, § 30, ¶ 1 (F.R.G.).
943   GmbH-Gesetz [GmbHG] [Limited Liability Companies Act] 1892, § 43, ¶ 3, sentence 1, alternative 1 (F.R.G.).
944   § 414 deals with the GmbH reform effected by the MoMiG.
945   Insolvenzordnung [InsO] [Insolvency Code] 1994, § 39, ¶ no. 5 (F.R.G.).
946   Insolvenzordnung [InsO] [Insolvency Code] 1994, § 135 (F.R.G.).

establish sufficient grounds to hold the general manager liable. However, the general manager may be held liable where the repayment caused the illiquidity of the GmbH.[947]

§ 586 Inadmissible acquisition of own shares

Although a GmbH is generally allowed to acquire its own shares to be held in treasury, this is not an unrestricted right: The law prohibits limited liability companies from acquiring their own shares or taking such shares as a pledge where the initial capital contribution has not yet been made in full.[948] A company may acquire its own shares only where sufficient financial means are available for this purpose within the company's registered capital and where the reserves stipulated by statute and in the articles of association are unaffected thereby. A company may also acquire its own shares in order to compensate shareholders in certain reorganization scenarios.[949] Should the company acquire its own shares in violation of these provisions, its general managers may be held liable and obligated to reimburse the company for the purchase price paid. In order to establish general managers' liability in this context, the company must show that it has suffered damages as a result of the acquisition of its own shares.[950] The general managers are generally entitled to claim from the company assignment of its rights *vis-à-vis* the seller of the shares of the GmbH.

§ 587 Waiver and settlement

A GmbH is not allowed to waive or settle a claim for damages arising from an inadmissible acquisition of own shares or violations of capital maintenance rules with a general manager if the desired payment of damages is necessary to satisfy the claims of the company's creditors.[951] A shareholders' resolution providing for an exemption of the general manager from liability will be null and void. This does not apply in the exceptional case where the general manager is unable to pay the damages and a settlement is reached in order to prevent the commencement of insolvency proceedings, or where the obligation to pay damages is settled in the context of an insolvency plan.

§ 588 Definition of damage

A general manager can be found liable for breach of duty only if a damage has occurred. Any deterioration in the monetary value of corporate assets qualifies as damage. That is, a damage has occurred where the actual value of the company's assets is lower than the value that those assets would have had if the breach had not occurred. The term "damage" also encompasses lost opportunities the company would have been able to pursue if the general manager had fulfilled his duties.

---

947   § 600 deals with payments made by the company in a crisis situation.
948   GmbH-Gesetz [GmbHG] [Limited Liability Companies Act] 1892, § 33, ¶ 1 (F.R.G.).
949   GmbH-Gesetz [GmbHG] [Limited Liability Companies Act] 1892, § 33, ¶ 3 (F.R.G.).
950   § 588 deals with the definition of damage.
951   GmbH-Gesetz [GmbHG] [Limited Liability Companies Act] 1892, § 43, ¶ 3, sentence 2 (F.R.G.) in conjunction with GmbH-Gesetz [GmbHG] [Limited Liability Companies Act] 1892, § 9b, ¶ 1, sentence 1 (F.R.G.).

§ 589 Examples of damage and relaxation of the company's burden of proof

A company has suffered a damage if, *e.g.*, a general manager settles a claim against the company before it became due, and this results in a loss of interest income. A company has also suffered a damage where a burden is imposed on the company's assets without the receipt of adequate consideration therefore or where the GmbH must pay to a third party an amount owed as a result of a general manager's misconduct.

The company generally bears the burden of proof with respect to the occurrence of a damage. However, pertinent case law has relaxed the burden of proof in certain cases.

§ 590 Requirements for joint and several liability

Where a GmbH has several general managers and each has breached a duty, then they are jointly and severally liable.[952] Joint and several liability is particularly likely to arise with respect to decisions taken jointly or omissions pertaining to a sphere of responsibilities that is assigned to everal general managers. Where areas of responsibility have been allocated among the general managers, each general manager is primarily liable in respect of the area assigned to him, although the other general managers may also incur some liability as a result of their general obligation to monitor the activities of their colleagues.[953] Joint and several liability may similarly apply in the event of a breach of general organizational duties.

§ 591 Consequences of joint and several liability

In the event of joint and several liability of the general managers, the company may claim the total amount of damages from one or all of the general managers.[954] This does not mean, however, that all liability is randomly borne by one of the general managers and that the remaining general managers may escape all liability. The general managers are obligated to settle the liability issue among themselves.[955] They are generally liable in equal parts, provided that no contrary arrangements have been made in this regard. A diverging allocation may be stipulated in the articles of association or in the service agreement or may result from differing levels of responsibility for the event giving rise to the damage claim. Thus, the general manager who is responsible for the area where the breach took place may ultimately have to compensate the company for the damage caused. Only if he is insolvent will the other general managers who have breached their duty to monitor his activities bear liability in a proportionate amount.

§ 592 Impact of contributory fault of other corporate bodies or employees

Any fault on the part of the shareholders' meeting or another corporate body will result in a reduction of the general manager's liability.[956] Such mitigation of liability is based on equitable considerations and is within the discretion of the courts. In extreme cases of contributory

---

952   GmbH-Gesetz [GmbHG] [Limited Liability Companies Act] 1892, § 43, ¶ 2 (F.R.G.) in conjunction with Bürgerliches Gesetzbuch [BGB] [Civil Code] 1896, §§ 421 *et seq.* (F.R.G.).

953   *Cf.* §§ 511 *et seq.* for more on the monitoring obligation in the case of an allocation of duties among the general managers.

954   *Cf.* Bürgerliches Gesetzbuch [BGB] [Civil Code] 1896, § 421 (F.R.G.).

955   Bürgerliches Gesetzbuch [BGB] [Civil Code] 1896, § 426 (F.R.G.).

956   *Cf.* Bürgerliches Gesetzbuch [BGB] [Civil Code] 1896, § 254 (F.R.G.).

fault by another corporate body, a damage claim against a general manager may be excluded entirely.

Fault on the part of the other general managers does not qualify as contributory fault and will not reduce the damages payable by the general manager who is found liable. The same holds true with respect to subordinated employees. Similarly, a general manager's liability will not be reduced as a result of a failure by the company's shareholders' meeting and/or its supervisory board to monitor the general manager's conduct.

§ 593 Assertion by a majority of shareholders

A shareholders' resolution is required before a GmbH can assert a claim for damages against a general manager.[957] Without such a resolution, the claim will automatically be deemed un-founded on the merits. Such a resolution may be passed on an informal basis if none of the shareholders has any objection to the course of action. The resolution must be passed with a simple majority of the votes cast.[958] The general manager against whom a claim is to be pursued and who is also a shareholder must not vote on the resolution.[959]

The shareholders' resolution must state that a claim against the general manager is being as-serted before the courts. The resolution must also address the issue of the representation of the company in the legal proceedings. The shareholders' meeting may appoint one or more share-holders or even third parties – in particular attorneys – as representatives of the company in this respect.[960] Where the GmbH has a supervisory board, this corporate body normally repre-sents the GmbH in connection with the enforcement of claims against a general manager.[961]

§ 594 Assertion by minority shareholders

The enforcement of a damage claim against a general manager by a minority of the sharehold-ers or by individual shareholders may only be considered under exceptional circumstances. It is subject to controversy whether a minority of the shareholders is entitled to assert claims against a general manager on behalf of the company or is able to compel the company to bring such an action. Pertinent case law allows a minority of shareholders to assert a claim for dam-ages on behalf of the company in cases where the majority of the shareholders has unconscion-ably prevented the assertion of the claim.

2.   Liability in respect of formation of the company
§ 595 Introduction

A company enjoys the privilege of limited liabilityx only upon registration of the GmbH with the competent commercial register. In the time period between notarization of the company's articles of association and its registration, the GmbH exists in the form of a GmbH in forma-

---

957   GmbH-Gesetz [GmbHG] [Limited Liability Companies Act] 1892, § 46, no. 8 (F.R.G.).
958   GmbH-Gesetz [GmbHG] [Limited Liability Companies Act] 1892, § 47, ¶ 1 (F.R.G.).
959   GmbH-Gesetz [GmbHG] [Limited Liability Companies Act] 1892, § 47, ¶ 4 (F.R.G.).
960   § 564 deals with the representation of the GmbH in cases of claims against general managers.
961   Aktiengesetz [AktG] [Stock Corporation Act] 1965, § 112 (F.R.G.) analogously.

tion. During that stage, the company is vested with legal capacity and may already enter into legal transactions.[962]

A GmbH should have a certain amount of capital at its disposal upon its formation. At the very least, the company must have access to capital in the amount of the nominal share capital that is registered with the commercial register. In order to ensure the company's access to the nominal share capital, the Limited Liability Companies Act sets forth precise requirements which the company must comply with in the context of its formation and registration with the commercial register.

In order to protect the company and its creditors, the law provides for liability of general managers (and also its shareholders) in respect of its formation. Such liability may not be waived in the articles of association.

§ 596 Prerequisites for liability of a general manager

In the context of liability in respect of the formation of the company, the liability of a general manager also applies to any person or persons to whom the application for registration with the commercial register may be attributed. Thus, not only a person who has been appointed a general manager or who functions as a general manager in respect of the registration of the GmbH may be regarded as a general manager of the company. Any form of participation in the process of registration of the GmbH may be sufficient in this regard.

The provision by a general manager of inaccurate information for the purpose of establishing the company, in particular with regard to the contribution of the company's share capital, may serve as a basis for the imposition of liability.[963] Information is considered inaccurate where it does not correspond to the truth from an objective standpoint or where it is incomplete despite the existence of a statutory duty of disclosure. The relevant moment in time for the evaluation of the correctness or completeness of the information provided is the point in time at which the application is submitted to the local court where the commercial register is located. In some cases, however, a revision of erroneous or incomplete information may be permitted between the application and the registration of the company.

§ 597 Consequences of liability in respect of the formation of the company

If a general manager is found liable in respect of the foundation of the company, he must place the company in the position it would have been in had the information been accurate. In practice, this generally means that the missing capital contributions must be made. In addition, the general manager must compensate the company for all damages it has suffered as a result of a missing capital contribution.

---

962   §§ 545 *et seq.* deal with specific duties and obligations of general managers during formation of the GmbH.
963   § 547 deals with specific disclosure requirements.

3.   Liability in crisis situations

§ 598 Obligation to file a petition for the commencement of insolvency proceedings

Should the company become insolvent, the general managers must apply for the commence-ment of insolvency proceedings as quickly as possible, at the latest within three weeks of the occurrence of the illiquidity. The same applies where the company is over-indebted.[964] A gen-eral manager may incur personal liability or even criminal charges by breaching his duty to file an insolvency petition in a timely manner.

§ 599 Untimely filing of a petition for the commencement of insolvency proceedings

A general manager may be held liable for damages suffered by the GmbH as a result of a delay in filing or a failure to file a petition for the commencement of insolvency proceedings.[965]

A prerequisite for liability in such a situation is a causal link between the conduct of the gen-eral manager and the damage caused. For example, it is possible that a failure by the general manager to file a petition for the commencement of insolvency proceedings within the ap-plicable time limit results in the creation of new liabilities, which causes a further reduction in the amount of the company's assets, so that a causal link could be established. A claim for damages may also arise from a premature filing of an insolvency petition, *e.g.*, where the gen-eral managers should have been aware of promising rescue efforts by the company within the three-week limitation period.

As soon as a general manager becomes aware of circumstances that may lead to the illiquidity or over-indebtedness of the GmbH, it is advisable to seek external expert advice. The utiliza-tion of such expert advice may lead to the liability of the general manager being excluded. According to pertinent case law, a general manager does not act in a culpable manner where he refrains from filing for insolvency based on the opinion of an independent expert who con-cludes that the GmbH is not in a state of insolvency, provided that the general manager has duly provided all facts to such expert and reviewed the expert opinion for plausibility.

Further, a general manager's liability is generally excluded where the delay of filing insolvency proceedings is due to binding instructions issued by the shareholders.[966]

§ 600 Payments in a crisis situation

General managers are liable to compensate the company for payments made after the occur-rence of the company's illiquidity or the determination of its over-indebtedness.[967] The fact that the general managers resign from office prior to the commencement of the insolvency proceedings does not remove the obligation to pay damages. Further, the MoMiG[968] intro-duced a new rule under which general managers may be held liable for payments made by the

---

964   §§ 538 *et seq*. deal with the duties of the general managers in case of a crisis situation.
965   GmbH-Gesetz [GmbHG] [Limited Liability Companies Act] 1892, § 43, ¶ 2 (F.R.G.).
966   §§ 613 *et seq*. deal with the exception of general managers from liability in case of instructions issued by share-holders.
967   GmbH-Gesetz [GmbHG] [Limited Liability Companies Act] 1892, § 64, sentence 1 (F.R.G.).
968   § 414 deals with the GmbH reform effected by the MoMiG.

company to its shareholders where such payments directly lead to the company's insolvency, unless this effect was not evident upon the exercise of due care.[969] Thus, under the new rule, general managers are responsible for the prevention of insolvency, at least as far as payments to shareholders are concerned.

Such payments include, in particular, monetary payments. It is irrelevant whether such payments are made in cash or by way of bank transfer. The delivery of property or the transfer of rights may also qualify. A company's claim for damages is excluded in respect of payments that are consistent with the exercise of due care.[970] For example, payments made within the filing period may be deemed consistent with the standard of due care where the payments are intended to facilitate the implementation of promising recapitalization measures. Payments that do not result in a reduction in the amount of the insolvency assets are generally permitted, as are payments in return for which the company receives immediate adequate consideration.

An additional requirement for establishing liability is that the general manager was at fault. It will be sufficient in this context if the general manager acted negligently.

The company's claim for damages will typically seek re-payment of the amount paid out by the general managers during the crisis situation. The company's claim for damages must be reduced by the amount of the consideration added to the company's assets, if any, in the course of the transaction. A waiver or settlement in respect of the damage claim is invalid where the receipt of damages is necessary in order to satisfy the claims of the company's creditors.[971]

B. Liability *vis-à-vis* the shareholders

§ 601 No liability as a basic principle
As a matter of principle, a general manager's obligation to conduct the company's business with due care only exists *vis-à-vis* the GmbH, not *vis-à-vis* the company's shareholders. The general managers do have certain obligations *vis-à-vis* the company's shareholders,[972] but non-compliance with these obligations does not automatically establish a claim for damages on the part of the shareholders.

§ 602 Liability for the breach of general manager duties and membership rights
In some cases, a general manager's breach of duties in connection with his corporate position or a related service agreement may establish liability to pay damages to the shareholders, provided that the breach inflicted damage on the shareholders. This may be the case, *e.g.*, where a shareholder sells his shareholding in the company for less than its value due to inaccurate information provided by the general manager. The law explicitly imposes an obligation on a general manager

---

969   GmbH-Gesetz [GmbHG] [Limited Liability Companies Act] 1892, § 64, sentence 3 (F.R.G.).
970   GmbH-Gesetz [GmbHG] [Limited Liability Companies Act] 1892, § 64, sentence 2 (F.R.G.).
971   GmbH-Gesetz [GmbHG] [Limited Liability Companies Act] 1892, § 64, sentence 4, § 43, ¶ 3, sentence 2,
        § 9b, ¶ 1 sentence 1 (F.R.G.).
972   §§ 528 *et seq.* deal with obligations of the general managers *vis-à-vis* the shareholders.

to pay damages to the shareholders where the general manager makes payments in violation of the capital maintenance rules,[973] or where he breached his obligation to submit an updated list of shareholders with the commercial register.[974] In the latter case, liability may in particular arise in cases where a shareholder whose position is not correctly reflected in the list may thus not exercise its rights in the company, including its participation in the distribution of profits.

C. Liability *vis-à-vis* third parties

§ 603 Introduction
General managers are generally not personally liable *vis-à-vis* third parties. However, certain sections of the Limited Liability Companies Act expressly provide for liability of the general managers *vis-à-vis* third parties. Further, general managers may be liable *vis-à-vis* the company's creditors in exceptional cases where a close relationship exists between the general managers and the creditors. Culpable breaches by the general managers of their duties may then give rise to claims for damages on the part of these creditors. Liability may additionally arise based on the principles of reliance or tort.

§ 604 Specific provisions of the Limited Liability Companies Act
Certain provisions of the Limited Liability Companies Act expressly provide for liability of the general managers. For example, in cases were the general managers violate their obligation to submit an updated list of shareholders with the commercial register,[975] the general managers are not only liable *vis-à-vis* the shareholders whose position is not correctly reflected in the list,[976] but also *vis-à-vis* the company's creditors.[977] Such liability may, *e.g.*, arise in cases where the creditor failed to assert a claim against a shareholder or to have claims of the company against shareholders pledged as security, since he was not aware of a change in the shareholder structure of the GmbH.

General managers generally act as representatives of the GmbH. Accordingly, the company on whose behalf they act bears the risks of liability for the consequences of the general managers' actions. However, general managers may incur personal liability in situations where they play a particularly important role in the conclusion of an agreement. This may occur in particular in two situations: Where the general manager exploits a special personal trust relationship and where the general manager pursues an economic self-interest.

§ 605 Exploitation of a special personal trust relationship
Where a general manager exploits a special personal relationship of trust and thereby gains influence in respect of the negotiation or conclusion of an agreement, the general manager may

---

973 *Cf.* GmbH-Gesetz [GmbHG] [Limited Liability Companies Act] 1892, § 31, ¶ 6 (F.R.G.).
974 *Cf.* GmbH-Gesetz [GmbHG] [Limited Liability Companies Act] 1892, § 40, ¶ 3 (F.R.G.). § 534 deals with the obligation to submit a list of shareholders and the legal consequences attached to such list.
975 § 534 deals with the obligation to submit a list of shareholders and the legal consequences attached to such list.
976 *Cf.* § 602 above.
977 *Cf.* GmbH-Gesetz [GmbHG] [Limited Liability Companies Act] 1892, § 40, ¶ 3 (F.R.G.).

incur personal liability,[978] provided that the general manager personally guarantees the integrity and the performance of the transaction or the accuracy and completeness of his statements in a way that goes beyond the normal expression of trust in the negotiation context. In order to establish personal liability, these personal statements must be material for the counterparty's decision. The general trust that is based on the executive and representative position of the general manager as such is not sufficient in this regard.

§ 606 Economic self-interest

According to the case law on the subject, a general manager may also incur personal liability where he has a significant economic self-interest in a particular transaction and he "acts *quasi* for his own account" in concluding the agreement in question or demonstrates a "qualified self-interest" in respect thereof. However, very strict requirements apply in such cases: If a general manager merely has a vested interest in performing well, *e.g.*, because he receives a commission for contracts he concludes, this is not sufficient to establish his personal liability.

§ 607 Main features

A general manager may incur liability where he gives the impression that a particular legal situation exists, *e.g.*, that he personally bears the liability for the consequences of his actions, and the other contractual party concludes the agreement in reliance upon that impression. A general manager is, as a general rule, only considered to have conveyed the existence of such a legal situation where he did not use the "GmbH" suffix in written correspondence. With regard to oral business transactions, liability may also arise under the principles of reliance. For example, personal liability was imposed in one case where the general manager used a business card that did not mention that the company was a GmbH. Therefore, it is advisable that a general manager always refers to the GmbH when doing business, unless he clearly intends to act on his own behalf.

§ 608 Liability on grounds of committing a tort

As a general rule, the German law of torts awards damages only for the violation of particular legal interests, including those in respect of property and health. Damages are not awarded for mere financial losses, such as a loss of profits. Thus, a prerequisite for an award of damages under the German law of torts is usually the violation of a legal interest of a third party. Exceptions apply for intentional infliction of damage and violations of specific protective laws (*Schutzgesetze*).[979]

One question is whether a general manager's breach of his organizational and monitoring duties in relation to the GmbH may give rise to tortious liability *vis-à-vis* the company's creditors. A general manager may be held liable whenever third-party property suffers damage as a result of the general manager's negligence with regard to the internal organization of the company. The same will apply to injury to the person or health of a customer, *e.g.*, as a result of a defective product.

---

978   *Cf.* Bürgerliches Gesetzbuch [BGB] [Civil Code] 1896, § 311, ¶ 3, sentence 2 (F.R.G.).
979   § 609 deals with violations of creditor protection rules.

Liability may also result from an intentional infliction of damage, *e.g.*, where the general manager misleads the other party to an agreement as to the willingness or ability of the company to make payments, or where he breaches his duty of disclosure when carrying out transactions on behalf of the GmbH. In such cases of intentional conduct, damages are exceptionally also awarded for mere financial losses. A requirement for liability in such cases is that the general manager is aware that he will cause injury to the other party.

Where the general manager merely considers the failure of the transaction in question to be a possibility, *e.g.*, in the case of recapitalization efforts in an economic crisis, such conduct does not give rise to personal liability *vis-à-vis* the company's creditors. The general manager must refrain from carrying out the transaction concerned only where he has serious doubts as to the success of the intended recapitalization efforts.

§ 609 Liability for violation of creditor protection rules
Certain legal provisions are specifically intended to protect the interests of a company's creditors. Where a general manager acts in violation of such rules, he is personally liable for the consequences of his actions. Even damages of a purely financial nature may give rise to a claim for damages in the case of a culpable violation of such a protective law.

The prohibitions contained in the Criminal Code (*Strafgesetzbuch*) qualify as such protective laws, including the provisions related to torts such as the fraudulent preference of a particular creditor or fraud.[980]

§ 610 Liability in other cases
In addition to the abovementioned cases of potential liability *vis-à-vis* the GmbH's creditors, a general manager may also incur personal liability towards third parties in other specified cases, *i.e.*, if he fails to file and pay tax returns.

§ 611 Liability for violations of competition law
German competition law imposes standards of conduct that apply in the market and prohibit certain anti-competitive activities.[981] Any contravention of these standards may result in the infringing party being subject to a claim for remediation, monetary fines and, where applicable, an injunction order.

Such a claim could also be brought against a general manager of a GmbH. A claim can be brought against a general manager where he has committed the violation of competition himself or through a third party. In light of older case law, it cannot be excluded that such a claim could be brought against a general manager even where he was unaware of the violation of competition law within the company. Recently there has been an increasing tendency of the courts towards limiting the responsibility of general managers in such cases.

---

980   *Cf.* Strafgesetzbuch [StGB] [Criminal Code] 1871, §§ 263, 283 (F.R.G.).
981   *Cf.* Gesetz gegen den unlauteren Wettbewerb [UWG] [Act against Unfair Competition] 2004, § 3 (F.R.G.).

D. Exemption and specific indemnification arrangements

§ 612 Introduction

In certain cases, the general managers of a GmbH are exempted from liability. It is also generally permitted to limit their liability towards the GmbH or to enter into indemnification and hold-harmless arrangements in their favor.

§ 613 Exemption

A general manager cannot be held liable *vis-à-vis* the GmbH where he acted on the basis of binding instructions issued by another corporate body, most notably the shareholders' meeting. In addition to the shareholders' meeting, any authorized corporate body (*e.g.*, the supervisory board or advisory council) is entitled to issue such instructions. Carrying out such instructions generally releases the general manager from potential liability for the consequences of the action. In order to exclude any doubts about the validity of such instructions, it is advisable that they be issued by way of a formal resolution.

§ 614 General limitations on the exemption from liability

If a general manager did not properly carry out the necessary preparatory measures for a corporate resolution, he is not granted exemption from liability. This may be the case, *e.g.*, where the general manager provides inadequate information to the competent corporate body (such as the shareholders' meeting or the supervisory board) about the risks or other concerns regarding a measure under consideration or where he otherwise influences the decision-making process of the corporate body in breach of his duty.

A general manager cannot be exempted from liability for payments made contrary to the rules for the maintenance of the company's registered capital or the prohibition against the acquisition of own shares,[982] if the general manager's payment of damages is necessary to satisfy the claims of the company's creditors. However, the general manager can be exempted from liability under the capital maintenance rules where a control and profit transfer agreement or a profit transfer agreement is in place with the company's parent.[983]

A general manager is also not exempted from liability where he carries out instructions that would entail a ruinous encroachment (*existenzvernichtender Eingriff*) upon the assets of the company. He must not follow such instructions in order to protect the interests of the company's creditors. This also means that the general manager may refuse to pay damages where the payment of damages is not necessary in order to satisfy the claims of the company's creditors.

§ 615 Limitation of the exemption from liability in the case of defective resolutions

With respect to defects in resolutions, a distinction must be drawn between resolutions that are null and void (*nichtig*) and resolutions that are merely challengeable (*anfechtbar*). A general manager carrying out shareholders' instructions that are based on a void shareholders' resolu-

---

982   In respect of these special cases, *cf.* §§ 585 *et seq.*
983   *Cf.* GmbH-Gesetz [GmbHG] [Limited Liability Companies Act] 1892, § 30, ¶ 1, sentence 2 (F.R.G.).

tion is generally not exempt from liability, because general managers are neither required nor permitted to carry out such void instructions. [984]

§ 616 Specific limitation and indemnification arrangements

The articles of association, the service agreement or shareholder resolutions may provide for a limitation of a general manager's liability *vis-à-vis* the GmbH and for an indemnification against third-party claims.

With respect to a general manager's liability *vis-à-vis* the company, it is subject to controversy whether the shareholders may stipulate a shorter statute of limitations period for claims against the general managers or a relaxation of the liability standard (*e.g.*, limiting liability to cases of gross negligence). Such contractual limitations may not, however, affect the liability of general managers *vis-à-vis* the company's creditors. For example, a contractual limitation of liability is subject to the provision of Section 43(3) of the Limited Liability Companies Act, which provides for liability of the general managers towards the company in the case of improper repayment of capital under the capital maintenance rules.

With respect to the general managers' liability towards third parties, the general managers may be granted (and may even be entitled to receive) indemnification from or be held harmless by the company against claims by third parties that are evidently unfounded or that do not coincide with a breach of a fiduciary duty *vis-à-vis* the GmbH.

In order to avoid problems with the interpretation of the indemnification provision, the provision should individually address each source of liability with regard to which indemnification shall be granted to the general manager (*e.g.*, liability arising from the general manager's corporate position, liability arising under the service agreement, and liability for tortious conduct).

E.   Liability *vis-à-vis* tax creditors and social security agencies

§ 617 Introduction

General managers are responsible for the GmbH's compliance with all of its obligations *vis-à-vis* the general public. This includes obligations that affect the internal organization of the company and that may arise from certain regulations, *e.g.*, statutory provisions in respect of trading in securities.[985] The general managers are in particular liable for the performance of the company's tax obligations and social security contributions.

1.   Liability for taxes payable by the GmbH
§ 618 Duties and liabilities of general managers

German tax law imposes an obligation on general managers to perform the tax-related duties

---

984   For a detailed discussion, *cf.* § 555.
985   *Cf.* Wertpapierhandelsgesetz [WpHG] [Securities Trading Act] 1994, § 32 (F.R.G.).

of the GmbH.[986] A breach of these duties may give rise to personal liability on the part of the general managers. This liability extends not only to the tax claim in question, but also to any penalties for late payment, interest, fines or other costs to the extent they accrue.[987] According to case law, a general manager also is required to ensure that the GmbH is capable of making tax payments at the point in time at which the taxes become due.

§ 619 Commencement, end and exclusion of liability for taxes

The liability of a general manager in connection with the GmbH's taxes generally commences upon his appointment, although it should be noted that a new general manager is also liable for any existing tax arrears (*Steuerrückstände*). A general manager does not incur any liability for taxes that accrue subsequent to his removal from office, because the general manager loses his authorization to represent the company.[988]

A general manager's liability in connection with taxes is excluded if the general manager is not at fault, *e.g.*, where he has not breached his duties in a grossly negligent or intentional manner.[989] A general manager acts in a grossly negligent manner where he fails to act with the necessary amount of care in a way that is exceptionally serious and extreme. The views expressed in the case law on the required standard of care are not always uniform. In some cases, high standards of care have been imposed, particularly relating to the payment of future tax debts. There is also a trend towards the imposition of very high standards of care relating to the payment of wage tax since it is the employer who must pay the employee's wage tax on his behalf; the amount of the wage tax constitutes money held in trust. If the liquidity of the company is low, the wages of its employees must, in the first instance, be decreased in order to enable the company to make wage tax payments.

2.   Liability for the payment of social security contributions

§ 620 Duty to pay the total amount of social security contributions

It has been recognized in the case law that the company's obligations under social security law are fundamentally borne by the general managers personally and that the general managers are liable for the non-performance of those obligations.[990]

§ 621 Consequences of general managers' non-compliance with obligations

General managers of a GmbH become liable under civil law when they are subject to a criminal prosecution for withholding employee social security contributions, because this criminal offense represents a protective law in favor of a company's creditors, the violation of which may give rise to tortious liability.[991] The claim must be brought by the competent social security agency, which must establish that the GmbH was in a position to pay the contributions at the

---

986 Abgabenordnung [AO] [General Tax Code] 1976, § 34, ¶ 1 (F.R.G.). § 536 deals with tax-related obligations of general managers.
987 Abgabenordnung [AO] [General Tax Code] 1976, §§ 152, 162, ¶ 4; §§ 233–237, 240, 329, 178, 337–345 (F.R.G.).
988 §§ 558 *et seq.* deal with the representation of the company.
989 *Cf.* Abgabenordnung [AO] [General Tax Code] 1976, § 69, ¶ 1 (F.R.G.).
990 § 537 deals with social and labor law obligations of the general manager.
991 *Cf.* Bürgerliches Gesetzbuch [BGB] [Civil Code] 1896, § 823, ¶ 2 (F.R.G.) in conjunction with Strafgesetzbuch [StGB] [Criminal Code] 1871, § 266a, ¶ 1 (F.R.G.).

time they became due. The GmbH will not be deemed to have been in a position to pay the contribution if it was already insolvent at that time.

Where the GmbH is in a crisis situation but has not yet become insolvent, recent case law of the Federal Supreme Court (*Bundesgerichtshof*) requires the general managers to ensure that they discharge the company's obligations under social security law before any other obligations of the company. The general managers are even required to cease efforts to secure the survival of the company if it is otherwise not possible for the company to discharge its foreseeable obligations under social security law. Even where separate sets of duties have been allocated among the general managers, all general managers should pay particular attention to the compliance with this priority for payments in a crisis situation, because all general managers are collectively obligated to ensure that the company's social security contributions are paid on time in the event of an imminent threat of insolvency.

Once the company has become insolvent, the general managers are faced with a dilemma: On the one hand, German criminal law requires the payment of the company's social security contributions;[992] on the other hand, German corporate law prohibits payments which reduce the amount of the company's assets in the context of the insolvency proceedings.[993] The most recent case law on the subject has resolved this conflict by establishing that civil liability will be excluded where a general manager makes payments in order to avoid becoming subject to criminal prosecution.

F.   Particularities relating to GmbH & Co. KGs

§ 622 The GmbH & Co. KG

The KG whose general partner is a GmbH as a hybrid corporate form has been recognized in Germany since the beginning of the 20th century. The GmbH in this constellation is (at least) the general partner (*Komplementär*) of a KG. In a KG, the general partner is personally liable with his entire assets and assumes management of the company. The liability of the other partners is limited to the sum of their contributions, and any authority to manage the company on their part is excluded as a matter of principle.[994] These shareholders are referred to as the limited partners (*Kommanditisten*). Thus, in respect of a GmbH & Co. KG, the GmbH is generally the sole personally liable shareholder. However, because the GmbH itself is a legal person, which is only liable with its corporate assets and generally does not provide for personal liability of its shareholders, no natural person ultimately bears unlimited liability in respect of a GmbH & Co. KG.

§ 623 Particularities regarding liability of general managers

The duties of a general manager of a GmbH being the general partner of a KG also comprise

---

992   Strafgesetzbuch [StGB] [Criminal Code] 1871, § 266a (F.R.G.); in this regard, *cf.* § 620.
993   Bürgerliches Gesetzbuch [BGB] [Civil Code] 1896, § 64, ¶ 2, sentence 1 (F.R.G.).
994   Handelsgesetzbuch [HGB] [Commercial Code] 1897, § 164 (F.R.G.).

the management duties of the GmbH in respect of the KG. The GmbH may be held liable in this constellation *vis-à-vis* the KG for any damage caused by its general managers.[995]

The issue of liability of a general manager of the GmbH *vis-à-vis* the KG is more problematic. Such liability arises as a result of non-permitted actions by the general manager *vis-à-vis* the KG, which are actions that include, in particular, criminal offenses such as misappropriation or embezzlement.

A breach of duties arising out of the service agreement of a general manager may also result in liability for damages on the part of that general manager *vis-à-vis* the KG. This may be the case where the service agreement of the general manager of the GmbH was concluded with the KG, or where the general manager is simultaneously a limited partner of the KG.

G. Insurability of liability risks

§ 624 D&O insurance

Limited liability companies may maintain D&O insurance (Directors and Officers Liability Insurance) for its general managers in respect of financial losses (*Vermögensschaden-Haftpflichtversicherung*) in Germany. In certain cases, depending on the risk profile of the company's operations and the probability of claims being asserted against the general managers, such insurance may even be required from a corporate law perspective. The available types of D&O insurance vary greatly, and the insurance coverage can be adapted to the requirements of the company in question. Advantages and disadvantages of the retention of a D&O insurance should be diligently assessed in each individual case prior to a final decision in this respect. A shareholder resolution is required before an insurance policy can be concluded between the company and the insurance provider.[996]

It should be noted in this context that the rules for AGs adopted by the German Federal Parliament on June 18, 2009[997] in the wake of the financial crisis and criticism of management compensation – in particular the rules with regard to mandatory deductibles in D&O insurance contracts in favor of managing directors of corporations – do not apply to D&O insurance retained in favor of general managers of a GmbH.

---

995   Bürgerliches Gesetzbuch [BGB] [Civil Code] 1896, § 31 (F.R.G.), analogously.
996   GmbH-Gesetz [GmbHG] [Limited Liability Companies Act] 1892, § 46, nos. 5, 8 (F.R.G.), analogously.
997   Gesetz zur Angemessenheit der Vorstandsvergütung [VorstAG] [Act on the Adequacy of Management Board Compensation] 2009 (F.R.G.). The new act entered into force on August 5, 2009. *Cf.* also press release of the German Federal Government of June 18, 2009 (http://www.bmj.de). §§ 44 *et seq.* deal with the compensation of the management board members of a German AG.

VI. Responsibility under criminal law

§ 625 Responsibility of the general managers of a GmbH under criminal law

In respect of general managers' risk of criminal liability, unless explicitly mentioned in this Chapter, the same principles apply as to the management board of the German AG.[998]

---

998 *Cf.* §§ 172 *et seq.* above.

CHAPTER SEVEN
ANNEXES

I. Service agreements

A. Form of service agreement: Management board member of an AG

Management Board Member Service Agreement[999]
Between

[•] **AG**, represented by its supervisory board, which is represented by its chairman,

…,

(hereinafter referred to as "**AG**")

and

Mr./Ms. [•],

…,

(hereinafter referred to as "**Management Board Member**")

The AG and the Management Board Member are hereinafter individually referred to as a "**Party**" and, collectively, as the "**Parties**".

---

[999] This form of a management board member service agreement is intended to serve illustrative purposes and includes terms and conditions that can be typically found in agreements of this type. The compensation package offered to a management board member, in particular, short-term and long-term incentive schemes as well as retirement benefits, will usually depend on the practices that have been established by the AG.

Section 1
Appointment to the Management Board

1.   Mr./Ms. [•] has been appointed management board member of the AG for the period
      from ... until ... by resolution of the supervisory board dated ...

2.   The purpose of this service agreement (the "**Agreement**") is to set forth the terms and
      conditions governing the Parties' service relationship.

Section 2
Duties and Responsibilities

1.   Mr./Ms. [•] shall conduct the business of the AG together with the other members of the
      management board. In this context, he/she shall be responsible for the business areas that
      are specified in the business organization plan for the management board of the AG as
      applicable from time to time.[1000]

2.   The Management Board Member shall fulfill the duties and responsibilities assigned to
      him/her with the diligence of a prudent business person, to the best of his/her ability
      and in the best interest of the AG. When performing his/her services, the Management
      Board Member shall at all times comply with statutory law, the Corporate Governance
      Code, the articles of association of the AG, the rules of procedure issued for the manage-
      ment board from time to time (including the business organization plan) and the provi-
      sions of this Agreement.

3.   The Management Board Member shall represent the AG jointly with another member
      of the management board or jointly with a Prokurist.[1001]

4.   At the request of the AG, the Management Board Member shall accept appointments
      to supervisory, advisory, executive or management bodies of enterprises that are affiliated
      with the AG within the meaning of Section 15 of the Stock Corporation Act (col-
      lectively, "**Affiliates**") as well as memberships in professional associations and similar
      organizations, without being entitled to additional compensation. To the extent legally
      permissible, the Management Board Member will resign from such positions at any time
      if so requested by the AG, but in any event no later than upon revocation of his/her ap-
      pointment as member of the management board of the AG.

1000 Alternatively, the service agreement may also allocate a specified area of responsibility to the management board
     member.
1001 The representation authority of the management board member need not be explicitly addressed, but many service
     agreements include a provision to this effect.

5. The Management Board Member shall devote his/her full working capacity and professional knowledge exclusively to the AG, and shall not carry out any ancillary professional activities, whether on an honorary basis, paid or unpaid, including memberships in supervisory, advisory, executive, management or similar bodies of enerprises that are not affiliated with the AG, without the prior consent of the supervisory board, which may revoke its consent at any time in its discretion.[1002] No such consent shall be required for publication or lecturing activities of the Management Board Member, provided that these do not interfere with his/her duties and responsibilities under this Agreement or with legitimate interests of the AG.

Section 3
Compensation

1. The Management Board Member receives a gross base salary of EUR [•] (in words: [•] Euros) per annum (the "**Base Salary**"), the net amount of which shall be paid in arrears in twelve equal monthly installments at the general payment date for salaries of the AG.

2. The Management Board Member is eligible for an annual variable bonus payment equal to [•] percent of the Base Salary (the "**Target Amount**") in the event that corporate and/or individual targets and objectives as set by the supervisory board at the beginning of a fiscal year are fully achieved (the "**Bonus**").[1003] In connection with the approval of the annual financial statements of the AG for the preceding fiscal year, the supervisory board will assess, in its discretion, to what extent the targets and objectives for such fiscal year were achieved. Should the overall target achievement rate exceed or fall below 100 percent, the Bonus shall be increased or decreased, as the case may be, accordingly in relation to the Target Amount; provided, however, that the Bonus payable with respect to a fiscal year shall in no event exceed an amount equal to [•] percent of the Base Salary; and further provided that no Bonus shall be payable at all if the overall target achievement rate with respect to a fiscal year is less than [•] percent. The net amount of any Bonus determined by the supervisory board will be paid to the Management Board

---

1002 In case that the management board member is actually holding memberships in supervisory or advisory boards of other enterprises at the time the service agreement is entered into, the present engagements should be expressly approved by the AG and listed in an annex to the service agreement. Additionally, the service agreement may provide that any income the management board member receives from ancillary professional activities must be set off against the compensation that the AG pays to him/her.

1003 Since the introduction of the Act on the Adequacy of Management Board Compensation, a special legal framework applies to an AG whose shares are listed and traded on a regulated market. In principle, any variable compensation granted to the management board members must be determined according to a long-term evaluation base covering several fiscal years. Short-term bonus payments that only consider the performance of the AG and/or the management board during a single fiscal year continue to be permissible as long as they are combined with a long-term bonus element and the overall variable compensation offers an adequate incentive for the management board to pursue a sustainable development of the AG with a longer perspective. In this context, the permissible ratio of short-term and long-term bonus elements remains subject to discussion of legal commentators.

Member at the end of the month following the shareholders' meeting in which the annual financial statements for the relevant fiscal year were available. [1004]

3.   Unless otherwise provided in this Agreement, any Bonus will be paid *pro rata temporis* in case that the Parties' service relationship commences or terminates during the course of a fiscal year.

4.   The Base Salary and the Target Amount shall be reviewed periodically, considering the individual performance of the Management Board Member and the economic situation of the AG. The supervisory board shall be entitled to reduce the remuneration of the Management Board Member to a reasonable amount in the case of a deterioration of the economic situation of the Company within the meaning of Secion 87(2) of the Stock Corporation Act.

5.   The supervisory board will decide, in its discretion, whether and to what extent the Management Board Member shall participate in stock option or similar long-term incentive plans of the AG.[1005]

6.   The remuneration payable to the Management Board Member hereunder constitutes compensation for any and all services that he/she performs under this Agreement. Any income that the Management Board Member receives from activities pursuant to Section 2(4) shall be offset against, and deducted from, the Base Salary and/or any Bonus.[1006]

7.   To reward exceptional performance on the part of the Management Board Member, the supervisory board may, in its discretion, decide to grant him/her additional non-recurring payments over and above the aforementioned compensation elements from time to time.

1004 The terms and conditions concerning the variable compensation to be granted to a management board member depend on the circumstances of the AG and the practices it has established in this respect. If the supervisory board of the AG has adopted general short-term and long-term incentive schemes for the management board, the service agreement will frequently only include a reference to the relevant rules and regulations as applicable from time to time. In the event that the service agreement itself sets out the bonus metrics, it will usually define a target bonus as well as the rules for determining the final bonus payment. The bonus provision included in this form is an example of the types of provisions that can be found in agreements with management board members.

1005 Alternatively, the service agreement itself may provide for a specific grant of stock option, stock appreciation or similar equity-based rights to the management board member.

1006 The purpose of this provision is to implement the general rule in Section 2(4) of this form in case that the management board member actually receives additional compensation in connection with his/her appointment to the corporate body of an affiliated enterprise or to a professional association.

Section 4
Additional Benefits[1007]

1. For the term of his/her appointment, the AG shall provide an adequate car of the luxury segment to the Management Board Member, which he/she may also use for private purposes. The AG shall bear all operating costs, including liability insurance, vehicle tax, repair and maintenance work as well as gas and oil. Additionally, the company car policy of the AG as amended from time to time shall apply.[1008]

2. The AG shall take out accident insurance for the Management Board Member covering both business related and private accidents with the following amounts: [1009]

   a) EUR [•] (in words: [•] Euros) in the event of accidental death;

   b) EUR [•] (in words: [•] Euros) in the event of disability.

3. The AG shall arrange for the Management Board Member to be covered by directors' and officers' liability insurance with a minimum amount insured of EUR [•] (in words: [•] Euros), which shall also apply to any positions and memberships pursuant to Section 2(4) that the Management Board Member accepts during the term of this Agreement, extend to claims that are asserted against the Management Board Member under foreign laws, including punitive or exemplary damages, and cover customary legal expenses that the Management Board Member incurs in connection with his/her defense against a claim that is asserted against him/her. The directors' and officers' liability insurance will provide for the statutory deductible as required by the Stock Corporation Act and the Corporate Governance Code from time to time.

4. In addition, the AG will pay the Management Board Member an allowance for health and nursing care insurance[1010] in accordance with Section 257 of the Social Security Code V and Section 61 of the Social Security Code XI, up to the maximum amounts that the AG would have to contribute if the Management Board Member was subject to statutory social security.[1011]

1007 While a company car and insurance coverage will be the most common fringe benefits granted to a management board member, service agreements frequently provide for additional benefits such as the AG's assumption of relocation costs, the rent for a private apartment or the costs of a home office.

1008 Further details may be set out in a separate company car agreement between the AG and the management board member.

1009 Alternatively, the service agreement may provide a maximum annual insurance premium to be borne by the AG and allow the management board member to determine the composition of the insurance benefits at his/her discretion.

1010 In Germany, nursing care insurance covers costs and expenses if a person becomes in need of care.

1011 Such a provision may be included in the service agreement if the management board member takes out (private) health and nursing care insurance on a voluntary basis.

5. The Management Board Member shall be responsible for any income tax that is payable on the non-cash benefits he/she receives hereunder.

Section 5
Retirement Benefits[1012]

1. The AG shall grant retirement benefits to the Management Board Member or his/her surviving dependants in accordance with the provisions of this Section 5; provided that he/she had been appointed to the management board of the AG for a minimum period of [five] years at the termination date of this Agreement; and further provided that any entitlement under this Section 5 will become forfeited in the event that this Agreement is terminated by the AG for good cause within the meaning of Section 84(3) of the Stock Corporation Act or Section 626 of the Civil Code.

2. The Management Board Member shall be entitled to receive retirement benefits as from the end of the month in which he/she

    a) reaches the age of [65]; or

    b) becomes permanently disabled within the meaning of Section 12(2) prior to reaching the retirement age.

3. The annual retirement benefits shall amount to [•] percent of the average Base Salary[1013] that the Management Board Member received over the last three-year period prior to the termination date of this Agreement and shall further increase by another [•] percent for each full year that the Management Board Member has served on the management board of the AG over and above the five-year period referred to in Section 5(1). The maximum amount of the retirement benefits payable to the Management Board Member under this Agreement shall not exceed [•] percent of the average Base Salary. Retirement benefits will be paid in arrears in twelve equal monthly installments at the general payment date for salaries of the AG as from the month following the month in which the Management Board Member reached the retirement age or in which his/her permanent disability was established.

1012 Since management board members of an AG are not subject to compulsory pension insurance in Germany, they are frequently granted retirement benefits in connection with their service relationship. In most cases, retirement benefits are determined according to a defined benefit scheme (i.e., the management board member earns a certain portion of his/her pensionable salary for each completed year of service subject to an overall cap) or according to a defined contribution scheme (i.e., the AG contributes a certain amount to an insurance, a pension fund or a similar institution). As is the case with the variable compensation, the level of retirement benefits and the underlying terms and conditions will usually depend on the practices that the AG has established in this respect. The retirement benefits of a management board member may be governed by a specific provision in the service agreement, or a separate pension agreement, or a general company pension plan to which the service agreement refers.

1013 Alternatively, the reference basis for determining the amount of the retirement benefits may be limited to a certain pensionable portion of the management board member's base salary.

4. Benefits that the Management Board Member receives from the statutory pension in-
    surance system and/or any other company pension scheme shall be set off against and
    deducted from the retirement benefits payable by the AG within the limits provided by
    Section 5 of the Improvement of Company Pension Schemes Act. The same shall apply
    to any kind of income received by the Management Board Member from an employ-
    ment, service, consulting or similar relationship as well as on a self-employed basis. In
    this context, the Management Board Member shall be required to exercise his/her claim
    to benefits from the statutory pension insurance system and/or any other company pen-
    sion scheme, and to furnish such information to the AG as is necessary for the determi-
    nation of his/her retirement benefits under this Agreement.

5. Should the Management Board Member pass away, the AG will pay survivor benefits to
    his/her spouse as well as any children entitled by statute to financial support according to
    the following terms and conditions[1014]:

    a) The survivor benefits of the spouse shall amount to [60] percent of the last retirement
        benefits that the Management Board Member received prior to his/her death or that
        the Management Board Member would have received had he/she retired at the time
        of his/her death. If the spouse was more than [ten] years younger than the Manage-
        ment Board Member, the survivor benefits shall be reduced by [four] percent for each
        full year over and above such age difference, unless the marriage had already lasted
        for at least [15] years, in which case no reduction shall take place. The entitlement to
        receive survivor benefits terminates if and when the spouse enters into a new marriage
        or a registered partnership.

    b) The survivor benefits of each child of the Management Board Member being entitled
        by statute to financial support shall amount to [ten] percent of the last retirement
        benefits that the Management Board Member received prior to his/her death or that
        the Management Board Member would have received had he/she retired at the time
        of his/her death, and shall increase to [20] percent of such reference basis in case that
        the child is or becomes an orphan. The entitlement to receive survivor benefits ter-
        minates if and when a child reaches age 18 or, if later, completes his or her vocational
        training, but in any event at the latest upon reaching age 27.

    c) The aggregate amount of any survivor benefits payable by the AG under this Agree-
        ment must not exceed the retirement benefits which the Management Board Member
        was entitled to at the time of his/her death.

1014 The terms and conditions for paying survivor benefits that are used in this form only serve illustrative purposes;
     provisions to this effect are frequently included in pension agreements or company pension plans.

d) Survivor benefits shall be paid as from the month following the month of death; provided that payments under this Section 5(5) shall be suspended during the period of time during which the AG grants a continuation of salary pursuant to Section 8(3).

e) Section 5(4) shall apply *mutatis mutandis* with respect to any survivor benefits that are paid by the AG.

6.   The AG shall review the amount of the retirement benefits and/or the survivor benefits every three years and decide on an adjustment in its discretion.

Section 6
Reimbursement of Expenses

Reasonable disbursements that the Management Board Member incurs while performing services under this Agreement, including travel, entertainment and other out-of-pocket expenses, shall be reimbursed to him/her in accordance with internal policies. The Management Board Member shall submit regular expense reports together with appropriate supporting documentation for tax purposes.

Section 7
Vacation Leave

1.   The Management Board Member is entitled to an annual vacation leave of 30 working days (based on a five-day working week). If the service relationship commences or terminates in the course of a calendar year, vacation leave is granted on a *pro rata temporis* basis.[1015]

2.   The Management Board Member shall coordinate his/her vacation leave with the other members of the management board, while reasonably considering business requirements and ensuring that the AG is at all times adequately represented. The Management Board Member shall notify the chairman of the supervisory board in good time of any leave of absence that exceeds one week.

1015 The service agreement may additionally provide that a portion of the vacation leave can be carried over to the subsequent calendar year until a certain cut-off date (*e.g.*, March 31 or June 30) if business requirements prevented the management board member from using the vacation leave in the calendar year in which it accrued.

Section 8
Continuation of Salary in the Event of Sickness and Death

1. Should the Management Board Member be temporarily unable to perform his/her duties and responsibilities under this Agreement due to sickness, an accident or any other reason for which he/she is not responsible, the AG will continue to pay the Base Salary for a maximum period of [•][1016] months, however, in no event beyond termination of this Agreement. Any benefits that the Management Board Member receives from third parties for the duration of or in connection with his/her inability to perform services shall be fully credited against the continuing salary payments and reduce the payment obligations of the AG accordingly.

2. In the event that the Management Board Member's inability to perform his/her duties and responsibilities pursuant to Section 8(1) exceeds a period of twelve weeks, any Bonus payable by the AG pursuant to Section 3(2) shall be reduced *pro rata temporis* in proportion to the aggregate period of his/her absence during the relevant fiscal year.

3. Should the Management Board Member pass away during the term of this Agreement, his/her spouse and any other persons entitled by statute to financial support shall, as joint and several creditors, be entitled to receive the Base Salary for the month of death and the following [•][1017] months, however, not beyond the date on which this Agreement would have terminated notwithstanding the Management Board Member's passing away.

Section 9
Confidentiality

1. The Management Board Member shall maintain secrecy with respect to the content of this Agreement as well as all confidential matters of the AG and its Affiliates, particularly business and trade secrets, that come to his/her attention in connection with the performance of the duties and responsibilities assigned to him/her.

2. To the extent legally permissible, the obligation to maintain secrecy survives termination of this Agreement.

1016 Continuing salary pay in the event of sickness is usually granted for a period of time between six and twelve months.

1017 A period between three and six months would be customary.

Section 10
Non-compete Undertaking

1. During the term of this Agreement, the Management Board Member shall neither be entitled to work for a competitor of the AG or any of its Affiliates (including in a freelance or advisory capacity), nor to directly or indirectly participate in such a competitor, irrespective of the form of the participation. In addition, the Management Board Member shall notify the chairman of the supervisory board if a party that is closely related to him/her pursuant to Section 15 of the Tax Code participates in a competitor within the meaning of the foregoing sentence. Investments that are made in the context of private asset management and do not permit exercising influence on a company's management or supervisory bodies are not subject to this non-compete undertaking. When conducting private investments, the Management Board Member shall, however, avoid any conflict of interests and strictly comply with any guidelines and policies that the AG establishes in this respect from time to time. The statutory obligations imposed on the Management Board Member under Section 88 of the Stock Corporation Act shall remain unaffected.

2. The non-compete undertaking pursuant to Section 9(1) sentence 1 shall also apply during a period of [•] year[s][1018] after termination of this Agreement, unless this Agreement terminates due to a permanent disability on the part of the Management Board Member pursuant to Section 12(2). The scope of the post-termination non-compete undertaking shall relate to the field of business of the AG and its Affiliates at the termination date of this Agreement, and its territorial application shall be unrestricted; provided that countries in which neither the AG nor any of its Affiliates conduct business shall be excluded.

3. For the duration of the post-termination non-compete undertaking, the AG shall pay to the Management Board Member, in arrears in twelve equal monthly installments at its general payment date for salaries, financial compensation equal to [50] percent of the sum of (i) his/her last Base Salary and (ii) the average Bonus granted to the Management Board Member over the last three-year period prior to the termination date of this Agreement.[1019] Stock options and similar long-term incentive awards as well as any benefits in kind shall not be taken into account when determining the aforementioned financial compensation.

1018 A post-termination non-compete undertaking in a management board member service agreement will usually have a term of between one year and two years.

1019 There is no statutory requirement as to the amount of the financial compensation to be granted to a management board member during the term of a post-termination non-compete undertaking. Contrary to the reference base used in this form, the financial compensation payable by the AG may also be equal to a certain percentage of the last base salary received by the management board member, without taking any variable compensation into account. Further, management board member service agreements occasionally provide that the AG will pay a higher financial compensation during the period of a post-termination non-compete undertaking if the management board member was not responsible for the termination of the service relationship.

4. Any retirement benefits that the AG pays to the Management Board Member pursuant to Section 5 as well as any other kind of income which the Management Board Member receives from an employment, service, consulting or similar relationship as well as on a self-employed basis during the period of the post-termination non-compete undertaking shall be fully credited against, and thus reduce the amount of, the financial compensation to be paid by the AG. Upon request, the Management Board Member shall provide information on any creditable income.

5. The AG shall be entitled to waive the post-termination non-compete undertaking at any time in writing with the effect that it shall become released from the obligation to pay the financial compensation pursuant to Section 10(3) upon expiration of a period of [six] months after a written waiver has been received by the Management Board Member. If this Agreement terminates for good cause in accordance with Section 12(3), the AG may cancel the post-termination non-compete undertaking with immediate effect during the subsequent one-month period by means of a written notification to the Management Board Member.

6. For each violation of the non-compete undertaking in this Section 11, the Management Board Member shall incur a contractual penalty equal to [three times][1020] a month's Base Salary, and the AG shall not be required to pay him/her any financial compensation pursuant to Section 10(3) for the month in which the violation occurred. In the event that a violation is not limited to a single event and the Management Board Member maintains his/her non-complying behavior during a continuous period of time, the full amount of the contractual penalty shall be incurred again at the beginning of each new month in which the violation of the non-compete undertaking persists.

Section 11
Work Results[1021]

1. The AG shall be exclusively entitled to all work results (including, drafts, documents, designs, concepts, methods, reports and computer software), know-how, technical improvements, inventions and rights attached (collectively, **"Work Results"**) that the Management Board Member develops during the term of this Agreement and which originate from the performance of the duties and responsibilities assigned to him/her under this Agreement or relate to the business area of the AG. The Management Board Member undertakes to notify the supervisory board of any Work Results so developed without undue delay and to provide all information required in this respect.

1020 The amount of the contractual penalty that a management board member shall incur for the violation of the non-compete undertaking usually ranges from one month's to one year's base salary.

1021 For illustrative purposes, this form includes a rather detailed provision on work results. Depending on the business area in which the AG is engaged and the duties and responsibilities assigned to the management board member, there may be no need for such a comprehensive regulation.

2.   To the extent that Work Results are or can be protected by intellectual property rights (such as patents, utility models or copyrights), the Management Board Member hereby transfers and assigns to the AG any and all rights related thereto. The AG is under no obligation to register or exploit the Work Results or to identify and name the Management Board Member as the author. Any right of revocation by reason of non-exercise on the part of the Management Board Member within the meaning of Section 41 of the Copyright Act shall be suspended for a period of five years from the effective date of the transfer and assignment. In the event that a transfer and assignment of Work Results is not feasible for legal reasons, the Management Board Member hereby grants the AG the exclusive and unrestricted right of use for all present and future types of exploitation, which right shall be as broad as legally possible in terms of content and geographical scope and shall survive termination of this Agreement. The Management Board Member shall reasonably cooperate with and support the AG in obtaining legal protection of any type for the Work Results developed by him/her and assist the AG with respect to all formalities that are required to have its rights to the Work Results registered.

3.   The Management Board Member agrees that he/she will not receive a separate remuneration for any such Work Results in addition to the compensation paid to him/her under this Agreement.

Section 12
Term of the Agreement

1.   Without prejudice to the following provisions, this Agreement is entered into for the term of the Management Board Member's appointment pursuant to Section 1(1). Unless the Parties agree otherwise, this Agreement shall be extended by any subsequent terms for which the supervisory board renews the appointment of the Management Board Member.[1022]

2.   This Agreement shall automatically terminate as of the end of

      a) the calendar month in which the Management Board Member reaches age [65][1023];

      b) the calendar quarter in which a permanent disability of the Management Board Member has been established. Permanent disability shall be deemed to exist if the Management Board Member has been prevented from performing services hereunder during a consecutive period of more than six months and it is unlikely that he/she will resume his/her duties and responsibilities within another six-month period. In

---

1022 A management board member service agreement is usually entered into for a fixed term without a prior termination possibility other than for good cause. Alternatively, the agreement may run for an indefinite period of time subject to ordinary termination by either party.

1023 It is common practice to align the relevant age limit to the retirement age as per the company pension scheme of the AG, if any.

cases of doubt, the permanent disability of the Management Board Member shall be determined on the basis of the expert opinion of a medical examiner to be agreed between the Parties. If the Parties fail to reach an agreement in this respect within a period of one month, the medical examiner shall be appointed by the President of the Medical Association (*Ärztekammer*) that is competent for the registered seat of the AG.

3. If the supervisory board revokes the Management Board Member's appointment for a reason that constitutes good cause within the meaning of Section 84(3) of the Stock Corporation Act[1024] or Section 626 of the Civil Code, the revocation shall simultaneously constitute a termination of this Agreement with immediate effect. In such an event, the Management Board Member shall not be entitled to receive any Bonus pursuant to Section 3(2) with respect to the fiscal year in which his/her appointment is revoked.

4. The AG shall be entitled to put the Management Board Member on garden leave and release him/her from the obligation to perform services during the remaining term of his/her office, setting off any outstanding vacation leave. Any income that the Management Board Member receives from an employment, service, consulting or similar relationship as well as on a self-employed basis shall be fully credited against, and thus reduce, the payment obligations of the AG pursuant to Section 2 during the period of release.

Section 13
Return of Documents and Company Property

1. Upon termination of this Agreement or a release from the obligation to perform services pursuant to Section 12(4), the Management Board Member shall return to the AG without undue delay all written materials, documents, files, correspondence, records, drafts as well as electronically saved information and similar items relating to the business matters of the AG or any of its Affiliates that are still in his/her possession at such point in time, without retaining any copies.

2. The same shall apply to the return of any other company property that has been made available to the Management Board Member, including a company car, technical devices, keys, tools, office equipment and supplies.

1024 Alternatively, the agreement may provide that the management board member will receive a severance payment if his/her appointment is revoked without good cause within the meaning of Section 626 of the Civil Code, being the stricter test as compared to the standard of Section 84(3) Stock Corporation Act. Such severance will usually comprise the discounted compensation that the management board member would have received until the expiration date of the original term of appointment (including a flat-rate percentage of the target value of the variable bonus payment).

3.   The Management Board Member shall not be entitled to any kind of retention right with respect to his/her obligations under this Section 13. At the request of the supervisory board, the Management Board Member shall confirm compliance with the obligation to return in writing.

Section 14
Data Protection

1.   The Management Board Member agrees that his/her personal data may be stored and processed in physical or electronic files kept by the AG or any external service providers retained by it in connection with the performance of the Parties' service relationship. The AG will obligate its employees and any third parties having access to such data to keep them confidential.

2.   The Management Board Member further agrees that the compensation granted to him/her under this Agreement may be disclosed individually in the annual financial statements of the AG.[1025]

Section 15
Final Provisions

1.   This Agreement represents the entire agreement and understanding of the Parties with respect to its subject matter and supersedes all prior negotiations, discussions, correspondence, communications, understandings and agreements of any form or nature between the Parties, whether oral or written, and whether express or implied.

2.   Any amendments of or supplements to this Agreement shall be made in writing, unless a stricter legal form is required. This shall also apply to any modifications of this written form requirement.

3.   This Agreement shall be governed by and construed in accordance with the laws of Germany. To the extent legally permissible, place of venue shall be the registered seat of the AG.

4.   Neither Party may assign this Agreement, or any right or obligation hereunder without the written consent of the other Party.

5.   Should any provision of this Agreement be or become invalid, ineffective or unenforceable as a whole or in part, the validity, effectiveness and enforceability of the remaining

---

1025 Such a provision may particularly be included in a management board member service agreement of an AG whose shares are listed and traded on a regulated market.

provisions shall not be affected thereby. Any such invalid, ineffective or enforceable provision shall be deemed replaced by such valid, effective and enforceable provision as comes closest to the economic intent and purpose of such invalid, ineffective or unenforceable provision. This shall apply accordingly to gaps in this Agreement of which the Parties become aware in connection with its performance.

6. This Agreement shall be executed in duplicate.

_____, the _____

_____

Chairman of the Supervisory Board of [•] AG

_____, the _____

_____

[•]

B. Form of service agreement: General manager of a GmbH

General Manager Service Agreement[1026]
Between

[•] GmbH, represented by its shareholders' meeting[1027]

...,

(hereinafter referred to as "**GmbH**")

and

Mr./Ms. [•],

...,

(hereinafter referred to as "**General Manager**"),

The GmbH and the General Manager are hereinafter individually referred to as a "**Party**" and, collectively, as the "**Parties**".

Section 1
Duties and Responsibilities

1.   Effective as of [•], Mr./Ms. [•] has been appointed general manager of the GmbH. In this capacity, he/she shall be responsible for the day-to-day management of the GmbH, particularly with a view to implementing the strategic goals and growth initiatives approved by the shareholders' meeting, creating sustainable year-over-year improvements as well as building up strong relationships with the suppliers, customers and other business partners in Germany. The GmbH reserves the right to specify the General Manager's duties and responsibilities in a separate job description from time to time and may, in its discretion, assign other duties and responsibilities to him/her, while considering his/her qualification and expertise.

2.   When performing services hereunder, the General Manager shall at all times comply with statutory law, the articles of association of the GmbH, any rules of procedure issued for the management from time to time, any schedule of responsibilities, the resolutions

---

1026 This form of a general manager service agreement is rather extensive for explanatory reasons and includes terms and conditions that can be typically found in agreements of this type. In practice, the service agreement between the general manager and the GmbH may be much shorter.
1027 In case that the GmbH is subject to the Co-Determination Act, the service agreement must be entered into by the company's supervisory board.

and instructions of the shareholders' meeting as well as the provisions of this service agreement (the "**Agreement**"). Irrespective of an internal allocation of responsibilities among the general managers of the GmbH, the General Manager shall remain subject to the statutory obligations of supervision and organization that are associated with the position of a general manager of a German company with limited liability.

3.   The General Manager shall fulfill the duties and responsibilities assigned to him/her with the diligence of a prudent business person, to the best of his/her ability and in the best interest of the GmbH. When managing the business of the GmbH, the General Manager shall abide by the code of business conduct as well as any pertinent policies and guidelines that have been adopted for the GmbH, to the extent that this is compatible with his/her duties and responsibilities under mandatory law.

4.   The General Manager shall represent the GmbH jointly with another general manager or jointly with a Prokurist. The shareholders' meeting may change the representation authority granted to the General Manager at any time.

5.   At the request of the GmbH, the General Manager shall accept appointments to supervisory, advisory, executive or management bodies of enterprises that are affiliated with the GmbH within the meaning of Section 15 of the Stock Corporation Act (collectively, "**Affiliates**") as well as memberships in professional associations and similar organizations, without being entitled to additional compensation. Unless expressly provided otherwise herein, any restriction of the General Manager's representation authorities and any consent requirements shall apply *mutatis mutandis* to positions that he/she assumes at Affiliates. To the extent legally permissible, the General Manager will resign from such positions at any time if so requested by the GmbH, but in any event no later than upon revocation of his/her appointment as general manager of the GmbH.

6.   The General Manager shall be required to obtain the consent of the shareholders' meeting prior to carrying out any management measures that go beyond the ordinary course of business of the GmbH, defined investment budgets, or any specific authorities delegated to him/her. [Without prejudice to the generality of the foregoing, the following transactions and management measures shall be subject to the prior consent of the shareholders' meeting for the time being:[1028]

   a) Holding shareholders' meetings and adopting corporate resolutions at the level of a subsidiary of the GmbH;

1028 Consent requirements in connection with certain transactions and other management measures are quite customary, but need not necessarily be included in the service agreement of the general manager. Alternatively, the articles of association of the GmbH, rules of procedure for the management, or a respective shareholders' resolution may provide for a catalogue with transactions and management measures that shall be subject to the prior consent of the shareholders' meeting.

b) Purchasing, selling, encumbering, leasing or renting real property or buildings, including entering into transactions constituting respective obligations;

c) Entering into, amending or terminating agreements that (i) contain exclusivity,
   non-compete or similar provisions capable of affecting the business operations of the
   GmbH, (ii) run for a term of more than one year, or (iii) create aggregate payment
   obligations for the GmbH in excess of EUR [•];

d) Entering into loan agreements (as borrower or lender) with the exception of customer loans in ordinary business transactions;

e) Hiring, or amending or terminating the employment and service agreements of, employees, freelancers or consultants with a salary in excess of EUR [•] per annum;

f) Agreements on debt accession, guaranties, suretyships and the creation of similar col-
   lateral;

g) Entering into domination and/or profit and loss pooling agreements, acceding to partnerships according to the Civil Code, cooperation agreements or joint ventures;

h) Establishing or setting up subsidaries, branch offices or representative offices of any
   kind;

The shareholders' meeting may, in its discretion, amend or extend this catalogue or establish
resolutions, policies or guidelines that further specify the transactions and the management
measures for which the General Manager requires its prior consent.]

Section 2
Working hours

1.   The General Manager shall devote his/her full working capacity and professional knowl-
     edge exclusively to the GmbH, and shall not carry out any ancillary professional activi-
     ties, whether on an honorary basis, paid or unpaid, including memberships in supervisory,
     advisory, executive, management or similar bodies of enterprises that are not affiliated
     with the GmbH, without the prior consent of the shareholders' meeting, which may
     revoke its consent at any time in its discretion.[1029] No such consent shall be required for
     publication or lecturing activities of the General Manager; provided that these do not
     interfere with his/her duties and responsibilities under this Agreement or with legitimate
     interests of the GmbH.

1029 Memberships and similar engagements that the general manager holds at the time the service agreement is entered
     into and that he/she would like to keep during his/her tenure should be expressly approved by the shareholders'
     meeting and listed in an annex to the service agreement.

2.   The General Manager shall work on a full-time basis and acknowledges that, due to the requirements of his/her position, he/she must be available as determined by operational requirements to attend to the interests of the GmbH.[1030] Any and all work performed by the General Manager hereunder, including beyond the usual business hours, shall be deemed fully compensated by the salary and other benefits paid to him/her under this Agreement.

Section 3
Compensation

1.   The General Manager shall receive a gross base salary of EUR [•] (in words: [•] Euros) per annnum (the "**Base Salary**"), the net amount of which shall be paid, less any applicable wage withholding taxes and social security contributions[1031], in arrears in twelve equal monthly installments at the general payment date for salaries of the GmbH. The Base Salary shall be reviewed periodically in accordance with company practice, it being understood that decisions regarding future increases in salary are made in the discretion of the shareholders' meeting without any legal entitlement whatsoever on the part of the General Manager.

2.   The GmbH will withhold and transfer the statutory contributions to health, nursing care[1032], pension and unemployment insurance in accordance with applicable laws. If the General Manager is exempt from compulsory health and nursing care insurance, the GmbH will bear 50 percent of any evidenced premiums under a private health and nursing care insurance taken out by the General Manager up to the relevant statutory contribution amounts that the GmbH would incur if the General Manager was subject to compulsory insurance in this respect.

3.   The General Manager shall be eligible for an annual variable compensation equal to [•] percent of the Base Salary (the "**Target Bonus**") in accordance with the following provisions:[1033]

1030 Alternatively, the service agreement may also stipulate a defined number of working hours to be performed by the general manager. Even in such an event, however, the agreement will usually provide that any additional work beyond the defined working hours shall be deemed compensated by the general manager's salary and other benefits, since it is not customary to grant overtime pay to a general manager of a GmbH.

1031 Other than a management board member of an AG, the general manager of a GmbH will usually be subject to statutory social security in Germany.

1032 In Germany, nursing care insurance covers costs and expenses if a person becomes in need of care.

1033 The bonus provision included in this form is only an example of the pertinent provisions that can be found in agreements of this type. The relevant terms and conditions under which a variable compensation is granted to general managers will depend on the practices that the GmbH has established in this respect. Besides regulating the bonus metrics in the individual service agreement, a GmbH may also operate a general bonus or incentive plan for its senior management. Alternatively, the service agreement may provide for the GmbH and the general manager to enter into target agreements on an annual basis, which will then set out the terms and conditions of the variable compensation in greater detail.

The amount of the variable compensation (the "**Bonus**") payable with respect to a fiscal year shall be subject to the rate by which corporate and/or individual targets and objectives as set by the shareholders' meeting have been achieved (the "**Target Achievement Rate**"). The determination of the Bonus shall generally be based on the pattern below; provided that the shareholders' meeting shall be entitled to amend or adjust such pattern from time to time depending on the nature of the targets and objectives set by it:

Target Achievement Rate (TAR)	Bonus
TAR < 80 percent	No payment
80 percent ≤ TAR < 85 percent	50 percent of Target Bonus
85 percent ≤ TAR < 90 percent	70 percent of Target Bonus
90 percent ≤ TAR < 95 percent	90 percent of Target Bonus
95 percent ≤ TAR < 105 percent	100 percent of Target Bonus
105 percent ≤ TAR < 115 percent	120 percent of Target Bonus
115 percent ≤ TAR < 130 percent	140 percent of Target Bonus
130 percent ≤ TAR < 150 percent	160 percent of Target Bonus
TAR ≥ 150 percent	200 percent of Target Bonus

The shareholders' meeting shall appraise the target achievement rate and determine the amount of the Bonus in its discretion after approval of the annual financial statements for the relevant fiscal year. In the event that the shareholders' meeting sets several targets and objectives, it shall also define their proportion of the Target Bonus.

4.   Unless regulated otherwise in this Agreement, any Bonus will be paid *pro rata temporis* in case that the Parties' service relationship commences or terminates during the course of a fiscal year.

5.   The General Manager may be eligible for participation in long-term incentive plans in the discretion of the shareholders' meeting. The shareholders' meeting will notify the General Manager in writing if he/she has been selected for participation in a long-term incentive plan, and the General Manager's accrual of rights thereunder shall exclusively be governed by the relevant plan rules as amended from time to time.

Section 4
Additional Benefits[1034]

1. For the term of his/her appointment, the GmbH shall provide the General Manager with an adequate car with a monthly lease rate of up to EUR [•] gross in accordance with its policies and guidelines as amended from time to time, which the General Manager may use for business related and, to a reasonable extent, also for private purposes.[1035] In the event that the General Manager is released from the obligation to perform services pursuant to Section 10(4) and the prerequisites for a business related use of the car do no longer exist, the General Manager shall be required to return such car together with any and all equipment and accessories in a state of good repair, without having any kind of retention right or being entitled to a financial compensation.

2. The GmbH shall arrange for the following insurances to be taken out for the benefit of the General Manager:

   a) Accident insurance covering business related and private accidents with insured sums of EUR [•] (in words: [•] Euros) in the event of accidental death and of EUR [•] (in words: [•] Euros) in the event of disability;

   b) Directors' and officers' liability insurance with a coverage reflecting industry standards.

3. The General Manager shall participate in the company pension scheme of the GmbH and earn pension entitlements in accordance with the terms and conditions of the underlying pension rules as amended from time to time.[1036]

4. The General Manager shall be responsible for any income tax that is payable on the non-cash benefits he/she receives hereunder.

1034 General manager service agreements occasionally provide for further benefits such as a housing allowance or the equipment of a home office at the cost of the GmbH.

1035 Alternatively, the service agreement may provide that the GmbH pays a monthly car allowance to the general manager, or refer to a separate company car agreement that the GmbH and the general manager will enter into in this respect.

1036 The amount of retirement benefits granted to a general manager and his/her surviving dependants as well as the underlying terms and conditions will usually depend on the pertinent practices of the GmbH. In addition to a reference to a general company pension scheme, the retirement benefits of a general manager may also be regulated in the service agreement itself or in a separate pension agreement.

Section 5
Reimbursement of Expenses

Reasonable disbursements that the General Manager incurs while performing services under this Agreement, including travel, entertainment and other out-of-pocket expenses, shall be reimbursed to him/her in accordance with internal policies. The General Manager shall submit regular expense reports together with appropriate supporting documentation for tax purposes.

Section 6
Vacation Leave

1. The General Manager shall be entitled to an annual vacation leave of 30 working days (based on a five-day working week). If the service relationship commences or terminates in the course of a calendar year, vacation leave is granted on a *pro rata temporis* basis. Vacation leave that is not taken in full during any one calendar year must be taken until the 31st of March of the succeeding calendar year in order not to become forfeited. Any further carry-over of unused vacation leave is excluded, unless the General Manager was prevented from taking his/her vacation leave in a timely manner due to an urgent project assigned to him/her, in which event the General Manager shall be granted an extension until the 30th of June of the succeeding calendar year. The General Manager shall not be entitled to any monetary compensation for unused vacation leave.[1037]

2. The General Manager shall coordinate his/her vacation leave with the other general managers of the GmbH, while reasonably considering business requirements and ensuring that the GmbH is at all times adequately represented.

Section 7
Continuation of Salary in the Event of Sickness and Death

1. The General Manager shall notify the GmbH of any incapability to work without undue delay, stating the reasons and the anticipated duration of his/her absence. Upon request, he/she is required to present a medical certificate.

2. Should the General Manager be temporarily unable to perform his/her duties and responsibilities under this Agreement due to sickness, an accident or any other reason for which he/she is not responsible, the GmbH will continue to pay the Base Salary for a maximum period of [•][1038] months, however, in no event beyond termination of this

---

1037 Although the Federal Leave Act does not apply to the general manager of a GmbH, it is quite customary to grant a certain grace period to take unused vacation leave that accrued in the preceding calendar year.

1038 Continuing salary pay in the event of sickness is usually granted for a period of six months. General manager service agreements occasionally provide that the GmbH will continue paying a certain portion of the base salary (*e.g.*, 60 percent) even beyond the expiration date of the six-month period up until a final cut-off date.

Agreement. In the event that the General Manager's inability to perform his/her duties and responsibilities exceeds a period of twelve weeks, any Bonus payable by the GmbH pursuant to Section 3(3) shall be reduced *pro rata temporis* in proportion to the aggregate period of his/her absence during the relevant fiscal year.

3. Any benefits that the General Manager receives from third parties for the duration of or in connection with his/her inability to perform services shall be fully credited against the continuing salary pay and reduce the payment obligations of the GmbH accordingly.

4. Should the General Manager pass away during the term of this Agreement, his/her spouse and any other persons entitled by statute to financial support shall, as joint and several creditors, be entitled to receive the Base Salary for the month of death and the following [•][1039] months, however, not beyond the date on which this Agreement would have terminated notwithstanding the General Manager's passing away.

Section 8
Confidentiality

1. The General Manager shall keep the content of this Agreement as well as all knowledge on confidential business matters of the GmbH and its Affiliates, which come to his/her attention in connection with fulfilling the duties and responsibilities assigned to him/her, strictly confidential and shall not use such knowledge in any manner for his own benefit or the benefit of third parties. The term "confidential business matters", in particular, includes all business and trade secrets, technical, operational and procedural know-how as well as all non-public information about (i) intellectual property, software and hardware, (ii) business development and marketing strategies, production and design processes, (iii) business plans, budgets, sales figures, prices, discount rates and profit margins, (iv) relationships with suppliers, customers, agents, distributors and similar business partners, as well as (v) personal data of, but not limited to, employees. A disclosure is only permitted in fulfillment of a contractual obligation of the GmbH or its relevant Affiliates or in safeguarding their interests.

2. To the extent legally permissible, the obligation to maintain secrecy survives termination of this Agreement.

1039 A period of three months would be customary.

Section 9
Inventions[1040]

1.   The General Manager shall promptly notify the GmbH in writing of any invention he/
     she makes during the term of this Agreement that originates from the performance of the
     duties and responsibilities assigned to him/her or significantly relates to the know-how or
     the work results of the business operations of the GmbH or its Affiliates, and shall pro-
     vide all required information in this respect. The GmbH is entitled to claim any such in-
     vention of the General Manager free-of-charge. Unless the GmbH informs the General
     Manager in writing within a period of four months after receipt of a proper notification
     that it releases the relevant invention, it shall be deemed to be claimed and any and all
     rights thereto shall transfer to the GmbH. If the GmbH releases an invention within the
     aforementioned time period, it shall be at the free disposal of the General Manager. The
     Parties agree that the right of the GmbH to use and exploit inventions of the General
     Manager shall be fully compensated by the salary and benefits paid to him/her under this
     Agreement and that he/she shall not be entitled to any additional remuneration in this
     respect.

2.   The General Manager shall further promptly notify the GmbH of any free invention
     within the meaning of Section 4(3) of the Act on Employee Inventions that he/she
     makes during the term of this Agreement. Before the General Manager may otherwise
     exploit a free invention, he/she must first offer to the GmbH an exclusive right of use
     on reasonable terms and conditions; provided that, at the time of such offer, the inven-
     tion falls within the existing or contemplated business areas of the GmbH. The priority
     right of the GmbH with respect to a free invention offered by the General Manager shall
     expire if it does not claim the invention within a period of three months after receipt of
     a proper notification.

3.   The GmbH shall be exclusively entitled to use any technical and organizational sug-
     gestions for improvement by the General Manager without having to pay an additional
     financial compensation.

1040 This provision largely implements the legal framework of the Act on Employee Inventions, except for its compensa-
     tion guidelines. Whether or not a more detailed regulation will be required depends on the business area in which
     the GmbH is engaged as well as the specific duties and responsibilities that are assigned to the general manager.

Section 10
Term and Termination

1. This Agreement shall run for an indefinite period of time and may be terminated in writing with [●] months' prior notice as of the end of a calendar month.[1041] Absent any declaration to the contrary, a resolution revoking the General Manager's appointment (of which the General Manager shall be informed in writing) shall be deemed a termination of this Agreement as of the earliest possible date.

2. The right to terminate this Agreement with immediate effect for good cause within the meaning of Section 626 of the Civil Code shall remain unaffected.[1042] A termination for good cause that is declared void in legal proceedings shall be deemed an ordinary termination as of the earliest possible date. In the event of a valid termination for good cause by the GmbH, the General Manager shall not be entitled to receive any Bonus pursuant to Section 3(3) with respect to the fiscal year in which the GmbH gave notice of termination.

3. This Agreement shall automatically terminate without prior notice upon the end of the calendar month in which the General Manager attains the statutory retirement age in Germany[1043]. If the General Manager becomes unable to practice his/her profession or permanently incapable to work in general, this Agreement shall automatically terminate without prior notice upon the end of the calendar month in which such disability is established by medical certificate or by notification of the social security authorities.

4. If notice of termination is given, the GmbH shall be entitled to put the General Manager on garden leave and release him/her from the obligation to perform services during the remaining term of this Agreement, with the proviso that the non-compete obligations pursuant to Section 11 shall continue to be binding on the General Manager. At the request of the GmbH, the General Manager shall take any outstanding vacation leave during his/her release. Any income that the General Manager receives from an employment, service, consulting or similar relationship as well as on a self-employed basis shall be fully credited against, and thus reduce, the payment obligations of the GmbH during the period of release.[1044]

1041 General manager service agreements that run for an indefinite period will frequently provide for a rather long notice period of between six and twelve months as of the end of a calendar month or a different effective date (*e.g.*, the end of a calendar half year). Alternatively, the service agreement may also be entered into for a fixed term without a prior termination possibility other than for good cause. Special rules apply in the case of a co-determined GmbH, whose general managers may only be appointed for a <u>maximum term of five years</u>. An extension of the tenure and the underlying service agreement beyond the five-year term will require a new supervisory board resolution.

1042 The agreement may set forth a catalogue of events that shall entitle the parties to termination for good cause. Since a court will usually carry out a balance of interests test based on the facts and circumstances at hand, it is not certain that the termination reasons stipulated in such a catalogue will always be acknowledged in court.

1043 If the general manager participates in a company pension scheme, the age limit will usually correspond to the retirement age provided in the underlying pension rules.

1044 General manager service agreements occasionally require the GmbH to pay severance to the general manager if it does not renew the service relationship (in case of a fixed-term agreement), or if it serves ordinary termination without a reason for which the general manager is responsible.

Section 11
Non-compete Undertaking

1. During the term of this Agreement, the General Manager shall neither be entitled to work for a competitor of the GmbH or any of its Affiliates (including in a freelance or advisory capacity), nor to directly or indirectly participate in such a competitor, irrespective of the form of the participation. Investments that are made in the context of private asset management and do not permit exercising influence on a company's management or supervisory bodies are not subject to this non-compete undertaking. When conducting private investments, the General Manager shall, however, avoid any conflict of interests and strictly comply with any guidelines and policies that the GmbH establishes in this respect from time to time. The General Manager shall further notify the shareholders' meeting if a party that is closely related to him/her pursuant to Section 15 of the Tax Code participates in a competitor of the GmbH or any of its Affiliates.

2. The non-compete undertaking pursuant to Section 11(1) sentence 1 shall also apply during a period of [•] year[s][1045] after termination of this Agreement, unless this Agreement terminates due to a permanent disability on the part of the General Manager pursuant to Section 10(3). The scope of the post-termination non-compete undertaking shall relate to the field of business of the GmbH and its Affiliates at the termination date of this Agreement, and its territorial application shall be unrestricted; provided that countries in which neither the GmbH nor any of its Affiliates conduct business shall be excluded.

3. For the duration of the post-termination non-compete undertaking, the GmbH shall pay to the General Manager, in arrears in twelve equal monthly installments at its general payment date for salaries, financial compensation equal to [50] percent of the sum of (i) his/her last Base Salary and (ii) the average Bonus paid to the General Manager over the last three-year period prior to the termination date of this Agreement.[1046] Any other benefits that the GmbH grants to the General Manager hereunder shall not be taken into account when determining the aforementioned financial compensation.

4. Any retirement benefits that the GmbH pays to the General Manager as well as any other kind of income which the General Manager receives from an employment, service, consulting or similar relationship as well as on a self-employed basis during the period of the post-termination non-compete undertaking shall be fully credited against, and thus reduce the amount of, the financial compensation payable by the GmbH. During the period of the post-termination non-compete undertaking, the General Manager shall provide information on any creditable income received by him/her on a quarterly basis and furnish evidence upon request.

1045 A period of between one year and two years would be customary.
1046 Contrary to the reference base used in this form, the financial compensation payable may also amount to a certain percentage of the last base salary, without taking any variable compensation into account.

5. The GmbH shall be entitled to waive the post-termination non-compete undertaking at any time in writing with the effect that it shall become released from the obligation to pay the financial compensation pursuant to Section 11(3) upon expiration of a period of [six] months after a written waiver has been received by the General Manager. If this Agreement terminates for good cause in accordance with Section 10(2), the GmbH may cancel the post-termination non-compete undertaking with immediate effect during the subsequent one-month period by means of a written notification to the General Manager.

6. For each violation of the non-compete undertaking in this Section 11, the General Manager shall incur a contractual penalty equal to [one month's] Base Salary, and the GmbH shall not be required to pay him/her any financial compensation pursuant to Section 11(3) for the month in which the violation occurred. In the event that a violation is not limited to a single event and the General Manager maintains his/her non-complying behavior during a continuous period of time, the full amount of the contractual penalty shall be incurred again at the beginning of each new month in which the violation of the non-compete undertaking persists. To the extent permitted by applicable laws, the Parties shall be entitled to offset claims for contractual penalties and claims for payment of the financial compensation against each other.

7. If and to the extent that any provisions of this post-termination non-compete undertaking should be invalid due to their being too broad or too narrow, they shall be replaced by valid provisions that, based on the economic purpose of this Agreement, come closest to what the Parties had intended in connection with the post-termination non-compete undertaking.

Section 12
Return of Documents and Company Property

1. Any documents and files that are in the possession of the General Manager and relate to the business matters of the GmbH or any of its Affiliates shall be kept in safe custody and protected against unauthorized inspection by third parties.

2. All business related documents, files, correspondence, records, drafts as well as electronically saved information and similar items pertaining to the GmbH or any of its Affiliates are the exclusive property of the GmbH or the relevant Affiliate, as applicable, irrespective of the addressee. The same shall apply to any technical devices, keys, tools, office equipment and supplies that have been made available to the General Manager. The General Manager shall return any such documents, files and other company property upon termination of this Agreement or upon a release from the obligation to perform services pursuant to Section 10(4), without retaining any copies.

3.   The General Manager shall not be entitled to any kind of retention right with respect to his/her obligations under this Section 12. At the request of the shareholders' meeting, the General Manager shall confirm compliance with the obligation to return in writing.

Section 13
Data Protection

The General Manager agrees that his/her personal data may be stored and processed in physical or electronic files kept by the GmbH or any external service providers retained by it in connection with the performance of the Parties' service relationship. The GmbH will obligate its employees and any third parties having access to such data to keep them confidential.

Section 14
Final Provisions

1.   This Agreement represents the entire agreement and understanding of the Parties with respect to its subject matter and supersedes all prior negotiations, discussions, understandings and agreements of any form or nature between the Parties, whether oral or written, and whether express or implied. [Henceforth, the legal relationship between the General Manager and the GmbH shall exclusively be governed by the terms and conditions of this Agreement. The Parties agree, in particular, that there is no suspended employment relationship in place.][1047]

2.   Any amendments of or supplements to this Agreement shall be made in writing, unless a stricter legal form is required. This shall also apply to any modifications of this written form requirement.

3.   This Agreement shall be governed by and construed in accordance with the laws of Germany. To the extent legally permissible, place of venue shall be the registered seat of the GmbH.

4.   Neither Party may assign this Agreement, or any right or obligation hereunder without the written consent of the other Party.

5.   Should any provision of this Agreement be or become invalid, ineffective or unenforceable as a whole or in part, the validity, effectiveness and enforceability of the remaining provisions shall not be affected thereby. Any such invalid, ineffective or enforceable provision shall be deemed replaced by such valid, effective and enforceable provision as

---

1047 Such a provision may, in particular, be introduced in the event that a former employee of the GmbH is appointed general manager later on. Alternatively, the parties may agree that the original employment relationship of the general manager shall be suspended during his/her tenure and be revived upon termination of the appointment.

comes closest to the economic intent and purpose of such invalid, ineffective or unenforceable provision. This shall apply accordingly to gaps in this Agreement of which the Parties become aware in connection with its performance.

6. This Agreement shall be executed in duplicate.

_____, the _____

_____

Shareholders' Meeting of [•] GmbH

_____, the _____

_____

[•]

II. Statutory Provisions

A. Sections 76 through 117 Stock Corporation Act

MANAGEMENT BOARD

Section 76 Management of the Stock Corporation

(1) The management board shall be immediately responsible for managing the company.

(2) [1]The management board may consist of one or more persons. [2]It must consist of at least two persons at companies with a nominal share capital of over three million euro unless the articles of association stipulate that it shall consist of one person. [3]The provisions regarding the appointment of a labor director shall remain unaffected.

(3) [1]Only a natural person having a full legal capacity may be a member of the management board. [2]A member of the management board may not be anyone who

1. as a person under custodianship is fully or partially subject to consent in regard to the management of his assets (Section 1903 of the Civil Code),

2. has been prohibited from practicing a profession, branch of a profession, trade or branch of a trade by a court judgment or enforceable decision by an administrative authority, if the purpose of the company coincides in full or in part with that of the subject of the prohibition,

3. has been sentenced for one or more intentionally committed criminal acts

    a) of failing to file the application for the opening of the insolvency proceeding (delaying insolvency),

    b) under Sections 283 through 283d of the Criminal Code (criminal insolvency offenses),

    c) of falsifying information under Section 399 of this Act or Section 82 of the Act concerning Limited Liability Companies,

    d) of misrepresentation under Section 400 of this Act, Section 331 of the Commercial Code, Section 313 of the Merger and Reorganization Act or Section 17 of the Public Disclosure Act,

    e) under Sections 263 through 264a or Sections 265b through 266a of the Criminal Code to imprisonment for at least one year;

this exclusion shall apply for a period of five years from the date on which the judgment becomes final, while the period during which the offender has been held in custody in an institution by order of authority shall not be included.

[3]Sentence 2 no. 3 shall apply *mutatis mutandis* in the event of being sentenced in a foreign country for an offense comparable to the offenses specified in sentence 2 no. 3.

Section 77 Management

(1) [1]If the management board consists of several persons, all management board members are authorized to manage the company solely on a joint basis. [2]The articles of association or the rules of procedure of the management board may provide otherwise; however, it cannot be stipulated that one or more management board members may resolve differences of opinion in the management board in opposition to the majority of its members.

(2) [1]The management board may issue rules of procedure for the management board, unless the articles of association transfer the issuance of rules of procedure to the supervisory board or the supervisory board issues rules of procedure for the management board. [2]The articles of association may regulate individual aspects of the rules of procedure on a binding basis. [3]Resolutions of the management board regarding the rules of procedure must be adopted unanimously.

Section 78 Representation

(1) [1]The management board shall represent the company both in and out of court. [2]If a company does not have a management board (vacancy of the position of management board), the company shall be represented by the supervisory board in the event that declarations of intent are submitted to it or documents are served upon it.

(2) [1]If the management board consists of several persons, unless the articles of association specify otherwise, all management board members are only authorized to represent the company jointly. [2]If a declaration of intent is submitted to the company, the submission to one management board member suffices or, in the event of paragraph 1 sentence 2, to one supervisory board member. [3]Declarations of intent may be submitted to the company or documents served for the company to the representatives of the company under paragraph 1 at the business address registered in the commercial register. [4]Irrespective thereof, the submission and service may also be effectuated to the person authorized for receipt pursuant to Section 39 paragraph 1 sentence 2 at the registered address.

(3) [1]The articles of association may also specify that individual management board members are authorized to represent the company alone or jointly with a holder of a general commercial power of attorney. [2]The supervisory board may specify the same if the articles of association have authorized it to do so. [3]In such cases paragraph 2 sentence 2 shall apply *mutatis mutandis*.

(4) [1]Management board members having joint representational powers may authorize individual management board members to engage in certain business transactions or certain types of business transactions. [2]This shall apply accordingly if an individual management board member is authorized to represent the company jointly with a holder of a general commercial power of attorney.

Section 79 (repealed)

Section 80 Information included in Business Letters

(1) [1]Irrespective of form all business letters addressed to a specific recipient must include the legal form and the registered office of the company, the court of register of the registered office of the company and the number, under which the company is registered in the commercial register, as well as all management board members and the chairman of the supervisory board, including their last names and at least one first name written out in full. [2]The chairman of the management board shall be designated as such. [3]If information about the capital of the company is included, it is required in any case to include the nominal share capital and, if the issue price of the shares has not been fully paid in, the total amount of outstanding contributions.

(2) The information under paragraph 1 sentence 1 and 2 need not be included in notifications or reports issued in connection with an existing business relationship and for which preprinted forms are customarily used that only call for filling in the particular information required in the individual circumstance.

(3) [1]Order forms shall be deemed business letters within the meaning of paragraph 1. [2]Paragraph 2 shall not be applicable to them.

(4) [1]All business letters and order forms used by a branch office of a stock corporation with a registered office in a foreign country must include the register at which the branch office is registered, and the number of the register entry; the provisions set forth in paragraphs 1 through 3 with respect to the information regarding the main office and the branch office shall otherwise apply to the extent that foreign law does not call for other information. [2]If the foreign company is in the process of liquidation this fact and the names of all liquidators should also be included.

Section 81 Changes in the Management Board
and the Powers of Representation of its Members

(1) Any change in the management board or the powers of representation of a management board member must be registered by the management board for entry in the commercial register.

(2) The registration must include the deeds regarding the change in the original or in an officially certified copy.

(3) [1]The new management board members shall affirm in the registration that there are no circumstances opposing their appointment under Section 76 paragraph 3 sentence 2 no. 2 and 3 as well as sentence 3, and that they have been instructed of their unrestricted duty of information to the court. [2]Section 37 paragraph 2 sentence 2 shall apply.

(4) (repealed)

Section 82 Restrictions of the Powers of Representation
and Management of the Company

(1) The powers of representation of the management board may not be restricted.

(2) In the relationship of the management board members to the company, they must comply with the restrictions of the powers of authority to manage the company that are specified in the provisions of stock corporation law regarding the articles of association, the supervisory board, the shareholders' meeting and the rules of procedure of the management board and of the supervisory board.

Section 83 Preparation and Execution of Shareholders' Meeting Resolutions

(1) [1]At the request of the shareholders' meeting, the management board is required to prepare measures within the competence of the shareholders' meeting. [2]This also applies to the preparation and conclusion of agreements, the validity of which is subject to the consent of the shareholders' meeting. [3]The resolution of the shareholders' meeting requires the majorities necessary for the measures or the consent to the agreement.

(2) The management board is required to execute the measures resolved by the shareholders' meeting within the scope of its competence.

Section 84 Appointment and Removal from office of the Management Board

(1) [1]Management board members shall be appointed by the supervisory board for a maximum term of five years. [2]A renewed appointment or extension of the term of office is permitted for a maximum term of five years respectively. [3]This requires a renewed supervisory board resolution, which may be adopted at the earliest one year prior to expiration of the previous term of office. [4]Only in the case of an appointment for fewer than five years may an extension of the term of office be allowed without a new supervisory board resolution, provided the complete term of office does not thereby exceed five years. [5]This applies accordingly for the service agreement; however, the service agreement may provide that it shall continue to apply in the event of an extension until the expiration of the term of office.

(2) If several persons are appointed as management board members, the supervisory board may appoint one member as the chairman of the management board.

(3) [1]The supervisory board may revoke the appointment as a management board member and the appointment as the chairman of the management board, provided there is due cause. [2]Such cause means specifically gross negligence, incapacity to manage the company on an orderly basis or the withdrawal of the confidence of the shareholders' meeting, unless the confidence has been withdrawn for obviously unfounded reasons. [3]This shall also apply to the management board appointed by the first supervisory board. [4]The revocation is valid until its invalidity is determined on a legally binding basis. [5]General regulations shall apply to rights arising out of the service agreement.

(4) The provisions of the Act Concerning the Co-Determination of Employees in Supervisory Boards and Management Boards of Companies of the Mining Industry and the Iron and Steel Producing Industry of May 21, 1951 (Federal Law Gazette I p. 347) – the "Coal and Steel-Co-Determination Act" – regarding the special majority requirements for a supervisory board resolution regarding the appointment of a labor director or the revocation of his appointment shall remain unaffected.

Section 85 Appointment by the Court

(1) [1]In the absence of a required management board member, in urgent cases the court shall appoint the member at the request of a participant. [2]The decision may be challenged by complaint.

(2) The office of the court-appointed management board member shall expire as soon as the deficiency is remedied.

(3) [1]The court-appointed management board member shall be entitled to reimbursement of appropriate cash outlays and to compensation for his activity. [2]If the court-appointed management board member and the company fail to agree, the court shall determine the outlays and

the compensation. [3]The decision may be challenged by complaint; the appeal is excluded. [4]The legally binding decision shall be enforced pursuant to the Code of Civil Procedure.

Section 86 (repealed)

Section 87 Principles regarding the Compensation of Management Board Members

(1) [1]In determining the total compensation of the individual management board member (salary, profit participations, expense reimbursements, insurance premiums, commissions, incentive pay schemes such as subscription rights and ancillary benefits of all kinds), the supervisory board shall ensure that the total compensation is in an appropriate relationship to the management board member's tasks and performance, as well as the status of the company and that total compensation does not exceed this amount unless there are unusual circumstances warranting otherwise. [2]For companies listed on the stock exchange, the compensation structure is geared towards the long-term development of the company. [3]Variable pay components therefore shall be structured for longer periods of time; the supervisory board shall agree on possible restrictions that apply for extraordinary circumstances. [4]Sentence 1 applies accordingly for pension payments and payments to dependants of deceased members and other related benefits.

(2) [1]If after determining that the status of the company has deteriorated so significantly that the further granting of the compensation specified in paragraph 1 would be grossly unfair to the company, the supervisory board is authorized, or in the event of Section 85 paragraph 3, the court at the request of the supervisory board, to effectuate an appropriate reduction. [2]Pension payments, orphan's/widow's pensions and other related benefits can only be reduced pursuant to sentence 1 within the first three years after a member has left the company. [3]The service agreement shall otherwise remain unaffected by the reduction. [4]The management board member may, however, terminate his service agreement as of the end of the next calendar quarter with a notice period of six weeks.

(3) If the insolvency proceeding is opened concerning the assets of the company and the insolvency receiver terminates the service agreement of a management board member, he may only claim damages arising for him due to the cancellation of the service relationship for two years as of the expiration of the service relationship.

Section 88 Non-compete obligation

(1) [1]The management board members may neither, without the consent of the supervisory board, operate a commercial activity nor engage in business transactions in the branch of business of the company for their own or a third-party account. [2]They are also not permitted without consent to be a member of the management board or a general manager or general

partner of any other company. [3]The consent of the supervisory board may only be granted for specific commercial activity or company or for certain types of business transactions.

(2) [1]If a management board member violates this prohibition, the company may demand compensation for damages. [2]*In lieu* thereof it may demand that the member allows the business transacted for his own account to be credited to the account of the company, and relinquishes the compensation received for business transacted for the account of a third party, or assigns his entitlement to the compensation.

(3) [1]Any claims of the company shall be subject to the statute of limitations in three months as of the date on which the remaining management board members and supervisory board members learn of the act requiring the compensation for damages or should have learned of without being grossly negligent. [2]They shall be subject to the statute of limitations, irrespective of this knowledge or grossly negligent lack of knowledge, in five years as of the date of arising.

Section 89 Granting Loans to Management Board Members

(1) [1]The company may grant loans to management board members only on the basis of a resolution of the supervisory board. [2]The resolution may only be adopted for certain loan transactions or types of loan transactions and not longer than three months in advance. [3]It shall regulate the interest and repayment of the loan. [4]The granting of a loan is equivalent to the permission for a withdrawal exceeding the compensation to which the management board member is entitled, specifically including the permission to withdraw compensation advances. [5]This shall not apply to loans that do not exceed one month's salary.

(2) [1]The company may only grant its holder of a general commercial power of attorney (*Prokurist*) and its commercial agents (*Handlungsbevollmächtigter*) loans with the consent of the supervisory board. [2]A dominating company may grant loans to legal representatives, holders of a general commercial power of attorney or commercial agents of a dependent company only with the consent of their supervisory board, a dependent company may only grant loans to legal representatives, holders of a general commercial power of attorney or commercial agents of the dominating company only with the consent of the supervisory board of the dominating company. [3]Paragraph 1 sentence 2 through 5 shall apply *mutatis mutandis*.

(3) [1]Paragraph 2 shall also apply to loans to the spouses, domestic partners or to an underage child of a management board member, of another legal representative, of a holder of a general commercial power of attorney or of a commercial agent. [2]It shall also apply to loans to a third party acting for the account of these persons or for the account of a management board member, of any other legal representative, of a holder of a general commercial power of attorney or of a commercial agent.

(4) [1]If a management board member, a holder of a general commercial power of attorney or a commercial agent is simultaneously a legal representative or member of the supervisory board

of another legal person or shareholder of a partnership, the company may only grant loans to the legal person or partnership with the consent of the supervisory board; paragraph 1 sentence 2 and 3 shall apply *mutatis mutandis*. [2]This shall not apply if the legal person or partnership is associated with the company or if the loan is granted for the payment of goods delivered by the company to the legal person or partnership.

(5) If a loan is granted contrary to paragraphs 1 through 4, the loan shall be returned immediately irrespective of any agreements to the contrary unless agreed to by the supervisory board retroactively.

(6) If the company is a credit institution or financial services institution, to which Section 15 of the Banking Act is applicable, the provisions of the Banking Act shall apply *in lieu* of paragraphs 1 through 5.

Section 90 Reports to the Supervisory Board

(1) [1]The management board must report to the supervisory board on

1.   the proposed business policy and other fundamental issues of corporate planning (in particular the financial, investment and personnel planning), while any deviations in actual developments from previously reported objectives shall be furnished including information regarding the grounds;

2.   profitability, in particular on the profitability of equity;

3.   the course of business transactions, in particular the turnover and the status of the company;

4.   business transactions that may be of material significance for the profitability or liquidity of the company.

[2]If the company is a parent company (Section 290 paragraph 1, 2 of the Commercial Code), the report shall also include subsidiaries and joint ventures (Section 310 paragraph 1 of the Commercial Code). [3]The chairman of the supervisory board should also receive reports if there are any other important reasons for doing so; important reasons for doing so shall also include any business conducted at an affiliated company of which the management board has become aware that is of material significance to the company.

(2) The reports under paragraph 1 sentence 1 no. 1 through 4 shall be submitted as follows:

1.   the reports under number 1 at least once annually, unless changes in the status or new issues call for prompt reporting;

2.   the reports under number 2 in the meeting of the supervisory board, in which negotiations regarding the annual financial statements take place;

3.   the reports under number 3 regularly, at least on a quarterly basis;

4.   the reports under number 4 as far as possible on a timely basis allowing the supervisory board the opportunity to comment prior to undertaking the business transactions.

(3) [1]The supervisory board may at any time request a report from the management board in regard to the affairs of the company, its legal and business relationships to affiliated companies and in regard to the course of business at these companies that may have a significant influence on the status of the company. [2]An individual member may also request a report, but only to the supervisory board.

(4) [1]The reports shall comply with the principles of a conscientious and truthful account. [2]They shall be submitted as timely as possible and, with exception of the report under paragraph 1 sentence 3, generally issued in writing.

(5) [1]Each of the supervisory board members shall have the right to inspect the reports. [2]To the extent the reports are issued in written form, they shall be furnished to each supervisory board member on request to the extent the supervisory board has not resolved otherwise. [3]The chairman of the supervisory board shall inform the supervisory board members of the reports under paragraph 1 sentence 2 at the latest in the next meeting of the supervisory board.

Section 91 Organization. Accounting

(1) The management board shall ensure that the required trading books are kept.

(2) The management board shall take appropriate measures, in particular by setting up a monitoring system enabling developments threatening the continued existence of the company to be recognized early.

Section 92 Management Board Duties in the Event of Loss, Overindebtedness or Insolvency

(1) If it results from the preparation of the annual balance sheet or an interim balance sheet, or if it can be assumed on exercising due discretion that there is a loss in the amount of half of the nominal share capital, the management board shall promptly call and report this to the shareholders' meeting.

(2) [1]After the company has become insolvent or its overindebtedness has resulted, the management board may not make any further payments. [2]This shall not apply to payments that are also

made after this date in keeping with the due care of a diligent and conscientious general manager. [3]The same obligation shall apply to the management board for payments to shareholders to the extent these would have to lead to the insolvency of the company, unless this was not recognizable even in consideration of the due care referred to in Section 93 paragraph 1 sentence 1.

Section 93 Duty of Due Care and Responsibility of the Management Board Members

(1) [1]The management board members shall exercise the due care of a diligent and conscientious general manager in their management of the business. [2]The duty shall not be deemed violated if, at the time of taking the entrepreneurial decision, the management board member had good reason to assume that it was acting for the welfare of the company on the basis of the appropriate information. [3]The management board members shall maintain confidentiality with regard to confidential information and secrets of the company, particularly business and operating secrets of which they have gained knowledge through their activity on the management board. [4]The obligation set forth in sentence 3 shall not apply to an accredited auditing office pursuant to Section 342b of the Commercial Code in connection with an audit conducted by it.

(2) [1]Management board members who violate their duties are required to compensate the company for the resulting damages as joint and several debtors. [2]They shall bear the burden of proof if it is disputed whether they have exercised the due care of a diligent and conscientious general manager. [3]If the company insures a management board member against professional liability risk, it bears at least a 10 percent share of the risk and up to at least one and a half times the amount of the management board member's annual compensation.

(3) The management board members are specifically liable for compensation if, in violation of this Act,

1. contributions are returned to the shareholders,

2. the shareholders are paid interest or profit shares,

3. own shares of the company or of another company are subscribed, acquired, accepted as a pledge or redeemed,

4. shares are issued prior to the full payment of the issue price,

5. company assets are distributed,

6. payments are made in violation of Section 92 paragraph 2,

7. compensation is granted to supervisory board members,

8. a loan is granted,

9.   subscription shares are issued in the event of a conditional capital increase not consistent
        with the designated purpose or prior to full payment of their value in return.

(4) [1]The liability to the company for damages shall not apply if the act is based on a lawful
resolution of the shareholders' meeting. [2]The fact that the supervisory board consented to the
act does not exclude the liability for damages. [3]The company may only waive damages three
years after the claim arises and may only waive or settle damage claims if the shareholders'
meeting agrees and no minority, whose shares together comprise one-tenth of the nominal
share capital, raises an objection to be recorded in the minutes. [4]The time limit shall not apply
if the party liable for damages is insolvent and settles with its creditors to avert the insolvency
proceedings, or if the liability for damages is regulated in an insolvency plan.

(5) [1]The liability for damages of the company may also be claimed by the creditors of the
company to the extent they are unable to gain satisfaction from the company. [2]This shall,
however, only apply in cases other than those set forth in paragraph 3, if the management
board members have grossly violated the due care of a diligent and conscientious general manager; paragraph 2 sentence 2 shall apply *mutatis mutandis*. [3]The liability for damages shall not
be rescinded with respect to the creditors either by a waiver or settlement of the company nor
on the basis of the fact that the act was based on a resolution of the shareholders' meeting.
[4]If the insolvency proceeding concerning the assets of the company is opened, the insolvency
receiver or the trustee shall thus exercise the rights of the creditors against the management
board members for the duration of the proceeding.

(6) The rights based on these provisions shall be subject to the statute of limitations in ten
years in the case of companies listed on the stock exchange at the time of the violation of the
duty, and in the case of other companies, after five years.

Section 94 Substitutes of the Management Board Members

The provisions applying to the management board members also apply to their substitutes.

SUPERVISORY BOARD

Section 95 Number of Supervisory Board Members

[1]The supervisory board shall consist of three members. [2]The articles of association may specify
a larger number. [3]The number must be divisible by three. [4]The maximum number of supervisory board members shall be for companies with a nominal share capital of

up to   1,500,000 euro, nine members,
over   1,500,000 euro, fifteen members,
over   10,000,000 euro, twenty-one members.

[5]Conflicting provisions of the Act Concerning the Co-Determination of Employees of May 4, 1976 (Federal Law Gazette I p. 1153), the Coal and Steel-Co-Determination Act and the Act Supplementing the Act Concerning the Co-Determination of Employees in the Supervisory Boards and Management Boards of Companies in the Mining and Iron and Steel Producing Industries of August 7, 1956 (Federal Law Gazette I p. 707) – the "Co-Determination Amendment Act" shall remain unaffected.

Section 96 Composition of the Supervisory Board

(1) The supervisory board shall be composed

at companies for which the Co-Determination Act applies, of supervisory board members of the shareholders and of the employees,

at companies for which the Coal and Steel-Co-Determination Act applies, of supervisory board members of the shareholders and of the employees and of further members,

at companies for which Sections 5 through 13 of the Co-Determination Amendment Act applies, of supervisory board members of the shareholders and of the employees and of one further member,

at companies for which the One-Third Participation Act applies, of supervisory board members of the shareholders and of the employees,

at companies for which the Act on the Co-Determination of Employees in a Cross-Border Merger applies, of supervisory board members of the shareholders and of the employees,

at any other companies only of supervisory board members of the shareholders.

(2) The supervisory board may only be composed according to provisions other than those previously applied if under Section 97 or under Section 98 the statutory provisions are applicable as indicated in the announcement of the management board or in the court decision.

Section 97 Announcement of the Composition of the Supervisory Board

(1) [1]If the management board believes that the composition of the supervisory board does not comply with the relevant statutory provisions applying to the supervisory board, it shall announce this promptly in the publications designated for company notices and at the same time post the announcement in all businesses of the company and its group companies. [2]The announcement shall specify the statutory provisions that the management board considers definitive. [3]The announcement shall note that the supervisory board will be composed in accordance with these provisions, unless parties eligible to apply under Section 98 paragraph 2

appeal to the competent court pursuant to Section 98 paragraph 1 within one month of the announcement in the electronic Federal Gazette.

(2) [1]If no appeal is filed with the competent court pursuant to Section 98 paragraph 1 within one month of the announcement in the electronic Federal Gazette, the new supervisory board shall be composed in accordance with the statutory provisions cited in the announcement of the management board. [2]The provisions of the articles of association regarding the composition of the supervisory board, the number of supervisory board members and the election, removal and appointment of supervisory board members shall become invalid after the first shareholders' meeting has ended that was called following the expiration of the appeal period, at the latest six months following the expiration of this period to the extent that the provisions contradict the statutory provisions valid at the time. [3]At the same point in time, the office of the previous supervisory board members shall expire. [4]A shareholders' meeting taking place within the period of six months may resolve by a simple majority to adopt new provisions of the articles of association *in lieu* of the provisions of the articles of association that are no longer valid.

(3) No announcements regarding the composition of the supervisory board may be made for as long as a court proceeding is pending under Sections 98, 99.

Section 98 Court Decision regarding the Composition of the Supervisory Board

(1) [1]If the statutory provisions according to which the supervisory board should be composed are disputed or uncertain, this shall be exclusively decided by filing an application with the regional court in the district of which the company has its registered office.

(2) [1]Eligible to file an application are

1. the management board,

2. each of the supervisory board members,

3. each shareholder,

4. the central works council of the company or the works council if there is only one works council at the company,

5. the central or corporate executive committee of the company or the executive committee if there is only one executive committee at the company,

6. the central works council of any other company, whose employees participate themselves or through delegates in the election of supervisory board members of the company pursuant to the statutory provisions, the application of which is disputed or uncertain, or, if in the other company there is only one works council, the works council,

7.   the central or corporate executive committee of any other company, whose employees participate themselves or through delegates in the election of supervisory board members of the company pursuant to the statutory provisions, the application of which is disputed or uncertain, or, if in the other company there is only one executive committee, the executive committee,

8.   at least one-tenth or one hundred of the employees, who themselves or through delegates participate in the election of supervisory board members of the company pursuant to the statutory provisions, the application of which is disputed or uncertain,

9.   umbrella organizations of the trade unions, which would have a nomination right pursuant to the statutory provisions, the application of which is disputed or uncertain,

10.   trade unions, which would have a nomination right pursuant to the statutory provisions, the application of which is disputed or uncertain.

²If the application of the Co-Determination Act or the application of provisions of the Co-Determination Act is disputed or uncertain, beside the eligible filing parties under sentence 1 also respectively eligible to file are one-tenth of the employees who are eligible to vote as provided in Section 3 paragraph 1 no. 1 of the Co-Determination Act, or of the executive officers eligible to vote within the meaning of the Co-Determination Act.

(3) Paragraphs 1 and 2 shall apply *mutatis mutandis* if the correct calculation of the decisive turnover relationship by the auditor pursuant to Section 3 or Section 16 of the Co-Determination Amendment Act is disputed or uncertain.

(4) ¹If the composition of the supervisory board does not correspond to the court decision, the new supervisory board shall be composed pursuant to the statutory provisions specified in the decision. ²Section 97 paragraph 2 shall apply *mutatis mutandis*, with the proviso that the period of six months shall not begin until the decision becomes legally binding.

Section 99 Proceedings

(1) The Act on Proceedings in Family Matters and Matters of Non-contentious Jurisdiction shall apply to the proceedings unless provided otherwise in paragraphs 2 through 5.

(2) ¹The regional court shall announce the application in the publications designated for company notices. ²The management board and each supervisory board member, as well as the works councils, executive committees, umbrella organizations and trade unions eligible to file an application under Section 98 paragraph 2 shall be heard.

(3) ¹The regional court shall decide by resolution including the grounds. ²The decision of the regional court may be challenged by complaint. ³The complaint may only be based on a viola-

tion of the law; Section 72 paragraph 1 sentence 2 and Section 74 paragraphs 2 and 3 of the Act on Proceedings in Family Matters and Matters of Non-contentious Jurisdiction as well as Section 547 of the Code of Civil Procedure shall apply *mutatis mutandis*. [4]The complaint may only be lodged by submitting a complaint brief signed by an attorney-at-law. [5]The federal government may transfer the decision regarding the complaint to one of the higher regional courts or the highest regional court by statutory order for the districts of several higher regional courts if this serves to safeguard uniform adjudication. [6]The federal government may transfer this power to the department of administration justice of the federal state.

(4) [1]The court shall serve its decision upon the applicant and the company. [2]It shall also announce the decision, without stating the grounds, in the publications designated for company notices. [3]All of the parties eligible to apply under Section 98 paragraph 2 are entitled to the complaint. [4]The complaint period shall commence on the announcement of the decision in the electronic Federal Gazette, for the applicant and the company, however, not prior to the service of the decision.

(5) [1]The decision shall not become valid until it is legally binding. [2]It shall be effective for and against all parties. [3]The management board shall promptly submit the final decision to the commercial register.

(6) [1]The Order Regulating Court Fees shall apply to the costs of the proceedings. [2]Four times the full fee shall be levied for the proceedings of the first legal instance. [3]The same fee shall be levied for the proceeding because of an appeal; this also applies if the appeal succeeds. [4]If the application or the appeal is withdrawn prior to a decision, the fee shall be reduced by half. [5]The value of the matter in controversy shall be determined ex officio. [6]It shall be calculated according to Section 30 paragraph 2 of the Order Regulating Court Fees with the proviso that the value of 50,000 euro shall be routinely assumed. [7]The company shall be the debtor of the costs. [8]The costs may, however, be levied on the applicant in full or in part if this is equitable. [9]The participants' costs shall not be reimbursed.

Section 100 Personal Qualifications of Supervisory Board Members

(1) [1]Only a natural person having a full legal capacity may be a member of the supervisory board. [2]A person under custodianship who is fully or partially subject to consent in regard to the management of his assets (Section 1903 of the Civil Code) may not be a member of the supervisory board.

(2) [1]A member of the supervisory board may not be anyone who

1. already is a supervisory board member in ten companies required to form a supervisory board by law,

2. is a legal representative of a company that is dependent on the company

3.	is a legal representative of another corporation to whose supervisory board a management board member of the company belongs, or

4.	in the last two years was a member of the management board unless he was appointed upon the recommendation of shareholders who have more than a 25 percent share of voting rights.

[2]Not included in the maximum number under sentence 1 no. 1 are up to five supervisory board seats in companies belonging to the corporate group that are required to form a supervisory board by law that are held by a legal representative (in the case of a sole proprietorship, the owner) of the dominant company of a corporate group. [3]Double the number of supervisory board offices within the meaning of number 1 for which the member has been elected to chairman shall be included in the maximum number under sentence 1 no. 1.

(3) The other personal qualifications of supervisory board members representing the employees and any further members are defined under the Co-Determination Act, the Coal and Steel-Co-Determination Act, the Co-Determination Amendment Act, the One-Third Participation Act and the Act on the Co-Determination of Employees in a Cross-Border Merger.

(4) The articles of association may only specify personal qualifications for supervisory board members elected by the shareholders' meeting without being bound to nominations, or appointed to the supervisory board on the basis of the articles of association.

(5) At companies within the meaning of Section 264d of the Commercial Code, at least one independent member of the supervisory board must have a professional knowledge of the areas of accounting or the auditing of financial statements.

Section 101 Appointment of the Supervisory Board Members

(1) [1]The members of the supervisory board shall be elected by the shareholders' meeting to the extent they are not appointed to the supervisory board or elected as supervisory board members representing the employees under the Co-Determination Act, the Co-Determination Amendment Act, the One-Third Participation Act or the Act on the Co-Determination of Employees in a Cross-Border Merger. [2]The shareholders' meeting is only bound to nominations pursuant to Sections 6 and 8 of the Coal and Steel-Co-Determination Act.

(2) [1]A right to appoint members to the supervisory board may only be vested in the articles of association and only for certain shareholders or for the respective holders of certain shares. [2]The appointment right may only be granted to holders of certain shares if the shares are registered and their transfer is subject to the consent of the company. [3]The shares of the those eligible to make appointments shall not form a special class. [4]The appointment rights may be granted in total for a maximum of one-third of the number of supervisory board members representing the shareholders based on the law or articles of association.

(3) [1]Substitute supervisory board members may not be appointed. [2]However, a substitute member may be appointed who becomes a supervisory board member if the supervisory board member leaves office before his term of office expires, with exception of further members nominated by the other supervisory board members and elected pursuant to the Coal and Steel-Co-Determination Act or the Co-Determination Amendment Act. [3]The substitute member may only be appointed simultaneously with the supervisory board member. [4]The provisions applying to the supervisory board member's appointment shall also apply to the nullity and avoidance of the substitute supervisory board member's appointment.

Section 102 Term of Office of the Supervisory Board Members

(1) [1]Supervisory board members may not be appointed for any period of time longer than as of the close of the shareholders' meeting resolving on discharging the members of the supervisory board from their responsibilities for the fourth financial year after the commencement of their term of office. [2]The financial year in which the term of office commences shall not be included.

(2) The office of the substitute member shall expire at the latest on the expiration of the term of office of the departing supervisory board member.

Section 103 Removal of the Supervisory Board Members

(1) [1]Supervisory board members who have been elected by the shareholders' meeting without being bound to a nomination may be removed by it prior to the expiration of their term of office. [2]The resolution requires a majority of at least three-quarters of the votes cast. [3]The articles of association may specify another majority and further requirements.

(2) [1]A supervisory board member appointed to the supervisory board on the basis of the articles of association may be removed from office and replaced by another member at any time by the parties entitled to make appointments. [2]If any specific qualifications of the appointment right in the articles of association are repealed, the shareholders' meeting may remove the appointed member with a simple majority.

(3) [1]At the request of the supervisory board, the court shall remove a supervisory board member from office if there is due cause related to his person. [2]The supervisory board shall resolve in regard to the application by simple majority. [3]If the supervisory board member is appointed to the supervisory board on the basis of the articles of association, shareholders whose shares together comprise one-tenth of the nominal share capital, or the pro rata share of one million euro, may also file the application. [4]The decision may be challenged by complaint.

(4) In addition to paragraph 3, the Co-Determination Act, the Coal and Steel-Co-Determination Act, the Co-Determination Amendment Act, the One-Third Participation Act, the

SE-Participation Act and the Act on the Co-Determination of Employees in a Cross-Border Merger also apply to the removal of the supervisory board members appointed to the supervisory board neither by the shareholders' meeting not bound to a nomination nor on the basis of the articles of association.

(5) The provisions regarding the removal of the supervisory board member for whom he has been appointed shall apply to the removal of a substitute member.

Section 104 Appointment by the Court

(1) [1]If the supervisory board does not have the number of members required for a quorum, the court may supplement this number at the request of the management board, a member of the supervisory board or a shareholder. [2]The management board is required to file the application promptly unless the supplementation is anticipated prior to the next supervisory board meeting. [3]If the supervisory board must also have supervisory board members representing the employees, the following may also file the application

1.   the central works council of the company, or the works council if there is only one works council at the company, and if the company is the dominant company of a corporate group, the corporate group works council,

2.   the central or corporate executive committee of the company, or the executive committee if there is only one executive committee at the company, and if the company is the dominant company of a corporate group, the corporate group executive committee,

3.   the central works council of any other company whose employees participate in the election themselves or through delegates, or the works council if there is only one works council at the other company,

4.   the central or corporate executive committee of any other company or the executive committee if there is only one executive committee at the other company,

5.   at least one-tenth or one hundred employees who participate in the election themselves or through delegates,

6.   umbrella organizations of trade unions that have the right to nominate supervisory board members representing the employees,

7.   trade unions who have the right to nominate supervisory board members representing the employees.

[4]If, according to the Co-Determination Act, the supervisory board must also be comprised of supervisory board members representing the employees, in addition to those referred to in

sentence 3, respectively also eligible to file are one-tenth of the employees who are eligible to vote as provided in Section 3 paragraph 1 no. 1 of the Co-Determination Act, or the executive officers within the meaning of the Co-Determination Act eligible to vote. [5]The decision may be challenged by complaint.

(2) [1]If the supervisory board is comprised of fewer members than the number specified by law or the articles of association for longer than three months, this number shall be supplemented by the court on application. [2]On application in urgent cases, the court shall supplement the supervisory board even prior to the expiration of this period. [3]The right of application is defined under paragraph 1. [4]The decision may be challenged by complaint.

(3) Paragraph 2 shall apply to a supervisory board, in which the employees have a co-determination right under the Co-Determination Act, the Coal and Steel-Co-Determination Act or the Co-Determination Amendment Act provided that

1.   the court may not supplement the supervisory board in regard to the further member nominated by the other supervisory board members pursuant to the Coal and Steel-Co-Determination Act or the Co-Determination Amendment Act,

2.   it is always defined as an urgent case if the supervisory board does not have the total number of members according to which it should be comprised by law or the articles of association, except for the further member referred to in number 1.

(4) [1]If the supervisory board must also be comprised of supervisory board members representing the employees, the court shall supplement it to the extent that the numerical relationship required of its composition is constituted. [2]If the supervisory board is supplemented to constitute a quorum, this shall only apply to the extent that the number of supervisory board members required for a quorum makes it possible to maintain this relationship. [3]If a supervisory board member is to be replaced who is required to meet special personal qualifications by law or the articles of association, the supervisory board member appointed by the court must also meet these qualifications. [4]If a supervisory board member is to be replaced, in the election of which an umbrella organization of the trade unions, a trade union or the works council has a nomination right, the court shall take the nominations made by these organizations into account to the extent that no overriding concerns of the company or of the general public oppose the appointment of the nominee; this shall also apply if the supervisory board member would be required to be elected by delegates, for joint nominations by the works councils of the company, in which delegates are to be elected.

(5) The office of the court-appointed supervisory board member shall expire in any case as soon as the deficiency is remedied.

(6) [1]The court-appointed supervisory board member shall be entitled to reimbursement of appropriate cash outlays and, if the supervisory board members of the company are granted compensation, to compensation for his activity. [2]At the application of the supervisory board

member, the court shall specify the outlays and compensation. [3]The decision may be challenged by complaint; any further appeal is excluded. [4]The legally binding decision shall be enforced pursuant to the Code of Civil Procedure.

Section 105 Irreconcilability of Membership on the Management Board and the Supervisory Board

(1) A supervisory board member may not at the same time be a management board member, permanent representative of management board members, holder of a general commercial power of attorney or commercial agent of the company.

(2) [1]Only for a period of time limited in advance, at the most for one year, may the supervisory board appoint individual members as substitutes for absent or indisposed management board members. [2]A renewed appointment or extension of the term of office is permitted if the term of office as a whole does not thereby exceed one year. [3]During their terms of office as substitutes for management board members, the supervisory board members may not perform any activities as a supervisory board member. [4]The non-compete obligation set forth in Section 88 shall not apply to them.

Section 106 Announcement of Changes in the Supervisory Board

The management board shall promptly submit a list of the members of the supervisory board in the event of each change in the persons of the supervisory board members, including the name, first name, profession pursued by and place of residence of the members to the commercial register; pursuant to Section 10 of the Commercial Code the court shall thereupon announce that the list has been submitted to the commercial register.

Section 107 Internal Organization of the Supervisory Board

(1) [1]The supervisory board shall elect from among its members a chairman and at least one substitute chairman pursuant to the details specified in the articles of association. [2]The management board shall register the person elected with the commercial register. [3]The substitute chairman shall only have the rights and duties of the chairman if the latter is indisposed.

(2) [1]Minutes shall be prepared of the meetings of the supervisory board, which the chairman shall sign. [2]The minutes shall include the place and the date of the meeting, the participants, the items on the agenda, the main topics of the negotiations and the resolutions of the supervisory board. [3]A breach of sentence 1 or sentence 2 does not render a resolution invalid. [4]Each member of the supervisory board shall receive a copy of the minutes on request.

(3) [1]The supervisory board may from among its members appoint one or more committees, in particular to prepare its negotiations and resolutions or to monitor the execution of its resolutions. [2]It may in particular appoint an audit committee responsible for the supervision of the accounting processes, the effectiveness of the internal control system, of the risk management system and of the internal auditing system and the audit of the annual financial statements, here in particular the independence of the auditor of the annual financial statements and of additionally rendered services of the auditor of the annual financial statements. [3]The tasks under paragraph 1 sentence 1, Section 59 paragraph 3, Section 77 paragraph 2 sentence 1, Section 84 paragraph 1 sentence 1 and 3, paragraph 2 and paragraph 3 sentence 1, Section 87 paragraphs 1 and 2 sentences 1 and 2, Section 111 paragraph 3, Sections 171, 314 paragraph 2 and 3 and any resolutions that certain types of business transactions may only be undertaken with the consent of the supervisory board, may not be assigned to a committee for resolution *in lieu* of the supervisory board. [4]The supervisory board shall receive regular reports on the work of the committees.

(4) If the supervisory board of a company within the meaning of Section 264d of the Commercial Code sets up an audit committee within the meaning of paragraph 3 sentence 2, at least one member must meet the qualifications set forth in Section 100 paragraph 5.

Section 108 Resolutions of the Supervisory Board

(1) The supervisory board shall decide by resolution.

(2) [1]The quorum of the supervisory board may, to the extent this is not regulated by law, be specified by the articles of association. [2]If this is neither regulated by law nor the articles of association, the supervisory board shall only have a quorum if at least half of its members, of which it must consist by law or articles of association as a whole, participate in the adoption of the resolution. [3]In any case at least three members must participate in the adoption of the resolution. [4]The quorum is not opposed by the fact that fewer members belong to the supervisory board than the number specified by law or articles of association, even if the numerical ratio definitive to its composition is not warranted.

(3) [1]Absent supervisory board members may participate in the adoption of resolutions of the supervisory board and its committees by having their votes submitted in writing. [2]The votes cast in writing may be submitted by other supervisory board members. [3]They may also be submitted by other persons who do not belong to the supervisory board, if they are entitled to participate in the meeting under Section 109 paragraph 3.

(4) The adoption of resolutions of the supervisory board and its committees in writing, by means of telecommunication or other comparable forms is only permitted subject to being regulated in more detail in the articles of association or rules of procedure of the supervisory board if none of the members object to this procedure.

Section 109 Participation in Meetings of the Supervisory Board and its Committees

(1) [1]Persons who neither belong to the supervisory board nor the management board shall not participate in the meetings of the supervisory board and its committees. [2]Professional experts and persons providing information may be called upon to attend for the purpose of being consulted in regard to specific items.

(2) Supervisory board members who do not belong to the committee may participate in the committee meetings, unless the chairman of the supervisory board determines otherwise.

(3) The articles of association may permit persons who do not belong to the supervisory board to participate in the meetings of the supervisory board and its committees in lieu of indisposed supervisory board members if these members have authorized them to do so in writing.

(4) Any conflicting statutory provisions shall remain unaffected.

Section 110 Calling of Meetings of the Supervisory Board

(1) [1]Each of the supervisory board members or the management board may submit a request which includes the purpose and reasons for doing so to the chairman of the supervisory board to promptly call a meeting of the supervisory board. [2]The meeting must take place within two weeks of being called.

(2) If the request is not answered, the supervisory board member or the management board may call the meeting of the supervisory board itself, including the subject matter and a statement of the agenda.

(3) [1]The supervisory board must hold two meetings in each calendar half-year. [2]In companies not listed on the stock exchange, the supervisory board may resolve that one meeting is held in each calendar half-year.

Section 111 Duties and Rights of the Supervisory Board

(1) The supervisory board shall supervise the management of the company.

(2) [1]The supervisory board may inspect and examine the company's books and records, including its assets, in particular the cash on hand, securities portfolios and inventories of goods. [2]It may engage individual members to do so or in regard to certain special tasks professional experts. [3]It shall engage the auditor to audit the annual financial statements and consolidated financial statements pursuant to Section 290 of the Commercial Code.

(3) [1]The supervisory board shall call a shareholders' meeting if the welfare of the company requires doing so. [2]A simple majority suffices for the resolution.

(4) [1]Management measures may not be transferred to the supervisory board. [2]The articles of association or the supervisory board shall, however, specify that certain types of business transactions may only be undertaken with its consent. [3]If the supervisory board denies its consent, the management board may request the shareholders' meeting to resolve on the consent. [4]The resolution whereby the shareholders' meeting agrees requires a majority of at least three-quarters of the votes cast. [5]The articles of association may not specify any other majority nor any further requirements.

(5) The supervisory board members may not have its tasks performed by others.

Section 112 Representation of the company *vis-à-vis* the Members of the Management Board

[1]The supervisory board shall represent the company *vis-à-vis* the management board members in court and out of court. [2]Section 78 paragraph 2 sentence 2 shall apply *mutatis mutandis*.

Section 113 Compensation of the Supervisory Board Members

(1) [1]Compensation may be granted to the supervisory board members for their activities. [2]This may be specified in the articles of association or approved by the shareholders' meeting. [3]The compensation shall be in an appropriate relationship to the supervisory board member's tasks and the status of the company. [4]If the compensation is specified in the articles of association, the shareholders' meeting may resolve by simple majority to amend the articles of association, whereby the compensation shall be reduced.

(2) [1]A compensation of the members of the first supervisory board may only be approved by the shareholders' meeting. [2]The resolution may not be adopted until in the shareholders' meeting resolving to discharge the acts of the members of the first supervisory board.

(3) [1]If the supervisory board members are granted a share of the annual net income of the company, the share shall be calculated on the basis of the net profits reduced by an amount of at least four percent of the contributions made on the lowest issue price of the shares. [2]Any constrasting specifications shall be null.

Section 114 Contracts with Supervisory Board Members

(1) If a supervisory board member agrees outside of his activity on the supervisory board by virtue of a service agreement which does not establish an employment relationship, or by virtue

of a contract for work and labor *vis-à-vis* the company for an activity of a superior nature, the validity of the agreement shall be subject to the consent of the supervisory board.

(2) [1]If the company grants the supervisory board member any compensation on the basis of such a contract without the supervisory board consenting to the contract, the supervisory board member shall return the compensation, unless the supervisory board approves the agreement. [2]The right of the supervisory board member against the company to relinquishment of the enrichment achieved by virtue of the activity shall remain unaffected; this claim may, however, not be offset against the claim to the return.

Section 115 Granting of Loans to Supervisory Board Members

(1) [1]The company may grant loans to supervisory board members only with the consent of the supervisory board. [2]A dominating company may grant loans to supervisory board members of a dependent company only with the consent of its supervisory board, and a dependent company may grant loans to supervisory board members of the dominant company only with the consent of the supervisory board of the dominant company. [3]The consent may only be granted for certain loan transactions or types of loan transactions and no longer than three months in advance. [4]The resolution regarding the consent shall specify the rate of interest and terms of repayment of the loan. [5]If the supervisory board member operates commercial activities as a sole proprietor, the consent is not required if the loan is granted for the payment of goods delivered by the company to his business.

(2) Paragraph 1 shall also apply to loans to the spouses, domestic partners or to an underage child of a supervisory board member and to loans to a third party acting for the account of these persons or for the account of a supervisory board member.

(3) [1]If a supervisory board member is simultaneously a legal representative of another legal person or partner of a partnership, the company may only grant loans to the legal person or the partnership with the consent of the supervisory board; paragraph 1 sentence 3 and 4 shall apply *mutatis mutandis*. [2]This shall not apply if the legal person or the partnership is affiliated with the company or if the loan is granted for the payment of goods delivered by the company to the legal person or the partnership.

(4) If a loan is granted contrary to paragraphs 1 through 3, the loan shall be returned immediately irrespective of any agreements to the contrary unless agreed to by the supervisory board retroactively.

(5) If the company is a credit institution or financial services institution, to which Section 15 of the Banking Act is applicable, the provisions of the Banking Act shall apply *in lieu* of paragraphs 1 through 4.

Section 116 Duty of Due Care and Responsibility of the Supervisory Board Members

[1]Section 93, except for paragraph 2 sentence 3, on the duty of due care and responsibility of the management board members shall apply *mutatis mutandis* to the duty of due care and responsibility of the supervisory board members. [2]The supervisory board members are in particular required to maintain confidentiality in regard to any confidential reports they receive and confidential consultation. [3]They are obligated to pay damages where compensation is inadequate (Section 87 paragraph 1).

EXERTION OF INFLUENCE ON THE COMPANY

Section 117 Liability for Damages

(1) [1]Anyone intentionally using his influence on the company to prompt a member of the management board or of the supervisory board, a holder of a general commercial power of attorney or a commercial agent to damage the company or its shareholders, is liable to the company for the compensation of the resulting damages. [2]He is also liable to the shareholders for the compensation of the resulting damages if they sustain damages apart from the damages sustained due to the damaging of the company.

(2) [1]Apart from such a person, the members of the management board and of the supervisory board shall be liable as joint and several debtors if they have acted in breach of their duties. [2]If it is disputed whether they have applied the due care of a diligent and conscientious manager they shall bear the burden of proof. [3]The members of the management board and of the supervisory board shall not be liable for damages to the company nor to the shareholders if the act is based on a lawful resolution of the shareholders' meeting. [4]The fact that the supervisory board approved the act does not exclude the duty to pay damages.

(3) Apart from such a person, anyone who has benefited from the damaging act shall be liable as joint and several debtors to the extent that the exercising of the influence was caused intentionally.

(4) Section 93 paragraph 4 sentence 3 and 4 shall apply *mutatis mutandis* for the rescission of the duty to pay damages to the company.

(5) [1]The damage claim of the company may also be filed by the creditors of the company provided that they cannot be satisfied by the company. [2]The liability for damages shall not be abolished with respect to the creditors either by a waiver or settlement of the company nor on the basis of the fact that the act was based on a resolution of the shareholders' meeting. [3]If the insolvency proceeding concerning the assets of the company is opened, the insolvency receiver or the trustee shall thus exercise the rights of the creditors.

(6) The claims based on these provisions shall be subject to the statute of limitations in five years.

(7) These provisions shall not apply if the member of the management board or of the supervisory board, the holder of a general commercial power of attorney or the agent was designated to perform the damaging act by exercising

1.   the managerial power based on a control agreement,

2.   the managerial power of a parent company (Section 319), in which the company is integrated.

B. Articles 38 through 60 SE Regulation (EC) No. 2157/2001

Article 38

Under the conditions laid down by this Regulation an SE shall comprise:

(a) a general meeting of shareholders and

(b) either a supervisory body and a management body (two-tier system) or an administrative body (one-tier system) depending on the form adopted in the statutes.

TWO-TIER SYSTEM

Article 39

1. The management body shall be responsible for managing the SE. A Member State may provide that a managing director or managing directors shall be responsible for the current management under the same conditions as for public limited-liability companies that have registered offices within that Member State's territory.

2. The member or members of the management body shall be appointed and removed by the supervisory body.

A Member State may, however, require or permit the statutes to provide that the member or members of the management body shall be appointed and removed by the general meeting under the same conditions as for public limited-liability companies that have registered offices within its territory.

3. No person may at the same time be a member of both the management body and the supervisory body of the same SE. The supervisory body may, however, nominate one of its members to act as a member of the management body in the event of a vacancy. During such a period the functions of the person concerned as a member of the supervisory body shall be suspended. A Member State may impose a time limit on such a period.

4. The number of members of the management body or the rules for determining it shall be laid down in the SE's statutes. A Member State may, however, fix a minimum and/or a maximum number.

5. Where no provision is made for a two-tier system in relation to public limited-liability companies with registered offices within its territory, a Member State may adopt the appropriate measures in relation to SEs.

Article 40

1. The supervisory body shall supervise the work of the management body. It may not itself exercise the power to manage the SE.

2. The members of the supervisory body shall be appointed by the general meeting. The members of the first supervisory body may, however, be appointed by the statutes. This shall apply without prejudice to Article 47(4) or to any employee participation arrangements determined pursuant to Directive 2001/86/EC.

3. The number of members of the supervisory body or the rules for determining it shall be laid down in the statutes. A Member State may, however, stipulate the number of members of the supervisory body for SEs registered within its territory or a minimum and/or a maximum number.

Article 41

1. The management body shall report to the supervisory body at least once every three months on the progress and foreseeable development of the SE's business.

2. In addition to the regular information referred to in paragraph 1, the management body shall promptly pass the supervisory body any information on events likely to have an appreciable effect on the SE.

3. The supervisory body may require the management body to provide information of any kind which it needs to exercise supervision in accordance with Article 40(1). A Member State may provide that each member of the supervisory body also be entitled to this facility.

4. The supervisory body may undertake or arrange for any investigations necessary for the performance of its duties.

5. Each member of the supervisory body shall be entitled to examine all information submitted to it.

Article 42

The supervisory body shall elect a chairman from among its members. If half of the members are appointed by employees, only a member appointed by the general meeting of shareholders may be elected chairman.

ONE-TIER SYSTEM

Article 43

1. The administrative body shall manage the SE. A Member State may provide that a managing director or managing directors shall be responsible for the day-to-day management under the same conditions as for public limited-liability companies that have registered offices within that Member State's territory.

2. The number of members of the administrative body or the rules for determining it shall be laid down in the SE's statutes. A Member State may, however, set a minimum and, where necessary, a maximum number of members.

The administrative body shall, however, consist of at least three members where employee participation is regulated in accordance with Directive 2001/86/EC.

3. The member or members of the administrative body shall be appointed by the general meeting. The members of the first administrative body may, however, be appointed by the statutes. This shall apply without prejudice to Article 47(4) or to any employee participation arrangements determined pursuant to Directive 2001/86/EC.

4. Where no provision is made for a one-tier system in relation to public limited-liability companies with registered offices within its territory, a Member State may adopt the appropriate measures in relation to SEs.

Article 44

1. The administrative body shall meet at least once every three months at intervals laid down by the statutes to discuss the progress and foreseeable development of the SE's business.

2. Each member of the administrative body shall be entitled to examine all information submitted to it.

Article 45

The administrative body shall elect a chairman from among its members. If half of the members are appointed by employees, only a member appointed by the general meeting of shareholders may be elected chairman.

RULES COMMON TO THE ONE-TIER AND TWO-TIER SYSTEMS

Article 46

1. Members of company bodies shall be appointed for a period laid down in the statutes not exceeding six years.

2. Subject to any restrictions laid down in the statutes, members may be reappointed once or more than once for the period determined in accordance with paragraph 1.

Article 47

1. An SE's statutes may permit a company or other legal entity to be a member of one of its bodies, provided that the law applicable to public limited-liability companies in the Member State in which the SE's registered office is situated does not provide otherwise.

That company or other legal entity shall designate a natural person to exercise its functions on the body in question.

2. No person may be a member of any SE body or a representative of a member within the meaning of paragraph 1 who:

(a)   is disqualified, under the law of the Member State in which the SE's registered office is situated, from serving on the corresponding body of a public limited-liability company governed by the law of that Member State, or

(b)   is disqualified from serving on the corresponding body of a public limited-liability company governed by the law of a Member State owing to a judicial or administrative decision delivered in a Member State.

3. An SE's statutes may, in accordance with the law applicable to public limited-liability companies in the Member State in which the SE's registered office is situated, lay down special conditions of eligibility for members representing the shareholders.

4. This Regulation shall not affect national law permitting a minority of shareholders or other persons or authorities to appoint some of the members of a company body.

Article 48

1. An SE's statutes shall list the categories of transactions which require authorisation of the management body by the supervisory body in the two-tier system or an express decision by the administrative body in the one-tier system.

A Member State may, however, provide that in the two-tier system the supervisory body may itself make certain categories of transactions subject to authorisation.

2. A Member State may determine the categories of transactions which must at least be indicated in the statutes of SEs registered within its territory.

Article 49

The members of an SE's bodies shall be under a duty, even after they have ceased to hold office, not to divulge any information which they have concerning the SE the disclosure of which might be prejudicial to the company's interests, except where such disclosure is required or permitted under national law provisions applicable to public limited-liability companies or is in the public interest.

Article 50

1. Unless otherwise provided by this Regulation or the statutes, the internal rules relating to quorums and decision-taking in SE bodies shall be as follows:

(a)   quorum: at least half of the members must be present or represented;

(b)   decision-taking: a majority of the members present or represented.

2. Where there is no relevant provision in the statutes, the chairman of each body shall have a casting vote in the event of a tie. There shall be no provision to the contrary in the statutes, however, where half of the supervisory body consists of employees' representatives.

3. Where employee participation is provided for in accordance with Directive 2001/86/EC, a Member State may provide that the supervisory body's quorum and decision-making shall, by way of derogation from the provisions referred to in paragraphs 1 and 2, be subject to the rules applicable, under the same conditions, to public limited-liability companies governed by the law of the Member State concerned.

Article 51

Members of an SE's management, supervisory and administrative bodies shall be liable, in accordance with the provisions applicable to public limited-liability companies in the Member State in which the SE's registered office is situated, for loss or damage sustained by the SE following any breach on their part of the legal, statutory or other obligations inherent in their duties.

GENERAL MEETING

Article 52

The general meeting shall decide on matters for which it is given sole responsibility by:

(a)   this Regulation or

(b)   the legislation of the Member State in which the SE's registered office is situated adopted in implementation of Directive 2001/86/EC.

Furthermore, the general meeting shall decide on matters for which responsibility is given to the general meeting of a public limited-liability company governed by the law of the Member State in which the SE's registered office is situated, either by the law of that Member State or by the SE's statutes in accordance with that law.

Article 53

Without prejudice to the rules laid down in this section, the organisation and conduct of general meetings together with voting procedures shall be governed by the law applicable to public limited-liability companies in the Member State in which the SE's registered office is situated.

Article 54

1. An SE shall hold a general meeting at least once each calendar year, within six months of the end of its financial year, unless the law of the Member State in which the SE's registered office is situated applicable to public limited-liability companies carrying on the same type of activity as the SE provides for more frequent meetings. A Member State may, however, provide that the first general meeting may be held at any time in the 18 months following an SE's incorporation.

2. General meetings may be convened at any time by the management body, the administrative body, the supervisory body or any other body or competent authority in accordance with the national law applicable to public limited-liability companies in the Member State in which the SE's registered office is situated.

Article 55

1. One or more shareholders who together hold at least 10% of an SE's subscribed capital may request the SE to convene a general meeting and draw up the agenda therefore; the SE's stat-

utes or national legislation may provide for a smaller proportion under the same conditions as those applicable to public limited-liability companies.

2. The request that a general meeting be convened shall state the items to be put on the agenda.

3. If, following a request made under paragraph 1, a general meeting is not held in due time and, in any event, within two months, the competent judicial or administrative authority within the jurisdiction of which the SE's registered office is situated may order that a general meeting be convened within a given period or authorise either the shareholders who have requested it or their representatives to convene a general meeting. This shall be without prejudice to any national provisions which allow the shareholders themselves to convene general meetings.

Article 56

One or more shareholders who together hold at least 10% of an SE's subscribed capital may request that one or more additional items be put on the agenda of any general meeting. The procedures and time limits applicable to such requests shall be laid down by the national law of the Member State in which the SE's registered office is situated or, failing that, by the SE's statutes. The above proportion may be reduced by the statutes or by the law of the Member State in which the SE's registered office is situated under the same conditions as are applicable to public limited-liability companies.

Article 57

Save where this Regulation or, failing that, the law applicable to public limited-liability companies in the Member State in which an SE's registered office is situated requires a larger majority, the general meeting's decisions shall be taken by a majority of the votes validly cast.

Article 58

The votes cast shall not include votes attaching to shares in respect of which the shareholder has not taken part in the vote or has abstained or has returned a blank or spoilt ballot paper.

Article 59

1. Amendment of an SE's statutes shall require a decision by the general meeting taken by a majority which may not be less than two thirds of the votes cast, unless the law applicable to public limited-liability companies in the Member State in which an SE's registered office is situated requires or permits a larger majority.

2. A Member State may, however, provide that where at least half of an SE's subscribed capital is represented, a simple majority of the votes referred to in paragraph 1 shall suffice.

3. Amendments to an SE's statutes shall be publicised in accordance with Article 13.

Article 60

1. Where an SE has two or more classes of shares, every decision by the general meeting shall be subject to a separate vote by each class of shareholders whose class rights are affected thereby.

2. Where a decision by the general meeting requires the majority of votes specified in Article 59(1) or (2), that majority shall also be required for the separate vote by each class of shareholders whose class rights are affected by the decision.

C. Sections 15 through 49 SE Implementation Act

TWO-TIER SYSTEM

Section 15 Exercising Management Responsibilities by Members of the Supervisory Body

[1]Assigning a member of the supervisory body to exercise the duties of a member of the management body in accordance with Article 39 paragraph 3 sentence 2 of the Regulation is only permissible for a limited period of time, set forth in advance, of no longer than one year. [2]A reappointment or extension of the term in office is permissible, if the entire term in office does thereby not exceed a period of one year.

Section 16 Number of Members of the Management Body

[1]The management body for companies with a nominal share capital of more than 3 million euros must consist of at least two persons, unless the articles of association provide that it shall consist of one person. [2]Section 38 paragraph 2 of the SE-Participation Act remains unaffected.

Section 17 Number and Composition of Members of the Supervisory Body

(1) [1]The supervisory body consists of three members. [2]The articles of association may stipulate a certain greater number of members. The number must be divisible by three. [3]The maximum number of members shall be for companies with a nominal share capital of

up to	1,500,000 euros	nine,
more than	1,500,000 euros	fifteen,
more than	10,000,000 euros	twenty-one.

(2) Employee participation in accordance with the SE-Participation Act remains unaffected.

(3) [1]An SE's works council also has the right to file a petition in proceedings under Sections 98, 99 or 104 of the Stock Corporation Act. [2]The SE's works council is also capable of being a party to a lawsuit in actions in accordance with Section 250 of the Stock Corporation Act; Section 252 of the Stock Corporation Act shall apply *mutatis mutandis*.

(4) [1]Section 251 of the Stock Corporation Act shall apply with the stipulation that asserting an unlawful adoption of candidate nominations for employee representatives in the supervisory body may only be invoked under the regulations of the Member States regarding the appointment of seats allocated to it. [2]National employee representatives are subject to Section 37 paragraph 2 of the SE-Participation Act.

Section 18 Information Requests by Individual Members of the Supervisory Body

Every member of the supervisory body may request information of any kind from the management body in accordance with Article 41 paragraph 3 sentence 1 of the Regulation, however, disclosure is only to occur to the supervisory body.

Section 19 Stipulating Transactions Requiring Authorization by the Supervisory Body

The supervisory body may itself stipulate which categories of transactions are subject to its authorization.

ONE-TIER SYSTEM

Section 20 Applicable Provisions

Should an SE select a one-tier system with one administrative body (administrative body) in its articles of association pursuant to Article 38 letter b of the Regulation, the following provisions apply *in lieu* of Sections 76 through 116 of the Stock Corporation Act.

Section 21 Application and Registration

(1) Application for registration of the SE for entry in the commercial register of the court is to be filed by all founders, members of the administrative body and managing directors.

(2) [1]The managing directors shall affirm in the registration that there are no circumstances opposing their appointment under Section 40 paragraph 1 sentence 4, and that they have been instructed of their unrestricted duty of information to the court. [2]The application for registration must state the type and scope of the powers of representation exercised by the managing directors. [3]The application for registration must include the deeds regarding the appointment of the administrative body and managing directors as well as the auditor's reports of the members of the administrative body.

(3) The court may reject the application for registration should the requirements of Section 38 paragraph 2 of the Stock Corporation Act with respect to the auditor's reports of the members of the administrative body be given.

(4) The registration shall specify the managing directors as well as their powers of representation.

(5) (repealed)

Section 22 Duties and Rights of the Administrative Body

(1) The administrative body shall manage the SE, develop the strategy of it's operation and supervise its implementation.

(2) [1]The administrative body shall call a shareholders' meeting if the welfare of the company requires doing so. [2]A simple majority suffices for the resolution. [3]Section 83 of the Stock Corporation Act shall apply *mutatis mutandis* to the preparation and implementation of resolutions by the shareholders' meeting; the administrative body can delegate related tasks to the managing directors.

(3) [1]The administrative body shall ensure that the required trading books are kept. [2]The administrative body shall take appropriate measures, in particular by setting up a monitoring system enabling developments threatening the continued existence of the company to be recognized early.

(4) [1]The administrative body may inspect and examine the company's books and records, including its assets, in particular the cash on hand, securities portfolios and inventories of goods. [2]It may engage individual members to do so or in regard to certain special tasks professional experts. [3]It shall engage the auditor to audit the annual financial statements and consolidated financial statements pursuant to Section 290 of the Commercial Code.

(5) [1]If it results from the preparation of the annual balance sheet or an interim balance sheet, or if it can be assumed on exercising due discretion that there is a loss in the amount of half of the nominal share capital, the administrative body shall promptly call and report this to the shareholders' meeting. [2]In the event of insolvency or over-indebtedness of the company, the administrative body must file for insolvency in accordance with Section 15a paragraph 1 of the Insolvency Act; Section 92 paragraph 2 of the Stock Corporation Act applies *mutatis mutandis*.

(6) Statutory provisions outside of this Act, which assign rights and duties to the management board or supervisory board of a stock corporation, apply *mutatis mutandis* to the administrative body, provided this Act does not contain special provisions for the administrative body and for managing directors.

Section 23 Number of Members of the Administrative Body

(1) [1]The administrative body consists of three members. [2]The articles of association may stipulate otherwise; however, administrative bodies for companies with a nominal share capital of more than 3 million euros must consist of at least three persons. [3]The maximum number of members of the administrative body shall be for companies with a nominal share capital of

up to	1,500,000 euros	nine,
more than	1,500,000 euros	fifteen,
more than	10,000,000 euros	twenty-one.

(2) Employee participation in accordance with the SE Participation Act remains unaffected.

Section 24 Composition of the Administrative Body

(1) The administrative body is composed of members of the administrative body representing the shareholders and, should it be provided for in an agreement in accordance with Section 21 or Sections 34 through 38 of the SE Participation Act, members of the administrative body representing the employees.

(2) The administrative body may only be composed according to contractual or statutory provisions other than those previously applied if under Section 25 or under Section 26 the contractual or statutory provisions are applicable as indicated in the announcement of the chairman of the administrative body or in the court decision.

Section 25 Announcement on the Composition of the Administrative Body

(1) [1]If the chairman of the administrative body is of the opinion that the composition of the administrative body does not comply with the relevant contractual or statutory provisions he shall announce this promptly in the publications designated for company notices and at the same time post the announcement in all businesses of the company and its group companies. [2]The announcement may also be made in electronic form. [3]The announcement shall specify the contractual or statutory provisions that the chairman of the administrative body considers relevant. [4]It shall be noted that the administrative body will be composed in accordance with these provisions, unless parties eligible to apply under Section 26 paragraph 2 appeal to the competent court pursuant to Section 26 paragraph 1 within one month of the announcement in the electronic Federal Gazette.

(2) [1]If no appeal is filed with the competent court pursuant to Section 26 paragraph 1 within one month of the announcement in the electronic Federal Gazette, the new administrative body shall be composed in accordance with the provisions cited in the announcement. [2]The provisions of the articles of association regarding the composition of the administrative body, the number of administrative body members and the election, removal and appointment of administrative body members shall become invalid after the first shareholders' meeting has ended that was called following the expiration of the appeal period, at the latest six months following the expiration of this period to the extent that the provisions contradict the provisions valid at the time. [3]At the same point in time, the office of the previous administrative body members shall expire. [4]A shareholders' meeting taking place within the period of six months may resolve

by a simple majority to adopt new provisions of the articles of association *in lieu* of the provisions of the articles of association that are no longer valid.

(3) No announcements regarding the composition of the administrative body may be made for as long as a court proceeding is pending under Section 26.

Section 26 Court Decision Regarding the Composition of the Administrative Body

(1) If the statutory provisions according to which the administrative body should be composed are disputed or uncertain, this shall be exclusively decided by filing an application with the regional court in the district of which the company has its registered office.

(2) Eligible to file an application are

1. each of the administrative body members,

2. each shareholder,

3. those parties eligible to file an application under Section 98 paragraph 2 sentence 1 no. 4 through 10 of the Stock Corporation Act,

4. the SE works council.

(3) ¹If the composition of the administrative body does not correspond to the court decision, the new administrative body shall be composed pursuant to the statutory provisions specified in the decision. ²Section 25 paragraph 2 shall apply *mutatis mutandis*, with the proviso that the period of six months shall not begin until the decision becomes legally binding.

(4) Section 99 of the Stock Corporation Act shall apply *mutatis mutandis* to the proceeding with the proviso that the submission of the legally binding decision shall be conducted by the chairman of the administrative body in accordance with paragraph 5 of the provision.

Section 27 Personal Qualifications of Members of the Administrative Body

(1) A member of the administrative body may not be anyone who

1. already is a member of the supervisory board or administrative body in ten companies required to form a supervisory board or administrative body by law,

2. is a legal representative of a company that is dependent on the company, or

3.   is a legal representative of another corporation to whose supervisory board or administrative body a management board member or managing director of the company belongs.

[1]Not included in the maximum number under sentence 1 no. 1 are up to five seats on the supervisory board or administrative body in companies belonging to the corporate group and required to form a supervisory board or administrative body by law which are held by a legal representative (in the case of a sole proprietorship, the owner) of the dominant company of a group. [2]Double the number of supervisory board or administrative body offices within the meaning of number 1 for which the member has been elected to chairman shall be included in the maximum number under sentence 1 no. 1. [3]In the case of an SE within the meaning of Section 264d of the Commercial Code, at least one member of the administrative body must meet the requirements of Section 100 paragraph 5 of the Stock Corporation Act.

(2) Section 36 paragraph 3 sentence 2 in conjunction with Section 6 paragraphs 2 through 4 of the SE-Participation Act or any agreements related to Section 21 of the of the SE-Participation Act in regard to the personal requirements of the workforce members shall remain unaffected.

(3) A legal person may not be a member of the administrative body.

Section 28 Appointment of the Members of the Administrative Body

(1) The appointment of the members of the administrative body shall be based on the Regulation.

(2) Section 101 paragraph 2 of the Stock Corporation Act shall apply accordingly.

(3) [1]Substitute administrative body members may not be appointed. [2]However, a substitute member may be appointed who becomes an administrative body member if the administrative body member leaves office before his term of office expires. [3]The substitute member may only be appointed simultaneously with the administrative body member. [4]The provisions applying to the administrative body member's appointment shall also apply to the appointment as well as the nullity and avoidance of the substitute administrative body member. [5]The office of the substitute administrative body member shall expire at the latest on the expiration of the office of the administrative body member leaving office.

Section 29 Removal of the Members of the Administrative Body

(1) [1]Members of the administrative body, who have been elected by the shareholders' meeting without being bound to a nomination may be removed by it prior to the expiration of their term of office. [2]The resolution requires a majority of at least three-quarters of the votes cast. [3]The articles of association may specify another majority and further requirements.

(2) [1]A member of the administrative body appointed to the administrative body on the basis of the articles of association may be removed from office and replaced by another member at any time by the person eligible to appointment. [2]If any specific qualifications of the appointment right in the articles of association are repealed, the shareholders' meeting may remove the appointed member with a simple majority.

(3) [1]At the request of the administrative body, the Court may remove a member from office, if there is due cause for doing so in regard to his person. [2]The administrative body shall resolve on his removal from office by simple majority. [3]If the member was appointed to the administrative body on the basis of the articles of association, shareholders whose shares collectively comprise one-tenth of the share capital, or a share in the amount of 1 million euro, may also submit the request. [4]The decision may be challenged by complaint.

(4) For the removal from office of a substitute member, the provisions regarding the removal from office of the member for which he has been appointed shall apply.

Section 30 Appointment by the Court

(1) [1]If the administrative body does not have the number of members required for a quorum, the court may supplement this number at the request of a member of the administrative body or a shareholder. [2]Members of the administrative body are required to file the application promptly unless the supplementation is anticipated prior to the next meeting of the administrative body. [3]If the administrative body must also have members representing the employees, the application may also be filed by

1. the parties eligible to file the application under Section 104 paragraph 1 sentence 3 of the Stock Corporation Act,

2. the SE works council.

The decision may be challenged by complaint.

(2) [1]If the administrative body is comprised of fewer members than the number specified by agreement, by law or the articles of association for longer than three months, this number shall be supplemented by the court on application. [2]On application in urgent cases, the court shall supplement the administrative body even prior to the expiration of this period. [3]The right of application is defined under paragraph 1. [4]The decision may be challenged by complaint.

(3) The office of the court-appointed member of the administrative body shall expire in any case as soon as the deficiency is remedied.

(4) [1]The court-appointed member of the administrative body shall be entitled to reimbursement of appropriate cash outlays and, if the members of the administrative body of the com-

pany are granted compensation, to compensation for his activity. [2]At the application of the member of the administrative body, the court shall specify the outlays and compensation. [3]The decision may be challenged by complaint; any further appeal is excluded. [4]The legally binding decision shall be enforced pursuant to the Code of Civil Procedure.

Section 31 Nullification of the Election of Members of the Administrative Body

(1) Except in the case of Section 241 nos. 1, 2 and 5 of the Stock Corporation Act, the election of a member of the administrative body by the general shareholders' meeting may only be nullified, if

1.   the administrative body is constituted in violation of Section 24 paragraph 2, Section 25 paragraph 2 sentence 1 or Section 26 paragraph 3;

2.   the statutory maximum number of members of the administrative body is exceeded as a result of the election (Section 23);

3.   the person elected is not permitted to be a member of the administrative body under Article 47 paragraph 2 of the Regulation on the commencement of his term of office.

(2) [1]Section 250 paragraph 2 of the Stock Corporation Act shall apply accordingly to being eligible to be a party to a declaratory judgment stating that the election of a member of the administrative bodies is null. [2]The SE works council is also eligible to be such a party.

(3) [1]If a shareholder, a member of the administrative body or a party eligible under paragraph 2 files for a declaratory judgment against the company declaring that the election of a member of the administrative body is null, Section 246 paragraph 2, paragraph 3 sentence 1 through 4, paragraph 4, Sections 247, 248 paragraph 1 sentence 2, Sections 248a and 249 paragraph 2 of the Stock Corporation Act shall apply *mutatis mutandis*. [2]It cannot be excluded that being null may be asserted by other means than filing for such a judgment.

Section 32 Avoidance of the Election of Members of the Administrative Body

[1]Section 251 of the Stock Corporation Act shall apply to the avoidance of the election of members of the administrative body subject to the proviso that whether the nominees have been proposed for the administrative body unlawfully may only be established in accordance with the regulations of the Members States in regard to filling the seats allotted to it. [2]Section 37 paragraph 2 of the SE Participation Act shall apply to employee representatives from Germany.

Section 33 Effectiveness of the Judgment

Section 252 of the Stock Corporation Act shall apply accordingly to the effectiveness of the judgment.

Section 34 Internal Organization of the Administrative Body

(1) [1]The administrative body shall elect from among its members a chairman and at least one substitute chairman pursuant to the details specified in the articles of association. [2]The substitute chairman shall only have the rights and duties of the chairman if the latter is indisposed. [3]If the administrative body is comprised of only one person, this person shall be responsible for the tasks assigned to the chairman of the administrative body by law.

(2) [1]The administrative body may issue rules of procedure for the administrative body. [2]The articles of association may regulate individual aspects of the rules of procedure on a binding basis.

(3) [1]Minutes shall be prepared of the meetings of the administrative body, which the chairman shall sign. [2]The minutes shall include the place and the date of the meeting, the participants, the items on the agenda, the main topics of the negotiations and the resolutions of the administrative body. [3]A breach of sentence 1 or sentence 2 does not render a resolution invalid. [4]Each member of the administrative body shall receive a copy of the minutes on request. [5]Sentences 1 through 4 shall not apply to an administrative body comprised of only one member.

(4) [1]The administrative body may from among its members appoint one or more committees, in particular to prepare its negotiations and resolutions or to monitor the execution of its resolutions. [2]The tasks under paragraph 1 sentence 1 and under Section 22 paragraphs 1 and 3, Section 40 paragraph 1 sentence 1 and Section 47 paragraph 3 of this Act and under Section 68 paragraph 2 sentence 2, Section 203 paragraph 2, Section 204 paragraph 1 sentence 1, Section 205 paragraph 2 sentence 1 and Section 314 paragraphs 2 and 3 of the Stock Corporation Act may not be assigned to a committee for resolution in lieu of the administrative body. [3]The administrative body shall receive regular reports on the work of the committees. [4]The administrative body may appoint an audit committee, to which may be assigned in particular the tasks under Section 107 paragraph 3 sentence 2 of the Stock Corporation Act. [5]It must be comprised of a majority of non-managing members. [6]If the administrative body of an SE within the meaning of Section 264d of the Commercial Code sets up an audit committee, at least one member of the audit committee must meet the qualifications set forth in Section 100 paragraph 5 of the Stock Corporation Act, and the chairman of the audit committee may not be a managing director.

Section 35 Adoption of Resolutions

(1) [1]Absent members may participate in the adoption of resolutions of the administrative body and its committees by having their votes submitted in writing. [2]The votes cast in writing may be submitted by other administrative body members. [3]They may also be submitted by other persons who do not belong to the administrative body, if they are entitled to participate in the meeting under Section 109 paragraph 3 of the Stock Corporation Act.

(2) The adoption of resolutions of the supervisory board and its committees in writing, by means of written form, telecommunication or other comparable forms is only permitted subject to being regulated in more detail in the articles of association or rules of procedure of the administrative body if none of the members object to this procedure.

(3) If a managing director who is simultaneously a member of the administrative body is prevented from participating in the adoption of a resolution in the administrative body for legal reasons, the chairman of the administrative body shall insofar have an additional vote.

Section 36 Participation in Meetings of the Administrative Body and its Committees

(1) [1]Persons who do not belong to the administrative body shall not participate in meetings of the administrative body and its committees. [2]Professional experts and persons providing information may be called upon to attend for the purpose of being consulted in regard to specific items.

(2) Members of the administrative body who not belong to the committee may participate in committee meetings unless specified otherwise by the chairman of the administrative body.

(3) The articles of association may permit persons who do not belong to the administrative body to participate in the meetings of the administrative body and its committees *in lieu* of indisposed members if these members have authorized them to do so in writing.

(4) Any conflicting statutory provisions shall remain unaffected.

Section 37 Calling of Meetings of the Administrative Body

(1) [1]Each member of the administrative body may submit a request to the chairman of the administrative body to promptly call a meeting of the administrative body which includes the purpose and reasons for doing so. [2]The meeting must take place within two weeks of being called.

(2) If the request is not answered, the administrative body member may call the meeting of the administrative body itself, including the subject matter and a statement of the agenda.

Section 38 Legal relationship of the Members of the Administrative Body

(1) Section 113 of the Stock Corporation Act shall apply *mutatis mutandis* to the compensation of the members of the administrative body.

(2) Sections 114 and 115 of the Stock Corporation Act shall apply *mutatis mutandis* to granting loans to members of the administrative body and to any other contracts with members of the administrative body.

Section 39 Duty of Due Care and Responsibility of the Members of the Administrative Body

Section 93 of the Stock Corporation Act shall apply accordingly to the duty of due care and responsibility of the members of the administrative body.

Section 40 Managing Directors

(1) [1]The administrative body shall appoint one or more managing directors. [2]Members of the administrative body may be appointed as managing directors, provided that the majority of the administrative body continues to consist of non-managing members. [3]The registration of the appointment shall be filed with the commercial register. [4]If third parties are appointed as managing directors, Section 76 paragraph 3 of the Stock Corporation Act shall apply to them *mutatis mutandis*. [5]The articles of association may also include rules regarding the appointment of one or more managing directors. [6]Section 38 paragraph 2 of the SE Participation Act shall remain unaffected.

(2) [1]The managing directors shall manage the business conducted by the company. [2]If several managing directors are appointed, they are only authorized to manage the company jointly; the articles of association or rules of procedure issued by the administrative body by law may provide otherwise. [3]Tasks assigned to the administrative body may not be transferred to the managing directors. [4]The managing directors shall file registrations and submit documents to the commercial register *in lieu* of the management board to the extent that the legal provisions applying to stock corporations require the management board to do so.

(3) [1]If it results from the preparation of the annual balance sheet or an interim balance sheet or on exercising due discretion that there is a loss in the amount of half of the nominal share capital, the managing directors shall inform the chairman of the administrative body thereof promptly. [2]This shall also apply if the company becomes insolvent or an overindebtedness of the company results.

(4) [1]If several managing directors are appointed, they may issue rules of procedure for the managing directors unless the articles of association transfer the issuing of rules of procedure to the

administrative body or the administrative body issues rules of procedure. [2]The articles of association may regulate individual aspects of the rules of procedure on a binding basis. [3]Resolutions regarding the rules of procedure must be adopted by the managing directors unanimously.

(5) [1]Managing directors may be removed from office at any time by resolution of the administrative body, unless the articles of association provide otherwise. [2]The general regulations shall apply to any claims based on the service agreement.

(6) Managing directors shall report to the administrative body in accordance with Section 90 of the Stock Corporation Act, unless the articles of association or rules of procedure provide otherwise.

(7) Sections 87 through 89 of the Stock Corporation Act shall apply *mutatis mutandis*.

(8) Section 93 of the Stock Corporation Act shall apply accordingly to the duty of due care and responsibility of the managing directors.

(9) The regulations applying to the managing directors shall also apply to their substitutes.

Section 41 Representation

(1) [1]The managing directors shall represent the company in and out of court. [2]If a company does not have any managing directors (vacancy of the position of managing director), the company shall be represented by the administrative body in the event that declarations of intent are submitted to it or documents are served upon it.

(2) [1]If there are several managing directors, those managing directors are only authorized to represent the company jointly unless provided otherwise in the articles of association. [2]If a declaration of intent is to be issued to the company, it is sufficient to issue such declaration of intent to one of the managing directors or in the case of paragraph 1 sentence 2 to a member of the administrative body. [3]Section 78 paragraph 2 sentence 3 and 4 of the Stock Corporation Act shall apply *mutatis mutandis*.

(3) [1]The articles of association may also specify that individual managing directors authorized to represent the company alone or jointly with a holder of a general commercial power of attorney. [2]Paragraph 2 sentence 2 shall apply *mutatis mutandis* in such cases.

(4) [1]Managing directors having joint representational powers may authorize individual managing directors to engage in certain business transactions or certain types of business transactions. [2]This shall apply accordingly if an individual managing director is authorized to represent the company jointly with a holder of a general commercial power of attorney.

(5) The administrative body shall represent the company *vis-à-vis* the managing directors in and out of court.

Section 42 (repealed)

Section 43 Information included in Business Letters

(1) [1]Irrespective of form, all business letters addressed to a specific recipient must include the legal form and the registered office of the company, the court of register of the registered office of the company and the number, under which the company is registered in the commercial register, as well as all managing directors and the chairman of the administrative body including their last names and at least one first name written out in full. [2]Section 80 paragraph 1 sentence 3 of the Stock Corporation Act shall apply *mutatis mutandis*.

(2) Section 80 paragraph 2 through 4 of the Stock Corporation Act shall apply accordingly.

Section 44 Restrictions of the Powers of Representation and Powers of Authority to Manage the Company

(1) The powers of representation of the managing directors may not be restricted.

(2) In the relationship of the managing directors to the company, they must comply with the instructions and restrictions of the powers of authority to manage the company that are specified in the provisions of SE law regarding the articles of association, the administrative body, the shareholders' meeting and the rules of procedure of the administrative body and the managing directors.

Section 45 Appointment by the Court

[1]In the absence of a required managing director, in urgent cases the court shall appoint the member at the request of a participant. [2]Section 85 paragraph 1 sentence 2, paragraphs 2 and 3 of the Stock Corporation Act shall apply accordingly.

Section 46 Announcement of Changes

(1) [1]The managing directors shall promptly announce any changes regarding the members of the administrative body in the publications designated for notices and submit the announcement to the commercial register. [2]They must submit each change regarding the managing directors or powers of representation of a managing director for registration in the commercial

register. [3]They must also register the election of the administrative body chairman and his substitute in the commercial register in addition to any changes regarding the person of the administrative body chairman or his substitute.

(2) [1]The new managing directors shall ensure in the registration that there are no circumstances opposing their appointment under Section 40 paragraph 1 sentence 4 and that they have been instructed of their unqualified duty of disclosure to the court. [2]Section 37 paragraph 2 sentence 2 of the Stock Corporation Act shall be applicable.

(3) Section 81 paragraph 2 of the Stock Corporation Act shall apply to the managing directors accordingly.

Section 47 Preparation of Annual Financial Statements

(1) [1]The managing directors must promptly submit the annual financial statements and the annual report to the administrative body following their preparation. [2]At the same time, the managing directors shall submit a proposal for the administrative body to submit to the general shareholders' meeting for the appropriation of the net income; Section 170 paragraph 2 sentence 2 of the Stock Corporation Act shall apply *mutatis mutandis*.

(2) [1]Each member of the administrative body shall be entitled to inspect these documents and audit reports. [2]The documents and audit reports shall be provided to each member of the administrative body, or if the administrative body has resolved to do so and there is an audit committee, to the members of such committee.

(3) Section 171 paragraphs 1 and 2 of the Stock Corporation Act shall apply *mutatis mutandis* to being audited by the administrative body.

(4) [1]Paragraph 1 sentence 1 and paragraph 3 shall apply accordingly to individual accounts pursuant to Section 325 paragraph 2a sentence 1 of the Commercial Code and in the case of parent companies (Section 290 paragraphs 1, 2 of the Commercial Code) to the consolidated annual financial statements and a consolidated annual report. [2]The individual accounts under Section 325 paragraph 2a sentence 1 of the Commercial Code may only be disclosed after being approved by the administrative body.

(5) [1]Once the administrative body issues its consent to the annual financial statements, these are thereupon approved unless the administrative body resolves to have the annual financial statements approved by the general shareholders' meeting. [2]The resolutions of the administrative body shall be included in the report by the administrative body to the general shareholders' meeting.

(6) [1]If the administrative body resolves to have the annual financial statements approved by the general shareholders' meeting, or the administrative body does not approve the annual fi-

nancial statements, the general shareholders' meeting shall approve the annual financial statements. [2]If the administrative body of a parent company (Section 290 paragraphs 1, 2 of the Commercial Code) does not approve the consolidated annual financial statements, the general shareholders' meeting shall decide the approval. [3]Section 173 paragraphs 2 and 3 of the Stock Corporation Act shall apply accordingly to the approval of the annual financial statements or approval of the consolidated annual financial statements by the general shareholders' meeting.

Section 48 Ordinary General Shareholders' Meeting

(1) Promptly after the report is sent to the managing directors, the administrative body shall call a general shareholders' meeting for the receipt of the approved annual financial statements and the annual report, an individual account approved by the administrative body pursuant to Section 325 paragraph 2a sentence 1 of the Commercial Code and to resolve on the appropriation of the net income, and in the case of a parent company (Section 290 paragraphs 1, 2 of the Commercial Code) also for the receipt of the consolidated annual financial statements and the consolidated annual report approved by the administrative body.

(2) [1]The provisions of Section 175 paragraphs 2 through 4 and Section 176 paragraph 2 of the Stock Corporation Act shall apply *mutatis mutandis*. [2]The administrative body shall grant the general shareholders' meeting access to the materials specified in Section 176 paragraph 1 sentence 1 of the Stock Corporation Act. [3]On commencing negotiations, the administrative body shall furnish an explanation of the materials. [4]It shall also comment on any annual deficits or losses that materially affected the annual result. [5]Sentence 4 shall not apply to credit institutions.

Section 49 Managerial Powers and Responsibilities in the Case of the Dependence of Companies

(1) In applying the provisions of Sections 308 through 318 of the Stock Corporation Act, the managing directors shall replace the management board members.

(2) In applying the provisions of Sections 319 through 327 of the Stock Corporation Act, the managing directors shall replace the management board members of the integrated company.

D.   Sections 35 through 54, 64 Limited Liability Companies Act

Section 35 Representation of the Company

(1) [1]The company shall be represented by the general managers in court and out of court. [2]If a company does not have a general manager (vacancy of the position of general manager), the company shall be represented by the shareholders in the event that declarations of intent are submitted to it or documents are served upon it.

(2) [1]In a case where several general managers are appointed, those general managers are only authorized to represent the company jointly, unless it is otherwise provided for in the articles of association. [2]If a declaration of intent is to be issued to the company, it is sufficient to issue such declaration of intent to one representative of the company in accordance with paragraph 1. [3]Declarations of intent may be submitted or documents for the company served to the representatives of the company under paragraph 1 at the business address registered in the commercial register. [4]Irrespective thereof, the submission and service may also be effectuated to the person authorized for receipt pursuant to Section 10 paragraph 2 sentence 2.

(3) [1]If all shares of the company are held by a sole shareholder or jointly held by the shareholder and the company, and if at the same time the shareholder is the sole general manager, then Section 181 of the Civil Code must be applied to his legal transactions with the company. [2]Even if the general manager is not the sole general manager, legal transactions between the general manager and the company he represents must be recorded in the written minutes immediately upon their execution.

Section 35a Information included in Business Letters

(1) [1]Irrespective of form all business letters addressed to a specific recipient must include the legal form and the registered office of the company, the court of register of the registered office of the company and the number, under which the company is registered in the commercial register, as well as all general managers and, provided that the company has established a supervisory board which has a chairman, the chairman of the supervisory board including his last name and at least one first name written out in full. [2]If information on the capital of the company is provided, it is required in any case to state the registered nominal share capital as well as, provided not all capital contributions to be effected in cash have been made, the total amount of the outstanding contributions.

(2) The information under paragraph 1 sentence 1 need not be included in notifications or reports issued in connection with an existing business relationship and for which preprinted forms are customarily used that only call for filling in the particular information required in the individual circumstance.

(3) [1]Order forms shall be deemed to be business letters within the meaning of paragraph 1. [2]Paragraph 2 shall not apply to them.

(4) [1]All business letters and order forms used by a branch office of a limited liability company with a registered office in a foreign country must include the register at which the branch office is registered, and the number of the register entry; regarding the main office and the branch office, to the extent that foreign law does not call for other information paragraphs 1 through 3 shall apply. [2]If the foreign company is in the process of winding up, this fact and the names of all liquidators should also be included.

Section 36 (repealed)

Section 37 Limitations on the power of representation

(1) The general managers are obligated to the company to comply with the limitations, which provide for the scope of their power to represent the company and have been set forth by the articles of association or, to the extent these do not determine otherwise, by the resolutions of the shareholders.

(2) [1]To third parties, limitations of the power of general managers to represent the company do not have any legal effect. [2]This shall apply particularly to cases in which the representation only covers certain transactions or types of transactions or where representation is to occur under certain circumstances or for a certain period of time, or at individual locations or when the approval by the shareholders or a corporate body of the company is required for individual transactions.

Section 38 Removal from office

(1) The appointment of the general managers may be revoked at any time, notwithstanding the claims for compensation arising from existing contracts.

(2) [1]The articles of association may provide that general managers may only be removed from office for due cause. [2]In particular, a gross breach of duty or inability to properly manage the company constitute due cause.

Section 39 Registration of general managers

(1) Any change in the persons of the general managers or termination of their powers of representation must be registered for entry in the commercial register.

(2) The registration must include the deeds regarding the appointment of the general managers or the termination of their powers of representation in the original or in an officially certified copy.

(3) [1]The new general managers shall affirm in the registration that there are no circumstances opposing their appointment under Section 6 paragraph 2 sentence 2 no. 2 and 3 as well as sentence 3, and that they have been instructed of their unrestricted duty of information to the court. [2]Section 8 paragraph 3 sentence 2 shall apply.

(4) (repealed)

Section 40 List of shareholders

(1) [1]The general managers must promptly submit a signed current list of shareholders to the commercial register upon the entry into force of any changes regarding the shareholders or the amount of their shares, which shall contain the last name, first name, date of birth and place of residence of the shareholders as well as the nominal amounts and sequential numbers of their acquired shares. [2]Upon notification and documentation, the general managers may change the list.

(2) [1]If a notary participated in the changes in accordance with paragraph 1 sentence 1, irrespective of any reasons resulting in invalidity that may arise in the future he must sign the list in place of the general managers, submit it to the commercial register and promptly provide the company with a transcript of the changed list. [2]The list must include an attestation by the notary that the amended entries correspond to those changes in which he participated and that the remaining entries correspond to the content of the list last registered with the commercial register.

(3) General managers who breach their duties described in paragraph 1 are liable, as joint debtors for damages incurred, to those parties whose shareholdings have changed and to the company's creditors.

Section 41 Bookkeeping

The general managers are required to ensure proper bookkeeping by the company.

Section 42 Balance sheet

(1) For the balance sheet of the annual financial statement to be prepared in accordance with Sections 242 and 264 of the Commercial Code, the nominal share capital must be accounted for as subscribed capital.

(2) [1]The right of the company to collect additional capital contributions from the shareholders is to be included in the balance sheet to the extent that the collection has already been resolved and that the shareholders do not have right to claim exemption from paying additional contributions by referring to their existing shareholding. [2]The amount of the additional capital contribution shall be accounted for separately on the asset side as a receivables item called "Additional capital contributions to be collected", at least to the extent that payment can be expected. [3]An amount corresponding to the asset item shall be accounted for separately on the liability side under "Capital reserve".

(3) Loans, receivables and liabilities to shareholders are principally to be accounted separately as such, or are to be included in an annex; if they are accounted for under different items, then this characteristics must be noted.

Section 42a Preparation of annual financial statements and annual report

(1) [1]The general managers must promptly submit the annual financial statements and the annual report following their preparation to the shareholders for their approval. [2]If the annual financial statements need to be examined by an auditor, the general managers must submit them together with the annual report and audit report promptly upon receipt. [3]If the company is vested with a supervisory board, then its report on the results of its audit must also be submitted promptly.

(2) [1]The shareholders must approve the annual financial statements and resolve the appropriation of the net income at the latest by the end of the first eight or, if it is a small company (Section 267 paragraph 1 of the Commercial Code), by the end of the first eleven months of the financial year. [2]The articles of association may not extend the deadline. [3]The approval of the annual financial statements is subject to the application of the provisions of their preparation.

(3) If an auditor has audited the annual financial statements, he must upon request of a shareholder participate in the discussions on the approval of the annual financial statements.

(4) [1]If the company is required to prepare consolidated annual financial statements and a consolidated annual report, then paragraphs 1 through 3 shall apply *mutatis mutandis*. [2]The same shall apply to individual accounts in accordance with Section 325 paragraph 2a of the Commercial Code if the shareholders have resolved that these shall be disclosed.

Section 43 Liability of general managers

(1) The general managers must exercise the due care of a diligent manager with respect to company matters.

(2) General managers who breach their obligations are jointly liable to the company for damages incurred.

(3) [1]They are in particular liable for damages when they pay out financial assets which are necessary for the maintenance of the stated capital of the company contrary to the provisions of Section 30, or when own shares of the company have been acquired contrary to the provisions of Section 33. [2]The provisions of Section 9b paragraph 1 shall apply *mutatis mutandis* to the claim for damages. [3]Insofar as damages are required to satisfy the company's creditors, the general managers shall not be absolved of liability by virtue of the fact that they acted in accordance with a shareholders' resolution.

(4) Claims for damages arising from the above provisions shall be subject to the statute of limitations in five years.

Section 43 a Granting loans from assets of the company

[1]General managers, other legal representatives, holder of a general commercial power of attorney or commercial agents authorized to act on behalf of the company in all matters may not be granted loans from assets which are necessary for the maintenance of the stated capital of the company. [2]A loan granted contrary to sentence 1 shall be repaid immediately and irrespective of any contravening agreements.

Section 44 Substitute general managers

The provisions issued for general managers also apply to the substitute general managers.

Section 45 Shareholder rights

(1) Rights to which shareholders are entitled with respect to company matters, in particular with respect to managing the business, as well as the exercising of such rights, are set forth by the articles of association, provided that there are no conflicting statutory provisions.

(2) The provisions of Sections 46 through 51 shall apply in the absence of specific provisions set forth in the articles of association.

Section 46 Shareholders' scope of responsibilities

Subject to shareholder identification are:

1. the approval of the annual financial statements and appropriation of the net income;

1a. the decision on disclosure of an individual account in accordance with international accounting standards (Section 325 paragraph 2a of the Commercial Code) and the approval of the annual financial statements prepared by the general managers;

1b. the approval of consolidated annual financial statements prepared by the general managers;

2. the collection of capital contributions;

3. the repayment of additional capital contributions;

4. the division, consolidation and confiscation of shares;

5. the appointment and removal from office of general managers as well as the discharging of the general managers from their responsibilities;

6. the rules with respect to auditing and supervising management of the company;

7. the appointment of holder of a general commercial power of attorney or commercial agents to act on behalf of the company in all matters;

8. the assertion of damage claims against general managers or shareholders to which the company is entitled from the foundation or management of the company, as well as the representation of the company in legal proceedings against the general managers.

Section 47 Voting

(1) Provisions drawn up by shareholders with regard to company matters are effected by resolution with a majority of the votes cast.

(2) Each euro of a share carries one vote.

(3) Only powers of attorney provided in written form are considered valid.

(4) [1]A shareholder who is to be released from an obligation by the resolution has no voting right and may not exercise such voting rights for others. [2]The same shall apply for a resolution concerning a legal transaction or initiating or settling a legal claim against a shareholder.

Section 48 Shareholders' meeting

(1) Shareholder resolutions shall be adopted in shareholders' meetings.

(2) A meeting shall not be required if all shareholders declare in writing or in a written statement that they agree to the relevant provision or the casting of votes in writing.

(3) If all company shares belong to one shareholder or aside belong to the company, this person must immediately record and sign the minutes after the resolution has been passed.

Section 49 Calling of a shareholders' meeting

(1) The general manager shall be responsible for calling the shareholders' meeting.

(2) The shareholders' meeting must be called where it appears to be in the interests of the company, in addition to certain defined cases set forth by statutory law.

(3) In particular, the shareholders' meeting must be called if it may be concluded on the basis of the annual or interim balance sheet that half of the company's registered nominal share capital has been lost.

Section 50 Minority shareholder rights

(1) Shareholders whose shareholdings collectively amount to at least one-tenth of the nominal share capital may also call the shareholders' meeting, stating the purpose and reasons for doing so.

(2) Similarly, shareholders have the right to request that issues to be resolved upon shall be announced in the meeting.

(3) [1]If this request is not complied with or if the persons to which this request should be directed are not available, the shareholders referred to under paragraph 1 may effectuate the call or the announcement themselves, including information regarding the circumstances. [2]The shareholders' meeting shall resolve whether the company shall bear the costs.

Section 51 Formal requirements of the calling

(1) [1]The calling of the shareholders' meeting shall be carried out by inviting the shareholders using registered mail. [2]It must take place with at least one week's notice.

(2) The purpose of the shareholders' meeting should always be announced when calling the meeting.

(3) Should the shareholders' meeting be called improperly, resolutions may only be passed if all shareholders are present.

(4) The same shall apply for resolutions on issues that were not communicated to shareholders in accordance with the prescribed procedure at least three days prior to the meeting.

Section 51 a Right to information and inspection

(1) The shareholders shall be entitled to promptly receive information from general managers on matters pertaining to the company as well as the right to inspect company accounts and records.

(2) [1]General managers shall be entitled to refuse to provide information or inspection where there is a concern that the shareholders will use the information obtained for non-company related purposes and thus cause considerable damage to the company or one of its affiliated companies. [2]Such a refusal must be supported by a shareholder resolution.

(3) The articles of association may not deviate from these provisions.

Section 51 b Court decisions on the right to information and inspection

[1]Section 132 paragraph 1 and 3 through 5 of the Stock Corporation Act shall apply *mutatis mutandis* to court decisions on the right to information and inspection. [2]Any shareholder who was denied information or inspection shall be entitled to file a claim.

Section 52 Supervisory board

(1) If the articles of association stipulate that a supervisory board shall be appointed, Section 90 paragraphs 3, 4 and 5 sentences 1 and 2, Section 95 sentence 1, Section 100 paragraphs 1 and 2 no. 2 and paragraph 5, Section 101 paragraph 1 sentence 1, Section 103 paragraph 1 sentences 1 and 2, Sections 105, 107 paragraph 4, Sections 110 through 114, 116 of the Stock Corporation Act in conjunction with Section 93 paragraphs 1 and 2 sentence 1 and 2 of the Stock Corporation Act, Section 124 paragraph 3 sentence 2, Sections 170, 171 of the Stock Coporation Act apply *mutatis mutandis* insofar as the articles of association do not provide otherwise.

(2) ¹If appointments are made to the supervisory board prior to registration of the company with the commercial register, Section 37 paragraph 4 no. 3 and 3 a of the Stock Corporation Act shall apply *mutatis mutandis*. ²Whenever the members of the supervisory board change, the general managers must immediately submit a list of the members of the supervisory board containing the last name, first name, profession and place of residence to the commercial register; pursuant to Section 10 of the Commercial Code, the court shall give notice that the list was submitted to the commercial register.

(3) Claims to damages against members of the supervisory board for breaching their obligations shall be subject to the statute of limitations in five years.

Section 53 Formal requirements for amending the articles of association

(1) Amendments may be made to the articles of association only by shareholder resolution.

(2) ¹The resolution must be notarized and requires a three-quarters majority of votes. ²The articles of association may also stipulate other requirements.

(3) Increasing shareholder capacity in accordance with the articles of association may only be resolved upon with the approval of all participating shareholders.

Section 54 Notification and registration of amendments of the articles of association

(1) ¹The commercial register must be informed of any amendments of the articles of association. ²The full text of the articles of association should be included with the application for registration; it must be furnished with the attestation of a notary with respect to the fact that the amended provisions of the articles of association correspond to the resolution to amend the articles of association, and that the text of the unamended provisions corresponds in full to the articles of association last submitted to the commercial register.

(2) For registration it shall suffice to refer to the documents submitted to the court that reflect the amendments, insofar as the amendments do not refer to the specifications mentioned under Section 10.

(3) The amendments shall not take legal effect prior to being recorded in the commercial register located at the company's registered office.

Section 64 Liability for payments after insolvency or overindebtedness

¹The general managers are required to compensate the company for payments that were made after insolvency or overindebtedness was evident. ²This does not apply for payments that were

made where the due care of a diligent manager was exercised. [3]The same obligation shall apply to general managers for payments to shareholders, insofar as this causes insolvency of the company, unless this could not have been foreseen when exercising the due care under sentence 2. [4]The provisions under Section 43 paragraphs 3 and 4 shall apply to claims to damages.

E. German Corporate Governance Code[1048]

1. Foreword

This German Corporate Governance Code (the "Code") presents essential statutory regulations for the management and supervision (governance) of German listed companies and contains internationally and nationally recognized standards for good and responsible governance. The Code aims at making the German Corporate Governance system transparent and understandable. Its purpose is to promote the trust of international and national investors, customers, employees and the general public in the management and supervision of listed German stock corporations.

The Code clarifies the obligation of the Management Board and the Supervisory Board to ensure the continued existence of the enterprise and its sustainable creation of value in conformity with the principles of the social market economy (interest of the enterprise).

A dual board system is prescribed by law for German stock corporations:

The Management Board is responsible for managing the enterprise. Its members are jointly accountable for the management of the enterprise. The Chairman of the Management Board coordinates the work of the Management Board.

The Supervisory Board appoints, supervises and advises the members of the Management Board and is directly involved in decisions of fundamental importance to the enterprise. The chairman of the Supervisory Board coordinates the work of the Supervisory Board.

The members of the Supervisory Board are elected by the shareholders at the General Meeting. In enterprises having more than 500 or 2000 employees in Germany, employees are also represented in the Supervisory Board, which then is composed of employee representatives to one third or to one half respectively. For enterprises with more than 2000 employees, the Chairman of the Supervisory Board, who, for all practical purposes, is a representative of the shareholders, has the casting vote in the case of split resolutions. The representatives elected by the shareholders and the representatives of the employees are equally obliged to act in the enterprise's best interests.

Alternatively the European Company (SE) gives enterprises in Germany the possibility of opting for the internationally widespread system of governance by a single body (board of directors).

The form that codetermination takes in the SE is established generally by agreement between the company management and the employee side. All employees in the EU Member States are included.

1048 Published with permission of the Government Commission on the German Corporate Governance Code.

In practice the dual board system, also established in other continental European countries, and the single-board system are converging because of the intensive interaction of the Management Board and the Supervisory Board in the dual-board system. Both systems are equally successful.

The accounting standards of German enterprises are oriented on the "true and fair view" principle and represent a fair picture of the actual conditions of the asset, financial and earnings situations of the enterprise.

The recommendations of the Code are marked in the text by use of the word "shall". Companies can deviate from them, but are then obliged to disclose this annually. This enables companies to reflect sector and enterprise-specific requirements. Thus, the Code contributes to more flexibility and more self-regulation in the German corporate constitution. Furthermore, the Code contains suggestions which can be deviated from without disclosure; for this the Code uses terms such as "should" or "can". The remaining passages of the Code not marked by these terms contain provisions that enterprises are compelled to observe under applicable law.

For Code stipulations relating to not only the listed company itself but also its group companies, the term "enterprise" is used instead of "company".

Primarily, the Code addresses listed corporations. It is recommended that non-listed companies also respect the Code.

As a rule the Code will be reviewed annually against the background of national and international developments and be adjusted, if necessary.

2. Shareholders and the General Meeting

2.1 Shareholders
2.1.1 To the extent provided for in the Articles of Association the shareholders exercise their rights before ore during at the General Meeting and, in this respect, vote.

2.1.2 In principle, each share carries one vote. There are no shares with multiple voting rights, preferential voting rights (golden shares) or maximum voting rights.

2.2 General Meeting
2.2.1 The Management Board submits to the General Meeting the Annual Financial Statements and the Consolidated Financial Statements. The General Meeting resolves on the appropriation of net income and the discharge of the acts of the Management Board and of the Supervisory Board and, as a rule, elects the shareholders' representatives to the Supervisory Board and the auditors.

Furthermore, the General Meeting resolves on the Articles of Association, the purpose of the company, amendments to the Articles of Association and essential corporate measures such as, in particular, inter-company agreements and transformations, the issuing of new shares and of convertible bonds and bonds with warrants, and the authorization to purchase own shares. It can resolve on the authorization of the remuneration system for the members of the Management Board.

2.2.2 When new shares are issued, shareholders, in principle, have pre-emptive rights corresponding to their share of the equity capital.

2.2.3 Each shareholder is entitled to participate in the General Meeting, to take the floor on matters on the agenda and to submit materially relevant questions and proposals.

2.2.4 The chair of the meeting provides for the expedient running of the General Meeting. In this, the chair should be guided by the fact that an ordinary general meeting is completed after 4 to 6 hours at the latest.

2.3 Invitation to the General Meeting, Proxies
2.3.1 At least once a year the shareholders' General Meeting is to be convened by the Management Board giving details of the agenda. A quorum of shareholders is entitled to demand the convening of a General Meeting and the extension of the agenda. The convening of the meeting, as well as the reports and documents, including the Annual Report and the Postal Vote Forms, required by law for the General Meeting are to be published on the company's internet site together with the agenda.

2.3.2 The company shall send notification of the convening of the General Meeting together with the convention documents to all domestic and foreign financial services providers, shareholders and shareholders' associations by electronic means if the approval requirements are fulfilled.

2.3.3 The company shall facilitate the personal exercising of shareholders' voting rights. The company shall also assist the shareholders in the use of postal votes and proxies. The Management Board shall arrange for the appointment of a representative to exercise shareholders' voting rights in accordance with instructions; this representative should also be reachable during the General Meeting.

2.3.4 The company should make it possible for shareholders to follow the General Meeting using modern communication media (*e.g.*, Internet).

3. Cooperation between Management Board and Supervisory Board
3.1 The Management Board and Supervisory Board cooperate closely to the benefit of the enterprise.

3.2 The Management Board coordinates the enterprise's strategic approach with the Supervisory Board and discusses the current state of strategy implementation with the Supervisory Board in regular intervals.

3.3 For transactions of fundamental importance, the Articles of Association or the Supervisory Board specify provisions requiring the approval of the Supervisory Board. They include decisions or measures which fundamentally change the asset, financial or earnings situations of the enterprise.

3.4 Providing sufficient information to the Supervisory Board is the joint responsibility of the Management Board and Supervisory Board.

The Management Board informs the Supervisory Board regularly, without delay and comprehensively, of all issues important to the enterprise with regard to planning, business development, risk situation, risk management and compliance. The Management Board points out deviations of the actual business development from previously formulated plans and targets, indicating the reasons therefor.

The Supervisory Board shall specify the Management Board's information and reporting duties in more detail. The Management Board's reports to the Supervisory Board are, as a rule, to be submitted in writing (including electronic form). Documents required for decisions, in particular, the Annual Financial Statements, the Consolidated Financial Statements and the Auditors' Report are to be sent to the members of the Supervisory Board, to the extent possible, in due time before the meeting.

3.5 Good corporate governance requires an open discussion between the Management Board and Supervisory Board as well as among the members within the Management Board and the Supervisory Board. The comprehensive observance of confidentiality is of paramount importance for this.

All board members ensure that the staff members they employ observe the confidentiality obligation accordingly.

3.6 In Supervisory Boards with codetermination, representatives of the shareholders and of the employees should prepare the Supervisory Board meetings separately, possibly with members of the Management Board.

If necessary, the Supervisory Board should meet without the Management Board.

3.7 In the event of a takeover offer, the Management Board and Supervisory Board of the target company must submit a statement of their reasoned position so that the shareholders can make an informed decision on the offer.

After the announcement of a takeover offer, the Management Board may not take any actions outside the ordinary course of business that could prevent the success of the offer unless the Management Board has been authorized by the General Meeting or the Supervisory Board has given its approval. In making their decisions, the Management and Supervisory Boards are bound to the best interests of the shareholders and of the enterprise.

In appropriate cases the Management Board should convene an extraordinary General Meeting at which shareholders discuss the takeover offer and may decide on corporate actions.

3.8 The Management Board and Supervisory Board comply with the rules of proper corporate management. If they violate the due care and diligence of a prudent and conscientious Managing Director or Supervisory Board member, they are liable to the company for damages. In the case of business decisions an infringement of duty is not present if the member of the Management Board or Supervisory Board could reasonably believe, based on appropriate information, that he/she was acting in the best interest of the company (Business Judgment Rule).

If the company takes out a D&O (directors' and officers' liability insurance) policy for the Management Board, a deductible of at least 10% of the loss up to at least the amount of one and a half times the fixed annual compensation of the Management Board member must be agreed upon.

A similar deductible shall be agreed upon in any D&O policy for the Supervisory Board.

3.9 Extending loans from the enterprise to members of the Management and Supervisory Boards or their relatives requires the approval of the Supervisory Board.

3.10 The Management Board and Supervisory Board shall report each year on the enterprise's Corporate Governance in the Annual Report (Corporate Governance Report). This includes the explanation of possible deviations from the recommendations of this Code. Comments can also be provided on the Code's suggestions. The company shall keep previous declarations of conformity with the Code available for viewing on its website for five years.

4. Management Board

4.1 Tasks and Responsibilities
4.1.1 The Management Board is responsible for independently managing the enterprise in the interest of the enterprise, thus taking into account the interests of the shareholders, its employees and other stakeholders, with the objective of sustainable creation of value.

4.1.2 The Management Board develops the enterprise's strategy, coordinates it with the Supervisory Board and ensures its implementation.

4.1.3 The Management Board ensures that all provisions of law and the enterprise's internal policies are abided by and works to achieve their compliance by group companies (compliance).

4.1.4 The Management Board ensures appropriate risk management and risk controlling in the enterprise.

4.1.5 When filling managerial positions in the enterprise the Management Board shall take diversity into consideration and, in particular, aim for an appropriate consideration of women.

4.2 Composition and Compensation

4.2.1 The Management Board shall be comprised of several persons and have a Chairman or Spokesman. By-Laws shall govern the work of the Management Board, in particular the allocation of duties among individual Management Board members, matters reserved for the Management Board as a whole, and the required majority for Management Board resolutions (unanimity or resolution by majority vote).

4.2.2 At the proposal of the committee dealing with Management Board contracts, the full Supervisory Board determines the total compensation of the individual Management Board members and shall resolve and regularly review the Management Board compensation system.

The total compensation of the individual members of the Management Board is determined by the full Supervisory Board at an appropriate amount based on a performance assessment, taking into consideration any payments by group companies. Criteria for determining the appropriateness of compensation are both the tasks of the individual member of the Management Board, his personal performance, the economic situation, the performance and outlook of the enterprise as well as the common level of the compensation taking into account the peer companies and the compensation structure in place in other areas of the company.

If the Supervisory Board calls upon an external compensation expert to evaluate the appropriateness of the compensation, care must be exercised to ensure that said expert is independent of respectively the Management Board and the enterprise.

4.2.3 The total compensation of management board members comprises the monetary compensation elements, pension awards, other awards, especially in the event of termination of activity, fringe benefits of all kinds and benefits by third parties which were promised or granted in the financial year with regard to management board work.

The compensation structure must be oriented toward sustainable growth of the enterprise. The monetary compensation elements shall comprise fixed and variable elements. The Supervisory Board must make sure that the variable compensation elements are in general based on a multi-year assessment. Both positive and negative developments shall be taken into account when determining variable compensation components. All compensation components must be appropriate, both individually and in total, and in particular must not encourage to take unreasonable risks.

For instance, share or index-based compensation elements related to the enterprise may come into consideration as variable components. These elements shall be related to demanding, relevant comparison parameters. Changing such performance targets or the comparison parameters retroactively shall be excluded. For extraordinary developments a possibility of limitation (cap) must in general be agreed upon by the Supervisory Board.

In concluding Management Board contracts, care shall be taken to ensure that payments made to a Management Board member on premature termination of his contract without serious cause do not exceed the value of two years' compensation (severance payment cap) and compensate no more than the remaining term of the contract. The severance payment cap shall be calculated on the basis of the total compensation for the past full financial year and if appropriate also the expected total compensation for the current financial year.

Payments promised in the event of premature termination of a Management Board member's contract due to a change of control shall not exceed 150% of the severance payment cap.

The Chairman of the Supervisory Board shall outline the salient points of the compensation system and any changes thereto to the General Meeting.

4.2.4 The total compensation of each one of the members of the Management Board is to be disclosed by name, divided into fixed and variable compensation components. The same applies to promises of benefits that are granted to a Management Board member in case of premature or statutory termination of the function of a Management Board member or that have been changed during the financial year. Disclosure may be dispensed with if the General Meeting has passed a resolution to this effect by three-quarters majority.

4.2.5 Disclosure shall be made in a compensation report which as part of the Corporate Governance Report describes the compensation system for Management Board members in a generally understandable way.

The compensation report shall also include information on the nature of the fringe benefits provided by the company.

4.3 Conflicts of interest
4.3.1 During their employment for the enterprise, members of the Management Board are subject to a comprehensive non-competition obligation.

4.3.2 Members of the Management Board and employees may not, in connection with their work, demand nor accept from third parties payments or other advantages for themselves or for any other person nor grant third parties unlawful advantages.

4.3.3 Members of the Management Board are bound by the enterprise's best interests. No member of the Management Board may pursue personal interests in his decisions or use business opportunities intended for the enterprise for himself.

4.3.4 All members of the Management Board shall disclose conflicts of interest to the Supervisory Board without delay and inform the other members of the Management Board thereof. All transactions between the enterprise and the members of the Management Board as well as persons they are close to or companies they have a personal association with must comply with standards customary in the sector. Important transactions shall require the approval of the Supervisory Board.

4.3.5 Members of the Management Board shall take on sideline activities, especially Supervisory Board mandates outside the enterprise, only with the approval of the Supervisory Board.

5. Supervisory Board

5.1 Tasks and Responsibilities
5.1.1 The task of the Supervisory Board is to advise regularly and supervise the Management Board in the management of the enterprise. It must be involved in decisions of fundamental importance to the enterprise.

5.1.2 The Supervisory Board appoints and dismisses the members of the Management Board. When appointing the Management Board, the Supervisory Board shall also respect diversity and, in particular, aim for an appropriate consideration of women. Together with the Management Board it shall ensure that there is a long-term succession planning. The Supervisory Board can delegate preparations for the appointment of members of the Management Board, as well as for the handling of the conditions of the employment contracts including compensation, to committees.

For first time appointments the maximum possible appointment period of five years should not be the rule. A re-appointment prior to one year before the end of the appointment period with a simultaneous termination of the current appointment shall only take place under special circumstances. An age limit for members of the Management Board shall be specified.

5.1.3 The Supervisory Board shall issue Terms of Reference.

5.2. Tasks and Authorities of the Chairman of the Supervisory Board
The Chairman of the Supervisory Board coordinates work within the Supervisory Board and chairs its meetings and attends to the affairs of the Supervisory Board externally.

The Chairman of the Supervisory Board shall also chair the committees that handle contracts with members of the Management Board and prepare the Supervisory Board meetings. He should not be Chairman of the Audit Committee.

The Chairman of the Supervisory Board shall regularly maintain contact with the Management Board, in particular, with the Chairman or Spokesman of the Management Board and consult with him on strategy, business development and risk management of the enterprise. The Chairman of the Supervisory Board will be informed by the Chairman or Spokesman of the Management Board without delay of important events which are essential for the assessment of the situation and development as well as for the management of the enterprise. The Chairman of the Supervisory Board shall then inform the Supervisory Board and, if required, convene an extraordinary meeting of the Supervisory Board.

5.3 Formation of Committees

5.3.1 Depending on the specifics of the enterprise and the number of its members, the Supervisory Board shall form committees with sufficient expertise. They serve to increase the efficiency of the Supervisory Board's work and the handling of complex issues. The respective committee chairmen report regularly to the Supervisory Board on the work of the committees.

5.3.2 The Supervisory Board shall set up an Audit Committee which, in particular, handles issues of accounting, risk management and compliance, the necessary independence required of the auditor, the issuing of the audit mandate to the auditor, the determination of auditing focal points and the fee agreement. The chairman of the Audit Committee shall have specialist knowledge and experience in the application of accounting principles and internal control processes. He should be independent and not be a former member of the Management Board of the company whose appointment ended less than two years ago.

5.3.3 The Supervisory Board shall form a nomination committee composed exclusively of shareholder representatives which proposes suitable candidates to the Supervisory Board for recommendation to the General Meeting.

5.3.4 The Supervisory Board can refer other factual issues to one or more committees for handling. They include the enterprise's strategy, the compensation of the members of the Management Board, investments and financings.

5.4 Composition and Compensation

5.4.1 The Supervisory Board has to be composed in such a way that its members as a group possess the knowledge, ability and expert experience required to properly complete its tasks.

The Supervisory Board shall specify concrete objectives regarding its composition which, whilst considering the specifics of the enterprise, take into account the international activities of the enterprise, potential conflicts of interest, an age limit to be specified for the members of the Supervisory Board and diversity. These concrete objectives shall, in particular, stipulate an appropriate degree of female representation.

Recommendations by the Supervisory Board to the competent election bodies shall take these objectives into account. The concrete objectives of the Supervisory Board and the status of the implementation shall be published in the Corporate Governance Report.

The members of the Supervisory Board shall on their own take on the necessary training and further education measures required for their tasks. They shall be supported by the company appropriately.

5.4.2 To permit the Supervisory Board's independent advice and supervision of the Management Board, the Supervisory Board shall include what it considers an adequate number of independent members. A Supervisory Board member is considered independent if he/she has no business or personal relations with the company or its Management Board which cause a conflict of interests. Not more than two former members of the Management Board shall be members of the Supervisory Board and Supervisory Board members shall not exercise director-ships or similar positions or advisory tasks for important competitors of the enterprise.

5.4.3 Elections to the Supervisory Board shall be made on an individual basis. An application for the judicial appointment of a Supervisory Board member shall be limited in time up to the next annual general meeting. Proposed candidates for the Supervisory Board chair shall be announced to the shareholders.

5.4.4 Management Board members may not become members of the Supervisory Board of the company within two years after the end of their appointment unless they are appointed upon a motion presented by shareholders holding more than 25% of the voting rights in the company. In the latter case appointment to the chairmanship of the Supervisory Board shall be an excep-tion to be justified to the General Meeting.

5.4.5 Every member of the Supervisory Board must take care that he/she has sufficient time to perform his/her mandate. Members of the Management Board of a listed company shall not accept more than a total of three Supervisory Board mandates in non-group listed companies or in supervisory bodies of companies with similar requirements.

5.4.6 Compensation of the members of the Supervisory Board is specified by resolution of the General Meeting or in the Articles of Association. It takes into account the responsibilities and scope of tasks of the members of the Supervisory Board as well as the economic situation and performance of the enterprise. Also to be considered here shall be the exercising of the Chair and Deputy Chair positions in the Supervisory Board as well as the chair and member-ship in committees.

Members of the Supervisory Board shall receive fixed as well as performance-related compensa-tion. Performance-related compensation should also contain components based on the long-term performance of the enterprise.

The compensation of the members of the Supervisory Board shall be reported individually in the Corporate Governance Report, subdivided according to components. Also payments made by the enterprise to the members of the Supervisory Board or advantages extended for services provided individually, in particular, advisory or agency services shall be listed separately in the Corporate Governance Report.

5.4.7 If a member of the Supervisory Board took part in less than half of the meetings of the Su-pervisory Board in a financial year, this shall be noted in the Report of the Supervisory Board.

5.5 Conflicts of Interest
5.5.1 All members of the Supervisory Board are bound by the enterprise's best interests. No member of the Supervisory Board may pursue personal interests in his/her decisions or use busi-ness opportunities intended for the enterprise for himself/herself.

5.5.2 Each member of the Supervisory Board shall inform the Supervisory Board of any con-flicts of interest which may result from a consultant or directorship function with clients, sup-pliers, lenders or other business partners.

5.5.3 In its report, the Supervisory Board shall inform the General Meeting of any conflicts of interest which have occurred together with their treatment. Material conflicts of interest and those which are not merely temporary in respect of the person of a Supervisory Board member shall result in the termination of his mandate.

5.5.4 Advisory and other service agreements and contracts for work between a member of the Supervisory Board and the company require the Supervisory Board's approval.

5.6 Examination of Efficiency
The Supervisory Board shall examine the efficiency of its activities on a regular basis.

6. Transparency
6.1 The Management Board must disclose insider information directly relating to the company without delay unless it is exempted from the disclosure requirement in an individual case.

6.2 As soon as the company becomes aware of the fact that an individual acquires, exceeds or falls short of 3, 5, 10, 15, 20, 25, 30, 50 or 75% of the voting rights in the company by means of a purchase, sale or any other manner, the Management Board will disclose this fact without delay.

6.3 The company's treatment of all shareholders in respect of information shall be equal. All new facts made known to financial analysts and similar addressees shall also be disclosed to the shareholders by the company without delay.

6.4 The company shall use suitable communication media, such as the Internet, to inform shareholders and investors in a prompt and uniform manner.

6.5 Any information which the company discloses abroad in line with corresponding capital market law provisions shall also be disclosed domestically without delay.

6.6 Beyond the statutory obligation to report and disclose dealings in shares of the company without delay, the ownership of shares in the company or related financial instruments by Management Board and Supervisory Board members shall be reported if these directly or indi-rectly exceed 1% of the shares issued by the company. If the entire holdings of all members of the Management Board and Supervisory Board exceed 1% of the shares issued by the company, these shall be reported separately according to Management Board and Supervisory Board.

The aforesaid disclosures shall be included in the Corporate Governance Report.

6.7 As part of regular information policy, the dates of essential regular publications (including the Annual Report, interim financial reports) and the date of the General Meeting shall be published sufficiently in advance in a "financial calendar".

6.8 Information on the enterprise which the company discloses shall also be accessible via the company's Internet site. The Internet site shall be clearly structured. Publications should also be in English.

7. Reporting and Audit of the Annual Financial Statements

7.1 Reporting
7.1.1 Shareholders and third parties are mainly informed by the Consolidated Financial Statements. During the financial year they are additionally informed by means of a half-year financial report and, in the first and second halves, by interim reports or quarterly financial reports. The Consolidated Financial Statements and the Condensed Consolidated Financial Statements in the half-year financial report and the quarterly financial report are prepared under observance of internationally recognised accounting principles.

7.1.2 The Consolidated Financial Statements must be prepared by the Management Board and examined by the auditor and Supervisory Board. Half-year and any quarterly financial reports shall be discussed with the Management Board by the Supervisory Board or its Audit Committee prior to publication. In addition, the Financial Reporting Enforcement Panel and the Federal Financial Supervisory Authority are authorized to check that the Consolidated Financial Statements comply with the applicable accounting regulations (enforcement). The Consolidated Financial Statements shall be publicly accessible within 90 days of the end of the financial year; interim reports shall be publicly accessible within 45 days of the end of the reporting period.

7.1.3 The Corporate Governance Report shall contain information on stock option programmes and similar securities-based incentive systems of the company.

7.1.4 The company shall publish a list of third party companies in which it has a shareholding that is not of minor importance for the enterprise. The trading portfolios of banks and financial services companies, on which voting rights are not exercised, are disregarded in this context. The following shall be provided: name and headquarters of the company, the amount of the shareholding, the amount of equity and the operating result of the past financial year.

7.1.5 Notes on the relationships with shareholders considered to be "related parties" pursuant to the applicable accounting regulations shall be provided in the Consolidated Financial Statements.

7.2 Audit of Annual Financial Statements
7.2.1 Prior to submitting a proposal for election, the Supervisory Board or, respectively, the Audit Committee shall obtain a statement from the proposed auditor stating whether, and

where applicable, which business, financial, personal and other relationships exist between the auditor and its executive bodies and head auditors on the one hand, and the enterprise and the members of its executive bodies on the other hand, that could call its independence into question. This statement shall include the extent to which other services were performed for the enterprise in the past year, especially in the field of consultancy, or which are contracted for the following year.

The Supervisory Board shall agree with the auditor that the Chairman of the Supervisory Board will be informed immediately of any grounds for disqualification or impartiality occurring during the audit, unless such grounds are eliminated immediately.

7.2.2 The Supervisory Board commissions the auditor to carry out the audit and concludes an agreement on the latter's fee.

7.2.3 The Supervisory Board shall arrange for the auditor to report without delay on all facts and events of importance for the tasks of the Supervisory Board which arise during the performance of the audit.

The Supervisory Board shall arrange for the auditor to inform it and/or note in the Auditor's Report if, during the performance of the audit, the auditor comes across facts which show a misstatement by the Management Board and Supervisory Board on the Code.

7.2.4 The auditor takes part in the Supervisory Board's deliberations on the Annual Financial Statements and Consolidated Financial Statements and reports on the essential results of its audit.

Index

Authors

Christof von Dryander studied law and economics at the University of Freiburg and received an LL.M. degree from Yale Law School in 1981. He joined Cleary Gottlieb Steen & Hamilton LLP in 1982 and became a partner in 1990. Prior to moving to Germany in 1991 to help establish the firm's German practice in Frankfurt, he was resident in the Brussels and London offices of Cleary Gottlieb. At the beginning of 2011, he relocated from the Frankfurt to the firm's Hong Kong office. Christof von Dryander's practice focuses on corporate and financial matters, mergers & acquisitions, private equity transactions and corporate governance issues. He lectures and is widely published on corporate and capital markets matters. Christof von Dryander is consistently listed as one of the leading banking and capital markets lawyers in Germany. Chambers Global ranks him in the top category of leading individuals for capital markets. Since 2000, JUVE, the leading publication on German law firms, has continuously ranked him among the top practitioners in several categories. Mr. von Dryander is a member of the German and Washington, D.C., bars and a Registered Foreign Lawyer at the Law Society in Hong Kong.

Tel: +852 2521 4122 (Hong Kong)
Tel: +49 69 971 030 (Frankfurt)
Email: cvondryander@cgsh.com

Klaus W. Riehmer studied law at the universities in Freiburg and Munich. He served as a research fellow at the Max-Planck-Institute for Comparative and International Private Law in Hamburg. Mr. Riehmer received a doctorate in law from the University of Kiel and an LL.M. degree from the University of Texas, Austin. In 1994, he started his career as a corporate lawyer in Frankfurt and, in 2004, joined Cleary Gottlieb Steen & Hamilton LLP as a partner. Klaus Riehmer's practice focuses on mergers & acquisitions and corporate law. He is distinguished as a leading German corporate and M&A lawyer by various independent directories and commentators including Chambers Global, Chambers Europe, Best Lawyers, IFLR 1000, PLC Which Lawyer?, JUVE, Wirtschaftswoche and the Guide to the World's Leading Mergers and Acquisitions Lawyers. Mr. Riehmer is widely published, particularly on German corporate law.

Tel: +49 69 971 030 (Frankfurt)
Email: kriehmer@cgsh.com

GLP
German Law Publishers
www.germanlawpublishers.com

Mergers & Acquisitions in Germany

edited by Dr. Christoph Louven, written by Dr. Tobias Böckmann
LL.M. (Minnesota), Dr. Tim Oliver Brandi LL.M. (Columbia), Kristina
Ernst LL.M. (Norwich), Annika Flues, Dr. Heiko Gemmel, Arnt Göppert
LL.M. (McGill), Dr. David Alexander Jüntgen LL.M. (NZ), Dr. Angela
Kölbl, Dr. Michael Leistikow, Dr. Barbara Lepper, Dr. Alexander Loos,
Dr. Kerstin Schmidt, Holger Stabenau, Dr. Martin Sura, Dr. Heiko
Tschauner, Jens Uhlendorf, Dr. Thorsten Volz

2011, about 450 pages, € 128,–

ISBN 978-3-941389-09-0

THE CONTENT:

This Manual in the English language outlines mergers & acquisitions
under German law. Every aspect of a M&A transaction considering
possible German peculiarities is illuminated by the authors: preparatory steps, the sale and purchase agreement as well as post-closing
measures. Furthermore, there is relevant information on taxation,
employment law und competition law issues. Some precious insight
is given on tactical strategies for companies in the forefront of a
takeover.

Please order at your convenient bookshop or go to www.germanlawpublishers.com

SWEET & MAXWELL    THOMSON REUTERS    BOORBERG